Star Wars
FAQ

Star Wars FAQ

Everything Left to Know About the Trilogy That Changed the Movies

Unofficial and Unauthorized

Mark Clark

APPLAUSE
THEATRE & CINEMA BOOKS
An Imprint of Hal Leonard Corporation

Published in 2015 by Applause Theatre and Cinema Books
An Imprint of Hal Leonard Corporation
7777 West Bluemound Road
Milwaukee, WI 53213

Trade Book Division Editorial Offices
33 Plymouth St., Montclair, NJ 07042

Except where otherwise specified, all images are from the author's personal collection.

The FAQ series was conceived by Robert Rodriguez and developed with Stuart Shea.

Printed in the United States of America

Book design by Snow Creative Services

Library of Congress Cataloging-in-Publication Data

Clark, Mark, 1966–
   Star Wars FAQ : everything left to know about the trilogy that changed the movies
/ Mark Clark.
      pages cm
   "Unofficial and unauthorized."
   Includes bibliographical references and index.
   ISBN 978-1-4803-6018-1 (pbk.)
1. Star Wars films—Miscellanea. I. Title.
   PN1995.9.S695C57 2015
   791.43'75—dc23
                                                      2015016071

www.applausebooks.com

In Memory of Mark A. Miller
Author, educator, musician, friend
You are still loved

Contents

Foreword

"The Merchandising Rights Are Worth Nothing" (And Other Mysterious Fables of Our Time)

I n a certain dimension, someone at a certain movie studio decided that the merchandising rights to STAR WARS and any subsequent sequels might be worth a few shekels. Consequently, George Lucas was given a modest increase in advance monies in return for those rights.

This is not that dimension.

Pioneered by Walt Disney, the world of movie merchandising was already well established by the time *Star Wars* appeared. It's safe to say that world would be a very different one had Lucas not retained control over the merchandising rights. So . . . many . . . toys. So . . . many . . . PEZ dispensers.

But . . . where do you go if you want to find out a little something about those toys and dispensers and the Chewbacca toothbrushes that all those PEZ dispensers made necessary (a connection, there, of Sith-like insidiousness)? Where can you find reference to everything *Star Wars* both known and elsewhere unreferenced? Yes, there is much to be sourced from the web. But you can't hold that information in your hands. For all its virtues, the Internet doesn't let you flip easily back and forth between the pictures and prose of *Star Wars* history.

Well, now you can do that. There's this here book.

To me, the best reference tomes as well as those that are the most fun are the ones that delve into topics that had never even occurred to me. Researching the history of the domesticated banana, for example, becomes even more interesting (if depressing) when you learn that a single variety (the Cavendish) is all that's available in your friendly nickel-squeezing local supermarket.

While it's interesting to learn that one of the primary influences on *Star Wars* is Akira Kurosawa's *Hidden Fortress*, how nice to have an image from that film accompanying the revelation. Just like with bananas, you're tempted by such marvelous information to delve further. About a thousand varieties of bananas exist (of which we get one). Similarly, young *Star Wars* fans may not realize that Akira Kurosawa is known for influencing other films besides *Star Wars* (note the American remake of *Seven Samurai* aka *The Magnificent Seven*). So if properly informed, a reader might go from *Star Wars* to *The Hidden Fortress* to *Seven Samurai* to *Yojimbo* and so on (or banana-wise, from the Cavendish to the sadly unavailable Ibota Ibota).

What I'm saying is that while there's a lot more to *Star Wars* than *Star Wars*, tracking down such references can be a bit of a pain in the search engine. Thankfully, in *Star Wars FAQ*, Mark Clark has done the work for you. There's so much to explore, and to use as springboards for additional searching.

Where else are you going to quickly find a picture of Han Solo (all right; Harrison Ford) wearing glasses and looking for all the world like a university grad student (or maybe a young Indiana Jones?). Or learn more about the influence of the great comic-book writer and artist Carl Barks (one of my own primary influences) on not only George Lucas but Steven Spielberg?

There's so much information bound up (pun intended) in *Star Wars FAQ* that I suggest reading it not in one sitting, but in bits and pieces, much as you'd fumble your way through a bowl of M&M's. Don't go searching for and picking out all the blue ones at once. Let them find you. One of the joys of a book such as this is the pleasure to be gained from jumping around and letting the surprises come to you, instead of the other way around. A map of a theme park is sometimes useful, but hardly necessary. Reading a book like *Star Wars FAQ* is a bit like strolling the streets of London without a guidebook. You know where Big Ben is, but stumbling across the first public drinking fountain in Britain is apt, in its own more modest way, to be even more enchanting.

Go now and delve. Let the force of Mark's research wash over you. I guarantee that the Force will be with you all the way to the last page, and to the last fragment of arcane information that you will use to awe your friends at the next convention, or party—or when your grandchildren ask you about a wonderful place not so long ago, and not so very far away.

Alan Dean Foster
Prescott, Arizona
June, 2014

Alan Dean Foster is the critically acclaimed author of more than a hundred science fiction and fantasy novels and short story collections, including the long-running Humanx Commonwealth and Pip and Flinx series. Star Wars *fans know him best as the author of* Splinter of the Mind's Eye, *the first original work of* Star Wars *fiction. He later penned a second original* Star Wars *novel,* The Approaching Storm. *Born in New York City and raised in Los Angeles, Foster has an MFA in cinema from UCLA and is also renowned for his masterful novelizations of dozens of screenplays. Foster ghost-wrote the best-selling novelization for the original* Star Wars *film, and wrote the novelization for the upcoming* Star Wars Episode VII: The Force Awakens.

Acknowledgments

I am deeply grateful to everyone who participated in the development of *Star Wars FAQ*, especially:

My Rogue Squadron of Alpha Readers, whose corrections, questions, and suggestions greatly improved this book: Bryan Senn, The Rev. Julie Fisher, and new recruits Robert James and Perry Olsen.

Steve Vertlieb, the Yoda of film music scholarship, for his assistance with Chapter 23.

David Zuzelo, the Jabba the Hutt of Eurotrash movie collectors, for his assistance with Chapter 13.

Stephen Ashcraft, the Han Solo of science educators, for his assistance with Chapter 28.

Preston Hewis, the Boba Fett of photography, who shot the memorabilia pictured in this book.

Publisher John Cerullo, the Obi-Wan Kenobi of the FAQ Series, who left me with no excuses not to undertake this project.

Marybeth Keating, the Chewbacca of editors (meaning that she's a loyal companion and fierce protector, not that she's big and furry), whose support and friendship have made writing three FAQ books a joy.

The Applause Books art department and promotional staff. Without their excellent work, this book would be stuck in the garbage masher.

A cantina full of friends who supported me in this endeavor, especially Ron and Margaret Borst, The Rev. Kip Colegrove, Phyllis Harbor and Linda Mayer McConnell, Ken Hardin, David Harnack, Joe and Jennifer Hans, Gregory Harris, David Hogan, Lynn Naron, The Rev. Cricket Park, Caren Prideaux, Ted Okuda, Marge Rutherford, and Nick Schlegel.

And, as always, my wife Vanessa, without whose support and encouragement I would accomplish nothing.

May the Force be with all of you.

Introduction

Star Wars and Me

When I was eleven years old, I was an insufferable snob. I had always been a precocious and voracious reader, and a couple of years earlier my Uncle Marty, whom I idolized, had suggested I try reading some of his favorite authors. So, beginning with things like Ray Bradbury's short story collections *R Is for Rocket* and *S Is for Space*, I quickly consumed many works by science fiction legends such as Isaac Asimov, Arthur C. Clarke, Robert A. Heinlein, Bradbury, and others. Even before that, Uncle Marty and I had often stayed up late watching television broadcasts of classic SF movies like *The Day the Earth Stood Still* (1951) and *Forbidden Planet* (1956). On my own I had discovered *2001: A Space Odyssey* (1968), which was then my favorite film. And yet, when *Star Wars* premiered in May 1977, despite the sensation it caused, I wasn't particularly interested in seeing it. I had heard it was "space fantasy," and I was a fan of *real* science fiction. The masses could have their *Star Wars*; I had Stanley Kubrick and *The Foundation Trilogy*.

Then, in late summer, shortly before I had to go back to school, my family went to visit Uncle Marty, who had married and moved out of state. When I told him I hadn't seen *Star Wars* (which, by this time, had been out for nearly three months), Marty looked at me as if I had sprouted antlers. "You *must* see *Star Wars*," he insisted. So the next day he dragged me to the local movie theater. Uncle Marty was right again, to put it mildly. I was stunned by the now-famous opening shot of the Star Destroyer rumbling across the screen in pursuit of Princess Leia's spaceship, and basically spent the next two hours staring awestruck at the spectacle unfolding before me. I think my uncle enjoyed watching my reaction as much as he enjoyed rewatching the movie. By the time I left the cinema, *2001* had to settle for second place.

I was at the perfect age to be swept up by *Star Wars* mania. Although I only saw the film a relatively modest five times during its original theatrical release, I also acquired the novelization, the comic books, the soundtrack, the *Story of Star Wars* record album, posters, and the action figures and other toys. I joined the Official Star Wars Fan Club (the only fan club I ever joined). But my personal connection with *Star Wars* went much deeper than my collection of memorabilia. I started middle school that fall. By enriching my fantasy life, *Star Wars* somehow made that difficult adolescent passage a little easier. I loved *Star Wars* so much that I decided I needed to see the Japanese movies that had inspired it. So I sought out the works of director Akira Kurosawa and was introduced to international art cinema, which broadened my mind and became another great passion. For years I had imagined becoming a writer, but *Star Wars* inspired me to actually begin writing stories—and what came out was colorful juvenile space opera that owed more to George Lucas than to Ray Bradbury. *Star Wars* also rekindled in me a spiritual curiosity, which had been nearly snuffed out by my alienating experiences at my grandparents' fire-and-brimstone Southern Baptist church. My spiritual journey was long and winding, but faith eventually became a central part of my life; my wife is an Episcopal priest. No other movie altered the course of my life so profoundly.

There are millions of other people who also feel deeply connected to *Star Wars*, for one reason or another. If you purchased this book or received it as a gift, you may be one of them. Because of this, *Star Wars* ranks among the most discussed and written-about movies of all time. It's been celebrated and denigrated, criticized, analyzed, and scrutinized almost nonstop for nearly forty years. Books, essays, websites, and documentaries have delved into every aspect of its creation and legacy. Authors have examined the film's implications—mythological, technological, psychological, political, economic, ethical, and religious (with separate Christian, Jewish, Muslim, Buddhist, and Hindu interpretations). So much has been written about it that there's even a book about how to write about *Star Wars*. If I'm doing this wrong, it must be because I neglected to read that volume. Sorry.

So why does the world need *Star Wars FAQ* when there are already so many other *Star Wars* books? Precisely *because* there are so many other *Star Wars* books. The volume you hold in your hands (or have stored in your tablet) is a single-shot distillation of all that other material. It's intended primarily for people who have great affection for *Star Wars* but don't have the time or inclination to excavate the mountain of books and other media already published on the subject. However, I believe that devoted fans who purchase every book about *Star Wars* that drops out of hyperspace will also find *Star Wars FAQ* rewarding. I spent the better part of two years searching for underreported stories and illuminating minutiae often overlooked in other works. Also, because this book is not authorized or approved by Lucasfilm, Disney, or anybody else, I was able to delve into areas often skimmed over or completely ignored by most histories, including the *Star Wars Holiday Special* debacle, the rise of *Star Wars* fiction and its importance in the revival of the franchise, and the wave of *Star Wars* imitators and parodies that flooded theaters and TV screens in the late 1970s and early 1980s. I also offer my own analysis of the *Star Wars* films—their relative merits, their thematic messages, their ongoing influence, and their cultural legacy—as well as my assessment of ancillary projects like the *Ewoks* TV movies and *Star Wars* cartoons. I call 'em like I see 'em. Your mileage may vary.

To keep the scope of my research manageable, *Star Wars FAQ* focuses exclusively on the earliest films, which for the sake of historical accuracy are referred to by their original titles: *Star Wars*, *The Empire Strikes Back*, and *Return of the Jedi*. The book begins with the conception of the first movie and continues through the release of the Special Edition versions of the Original Trilogy in 1997. *Star Wars FAQ* deals primarily with the writing and production of, and the critical and popular reaction to, these movies. It is not concerned with the details of franchise mythology. If you want to know the starship make and model of the *Millennium Falcon*, you will have to find another book; I recommend *The Star Wars Encyclopedia*, by Stephen J. Sansweet and Pablo Hidalgo. (Okay, just this once: the *Falcon* is a modified YT-1300f light freighter manufactured by the Corellian Engineering Corp.)

The toughest task in writing *Star Wars FAQ* was separating the truth from another sort of mythology—the revisionist history, rife with misconceptions and in some cases outright fabrications, that has collected around the making of these films over the decades. To present the story as accurately as it can be ascertained at this distance, I have relied on the earliest interviews and historical documents available. Fortunately, multiple corroborating sources were available for most aspects of the narrative. Sources for direct quotes or other unique information are cited within the text. In some cases, I present conflicting accounts and invite readers to draw their own conclusions.

Star Wars FAQ could not, given the scope of its topic and the brevity of its format, include every fascinating, amusing, or just plain kooky *Star Wars*–related subplot or anecdote. No single book could. I have tried to include as much of this material as possible, but some of it simply wouldn't fit (see Chapter 27). I'll sneak another item in here: Did you know that a likeness of Darth Vader resides among the gargoyles on the northwest tower of the Washington National Cathedral in D.C.? It's true; Google it.

Please be advised that despite its title, *Star Wars FAQ* is not a collection of Frequently Asked Questions. It is part of a series of similarly titled works published by Hal Leonard Corporation that deal with music, film, and other pop culture topics in a shared format. This is my third book in the series (following two volumes about *Star Trek*). Critics and readers unfamiliar with the FAQ Series often complain that the title is misleading, so consider this fair warning. One more note before you begin reading: *Star Wars FAQ* has been written so that readers can dip in and out of the book at will (so feel free to skip to that chapter on the *Star Wars Holiday Special* if your interest is piqued). However, the chapters dealing with the production and reception of the films (Chapters 3–11, 14–18, and 20–21) are best read in order, or at least as contiguous blocks.

I have endeavored to cover all aspects of the *Star Wars* phenomenon—everything from the books and movies that inspired Lucas to imagine the franchise, to early screenplay drafts that were never filmed, to short biographies of many people who made key contributions to the movies' success, to the winding (and, in ways, maddening) history of the Original Trilogy's home video releases. I have also endeavored to place events in their historical and pop cultural contexts, because otherwise it is difficult to appreciate how revolutionary *Star Wars* was. The overarching theme of *Star Wars FAQ* is the vast and enduring impact the *Star Wars* films have had on the movie industry, on popular culture, and on the lives of the people who made them, especially George Lucas. It's a story as thrilling and action-packed as the movies themselves, with bold characters facing apparently insurmountable odds, full of frantic chases, narrow escapes, daring victories, and tragic setbacks, culminating in an unlikely triumph that changed the course of the galaxy—or at least of Hollywood. So strap in; we're about to make the jump to lightspeed.

—*Mark Clark, Mentor on the Lake, Ohio, 2015*

This Will Be a Day Long Remembered

How *Star Wars* Changed the Movies

Every ten years, Britain's *Sight & Sound* magazine polls film critics and directors from around the world to compile a list of the ten greatest movies ever made. The most recent poll, published in 2012, named Alfred Hitchcock's *Vertigo* the all-time No. 1 movie. *Vertigo* (1958) dislodged Orson Welles' *Citizen Kane* (1941), which had held the top spot for the previous fifty years. Other films that have regularly appeared on the list include Jean Renoir's *The Rules of the Game* (1939), Federico Fellini's *8½* (1963), and Sergei Eisenstein's *Battleship Potemkin* (1925). *Star Wars* (1977), *The Empire Strikes Back* (1980), and *Return of the Jedi* (1983) have never cracked the *Sight & Sound* Top 10 and probably never will. Nor do they often appear on the multitude of similar, lesser-watched Greatest Movie lists except those such as the Internet Movie Database and American Film Institute polls, which accept input from fans.

If the cinematic virtues of George Lucas' original *Star Wars* trilogy remain debatable, however, their historical importance is indisputable. These pictures—the first one in particular—must be counted among the handful of the most pivotal movies ever made. *Star Wars* expanded the medium's audience more than anything since the comedies of Charlie Chaplin and the historical dramas of D. W. Griffith popularized moviegoing in the mid-teens, and they stimulated the greatest surge of technological innovation since *The Jazz Singer* (1927) spurred Hollywood's transition to sound. To fully appreciate how groundbreaking *Star Wars* truly was, it's necessary to consider where the film industry was in early 1977 and how it got there.

The Golden Age

Hollywood won the First World War. Before the war, it had competed on fairly equal terms with the vibrant film industries of France, Germany, Sweden, and other European nations to supply product to theaters in America and around the world. But the World War left European film studios in ruins, clearing the way for Hollywood to become the moviemaking capital of the planet. The advent of sound in the late 1920s enabled U.S. studios to virtually monopolize the domestic market, since American viewers (unlike audiences overseas) generally resisted subtitled pictures and dubbing technology took years to perfect. During this same era, Hollywood's major studios began what they called "vertical integration"—not only producing films but buying all the major theater chains and distribution hubs. MGM, Warner Brothers, Twentieth Century-Fox, Paramount, and RKO snapped up the theater chains; only Columbia, Universal, and United Artists were left out.

The Golden Age of Hollywood ensued. Depending on your perspective, this period (beginning in the late silent era and continuing through World War II) was comparable to either the glory days of Old Republic or the dark days of the Evil Empire—or perhaps both simultaneously. Hollywood made legendary pictures including *Citizen Kane, Casablanca* (1942), *Gone with the Wind*, and *The Wizard of Oz* (both 1939); employed directors such as Hitchcock, John Ford, and Billy Wilder; and featured stars such as Humphrey Bogart, Cary Grant, and Bette Davis. Since tickets were cheap (admission cost as little as a dime), a night at the movies was one of the few luxuries many people could afford during the Great Depression and amid the privation and rationing of World War II. The studios made money creating, distributing, and exhibiting their product, and cash poured in from all three links in the cinematic food chain. On the other hand, actors and creative personnel were sometimes treated abominably. Studios became factories, churning out movies like sausages. And independently owned theaters were forced to book entire blocks of films, including not only prestige productions with major stars but also B-budget programmers with less box office appeal.

Just when Hollywood seemed invincible, in 1948 the U.S. Supreme Court delivered a crushing blow to the industry with its decision *United States v. Paramount Pictures, Inc., et al.*, which found the eight major studios were in violation of federal antitrust laws. Through the auspices of the Motion Pictures Producers and Distributors of America (MPPDA), the eight major studios (Paramount, MGM, 20th Century-Fox, Warner Brothers, RKO, Universal, Columbia, and United Artists) not only enforced their Production Code (which regulated the content of films) but colluded to prevent any significant new competitor from entering the marketplace. The court ordered the companies to sell their theater chains and end block-booking and other monopolistic practices, but allowed the studios to remain in the film distribution business.

With a major revenue source eliminated, however, studio coffers dwindled. Movie moguls lost not only cash but clout. Independent producers found it much easier to distribute their films. Many stars opted to freelance rather than renew their exclusive studio contracts. Agents gained greater power and began bundling scripts with freelance talent (directors and actors) and selling packaged projects to the highest bidder. Although it would take nearly a decade for all of its provisions to be carried out, the Paramount decision sounded the death knell for the Hollywood studio system. The Golden Age was over.

The New Hollywood

Still reeling from these hardships, Hollywood soon faced a major new threat—television. As stations opened across the country and the sale of TV sets proliferated, the medium rapidly siphoned viewers away from movie theaters. For instance, the popularity of television Westerns decimated the audience for low-budget "oaters," which had been a bread-and-butter Hollywood staple since the early silent era. Hollywood responded by introducing Cinerama and various other widescreen processes, shooting more features in color, trying gimmicks like 3-D, and reviving "road show" exhibition spectacles (prestige productions offered at escalated ticket prices, with floor shows, live music. or other added attractions)—anything to differentiate its product from its black-and-white, small-screen rival. Another response was the rise of art house and drive-in theaters, both of which offered more exotic viewing experiences than those available on TV.

An unintended consequence of the Paramount decision was that with the MPPDA weakened, enforcement of the studios' Production Code became more difficult. Then in 1952 the U.S. Supreme Court ruled, in *Joseph Burstyn, Inc. v. Wilson*, that motion pictures were entitled to First Amendment protection, eliminating the threat of government censorship that had inspired the creation of the code in the first place. By the end of the 1960s the code was a thing of the past. Mainstream American movies began to include more explicit sexuality and graphic violence.

While Hollywood reconsidered its way of telling stories, it was also forced to reinvent its way of doing business. The major studios, once among the most successful privately owned businesses in history, were rapidly going broke in the mid-1960s. Cash-strapped moguls were forced to sell their companies to corporate behemoths. Gulf + Western began the corporate takeover of Hollywood by purchasing the tottering Paramount Pictures in 1966. The following year the Seven Arts conglomerate bought the iconic but destitute Warner Brothers Pictures, while Transamerica took over the enfeebled

THIS YEAR IT'S
EASY RIDER

PANDO COMPANY in association with RAYBERT PRODUCTIONS presents
EASY RIDER PETER FONDA · DENNIS HOPPER · JACK NICHOLSON
Written by   Directed by   Produced by   Associate Producer   Executive Producer
PETER FONDA   DENNIS HOPPER   PETER FONDA   WILLIAM HAYWARD   BERT SCHNEIDER   COLOR
DENNIS HOPPER
TERRY SOUTHERN   [R]RESTRICTED — Persons under 16 not admitted unless accompanied by parent or adult guardian.   Released by COLUMBIA PICTURES

The startling success of *Easy Rider* in 1969 sprung open the locked gates of Hollywood for a generation of young filmmakers, including George Lucas.

United Artists. The executives who authorized these deals knew nothing about movie-making (Transamerica, for example, was a life insurance company whose other investment properties included Budget Rent-a-Car), but they recognized that the studios were underperforming assets that might regain value over time.

Shortly afterward, the success of a handful of small, independently produced pictures—most notably Dennis Hopper's *Easy Rider* (1969)—encouraged the under-new-management studios to usher in a wave of young, fresh talent. These young filmmakers—including Francis Ford Coppola, Martin Scorsese, Robert Altman, William Friedkin, Steven Spielberg, and George Lucas—made more personal and experimental pictures that could be shot inexpensively but sometimes generated huge profits. *Easy Rider*, made for $360,000, grossed nearly $60 million worldwide. Other New Hollywood hits included Altman's *M*A*S*H* (1970), Friedkin's *The French Connection* (1971) and *The Exorcist* (1973), Coppola's first two *Godfather* films (1972 and '74), and Lucas' *American Graffiti* (1973).

Hollywood also received a crucial economic boost from generous new tax laws passed in 1971, designed to reinvigorate the industry. These allowed the studios to claim tax credits on production costs for films made in the United States, including projects dating back to the 1960s. The new regulations also created a tax shelter for private investors in American film productions, making such investments tax deductible. These laws were repealed in the early 1980s, but in the meantime, the major studios recouped hundreds of millions of dollars, while the tax shelter helped fund movies like Milos Forman's *One Flew Over the Cuckoo's Nest* (1975) and Scorsese's *Taxi Driver*

(1976), which probably wouldn't have been produced by a major studio during any other era.

The New Hollywood wave crested in the mid-1970s. Studio bosses remained skittish about the influx of young filmmakers—not without reason, considering the wildly uneven box office performance of these pictures, including the conspicuous failure *The Last Movie* (1971), Hopper's follow-up to *Easy Rider*. The movement's upstart auteurs demanded greater creative control than Hollywood executives were comfortable ceding, and when even the most celebrated of these wunderkind directors began to falter—like Altman with *Buffalo Bill and the Indians* (1976), Scorsese with *New York, New York*, and Friedkin with *Sorcerer* (both 1977)—the studios' commitment to this style of filmmaking crumbled. At just this moment *Star Wars* arrived and changed everything. Unintentionally, George Lucas, who had entered the studio gates with the rest of the New Hollywood crowd, slammed the door shut behind him.

The Age of the Blockbuster

Star Wars wasn't the first blockbuster of the 1970s. Movies as diverse as *Airport, Love Story* (both 1970), *The Godfather* (1972), *American Graffiti, The Sting, The Exorcist* (all 1973), and *The Towering Inferno* (1974) all earned more than $100 million in raw dollars (without adjustment for inflation) in the United States alone. Friedkin's *The Exorcist* earned $402 million worldwide, and Spielberg's *Jaws* raked in a record-setting $470 million the following year. Nor was *Star Wars* the only blockbuster of 1977, when four movies turned huge profits—Spielberg's *Close Encounters of the Third Kind* grossed $337 million worldwide, John Badham's *Saturday Night Fever* earned $282 million worldwide, and Hal Needham's *Smokey and the Bandit* made $126 million in the United States. But *Star Wars* dwarfed everything else,

Dear George,
Last week "Star Wars" moved ahead of "Jaws" in domestic film rentals.
Your hyper-space performance package really did the trick.
Congratulations to the Cantina crowd and all the forces of your imagination that made "Star Wars" so worthy of the throne.
Wear it well.
Your pal,

Steven Spielberg

When *Star Wars* surpassed *Jaws* (the first modern summer blockbuster) as the top-grossing movie of all time, director Steven Spielberg took out this trade ad to congratulate his "pal," George Lucas.

racking up nearly $800 million worldwide, as well as hundreds of millions more in ancillary revenue through the sale of T-shirts, posters, toys, books, soundtrack albums, and everything else imaginable. In inflation-adjusted terms, the movie grossed the equivalent of more than $3 billion, and at least another billion through its unprecedented merchandising onslaught.

"It wasn't really the movie itself that shook the world," wrote Jim Emerson in a piece for the MSN Movies website. "It was the popular response to the movie, and the motion picture industry's response to that response."

Star Wars gave Hollywood a vision of the future, and the new business model it had been searching for practically since the Paramount decision in 1948. Small, personal movies by talented but difficult filmmakers were all but forgotten. The Age of the Blockbuster had arrived. Like a new California Gold Rush, the studios raced to find the next special effects–laden spectacular that could be turned into a merchandising bonanza. These movies cost more to make, which made them riskier bets, but the potential payoff was astronomical.

"I'm not saying that it's George's fault, but he and Steven Spielberg changed every studio's idea of what a movie should do in terms of investment versus return," writer-director Lawrence Kasdan said in a 1997 article for *Playboy* magazine. "It ruined the modest expectations of the movie business. Now every studio film is designed to be a blockbuster."

Lucas pushed back on this idea, angrily responding to a 1996 *Esquire* magazine essay by David Thomson titled "Who Killed the Movies" during a 1999 press conference. "There's an ecosystem in the film business," said Lucas, as quoted in the *Los Angeles Times*. "I think the effect Steven and I have had on the business is to help promote the independent art film." Lucas explained that when his and Spielberg's movies earn hundreds of millions, much of that revenue goes to theater owners, who use it to open more theaters, introducing more available screens, which represent more potential venues for independent films. The number of movie screens in the United States doubled between the mid-70s and the late 1990s, according to Lucasfilm research.

Lucas is right about the increased number of screens, but the latest blockbuster is now likely to occupy four or more of those screens at a time. And the rise of the multiplex has driven independently owned single- and double-screen cinemas—the venues most amenable to independently produced art films—to the brink of extinction. Besides, the point that filmmakers like Kasdan and critics like Thomson (and me) are making has to do with major studio films, not independent productions. Small, personal films are still made—but not usually by the major studios, which have the marketing muscle to make sure such movies are not merely released but noticed.

Beginning in the 1980s, the emerging technologies of home video and video gaming, and the new profit-making opportunities they offered, only deepened Hollywood's commitment to the blockbuster model. In retrospect, *Star Wars* seems like it was created with these markets in mind. As of late 2012, the *Star Wars* franchise had rung up better than $3.7 billion in DVD sales and another $2.9 billion in video game sales, according to a report published by Forbes. Yet, when *Star Wars* premiered, both the home video and gaming industries were in their infancy. The great VHS/Betamax format war was still raging, a conflict that delayed the wide adoption of home video for years. *Star Wars* didn't make its home video debut until 1982, when it was issued on laser disc. (For more on the convoluted history of *Star Wars* home viewing, see Chapter 34.) That same year saw the release of the first officially licensed *Star Wars* video game cartridge, which was based on *The Empire Strikes Back* and created for the Atari 2600 system. (For more on *Star Wars* games, see Chapter 31.)

Today, Hollywood's blockbuster-fueled post-*Star Wars* business model has endured longer than the Golden Age dream factory system, and nothing suggests it will end anytime soon (although video streaming and other emerging media may someday force Hollywood to again reinvent its modus operandi).

On the Screen . . .

Star Wars changed more than the business of movies, however. It changed the movies themselves.

While these things are admittedly difficult to quantify, most of Hollywood's subsequent blockbusters and would-be blockbusters were escapist fare that emulated the crisply edited, propulsively paced *Star Wars* to at least some degree. Also, many of the projects on which the studios wagered their money were science fiction thrillers such as the *Alien*, *Star Trek*, *Terminator*, and *Predator* films, or heroic fantasies such as the *Superman* and *Batman* movies. On the other hand, long-running, formerly bankable genres such as the Western and the musical collapsed, unable to compete with the visual effects–laden action spectacles that came to dominate the American movie marketplace from the 1980s onward. *Star Wars'* influence was immediate and has yet to wane. Director J. J. Abrams' 2009 and 2013 *Star Trek* films not only emulated the style and pacing of *Star Wars*, they copied specific shots from both *Star Wars* and *The Empire Strikes Back*. For the most part, however, *Star Wars* changed the style of action filmmaking not because later filmmakers sought to emulate George Lucas, but because *Star Wars* altered audience expectations.

The Empire Strikes Back and *Return of the Jedi* also proved influential, if only because they validated the success of *Star Wars* and continued to alter audience expectations. Moviegoers became less forgiving of narrative lulls and began demanding a high degree of production polish even from sci-fi, horror, and fantasy pictures, most of which had previously originated from studio B-units or scrappy independent companies. England's Hammer Films and Amicus Productions, which had released modestly budgeted but well-crafted and profitable horror and science fiction films for over three decades, both essentially gave up in the wake of *Star Wars*. Hammer released just one more picture before closing shop, a remake of Hitchcock's *The Lady Vanishes* in 1979. Amicus shut down immediately, even though the production company had recently scored hits with a series of Edgar Rice Burroughs adaptations (*The Land That Time Forgot* [1974], *At the Earth's Core* [1976], and *The People That Time Forgot* [1977]). Amicus cofounder Milton Subotsky said he closed Amicus because he realized his small-budget operation could not compete in the post-*Star Wars* movie marketplace.

One of the most obvious and indisputable ways that the original *Star Wars* trilogy changed the film landscape was that it raised the bar for special visual effects. Stanley Kubrick's *2001: A Space Odyssey* (1968) had represented a major leap forward in special effects technology, but it didn't alter audience perceptions the way *Star Wars* did. Even after *2001*, audiences were still willing to attend SF and fantasy films featuring relatively sketchy visual effects. That ended with the *Star Wars* films, which offered visuals of groundbreaking acuity, artifice, and sophistication. Visually, each picture was more impressive than its predecessor. Companies founded by Lucas to help create *Star Wars*—including legendary visual effects shop Industrial Light & Magic, and audio editing and effects house Sprocket Systems (now called Skywalker Sound)—quickly became the film industry's gold standard. By the early 1980s, any sci-fi or action film with sub-ILM-level visuals was likely to get laughed off the screen. For nearly thirty-five years, ILM and Skywalker Sound have remained at the forefront of new technologies including computer-generated imaging that have, for better or worse, fundamentally altered the way films are conceived and created. One result of this has been that many subjects once considered unfilmable, including the works of J. R. R. Tolkien and the adventures of various Marvel Comics superheroes, have been adapted for the screen, sometimes with thrilling results.

"*Star Wars* smashed open the possibilities of what film could actually do," said *Lord of the Rings* director Peter Jackson, in an interview included on the *Star Wars Original Trilogy* DVD collection. "It was like a seismic shift in the cinemagoing experience."

And at the Multiplex

Star Wars also changed the moviegoing experience for theater patrons. To insure that the meticulously sculpted soundscapes and rousing score for *Return of the Jedi* (1983) would be heard properly by audiences, Lucas introduced the THX audio quality assurance system (see Chapter 27). With his second *Star Wars* trilogy, Lucas spearheaded the industry's transition to digital film production and exhibition.

Perhaps most importantly, *Star Wars* changed movie audiences. Many of the patrons who bought tickets in record numbers during the original film's first release were young, and many of those viewers paid to see the film over and over again. While young people have always attended movies, and some people have always elected to see a movie more than once, Hollywood had never witnessed such a youthful, ravenous, repeat-viewing clientele before. In the years afterward, the audience for blockbuster science fiction, fantasy, and action films continued to skew toward those in their early twenties or younger. This may have been because *Star Wars* broadened the appeal of moviegoing for a new generation of fans, or because Hollywood, by creating more fare in the style of *Star Wars*, was actively courting the same demographic. It's a chicken-and-egg conundrum. However, the impact has been real.

American film audiences have grown younger over the years, even as the average age of the country's population has increased. According to statistics released by the MPAA in 2012, 37 percent of those patrons who attended movies in the United States and Canada in 2011 were age twenty-four or younger, even though those people make up only 32 percent of the population. This was a 3 percent increase in under-twenty-five viewers from 2010. Since the mid-1970s, attendance by people under age twenty-five has increased (gradually, in fits and starts) while attendance by those forty or older has declined. Also, most of the young patrons who paid to see *Star Wars* time and again in 1977 were male. Many of today's Hollywood blockbusters, such as those based on comic book superheroes, are aimed at young men.

Hollywood has produced other influential movie series—the James Bond films, for instance. And as any *Sight & Sound* pollster will tell you, it has also produced many movies that have earned greater acclaim from critics and more respect from directors. But no other film franchise has fostered so much change to so many facets of the movie industry as *Star Wars*. In essence, the Hollywood we know today was born nearly forty years ago, in a galaxy far, far away.

The Force Is Strong with This One

A George Lucas Timeline, 1944–1976

 Before he invented *Star Wars*, George Lucas invented himself. Both creations became the stuff of Hollywood legend.

May 14, 1944

George Walton Lucas Jr. was born on May 14, 1944, to George and Dorothy Lucas in the sleepy California town of Modesto. He was a diminutive, socially awkward boy with a weak chin and protruding ears. Once he started school, his older sisters Ann and Katy often protected him from bullies. Perhaps as a result, Lucas never liked Modesto and for many years hesitated to claim it as his hometown. At the University of Southern California (USC), when fellow students asked Lucas where he was from, he would answer evasively, "Northern California." Lucas later recalled his yearning to escape the remote, agrarian Modesto while creating young Luke Skywalker, who aches to leave the backwater planet Tatooine.

Lucas joined the Boy Scouts and played Little League, but spent much of his childhood watching old movies on television and reading comic books. He and a neighbor boy started a newspaper written by and for children called the *Daily Bugle*, which lasted less than a week. He and another friend turned the family garage into an elaborate haunted house for Halloween.

Lucas' father owned and operated a profitable stationary store, providing business supplies to local shops and offices in an era long before the emergence of big box retailers such as Staples and Office Depot. He hoped to hand the business down to his son, but George Jr. wasn't interested. By high school, Lucas had become obsessed with rock 'n' roll and hot rods—pursuits his father considered a waste of time. His father tried to encourage Lucas' passing interest in photography, but the young man became sullen and withdrawn at age fifteen when the family moved from their house at 530

Ramona Avenue in downtown Modesto to a larger home on thirteen wooded acres on the outskirts of town.

Without question, the teenage Lucas' most prized possession was his Fiat Bianchina, a tiny Italian coupe with a two-cylinder motor. Shortly after his father bought him the car, Lucas had crashed and rolled it. Afterward, he removed the crumpled roof and installed a roll bar and a low windscreen, along with special racing seat belts, which were bolted to the floor of the car and supposedly infallible. It was a weird-looking vehicle, but Lucas found that it raced well, despite its puny motor, because it was so light and nimble. When Han Solo tells Luke Skywalker that the *Millennium Falcon* "may not look like much, but she's got it where it counts," he could be Lucas describing his beloved Bianchina.

Toward the end of his tenure at Modesto's Downey High School, Lucas carried a D+ grade average. He grew out his hair and slicked it back with Vaseline, and began hanging out with tough kids who cruised and raced their souped-up cars. George Sr. feared that his son was on the road to juvenile delinquency. Then everything changed.

June 12, 1962

By all rights, Lucas should have died on June 12, 1962, when he wrapped his Bianchina around a walnut tree near the family ranch. He had gone to the library to study for his final exams. He was on the way home in his tiny Fiat—speeding, as usual—when he turned into the path of an oncoming Chevy Impala and was blasted off the road, flipping four or five times before slamming into the tree with so much force that it uprooted the adult walnut and moved it nearly two feet. Miraculously, his heavy-duty seat belt broke, ejecting Lucas from the vehicle as it tumbled, saving his life. Still, Lucas (who was five-foot-six and barely one hundred pounds at the time) was left in critical condition with a broken shoulder blade and internal bleeding. His lungs were rapidly filling with blood. The driver of the Impala, one of Lucas' classmates, called an ambulance.

Lucas spent two weeks recuperating in the hospital. The high school staff took pity on the injured boy and passed him despite his low grades and even though he missed finals. His diploma was delivered to his hospital bed. In numerous interviews, Lucas has pointed to this incident as the moment when he turned his life around. "That's when I decided to go straight, to be a better student, to try to do something with myself," Lucas told biographer Dale Pollock. Tellingly, Lucas' semiautobiographical *American Graffiti* (1973) takes place in 1962, involves a group of recent high school graduates, and concludes with a fiery car crash.

Lucas began to reinvent himself. He abandoned his dream of becoming a professional race car driver and enrolled at Modesto Junior College, hoping to improve his grades so that he could eventually transfer to a four-year university and earn a degree. For the first time, he applied himself to his schoolwork, and his grades improved to As, Bs, and Cs. He became fascinated by anthropology and sociology, and began to regularly read books without word balloons. He also rekindled his interest in photography and began filming auto races with an 8mm movie camera his father purchased for him.

Lucas remained close with race car driver Alan Grant, who he had befriended in high school. Grant was four years older than Lucas and served as a big brother figure. Lucas helped Grant maintain his race car and often filmed his races. Through Grant, Lucas met Hollywood cinematographer Haskell Wexler, a racing fan who was shooting a documentary in Northern California. Lucas volunteered as a production assistant on the film (*The Bus*, 1965) and impressed the up-and-coming Wexler, who would later shoot classic pictures including *Who's Afraid of Virginia Woolf?* (1966), *In the Heat of the Night* (1967), and *One Flew Over the Cuckoo's Nest* (1975); win two Oscars; and direct the cult favorite *Medium Cool* (1969). According to some sources, Wexler pulled strings to get Lucas admitted into the film program at USC. By all accounts, however, Wexler stoked young Lucas' interest in movies and urged him to consider pursuing a career in film.

June 9, 1964

Lucas graduated from Modesto Junior College June 9, 1964, and soon enrolled in the film studies program at USC. This decision infuriated George Sr., who still wanted Lucas to take over the office supply business. He warned Lucas that if the young man wasted his time on film school, he would end up being "a ticket-taker at Disneyland." Lucas insisted he was going to USC and declared that he would become a millionaire before he was thirty.

Lucas arrived at USC at a fortuitous moment. The old Hollywood studio system was crumbling, opening up more opportunities for new filmmakers than had been available in decades (see Chapter 1). He was also part of a remarkable group of young filmmakers who would pass through the USC program from 1966 to 1968, including future directors John Carpenter, Robert Zemeckis, John Milius, Randal Kleiser, and Don Glut; Oscar-winning sound editor Walter Murch; and Oscar-winning screenwriter David S. Ward, among others. Steven Spielberg, a student at nearby Cal State-Long Beach, was a friend of the program who often attended screenings with his USC pals. Even in this distinguished crowd, however, Lucas stood out.

At first, the shy Lucas kept his head down, intimidated by the prospect of major college-level coursework, adjusting to the hippie-friendly culture of USC (where all the men seemed to have long hair, beards, and often walked barefoot—this was nothing like Modesto!), and bowled over by his first exposure to foreign and avant-garde movies. He was particularly impressed by Nouvelle Vague directors such as Jean-Luc Godard, by Japanese master Akira Kurosawa, and by the non-narrative shorts of experimental filmmakers like Stan Brakhage and Jean-Claude Labrecque. Godard visited USC and spoke to its film students in 1966.

Lucas separated himself from his classmates with a series of brilliant student films. His earliest works—*Look at Life* (1965), a montage of clips from *Life* magazine set to music and sound effects, and *Herbie* (1965), a three-minute short that combined footage of city lights reflected on the polished body of a moving car with jazz by Herbie Hancock— display an innate grasp of rhythmic editing and a gift for sound design. Lucas applied the work ethic his father had modeled and made as many movies as possible at USC, often collaborating with fellow students on their films too. His projects routinely earned top marks and won prizes in competitions. The most impressive work of his undergraduate tenure was *The Emperor* (1966), a clever and entertaining twenty-five-minute documentary about bombastic Los Angeles disc jockey Bob Hudson.

Lucas graduated from USC on August 6, 1966. Almost immediately he was drafted but declared 4-F (he was diagnosed with diabetes). Freed from the prospect of a tour of duty in Vietnam, Lucas reenrolled at USC as a graduate student, hoping to complete a master's of fine arts. He never completed the MFA program, but made his most acclaimed student film, *Electronic Labyrinth: THX 1138 4EB* (1967), with the assistance of a crew of Navy film students. Taking a cue from Godard, who had filmed his science fiction pastiche *Alphaville* (1965) on the streets of Paris, Lucas shot his futuristic tale about a man fleeing a dehumanizing, underground society in contemporary locations around Los Angeles. Sophisticated and daring, with striking visuals and innovative sound design, *THX* won a national competition for student films. The film also helped him earn a coveted internship at Warner Brothers Pictures, where he made another pivotal career connection.

June 3, 1967

Lucas began his Warner Brothers internship on June 3, 1967. Originally, he wanted to work with the Warner Brothers animation unit, home of Bugs Bunny, Daffy Duck, and some of the greatest animators in Hollywood history. Unfortunately, by the mid-1960s the department had been shuttered. The only movie in production on the Warner lot at the time was a Fred Astaire musical titled *Finian's Rainbow* (1968), directed by another film school prodigy, Francis Ford Coppola. Lucas and Coppola struck up a friendship—in large part because they were the only people under age forty working on the crew. Coppola felt he could understand and trust Lucas. When Lucas' six-month internship ran out, Coppola hired him to remain on as his administrative assistant and promised to add him to the crew of his next picture, *The Rain People* (1969).

This offbeat road movie, starring James Caan, Robert Duvall, and Shirley Knight, was shot with a small crew (Lucas recorded sound, decorated sets, and served as an assistant to both the cinematographer and production manager) at various locations in New York, Pennsylvania, West Virginia, Virginia, Tennessee, Colorado, and Nebraska. Lucas also made a revealing thirty-two-minute documentary about the production titled *Filmmaker: A Diary* (1969), which Coppola funded through *The Rain People*'s promotional budget. Meanwhile, Coppola convinced Warner Brothers to option *THX 1138* as a possible feature film. Lucas' $3,000 option payment also counted

This lobby card shows the entire cast and crew of director Francis Ford Coppola's film *The Rain People*, including George Lucas (that's him, with camera, standing on top of the RV in the back). Coppola sits atop the tall ladder just right of center.

as his salary for *The Rain People*. In addition to serving his other functions and shooting the documentary, Lucas also had to write the *THX* screenplay. The flamboyant Coppola and reserved Lucas were very different personalities, and as the weeks and miles wore on, *The Rain People* at times tested their friendship.

By now, Lucas also had another distraction: He had fallen in love with Marcia Griffin, a talented film editor he met while editing footage for *Journey to the Pacific* (1968), a government documentary about President Lyndon B. Johnson's recent tour of Southeast Asia. She helped him edit *Filmmaker: A Diary* and later cut *American Graffiti* and *Star Wars* and other features, including Martin Scorsese's *Alice Doesn't Live Here Anymore* (1974) and *Taxi Driver* (1976). Lucas and Griffin married in 1969 in a church just south of Monterey, California. The couple honeymooned by driving down to Big Sur and, after a short stay, doubling back to return to work. *Journey to the Pacific* was one of several side projects the industrious Lucas worked on in the late 1960s. Among other things, he created an unorthodox documentary about the making of director Carl Foreman's 1969 Western *Mackenna's Gold* (Foreman reportedly hated Lucas' short, titled *6.18.67*), and he worked as a cameraman on Albert and David Maysles' documentary *Gimme Shelter* (1970) about the Rolling Stones' ill-fated appearance at a music festival in Altamont, California.

Enthralled by the guerrilla filmmaking dynamic of *The Rain People*, Coppola and Lucas decided to form their own production company, which they envisioned as a countercultural filmmaking collaborative that would help talented young directors produce the kinds of adventurous, personal pictures Hollywood was reluctant to greenlight. American Zoetrope, as they named the company (Coppola rejected Lucas' suggested moniker, Transamerican Sprocket Works), was founded on November 14, 1969. Coppola, who supplied nearly all the front money, was the company's president; Lucas was vice president. Lucas wanted the company to operate out of a beautiful home in a pastoral setting (a dream realized when he eventually created Skywalker Ranch), but when a suitable location could not be found, American Zoetrope began in a warehouse in downtown San Francisco.

Even before all the equipment had been installed, Coppola struck a $3.5 million, five-picture development agreement with Warner Brothers, who were gobsmacked by the box office receipts Columbia was collecting for Dennis Hopper's scruffy motorcycle picture *Easy Rider*. The promised films included Coppola's paranoid thriller *The Conversation* and a Vietnam movie Lucas and his USC classmate John Milius were writing called *Apocalypse Now*. But the fledgling production company's first release would be Lucas' feature-length version of *THX 1138*.

March 11, 1971

THX 1138 premiered on March 11, 1971. For Lucas, it had been a challenging production and a frustrating postproduction. The movie was rushed forward even though American Zoetrope was still finding its way. "It's like trying to put together a bicycle on Christmas when the kids will be up in an hour—you've got to get the whole thing together quickly, things are going wrong, and there are no instructions," Lucas explained to Pollock. Lucas was paid a modest $15,000 to write, direct, and edit the film, which was assigned a meager budget of $777,777.77 (a figure Coppola thought would be lucky) and tight ten-week shooting schedule, about the same length of time it took to make the fifteen-minute student version of *THX*. Coppola assumed Lucas would ignore the budget and spend whatever was necessary (that was the Coppola way), but Lucas wanted to prove to executives that he could deliver a picture on time and on budget.

Once again Lucas employed contemporary locations and minimalist sets to evoke the story's sterile dystopia. He signed *Rain People* costar Robert Duvall for the title role and San Francisco stage actress Maggie McOmie and English heavy Donald Pleasence for the film's other major parts. He also brought in fellow USC alum Walter Murch, who had helped him complete the screenplay, to design the movie's innovative electronic soundtrack. The real trouble began when Lucas delivered the finished film to Warner Brothers. The studio was unimpressed and announced that they would recut the picture themselves. Lucas was apoplectic. Warner ultimately removed only four judiciously chosen minutes from the eighty-six-minute picture, but Lucas remained infuriated and never released another picture through Warner, even though ten years later the studio begged him for *Raiders of the Lost Ark*.

However, the studio's pessimistic appraisal of *THX 1138* was borne out at the box office. The movie mystified most critics and audiences, and exasperated Warner executives, who immediately canceled the rest of the American Zoetrope projects in development. *THX* earned about $945,000 in its initial release. Even when Warner reissued it in the wake of *Star Wars*, it still performed poorly. In 2004, Lucas released a director's cut with enhanced visual effects and other revisions. Given three chances to score with audiences, *THX* mustered a lifetime gross of only $2.4 million.

Although it contains some haunting ideas and gripping sequences, *THX 1138* is an icy, inaccessible picture. Set in a future where human beings lead drug-numbed, emotionless lives directed by an all-powerful computer, it's about a man designated THX 1138 (Duvall) who goes off his meds and falls in love with his roommate LUH 3417 (McOmie). But they are discovered by LUH's jealous superior SEN 3214 (Pleasence), who wants THX for himself.

The ensuing conflict leads to the arrest and conviction of all three for crimes including "drug evasion" and sexual deviancy (for pursuing love, not for homosexuality). THX resolves to escape from the subterranean city to the surface world, setting in motion the events depicted in Lucas' original student film. The movie's key strengths are the same as the student version: arresting visuals (especially its chrome-faced robotic policemen) and an eerie, unsettling soundscape. Although the leads perform capably, the characters remain thinly sketched, and *THX 1138* registers little emotional impact. Like *Alphaville*, the Godard film that inspired it, it's aimed at the mind, not the heart. Lucas never again attempted anything like it.

June 26, 1972

By the time production of his second film began, on June 26, 1972, Lucas was determined to avoid all the mistakes he had made with *THX 1138*. The new movie, titled *American Graffiti*, was a lighthearted, nostalgic tale, full of relatable characters and situations—far more accessible than his first feature. Even so, *American Graffiti* was a tough sell. It took Lucas nearly a year to find

George Lucas, who is famously sparing in his direction of actors, instructs Duvall in this publicity still from *THX 1138*.   *Photo courtesy of Ronald V. Borst/ Hollywood Movie Posters*

a taker for the film, in part because he was the guy who had just made *THX 1138*, and in part because executives didn't understand the screenplay, cowritten by Lucas and his friends Gloria Katz and Willard Huyck. United Artists supplied Lucas with the initial development funds for the project but backed out after seeing the script. The picture didn't have a single protagonist; the story shifted between four point-of-view characters. Also, Lucas pitched *American Graffiti* as a sort of musical, with classic rock 'n' roll songs playing wall to wall. Executives feared the music rights alone would cost hundreds of thousands of dollars. Loosely plotted ensemble-cast movies and pictures with rock soundtracks are commonplace today, but *American Graffiti* was the first Hollywood picture to take this approach. Executives were leery.

With *American Graffiti* still twisting in the wind, Lucas was offered the chance to direct a low-budget crime drama called *Lady Ice* (1973), filmed mostly in Florida and starring Donald Sutherland, Jennifer O'Neill, and Robert Duvall. Although he desperately needed the money, he passed. Later, he said that not making *Lady Ice* was the best decision of his career. The picture was a flop and damaged the career of its director, Robert Greis. Had Lucas followed *THX 1138* with *Lady Ice*, he may have never made another movie.

Eventually, after Warner, United Artists, Columbia, and other major studios rejected it, Universal's Ned Tanen agreed to take a chance on *American Graffiti*, provided that Lucas engage a high-profile producer. Coppola—suddenly a big deal following *The Godfather* (1972)—agreed to loan his name to the film, although he was not actively involved in line production of *American Graffiti* (that role belonged to Gary Kurtz). Working with an even smaller budget than *THX* (just $775,000), Lucas was forced to cast unknowns. But with assistance from casting director Fred Roos, Lucas assembled an (in retrospect) jaw-dropping lineup, including Ron Howard (the film's biggest name at the time), Richard Dreyfuss, Cindy Williams, Harrison Ford, Bo Hopkins, Mackenzie Phillips, Charles Martin Smith, Suzanne Somers, and Paul Le Mat. Lucas' greatest casting coup was scoring an on-screen appearance by legendary L.A. disc jockey Robert Weston Smith, aka Wolfman Jack, heretofore a notorious recluse. With help from Kurtz, who had connections in the music industry, Lucas also struck friendly deals for the movie's music rights—spending a total of $90,000 to secure the use of forty-one classic rock tunes, although he was forced to abandon some of his more expensive selections (including all the Elvis Presley numbers).

American Graffiti follows four friends through the course of a single extraordinary night. College-bound nice guy Steve (Howard) tells his girlfriend (Williams) that he thinks the two of them should date other people while he's away at school, which leads to unforeseen repercussions. He also loans his treasured Chevy Impala to his nerdy pal Terry (Smith), with catastrophic consequences. Meanwhile, Steve's brainy friend Curt (Dreyfuss) runs afoul of a gang of greasers while pursuing a gorgeous blonde (Somers) who flirts with him from a passing car. And hot-rodder John (Le Mat) gears up for a showdown with a drag racer from out of town (Ford), but first must babysit young Carol (Phillips). The movie hits all the right notes. It's warm, engaging, and funny, rich in endearing, well-sculpted characters. In short, it's everything *THX 1138* is not. Lucas uses the rock soundtrack imaginatively, both evoking nostalgia for the era and commenting (often ironically) on the action. The movie's soundtrack album also became a major hit.

However, *American Graffiti* was a far more challenging picture to shoot than *THX*. The trouble began after just two nights of production when the city of San Rafael, California, yanked Lucas' filming permit because a local barkeeper complained that the movie (being shot entirely on location, from 9:00 p.m. to 5:00 a.m. since the entire story takes place on a single night) was interfering with his business. *American Graffiti* was forced to relocate to nearby Petaluma, California. The travails continued there with a fire, a marijuana bust among the crew, technical glitches of all sorts, and other headaches. Lucas called in old pal Haskell Wexler, who worked without credit to solve lighting problems. The difficulties continued even after the film was complete. Lucas, Marcia Griffin, and editor Verna Fields labored to trim the unwieldy three-hour rough cut of the movie to an acceptable 112 minutes. And, even though test audiences loved *American Graffiti*, Universal studio boss Ned Tanen hated it. Famously, Tanen and Coppola got into a shouting match over the film in the lobby following a sneak preview screening in San Francisco on January 28, 1973. Tanen didn't understand the picture; he wanted to recut it and was hesitant to release it at all. Coppola later claimed that he offered to buy the film outright and release it himself, something Tanen denies. Either way, Universal delayed the movie's release for months.

August 20, 1973

In the meantime, Lucas had no choice but to move on to his next project. In the spring of 1973, he had two stories in the works. The first was a hallucinogenic Vietnam War drama he was cowriting with former USC classmate John Milius—*Apocalypse Now*. Coppola, who was preparing to direct the paranoid thriller *The Conversation* (1974), pressed Lucas to direct *Apocalypse Now* for American Zoetrope. But Lucas was unhappy with the terms Coppola proposed (with Coppola taking a 25 percent profit share, and Lucas and Milius splitting another 25 percent share). The Lucas-Coppola friendship had always been mercurial and was strained by the *Apocalypse Now* negotiations. It nearly ruptured months later amid a bitter dispute over profit sharing on *American Graffiti*. Coppola would eventually make *Apocalypse Now* himself, rewriting the screenplay so extensively that Lucas failed to receive credit. It proved to be a torturous production, running years over schedule before finally premiering in 1979.

Lucas' other idea was to make an old-fashioned space opera in the style of *Flash Gordon*. Although his concept remained fuzzy at this stage, he had already prepared a brief outline and was trying to secure a screenplay development deal. He was contractually obligated to offer the project, then titled *The Star Wars*, to Universal, but the studio passed. On August 20, 1973, up-and-coming executive Alan Ladd Jr. of Twentieth

American Graffiti became one of the greatest "sleeper" hits of the 1970s, quietly building an audience and playing week after week in many cities. This trade ad celebrated the films' long (then ongoing) theatrical engagements at venues from Cincinnati to Seattle.

Century-Fox, who had seen *American Graffiti* and was very impressed with it, entered into a modest agreement with Lucasfilm Ltd. to develop *The Star Wars*. Lucasfilm would receive $15,000 in development funds, and Lucas would be paid $50,000 for the completed screenplay and another $100,000 for directing the film, which initially was assigned a $3 million budget. Fox, which had made a fortune on its *Planet of the Apes* franchise, was more amenable to science fiction than most Hollywood Studios. Had Lucas held out a little longer, he could have negotiated far better terms, but in the summer of 1973 he was deep in debt and anxious to get cracking on his new project.

Universal had finally dumped *American Graffiti* onto the market August 11, 1973, with little fanfare. No one knew it yet, but it was on its way to becoming one of the most profitable movies of all time. It was the prototypical sleeper hit, with box office receipts steadily pouring in throughout its lengthy original release, thanks mostly to enthusiastic word of mouth and repeat business. Made for less than $1 million, *American Graffiti* pulled in $115 million (that's $605 million in inflation-adjusted terms). Lucas personally made $7 million. He was twenty-eight years old. As he had predicted, he had become a millionaire before age thirty. The film also earned four Academy Award nominations: Best Picture (it lost to *The Sting*), Best Director, Best Original Screenplay, and Best Film Editing. It won a Golden Globe for Best Motion Picture (Musical or Comedy). The movie's structure and tone were copied by many later films, and its success spawned a flurry of other nostalgic movies and TV shows, including *Happy Days* (1974–84), starring Howard, and its spin-off *Laverne & Shirley* (1976–83), starring Williams. Most importantly for Lucas, *American Graffiti*—and the money he made from it—gave him leverage with the studio and the flexibility to invest his own money in his next project if he needed to. Both would prove invaluable as *The Star Wars* began its winding road to the screen.

3

Here's Where the Fun Begins

The Origins of *Star Wars*

tar Wars didn't emerge from a vacuum, like a Star Destroyer dropping out of hyperspace. It came together slowly over the course of several screenplay drafts (see next chapter) and combined many elements George Lucas had absorbed over the years, some dating from his childhood, some from his tenure at USC, and some recently discovered. Generally speaking, the most pervasive influence on *Star Wars* was the untold number of classic movies Lucas consumed on television as a child and later in film school. In its final form, *Star Wars* incorporated homages to many of these pictures (see Chapter 9). But in specific terms, a handful of books and movies exerted a powerful influence on the development of *Star Wars*.

Flash Gordon

One of Lucas' favorite TV programs as a child was *Adventure Theater*, broadcast at 6:00 p.m. Monday through Friday on San Francisco's KRON-TV. The show aired episodes of classic Hollywood serials, mostly from the Hollywood Television Service library of vintage Republic Pictures "chapter plays." These included *The Fighting Devil Dogs* (1938) and *Zorro's Fighting Legion* (1939), sometimes cited as influences on *Star Wars* and *Indiana Jones*, respectively (*Devil Dogs*' costumed supervillain, the Lightning, looks remarkably like Darth Vader). *Adventure Theater* also broadcast serials that had fallen into public domain, including *Flash Gordon Conquers the Universe* (1940), which was a particular favorite of Lucas.

Cartoonist Alex Raymond's seminal space opera *Flash Gordon* remains one of the best-loved and most influential works in the history of science fiction. Virtually every space-faring sci-fi adventure owes a debt to Raymond's creation, which began as a newspaper comic strip, became one of the great movie serials, and was later adapted for radio, comic books, novels, TV, and feature films. The strip debuted on January 7, 1934. Raymond created the strip to compete with illustrator Dick Calkins' futuristic *Buck Rogers*, which had premiered five years earlier. Thanks to Raymond's wildly imaginative scenarios and beautifully rendered artwork, *Flash Gordon* eventually eclipsed *Buck Rogers* in terms of circulation and fan interest, although today casual fans sometimes confuse the two characters.

Universal Pictures' thirteen-chapter serial *Flash Gordon* (1936), starring former Olympic swimmer Charles "Buster" Crabbe in the title role, followed the plot of Raymond's strip with reasonable fidelity. The chapter play proved extremely successful and spawned two sequels, *Flash Gordon's Trip to Mars* (1938) and *Flash Gordon Conquers the Universe* (1940), both also headlined by Crabbe. Despite their low-budget production values and badly dated costumes and visual effects, the *Flash Gordon* serials feature some of the most iconic imagery in all of science fiction cinema, including their smoke-belching rocket ships and spark-spewing ray guns.

Lucas had revealed his affinity for classic SF serials by opening *THX 1138* (1971) with a one-minute snippet from the trailer for *Buck Rogers* (1939), inserted for ironic effect. Originally, Lucas wanted to remake *Flash Gordon* as a major Hollywood movie and tried to purchase the rights from King Features Syndicate in the early 1970s. Unfortunately, the film rights had already been sold to Italian producer Dino de Laurentiis, who was trying to woo Federico Fellini into directing a reimagined version of the character. So Lucas set out to create an original space

The single greatest inspiration for *Star Wars* was *Flash Gordon Conquers the Universe* (1940), Universal's third and final "chapter play" featuring Buster Crabbe as the planet-hopping hero. George Lucas saw this serial, and many others, thanks to *Adventure Theater*, broadcast at 6:00 p.m. Monday through Friday on San Francisco's KRON-TV.
Image courtesy of Ronald V. Borst/Hollywood Movie Posters

opera in the style of Alex Raymond's comic strip and the classic serials. In interviews during the writing and production of *Star Wars*, Lucas invariably compared his upcoming film to *Flash Gordon*. In 1974, for instance, he told interviewer Larry Sturhahn that his upcoming film was "science fiction—*Flash Gordon* genre."

What precisely that meant, however, remained to be defined. Lucas had a concept but no plot. Or, as he put it in an interview included in the original *Star Wars* souvenir program, the project was "what you might call a good idea in search of a story." In his early drafts, Lucas cobbled together a story out of elements borrowed from several other works.

The Hidden Fortress

Lucas has also frequently mentioned the samurai films of Akira Kurosawa, and specifically his 1958 epic *The Hidden Fortress*, as an inspiration for *Star Wars*. Lucas discovered Kurosawa's work at USC and was "completely hooked," he said in a 2001 interview for the Criterion Collection. Widely regarded as one of the grand masters of international cinema, Kurosawa was the first Japanese director whose films earned admiration in the West. His *Rashomon* (1951) became the first Japanese movie to win an Academy Award. Although he also made noir thrillers, medical dramas, social problem films, and other types of movies, Kurosawa remains best known for his samurai pictures, a genre known in Japan as *jidai-geki*. (Lucas' "Jedi" are a thinly veiled tribute to this source.) Kurosawa's *Rashomon*, *Seven Samurai* (1954), and *Yojimbo* (1961) were all remade as Westerns, which seems only appropriate since Kurosawa was profoundly influenced by American John Ford, best remembered as the director of classic Westerns such as *Stagecoach* (1939). *Star Wars*, not coincidentally, is often described as a Western set in outer space.

The Hidden Fortress, while not one of Kurosawa's mostly highly regarded films, is a crowd-pleasing, seriocomic adventure yarn set in war-torn sixteenth-century Japan. In it, a general (Toshiro Mifune), a princess (Misa Uehara), and two peasants (Minoru Chiaki and Kamatari Fujiwara) try to sneak a fortune in gold through enemy lines. The story is told from the point of view of the two squabbling peasants, Matashichi and Tahei. "I was beginning to write the screenplay and put it together and I remembered *The Hidden Fortress*," Lucas said in the Criterion interview. "The one thing that really struck me about *The Hidden Fortress* and I was really intrigued by, was the fact that the story is told by the two lowliest characters. I decided that would be a nice way to tell the *Star Wars* story, to take the two lowliest characters as Kurosawa did and tell the story from their point of view. In *Star Wars*' case it was the two droids. That was the strongest influence."

However, this was hardly the *only* influence. Numerous other parallels can be drawn. If Matashichi and Tahei are the models for C-3PO and R2-D2, then war-weary General Makabe and hard-nosed, no-nonsense Princess Yuki equate to Obi-Wan Kenobi and Princess Leia. *Star Wars* both opens and closes in similar fashion to *The Hidden Fortress*. The Kurosawa film begins by introducing Matashichi and Tahei, quarrelsome friends (one tall, one short) who separate at the beginning of the story but are soon reunited when both are captured by enemy patrols. *Star Wars* introduces the two droids, who separate once they arrive on Tatooine but are soon reunited when both are captured by Jawas. In both films, the final scene is a formal gathering of the heroes, at which the princess doles out rewards. There are many other similarities between these bookends.

Moreover, the influence of *The Hidden Fortress* extends beyond the first *Star Wars* film to the entire Original Trilogy and beyond. In Kurosawa's film, the heroes prevail because General Makabe convinces rival General Tokodoro, his former ally but current adversary, to switch sides and join him in striking out against the cruel Lord Yamana. In *Return of the Jedi*, Luke Skywalker defeats the evil Emperor only by convincing Darth Vader to turn away from the Dark Side and strike against his master. *The Hidden Fortress* features a scene in which Makabe races down a wooded trail on horseback, chasing down two enemy samurai—a sequence that plays much like the speeder bike chase in *Jedi*. The fire festival Makabe, Yuki, and the peasants attend could be an Ewok ritual. And, to hide her identity, Princess Yuki fools her enemies by employing a double and masquerading as a servant—a gambit mirrored by the Queen Amidala/Padme business in *The Phantom Menace* (1999). Moreover, the anti-greed message of *The Hidden Fortress* aligns with the ethics professed by Lucas in his *Star Wars* films (see Chapter 29). Some of these commonalities may not demonstrate influence, but simply identify the elements and themes that attracted Lucas to *The Hidden Fortress* in the first place, concerns that naturally resurface in his work. But even so, *The Hidden Fortress* appears to have been a profound and long-standing source of inspiration for Lucas.

Dune

During the writing of *Star Wars*, Lucas read stacks of science fiction paper-backs and comic books. One of those was Frank Herbert's 1965 masterpiece *Dune*. The novel is set on a desert planet and involves a young hero who gains power after being initiated into an ancient religious cult. Eventually, he overthrows a malevolent galactic empire. *Dune* features a Princess Alia (pronounced "Ah-Leia"), vehicles known as sandcrawlers, "dew collectors" (similar to "moisture vaporators"), indigenous sandworm-riding "Fremen" (similar to the Sandpeople), and a powerful religious order (the matriarchal Bene Gesserit) who fight with swords and can exert mental control over the weak-minded. Perhaps most strikingly, the villain turns out to be the hero's grandfather. There are several other remarkable similarities between the two works.

Because of all this, some critics have asserted that *Dune* served as the primary model for *Star Wars*. That, however, appears to be an overstatement. Lucas has never mentioned *Dune* as a source of inspiration, even though he has acknowledged all the other sources mentioned in this chapter, and has cited some of them many times. Moreover, there are many significant differences between *Dune* and *Star Wars*. Luke Skywalker is a poor farm boy—a nobody. The hero of *Dune* is a young man of privilege—Paul Atreides, whose father is a duke charged with overseeing the planet Arrakis. Unlike the backwater Tatooine, Arrakis is the most important planet in the galaxy, the lone world capable of producing the "spice" known as mélange, which extends human life, introduces psychic abilities, and enables space travel. It is the most precious resource known to humankind. Unlike *Star Wars*, *Dune*'s plot involves a complex web of political and religious intrigue. Perhaps more importantly, the tone of the piece is nothing like the rollicking, swashbuckling vibe of *Star Wars*. *Dune* is a sober, sometimes challenging work (it opens with an eighteen-page glossary of vocabulary Herbert invented for the novel). It was modeled after the works of Fyodor Dostoevsky and the classical Greek tragedies, rather than the comic strip adventures of Alex Raymond. Still, the early drafts of *Star Wars* contain some

E. E. "Doc" Smith's Lensmen, featured in novels such as *Galactic Patrol*, may have provided the model for George Lucas' Jedi knights.
Photography by Preston Hewis/East Bank Images

very *Dune*-like elements (in one version, Princess Leia is protecting a fortune in "spice"), some of which clearly made it into the final screenplay.

Galactic Patrol

Another of the SF novels Lucas read during this period was E. E. "Doc" Smith's *Galactic Patrol* (1950), and possibly other volumes in Smith's classic Lensman series, all of which were reprinted in paperback in the early 1970s by Pyramid Books. The seven-part Lensman saga, published in book form between 1948 and 1960, was the crowning achievement of venerable pulp sci-fi author Edward Elmer Smith, PhD. Smith was a prolific writer whose career began in the 1920s in publications such as *Amazing Stories*, which first serialized his early novels. In addition to the Lensman novels, Smith also created the four-volume *Skylark* series (published in book form from 1946 to 1966 but initially serialized in the late 1920s), some of the earliest novels to depict human exploration of deep space. He held a doctorate in chemistry. In 1966, when a special one-time Hugo Award was handed out for Best All-Time Series, Smith's Lensman books finished second to Isaac Asimov's *Foundation Trilogy*.

Galactic Patrol features a group of superpowered policemen known as the lensmen who protect the galaxy from space pirates, interstellar gangsters, and other evildoers. The lensmen possess "lenses" that focus the "Cosmic All," enabling them to read minds and perform other psychic feats. They were almost certainly the model for Lucas' Jedi knights. In his early drafts, the plot of *Star Wars* involved something called the Kiber Crystal, which helped focus the power of the Force, a device that sounds a lot like one of Smith's lenses. In *Galactic Patrol*, the third volume in the series, rookie lensman Kimball Kinnison acquires the plans to a new superweapon developed by "Boskonian" pirates (after jettisoning them in an escape pod). Eventually Kinnison, who practices his psychic powers by fighting in a helmet with the blast shield down, uses information gleaned from the stolen plans to destroy the enemy base in his one-man fighter.

Although Lucas has seldom mentioned Smith's Lensman books as an influence, author Michael Kaminski (in his excellent book *The Secret History of Star Wars*) observes that a copy of *Galactic Patrol* can be seen on Lucas' bookshelf in the first *Star Wars Episode I: The Phantom Menace* web documentary.

The Hero with a Thousand Faces

After two drafts, Lucas had a desk (and a screenplay) littered with ideas— enough sequences, characters, and backstory to fill two or three movies, maybe more. But his work still lacked a compelling, coherent structure. As he struggled to organize this jumbled material, Lucas discovered Joseph Campbell's 1949 book *The Hero with a Thousand Faces*, which he readily cites as a profound influence on the creation of *Star Wars*. Later, after *Star Wars* premiered, Lucas struck up a personal friendship with the scholar.

Campbell's erudite writings combined studies in mythology, comparative religions, and Freudian psychology. In *The Hero with a Thousand Faces*, Campbell delineates plot points and story structures common to ancient myths and legends of various cultures spanning the globe, and argues that this common archetypal narrative serves basic human psychological needs. He refers to this uber-yarn as "the Hero's Journey," which begins with "the Call to Adventure," includes encounters with "helper" characters, tests (he lists nine common variations), a flight (an escape or chase), and concludes with the discovery or capture of an "elixir" that rescues his or her people. Other story elements that often recur, according to Campbell, include battles with dragons or other magical creatures (including, presumably, Rancor monsters), dismemberment (such as losing a hand), and "father atonement."

In its final form, Lucas' *Star Wars* screenplay scrupulously conforms to Campbell's "Hero's Journey" structure, both in the story's general design and in many particulars. For example, Campbell writes that "the first encounter of the hero-journey is with a protective figure (often a little old crone or old man) who provides the adventurer with amulets against the dragon forces he is about to pass." This would seem to be an excellent description of Obi-Wan Kenobi, who gives Luke Skywalker his lightsaber. Discussing what he calls "the Road of Trials," Campbell writes that during his mythic tests and ordeals, the hero "is covertly aided by the advice, amulets and secret agents of the supernatural helper he met before . . . Or it may be that he here discovers for the first time that there is a benign power everywhere supporting him in his superhuman passage." Both of these conditions apply to *Star Wars*. Luke continues to be guided by Obi-Wan throughout the story (even after the Jedi master's death); simultaneously, he grows to understand the workings and power of the Force.

Lucas has freely acknowledged Campbell's influence many times, including in a 1999 PBS interview with Bill Moyers. "When I did *Star Wars*, I consciously set out to recreate myths, and the classic mythological motifs," Lucas said. "I tried to take the ideas that seem to cut across most cultures because I'm fascinated by that, and that's one of the things that I really got from Joe Campbell. . . . I'm telling an old myth in a new way. I'm just taking the core myth and localizing it . . . more for the end of the millennium than for any particular place."

Not only does *Star Wars* adhere to Campbell's "Hero's Journey" schematic, but so does the Original Trilogy, taken in its totality. Lucas' Indiana Jones films also incorporate many of Campbell's archetypal concepts. In a dust jacket blurb written for a 2008 reprinting of *The Hero with a Thousand Faces*, Lucas wrote, "In the three decades since I discovered *The Hero with a Thousand Faces*, it has continued to fascinate and inspire me."

Tales of Power

Lucas wanted his modern myth to have a moral/religious core; it was central to his entire concept (see Chapter 29). But Lucas' personal religious convictions remained nebulous. He once described his beliefs as "Buddhist Methodist," and there are Zen overtones in *Star Wars*. But no Earthly religion would make sense in the context of long ago in a galaxy far, far away. So, like science fiction and fantasy writers such as Frank Herbert and Ursula K. Le Guin before him, he set out to invent his own religion—what became the Force. "I put the Force into the movies in order to try to awaken a certain kind of spirituality in young people—more a belief in God than a belief in any particular religious system," Lucas told interviewer Bill Moyers. The Force developed over the course of several screenplay iterations of *Star Wars*, was greatly expanded in *The Empire Strikes Back* and *Return of the Jedi*, and then significantly altered in his second trilogy of *Star Wars* films. However, in many respects, especially in its embryonic form, the Force recalls the writings of Carlos Castaneda, dubbed by *Time* magazine as "the godfather of the New Age." Lucas has acknowledged that during the writing of *Star Wars* he read Castaneda's *Tales of Power* (1974).

Castaneda, an anthropologist in training at UCLA, wrote a series of books detailing his experiences studying with a reclusive Mexican "sorcerer" he referred to as Don Juan. Through a series of guided visions and conversations with Don Juan, sometimes after smoking peyote, Castaneda learns secrets of mystical power. *Tales of Power*, Castaneda's fourth book, depicts the conclusion of his apprenticeship with Don Juan. It's a product of its era, the kind of book that probably works better if the reader has also smoked a bowl of peyote. However, many of the "truths" Don Juan reveals to Castaneda bear intriguing similarities to the Force. "Do you know that at this very moment you are surrounded by eternity? And do you know that you can use that eternity, if you so desire?" Don Juan asks in *Tales of Power*. "Eternity" in this context refers to a binding life force that the sorcerer can tap into as a source of power. Later, he reveals that benevolent sorcerers are opposed by "black magicians" who misuse the power of eternity. All this clearly parallels the Force, with its Jedi Knights and Sith Lords. In fact, Lucas' handwritten notes on his third draft outline include the following description: "Old man [Kenobi] can do magic, read minds, talk to things like Don Juan."

The Castanenda influence became even clearer in *The Empire Strikes Back*, with the introduction of Yoda, a sawed-off, green Don Juan figure. "We are luminous beings," Don Juan explains. Yoda echoes this in *Empire*: "Luminous beings we are, not this crude matter." To grasp the hidden nature of eternity, Don Juan insists, the sorcerer must set aside his previous ideas about the way the world works. Or, as Yoda instructs Luke Skywalker, "You must unlearn what you have learned." Numerous other links can be made to Castaneda's writings.

In the late 1960s and early 1970s, Castaneda's books earned admiring reviews and sold briskly, turning the author into a countercultural celebrity even before he completed his studies at UCLA. His admirers included Doors singer Jim Morrison and beat author William S. Burroughs. Castaneda maintained his books were true and that the teachings of Don Juan derived from arcane practices passed down from ancient Toltec shamans. In the late 1970s, however, anthropologists specializing in Yaqui (descendants of the Toltecs) culture debunked Castaneda's claims, pointing to the lack of Yaqui vocabulary or phrases in Don Juan's lessons, as well as numerous inaccuracies and anachronisms. However, some of these skeptics granted that Castaneda's books remained valuable as works of philosophy or fiction. By the time his books came under fire, Castaneda had withdrawn from public life. He moved into a large house in Los Angeles with three female acolytes and became a recluse, although he published seven more works before his death in 1998 and founded Cleargreen Inc. to promote a practice he called Tensegrity, based on the lessons he had supposedly learned from Don Juan. Cleargreen remains in business, and none of Castaneda's books have ever gone out of print.

Uncle Scrooge

For more than three decades, beginning in 1942, onetime Disney animator Carl Barks wrote and drew enthralling and wildly imaginative Donald Duck and Uncle Scrooge comic books for Western Publishing. Like everyone else who produced Disney comics for Western, Barks worked anonymously; by contractual agreement, all stories were credited solely to Walt Disney. However, Barks' expressive artwork and inventive stories were distinctive, and readers came to refer to him as "the Good Duck Artist," a nickname that stuck even after his identity was revealed in the early 1960s. Although Barks also created short (one- to ten-page) humorous stories, done in the same style as a Donald Duck cartoon, he became renowned for his longer (twenty-four- to thirty-two-page) adventure yarns, starring Scrooge, Donald, and Huey, Dewey, and Louie, who Barks sent on thrilling quests to recover rare treasures from the Klondike, the Orient, Africa, South America, the sunken continent of Atlantis, and even outer space. To oppose Scrooge, Barks invented the nefarious Beagle Boys, unscrupulous sorceress Magica de Spell, and rival gazillionnaire Flintheart Glomgold, among many other characters. These were rollicking action epics that merely happened to star anthropomorphic waterfowl.

George Lucas whiled away many hours of his youth reading comic books, and Barks' Disney comics were particular favorites. He subscribed to *Walt Disney's Comics and Stories* and bought issues of *Uncle Scrooge* at the local newsstand. "The stories were very cinematic," Lucas wrote in his introduction to Fantagraphics Books' 2012 collection *Walt Disney's Uncle Scrooge: Only a Poor Old Man.* "They have a clear beginning, middle, and end, and operate in scenes, unlike many comic strips and books. Barks' stories don't just move from panel to panel, but flow in sequences—sometimes several pages long—that lead to new sequences." The influence of Barks' fluid, dynamic storytelling can be seen both in *Star Wars* and, more overtly, in Lucas' Indiana Jones series. Both Lucas and Steven Spielberg acknowledged, in a 1982 *Time* magazine interview, that *Raiders of the Lost Ark* (1981) was influenced by Barks. The famous scene in which Indy flees from a giant boulder, they confessed, was cribbed from the 1954 Uncle Scrooge adventure "The Seven Cities of Cibola." Lucas' love of Barks' duck tales also may have played a part in his decision to produce the ill-fated *Howard the Duck* (1986), based on a Marvel Comics character created by Steve Gerber.

Lucas was also inspired by Barks in subtler but more profound ways. While Uncle Scrooge always sought to increase his fortune, he found even greater reward in the companionship of his nephew and grandnephews, and in the thrill of adventure. "Carl Barks' worldview involves poking fun at the materialistic tendencies that all people have and praising their more sociable, brotherly aspects," Lucas wrote in his *Only a Poor Old Man* introduction. Lucas has often espoused similar views (sometimes referring to his own Scrooge-like extreme wealth as "a pain"), and this theme recurs in his films. In *Star Wars* it is embodied in the character of Han Solo. Although Solo claims "I'm in it for the money," at the climax of the film he risks his life to save Luke and prevent the Death Star from wiping out the rebellion. "I knew there was more to you than money," Princess Leia says afterward.

Other writers have argued for additional possible influences on *Star Wars*, including writer-artist Jack Kirby's early 1970s *New Gods* comic books (in which the heroic Orion is the son of the galactic tyrant Darkseid), and even J. R. R. Tolkien's *The Lord of the Rings* (with Obi-Wan Kenobi serving as the equivalent of Gandalf). But, as with the more similar *Dune*, it's unclear how much, if any, direct impact these sources had on the development of *Star Wars*. Lucas has never publically credited these as sources as an inspiration, and many of the perceived links between these works and *Star Wars* are common to virtually every work structured (consciously or otherwise) in the mold of Campbell's "Hero's Journey" archetype.

In any case, Lucas still had to assemble the bits and pieces he gleaned from these sundry inspirations into a cohesive, original configuration. That task proved extremely difficult.

4

From the Adventures of Luke Starkiller

Draft Screenplays

In January 1973, George Lucas sat down with a pad of paper and a pencil and began writing his space opera. The early results were not encouraging.

His first attempt was a two-page outline titled *Journal of the Whills*, which opened this way: "This is the story of Mace Windy, a revered Jedi-bendu of the Ophuchi, as related to us by C. J. Thorpe, padawan learner to the famed Jedi." Thorpe, known to his friends as Chuiee (pronounced "Chewie"), is a sixteen-year-old aspiring "Jedi-templar" whose master, warlord Mace Windy, is thrown out of the Alliance of Independent System's defense forces on charges trumped up by his political rivals. Chuiee remains loyal to his master and leaves with Mace. Four years later, while guarding a shipment of valuable materials being delivered to the jungle planet Yavin, Mace and Chuiee receive an urgent summons from the leadership of the Alliance.

The narrative ends there, unfinished. If the reader is familiar with the universe Lucas would eventually create, this scenario may make some degree of sense. But no one who read *Journal of the Whills* in early 1973 could make heads or tails of it. Alan Ladd Jr. of Twentieth Century-Fox eventually offered Lucas a development deal not on the strength of Lucas' outline but because he had screened the as-yet unreleased *American Graffiti* and believed in Lucas' talent.

Lucas himself was unsure where the project that would become *Star Wars* was going—it was, in his words, "a good idea in search of a story"—and he was deeply insecure about his ability to write the screenplay. He had always received poor marks in English and had farmed out the scripts for his first two films to other screenwriters. Eventually, he would hire Gloria Katz and Willard Huyck, who had cowritten *American Graffiti*, to polish the dialogue for *Star Wars*. But there was no way to delegate the bulk of the writing; no one else understood Lucas' vision for *Star Wars*. Lucas didn't yet fully understand it himself. He came to know it only through continual writing and rewriting over the course of three years and five screenplay drafts, along with an initial treatment, several summaries, and other documents. It its earliest incarnations, as *Journal of the Whills* demonstrates, the story bore few similarities to the *Star Wars* we know.

Rough Draft and First Draft

Lucas discarded *Journal of the Whills* and started over, virtually from scratch. Over the course of the next two years, he developed many elements—plot points, characters, settings, backstory ideas—but had great difficulty assembling them into a coherent shape. The popular conception—propagated by Lucas himself—that he outlined the entire epic saga and then selected a slice of it (Episode IV) to film as the first movie is inaccurate. The actual process was more akin to assembling a jigsaw puzzle; only, when Lucas had finished the puzzle, there were several intriguing pieces left over. Some of those—for instance, a city floating in the clouds and an escape through an asteroid belt—eventually were incorporated into the sequels, but in the beginning there was no master plan.

Lucas' original treatment, titled *The Star Wars*, served as a thumbnail sketch for the rough draft screenplay he delivered to Ladd in May 1974. The treatment and early script contain some familiar elements. Most notably, it begins with a serial-like rolling summary of the backstory, features the Death Star, and includes the squabbling robots R2-D2 and C-3PO. Artoo and Threepio would remain virtually unchanged from this point forward. The script also includes many recognizable character names, although in most cases the characters little resemble those with whom the names would later be associated.

In this version, the Jedi-bendu, formerly the guardians of the Galactic Empire, are a near-extinct society of warriors who were hunted down by the Black Knights of the Sith, a rival sect that overthrew the kindly old emperor and installed the evil new emperor. The story centers on eighteen-year-old Anakin Starkiller, whose father Kane is a Jedi in hiding in the remote Kessil system. The Starkillers are forced into action when a Sith assassin arrives and, during an attempt on Kane's life, murders Anakin's ten-year-old brother, Deak. The remaining Starkillers return to their home planet of Aquilae, where Anakin becomes the padawan learner of a famed warrior, General Luke Skywalker, a man in his sixties. But soon Aquilae is attacked by the Empire's new space fortress, the Death Star, and its king is killed. Skywalker and Anakin are assigned to effect the escape of the rightful heir to the Aquilaean throne, fourteen-year-old Princess Leia. They are accompanied by a pair of robots,

R2-D2 and C-3PO, and soon joined by Kane's old friend Han Solo, an alien whose appearance recalls the Creature from the Black Lagoon.

Space dogfights and daring escapes ensue, including a laser sword duel in a cantina and a daring trip through an asteroid belt. Our heroes' adventures take them to the jungle planet Yavin, home of the Wookiees ("huge gray and furry beasts"). There, Leia is captured by Wookiee-hunting "trappers," who turn her over to the Empire for bounty. She is whisked off to the Death Star. Skywalker, Anakin, and the robots befriend the Wookiees, with the assistance of human anthropologists Owen and Beru Lars. In the final act, Luke, Han, and the Wookiees (whom Luke instructs in the finer points of piloting a fighter) attack the Death Star, while Anakin sneaks aboard the space station to rescue the princess. Anakin's mission seems doomed until General Valorum—one of the imperial officers who have been pursuing Luke, Anakin, and Leia—switches sides and joins the rebels. Together they escape in a nick of time. Anakin and Leia, who have fallen in love, kiss as the

Director Akira Kurosawa's *The Hidden Fortress* was such a powerful influence on early drafts of *Star Wars* that George Lucas briefly considered acquiring the remake rights. Pictured are (from left to right) Misa Euhara as Princess Yuki, Toshiro Mifune as General Makabe, Minoru Chiaki as Tahei, and Kamatari Fujiwara as Matashichi. These characters served as the templates for Princess Leia, Obi-Wan Kenobi, and R2-D2 and C-3P0, respectively.

Death Star blows apart. The script concludes with Leia bestowing honors on the heroes, including Valorum.

At this stage, *The Star Wars* was a thinly veiled sci-fi adaptation of Akira Kurosawa's *The Hidden Fortress* (see previous chapter). Lucas briefly considered purchasing the remake rights from Japan's Toho studio and toyed with the idea of casting Toshiro Mifune as Luke Skywalker. Darth Vader in this version is a secondary villain, a goon under the command of Imperial Governor Hoedaak. Vader is killed when the Death Star explodes. General Valorum serves as the primary antagonist. The Jedi and Sith are simply skilled warriors; there is no religious/mystical aspect to their orders, and the Force is not yet part of the picture. Lucas completed a polished first draft of the screenplay in July 1974, but this version included few significant alterations. Many character names were changed—Kane Starkiller became Akira Valor, Anakin Starkiller became Justin Valor, and Prince Valorum became General Dodona, while the Jedi-bendu became the Dia Noga, the Sith became the Legions of Lettow, and the Wookiees were renamed Jawas. The plot remained both derivative and jumbled, and the dialogue stilted and corny. Also, Lucas came to believe that these early versions were too similar to his and John Milius' in-progress screenplay for *Apocalypse Now*, with its theme of "primitive" indigenous peoples (Wookiees/Jawas/Vietcong) defeating an incursion by technologically superior but morally bankrupt imperialists. And finally, the script was far too long, containing nearly two hundred scenes. The screenplay still needed a great deal of work, and major changes were forthcoming in the second draft.

Second Draft

Still struggling to find his way, Lucas shared the first draft of *The Star Wars* with several friends, including John Milius, Francis Ford Coppola, Haskell Wexler, and Gloria Katz and Willard Huyck. None of them proved to be of much help. "When people read *Star Wars* originally, they didn't have a clue, really," Huyck told author J. W. Rinzler for his book *The Making of Star Wars*. "It was really a universe that nobody could understand from the scripts."

That included Twentieth Century-Fox executives, who weren't satisfied with Lucas' first draft and delayed issuing a production contract (the next step beyond the initial script development deal) for *Star Wars*. They were also (rightly) concerned that the ambitious project would cost much more than the originally projected $3 million budget. Lucas and his attorneys took advantage of the ensuing delay to negotiate two key concessions from the studio. It was at this point (in the fall of 1974) that Lucas asked for full ownership of any sequels and for joint merchandising rights. Fox eventually agreed to these terms because executives (other than Ladd) had low expectations for the movie. Sequels and merchandising seemed irrelevant when executives hadn't even seen a filmable script.

Lucas continued to grind away on the screenplay, however, delivering a second draft in January 1975. This version, titled *Adventures of the Starkiller, Episode I: The Star Wars,* marked a major break from the previous ones, with a story further removed from *The Hidden Fortress.* Certain features were retained, such as the opening scroll and the presence of the two robots, but many important new elements were added, including the emergence of Lord Darth Vader (described as the "right hand of the Sith") as the primary villain, and the addition of an embryonic version of the Force, here known as the Force of Others. It's a mysterious energy source with two aspects—the Ashla (good side) and the Bogan (dark side)—which can be manipulated with magical objects. For the first time, the benevolent, ousted government is referred to as the Republic and the current corrupt one as the Empire. Imperial armored soldiers are called "stormtroopers."

Scrolling text informs us that the do-gooding Jedi-bendu are nearly extinct, wiped out by the nefarious Black Knights of the Sith. But a powerful Jedi known as the Starkiller has arisen and, leading a ragtag Rebel Alliance, has struck a powerful blow against the Empire, which will stop at nothing to eliminate him and crush the rebellion. In the opening scene, four imperial Star Destroyers overtake a small rebel ship captained by Deak Starkiller, son of the legendary rebel leader. Deak is captured by Vader, but not before Deak sends robots R2-D2 and C-3PO to the surface of a nearby desert planet, Utapu, home to his brother, Luke. On the surface of the planet, the robots argue and separate, but are reunited after being captured by Jawas (here the pint-sized scavengers of the finished film, not Wookiee-like giants). Luke, a teenager, is living on Utapu under the care and supervision of his aunt and uncle, Owen and Beru Lars, who are instructing him in the ways of the Force of Others. Luke has two younger brothers—Biggs and Windy. Leia, a bit player in this draft, is Luke's cousin, Owen and Beru's sixteen-year-old daughter. Artoo carries a holographic message from Deak instructing Luke to take the mystic Kiber Crystal to Organa Major, where the Starkiller family patriarch—the man known simply as The Starkiller—is hiding. The Kiber Crystal has the ability to greatly multiply the power of the Force of Others; it must be kept from the Sith at all costs.

Luke travels to a spaceport cantina, uses his laser sword in a bar fight, and meets space pirate Han Solo and his Wookiee copilot, Chewbacca, who agree to transport Luke to Organa Major. Since Han doesn't have a ship of his own, he steals one from a fellow pirate named Jabba the Hutt. When Luke, Han, Chewie, and the robots arrive at Organa Major, however, the planet has been

In the earliest screenplay drafts, use of the lightsaber was not reserved for Jedi knights and Sith lords, as this Ralph McQuarrie painting of a lightsaber-wielding stormtrooper demonstrates.

destroyed. So they change course and travel to the imperial capital planet of Alderaan in hopes of freeing Deak. There, Luke and Han disguise themselves as stormtroopers (and Chewie as their prisoner) and rescue Deak from his prison cell. Deak has been tortured and is dying, but the power of the Kiber Crystal restores him to health. While escaping from the imperial dungeons, they become trapped in a trash masher but are freed by the robots. They blast off from Alderaan and, after a dogfight with imperial fighters, flee to a secret base on the jungle moon of Yavin. Luke's father contacts him telepathically to give him the location of the hidden base.

The rebels are pursued by a giant imperial space fortress, the Death Star. At the rebel base, they learn that Luke's father survived the destruction of Organa Major but was grievously wounded. Luke heals his father with the Kiber Crystal, and the Starkiller leads the climactic attack against the Death Star. Darth Vader leads the imperial defense forces. Han refuses to join the rebels, so Luke (with the Kiber Crystal in his pocket) pilots the stolen spaceship as a gunner named Antilles fires a rocket into the Death Star's exhaust port, destroying the space fortress. Vader is killed during the battle. A closing screen roll would have informed audiences that following this great victory, "the Starkiller would once again strike fear in the hearts of the Sith knights, but not before his sons were put to many tests . . . the most daring of which was the kidnapping of the Lars family and the perilous search for: THE PRINCESS OF ONDOS."

Third Draft

Although it contained many situations and characters that soon would be discarded, and lacked many important features of the finished film, the broad outline of the *Star Wars* story began to take shape with the second draft. Yet the screenplay's structure remained cluttered and disjointed, and Lucas continued to struggle to make other people understand the ideas he was trying to get across. So he moved on to a third draft, this time using the work of mythologist Joseph Campbell (see previous chapter) as a guide as he pruned and shaped the story. "About the time I was doing the third draft I read *The Hero with a Thousand Faces*, and I started to realize that I was following those rules unconsciously," said Lucas, as quoted in Laurent Bouzereau's *Star Wars: The Annotated Screenplays*. "So I said, I'll make it fit more into that classic mold." At this stage Lucas also hired production artist Ralph McQuarrie to create some concept paintings for the project. McQuarrie's art not only helped convince Fox executives, who were still dragging their feet, to finally issue a contract for *Star Wars*, but also helped Lucas crystalize some of his own ideas. (For more on McQuarrie and his contributions, see Chapter 22.)

Another issue with the second draft of *The Star Wars* was that it included no important female characters. To rectify this problem, Lucas considered changing Luke Starkiller's gender. McQuarrie dutifully produced paintings featuring a female version of the character that evolved into Luke Skywalker. About a month later, however, as he began writing draft three, Lucas changed his mind and made Luke male again, and revived Princess Leia as a major character—she, essentially, took the place occupied by Deak Starkiller in the second draft. He also introduced a new character: an old man named Ben Kenobi—a former Jedi general with mystical powers, modeled after Don Juan from the books of Carlos Castaneda (see previous chapter). Luke meets Kenobi as he travels to the spaceport town now known as Mos Eisley (formerly named Gordon). Many of these alterations were first noted in a story synopsis Lucas wrote for Fox executives in between drafts two and three of the screenplay. Also in this synopsis, it is Luke who destroys the Death Star.

Lucas—who was simultaneously recruiting key crew members, engaging composer John Williams, and founding Industrial Light & Magic, among other minor details—delivered his third draft screenplay in August 1975. It was titled *The Star Wars: From the Adventures of Luke Starkiller*. This version streamlined the preceding one, eliminating several characters—most notably Luke's father, who is now deceased. Also, for the first time, the screenplay shows some awareness of real-world budget constraints. For instance, a single Star Destroyer rather than a quartet of them overtakes the rebel ship at the opening of the film. Here it is sixteen-year-old Leia Organa who is captured during this raid and who sends the droids (no longer "robots") to Utapu. Uncle Owen in this version is a brutal taskmaster who keeps his nephew as a virtual slave. He steals eighteen-year-old Luke's life savings—the boy has been squirreling money away to pay for entry into the space academy—and uses those funds to buy R2-D2 and C-3PO. Biggs and Windy are Luke's friends in this telling, not his brothers. Artoo is found to be carrying a secret message from the princess—the droid has information vital to the rebel cause and must deliver it to Organa Major at once.

Luke and the droids set off for Mos Eisley but are waylaid by Tusken Raiders. He is left for dead on the side of the road but is aided by an old man who reveals himself to be Ben Kenobi, who "commanded the White Legions in the Clone Wars." Luke introduces himself as the son of Anakin Starkiller, a former comrade of Kenobi's. Back at Kenobi's hut, the old man instructs Luke on the power of the Force, which "can be collected and transmitted through the use of a Kiber Crystal. It's the only way to amplify the power of the Force within you." Naturally, Kenobi possesses a Kiber Crystal. Luke and Ben continue to the Mos Eisley cantina, where Kenobi (not Luke) settles a bar fight with his laser sword—for the first time called a "lightsaber." There they meet Chewbacca and Han, who this time owns his own ship—but is in hock to Jabba the Hutt, who funded the construction of Solo's vessel.

As in draft two, they discover Organa Major has been destroyed and decide to travel to the imperial capital, Alderaan—this time to rescue the princess. In this version, Kenobi uses a Vader-style telekinetic choke hold against the enemy (he raises his hands and the imperials "begin coughing and grabbing at their throats. They are unable to breathe, and eventually collapse on the floor"). Han, Luke, and Chewie use the same fake-prisoner gambit to rescue the princess and once again wind up in the trash masher, while Kenobi duels with Vader. Kenobi is wounded, but Luke returns in time to rescue the old man before they blast off from Alderaan and head for Yavin, pursued by the Death Star. Kenobi uses the Kiber Crystal to heal himself and then gives the crystal to Luke. Luke, this time aboard a single-pilot fighter, carries the Kiber Crystal with him into the climactic battle. Vader, leading the imperial defenses, senses the presence of the crystal and attacks, but Han, who had initially declined to join the rebels, zooms in at the last minute and prevents Vader from killing Luke. Luke destroys the Death Star, but Vader survives. The film concludes with Leia handing out medals and without any further scrolling text.

Originally, Lucas considered an alternate climax. In a story summary produced between the second and third draft screenplays, Lucas wrote a version in which Luke landed on the surface of the Death Star and dropped down a hatch into the space station to plant a bomb. On the way back to his ship, however, he would encounter Darth Vader. The two would duel with lightsabers as the space battle raged overhead. Lucas nixed this idea, worried that intercutting between the duel and the space battle might slow down the action when the film should be speeding to its climax. Although he abandoned this device for *Star Wars*, he revived it for *Return of the Jedi*, which cuts between Luke's duel with Vader and the emperor, Han and Leia's efforts to knock out the shield generator, and the rebel attack on the second Death Star.

In any case, the third draft screenplay marked a major step forward. But a few final changes were forthcoming before Lucas completed the script with a fourth draft, dated January 1, 1976.

Final Draft

The fourth draft, which became the shooting script, incorporated nearly all the remaining revisions to the scenario. The screenplay, which bore the unwieldy title *The Adventures of Luke Starkiller as Taken from the "Journal of the Whills" (Saga 1): Star Wars*, opens with the words, "A long, long time ago, in a galaxy far, far away, an incredible adventure took place. . . ." Uncle Owen becomes a more sympathetic character in this version, but he and Aunt Beru (and many Jawas) are murdered by stormtroopers. The presence of imperial troops searching for the droids was added to ratchet up the dramatic tension in the story's first act. Draft four eliminates the Kiber Crystal and simplifies the workings of the Force. It is in this version that Kenobi first informs Luke that Darth Vader betrayed and murdered his father. Also, this is the first script to portray Vader as half-machine; in previous drafts, he was completely human. Han Solo, here, owns his own ship but owes Jabba for a lost shipment. The planet Luke, Ben, Han, and Chewie are headed for is renamed Alderaan, and they are captured and taken aboard the Death Star rather than traveling to the imperial capital. On the Death Star, while Luke, Han, and Chewie rescue the princess, Ben disables the space station's tractor beam and duels with Darth Vader. Luke and Leia's swing across an abyss during their Death Star escape debuts here. Again, after their escape, the rebels make for a secret base on the fourth moon of Yavin. Several minor characters are introduced, including a rebel pilot named Wedge Antilles. Grand Moff Tarkin—the name of a rebel leader in drafts two and three—becomes an imperial governor. And the rebel fighters are referred to as X-wings and Y-wings for the first time.

Of all these alterations, however, the most important was the further development of Ben Kenobi, who becomes a central player in the story. Leia sends R2-D2 to the desert planet, now renamed Tatooine, to find General Kenobi and enlist his help. Kenobi connects Luke with Vader, and with Leia and the droids. He also introduces Luke to Han and Chewbacca, and explains both the workings of the Force and the historical backstory. As author Michael Kaminski points out in his book *The Secret History of Star Wars*, "With Ben Kenobi the story of *Star Wars* took on a new dynamic, and the character centered the plot much more than the previous drafts Lucas had struggled through. . . . Kenobi ties the story together and without him, the story would fall apart." Plus, eventually, having the character in the film enabled Lucas to hire the esteemed Sir Alec Guinness, whose presence in the cast raised the picture's profile and reassured skittish studio executives.

Even so, this was not quite the *Star Wars* that reached movie screens. Some final changes were made for a revised fourth draft, delivered March 15, 1976. It was at this late date that Han's ship was dubbed the *Millennium Falcon* and the scene of Han shooting a bounty hunter in the Mos Eisley cantina was added. In the first version of the fourth draft, Han and Luke battle imperial TIE fighters *before* being trapped by the Death Star's tractor beam. This sequence was moved to later in the story to improve the pacing of the film. Lucas made still more changes during production. Perhaps most importantly, Kenobi had survived the revised fourth draft script. Not until production was underway did Lucas decide that Vader should kill Kenobi, only to have the Jedi master return as a spectral guide for Luke. And it wasn't until the eleventh hour, a month into shooting, that Lucas finally discarded the surname Starkiller, which he decided sounded too bloodthirsty, and revived the name Skywalker. Lucas made his final revisions to the screenplay while shooting at EMI Studios in London, after returning from location work in Tunisia. Gloria Katz and Willard Huyck traveled to London to assist with the final polish. By then, however, Lucas faced a whole new collection of problems.

5

Light and Magic

Founding a Visual Effects Empire

ven though his *Star Wars* screenplay was not complete in the spring of 1975 (it wouldn't be finished until midway through production), George Lucas knew his story would involve dogfighting spaceships, laser sword duels, a cantina full of monsters, and other elements more elaborate than anything seen—or even attempted—on-screen before. In many cases, the equipment and techniques to realize what Lucas envisioned did not yet exist; they would have to be invented. *Star Wars* would also require enough visual effects footage for three movies. To reduce overhead at the cash-strapped studio, Twentieth Century-Fox's photographic effects department had been shuttered, and no standing shop had the know-how and capacity to handle the project. This left Lucas with only one solution: start his own company.

This decision presented a new set of challenges. Perhaps the greatest of these was, where would he find the talent he needed, and who would run the place?

Lucas' first choice to lead the company he christened Industrial Light & Magic was Douglas Trumbull, whose work on *2001: A Space Odyssey* (1968) represented a quantum leap in the art and science of visual effects. Lucas knew *Star Wars* would require a similar forward vault. But Trumbull, who had produced and directed the ecologically minded SF film *Silent Running* (1972), demurred because he wanted the freedom to pursue other directorial assignments. Besides, he had already agreed to provide visual effects for director Steven Spielberg's *Close Encounters of the Third Kind* (1977). As it turned out, Trumbull would helm only one more feature film—the snake-bitten sci-fi thriller *Brainstorm* (1983); star Natalie Wood died during production and the movie flopped. In his stead, Trumbull recommended a talented newcomer who had assisted him on *Silent Running*: John Dykstra.

John Dykstra

Dykstra, born June 3, 1947, in Long Beach, California, was the son of a mechanical engineer who began making 8mm home movies at age nine. He studied industrial design at Cal State-Long Beach but continued making experimental movies, now in 16mm. After graduation, he landed a position creating special photographic effects, under Trumbull's supervision, for *Silent Running*. He was just twenty-three years old. When he saw the finished film, which was a box office disappointment, Dykstra realized many shots had not come off as well as he hoped. He was especially let down by the ponderous and stilted motion of the spaceship and envisioned an entirely new way of achieving such shots. Dykstra realized that rather than moving a spaceship model past a static camera, a camera could pan past a stationary model to create the illusion of movement. If the motion of the camera were controlled by a computer, it could execute elaborate maneuvers without shaking or losing focus, and, once programmed, the movements could be easily repeated or modified. It was a revolutionary idea, but he needed funds to develop and prove his system (which he eventually named Dykstraflex).

When Lucas and producer Gary Kurtz met with Dykstra, they realized his proposed technology (if it worked) would enable them to create the outer space dogfights Lucas imagined but was unsure how to film. Dykstra also impressed them as the kind of energetic, innovative mind they needed to run ILM. The company was officially formed in May 1975, and Dykstra was hired to oversee operations.

Originally, Lucas wanted to locate ILM in Northern California, a setting both more picturesque and further removed from potential interlopers from Fox. Unfortunately, a suitable existing site could not be located, and Lucas didn't (yet) have the money to build from scratch. Dykstra found an empty warehouse for rent in Van Nuys, California, just north of Los Angeles. Although the site wasn't ideal—among other drawbacks, the place wasn't air conditioned—it had all the necessary infrastructure and was conveniently located near Hollywood's film processing labs. ILM worked out of this location, at 6842 Valjean Avenue, throughout the making of *Star Wars*.

The success of *Star Wars* gave Lucas the wherewithal to relocate the company to a new facility in San Rafael, California. Dykstra, whose working relationship with Lucas deteriorated throughout his time at ILM (see Chapters 7 and 8), left the company. Working with a half-dozen other former ILM employees, he founded his own studio, Apogee, which also became a respected visual effects shop. Almost immediately, Apogee landed a contract to provide visual effects for the television series *Battlestar Galactica* (1978–79), a *Star Wars* knockoff. Dykstra also received a producer's credit for the series.

Lucas and Twentieth Century-Fox sued Universal Pictures, producers of *Battlestar Galactica*, for plagiarism, and the acrimony between Lucas and Dykstra increased exponentially. Apogee went on to provide groundbreaking visual effects for *Star Trek: The Motion Picture* (1979) and *Firefox* (1982), among other films, before Dykstra closed the shop in 1992 and joined Eggers Films. Since then, Dykstra has continued to create impressive visual effects footage. In his career, Dykstra has earned five Academy Award nominations, winning two Oscars (for *Star Wars* and *Spider-Man 2*), as well as an Emmy (for *Battlestar Galactica*) and numerous other honors. But he still harbors resentment for Lucas. "I know that George was disappointed in the work and I'm disappointed that he was disappointed," Dykstra said, in the *Star Wars* documentary *Empire of Dreams*. "I wish he'd been happier but I think ultimately the work did the job."

George Lucas selected John Dykstra to lead the fledgling Industrial Light & Magic. Dykstra is seen here with supermodel Christy Turlington during the Coty International "Space" shoot at his post-ILM studio, Apogee Productions, in the late 1970s.

Photo courtesy of Ronald V. Borst/ Hollywood Movie Posters

The Rebel Band

In an article written for *American Cinematographer* magazine, Dykstra recalls that his first priority upon assuming control at ILM was recruiting. "First I sought out the personnel that I felt were necessary to carry out the special requirements of this project," he said. Early in his tenure at ILM, Dykstra assembled a team of like-minded, up-and-coming visual effects artists, few of whom had extensive industry experience. Some had never worked on a major motion picture before. Nevertheless, the staff Dykstra assembled included five men who would share credit for Academy Awards with him, as well as an electronics genius and two future industry legends.

Alvah Miller and **Jerry Jeffress** worked with Dykstra to design and build the Dykstraflex camera system. They earned a special Scientific and Technical Award at the 50th Academy Awards ceremony in 1978 for "the engineering of the Electronic Motion Control System used in concert for multiple exposure visual effects motion picture photography." When Dykstra split from ILM to form Apogee, he took Miller with him. Miller's other screen credits include *Close Encounters, Battlestar Galactica,* and *Star Trek: The Motion Picture.* He went on to win three more Oscars. Jeffress, who stuck with ILM, worked on *The Empire Strikes Back, Return of the Jedi, Raiders of the Lost Ark,* and *E.T: The Extra-Terrestrial,* among other films, and won two more Oscars. He then retired and moved to Northern Australia.

Camera operator **Richard Edlund** shot much of the Oscar-winning visual effects footage for *Star Wars.* Born in 1940 in Fargo, North Dakota, Edlund served in the Navy before enrolling in the film program at USC and making a series of experimental films. On the strength of his student work, Dykstra hired him to shoot effects footage at ILM. Edlund was another of the ILM staff members Dykstra retained when he established Apogee, but Edlund returned to ILM when Lucas asked him to work on *The Empire Strikes Back.* He remained with the company until 1983, when he left to establish his own firm, Boss Films, which supplied visual effects for movies including *Ghostbusters* (1984) and *Die Hard* (1988) before closing in 1997. Edlund, among the most distinguished alumni of Industrial Light & Magic, remains active and has racked up forty film and television credits since *Star Wars.* He won Oscars for *Star Wars, Empire, Jedi,* and *Raiders,* and was nominated for *Poltergeist.* He is chairman of the Academy's Visual Effects Branch and served on its Scientific and Technical Awards Committee for eight years. He also serves on the boards of the American Society of Cinematographers and the Visual Effects Society. He was honored with the ASC's President's Award in 2008.

In 1975, **Grant McCune** was a thirty-four-year-old graduate of Cal State-Northridge who had worked without credit on the construction of the mechanical shark nicknamed Bruce for Spielberg's *Jaws* (1975). Dykstra selected him to serve as one of ILM's chief model-makers. He is credited with, among other things, building R2-D2 (based on production artist Ralph McQuarrie's paintings). He also made an uncredited cameo in the film, playing an imperial gunner. Like Miller and Edlund, McCune also joined Dykstra's Apogee team, where he earned an Oscar nomination for his work on *Star Trek: The Motion Picture.* He left Apogee to launch McCune Designs, which remains in business and has provided visuals for thirty-five films. He died of pancreatic cancer in 2010 at age sixty-seven, survived by his wife, a son, and a daughter.

Robert Blalack earned an Oscar for his first show business job: filming composite optical shots for *Star Wars*. Blalack was born December 9, 1948, in the Panama Canal Zone. He graduated from St. Paul's School in London, earned a BA in English from Pomona (California) College in 1970, and an MFA in film from Cal-Arts in 1973. After *Star Wars*, he worked on eighteen more feature films and television series, including *Airplane!*, *Altered States* (both 1980), and *Robocop* (1987). He earned an Emmy Award for Outstanding Individual Achievement—Visual Effects for the hair-raising apocalyptic telefilm *The Day After* (1984). Since 2003, he has been employed by Praxis Film Works in Paris.

John Stears, one of the few special effects veterans who worked on *Star Wars*, was not hired by Dykstra and worked in his native England. Stears, born in Uxbridge, Middlesex, in 1934, studied at Harrow College of Art and Southall Technical School, served as a draftsman with the Royal Air Ministry, and worked at an architectural firm before moving into the film industry. Stears immediately gained prominence by designing vehicles and gadgets for the James Bond film series, including 007's tricked-out Aston Martin DB5 in *Goldfinger* (1964). He won an Oscar for his work on the Bond film *Thunderball* (1965) but parted ways with the franchise following *The Man with the Golden Gun* (1974). Lucas—an ardent fan of the Bond films—invited him to work on *Star Wars*. Stears accepted and went on to create C-3PO (based on McQuarrie's paintings), the lightsaber, and Luke Skywalker's landspeeder, among other iconic items. He was named alongside Dykstra, Edlund, McClune and Blalack on *Star Wars*' Academy Award for Best Visual Effects. In all, Stears' career spanned thirty-five years and thirty-three movies and television series. He died in 1999 following a stroke, survived by his wife and two daughters.

Lorne Peterson didn't win an Academy Award for *Star Wars*, but the movie's visual effects Oscar would never have been possible without Peterson's efforts as one of ILM's chief model builders. Peterson, born in British Columbia, was hired with a freshly minted BA in art from Cal State-Long Beach. Like Blalack, *Star Wars* was Peterson's first movie. Afterward, Peterson stuck with ILM and worked on all five subsequent *Star Wars* sequels and prequels, and codesigned Boba Fett's spaceship, the Slave 1. He also worked on blockbusters such as *E.T.: The Extra Terrestrial*, *Jurassic Park* (1993), and the Indiana Jones films, earning an Oscar for *Indiana Jones and the Temple of Doom* in 1984. He also authored the 2006 book *Sculpting a Galaxy: Inside the Star Wars Model Shop*. Peterson also had a cameo in *Star Wars*: That's him in the recon tower overlooking the jungle in the establishing shots of the hidden rebel base on Yavin 4.

Dennis Muren

The power struggle that eventually engulfed ILM during the making of *Star Wars* had its winners and its losers. Although no one was fired, and only two employees quit, some contributors lost stature while others gained respect. One of the winners was Dennis Muren, who emerged as an innovative problem-solver and a natural leader during the company's struggle to finish hundreds of shots under intense deadline pressure.

Muren was born November 1, 1946, in Glendale, California, and was fascinated by fantasy and science fiction films since childhood. He began making 8mm home movies in high school, some featuring crude Claymation dinosaurs and monsters. While studying at Pasadena City College, he and a group of school buddies (including future television actors Frank Bonner and Ed Begley Jr.) wrote and shot a scruffy but wildly imaginative horror film titled *Equinox*. Self-funded on a meager $6,500 budget, the picture featured stop-motion animated creatures and other ambitious visual effects created by

Muren. He and his friends sold the film to producer-director Jack H. Harris, who shot additional scenes and released *Equinox* theatrically in 1970. Although critical and box office results at the time were mixed, the film developed a cult following and was eventually released on DVD as part of the Criterion Collection. All in all, it was not a bad start.

Unfortunately, despite his obvious talent, after graduation Muren was turned down by every major studio special effects department in Hollywood. He had difficulty finding consistent work mostly because in the early 1970s there simply weren't many projects going that suited his abilities. He worked without credit on the softcore porn spoof *Flesh Gordon* in 1972.

Dennis Muren, pictured here with a model of one of the dinosaurs from *Jurassic Park* (1992), quickly rose through the ranks and eventually became the chief of ILM. *Photo courtesy of Ronald V. Borst/ Hollywood Movie Posters*

When Dykstra offered him a job at the embryonic ILM, Muren leaped at the opportunity.

After *Star Wars*, Muren followed Dykstra to Apogee but quickly returned to ILM, where he is still employed, now as Senior Visual Effects Supervisor. He led the company's transition from mechanical and optical effects to computer-generated imagery for movies such as *Terminator 2: Judgment Day* (1990) and *Jurassic Park*. Although he was not named on *Star Wars*' Academy Award for visual effects, he was a named recipient on the visual effects Oscars that went to *The Empire Strikes Back* and *Return of the Jedi*. In his career (so far), Muren has raked in nine Academy Awards, the most of any living person, and in 1999 became the first visual effects artist to be honored with a star on the Hollywood Walk of Fame.

Rick Baker

Rick Baker was hired almost as an afterthought. When Lucas wasn't satisfied with the initial footage shot for the cantina scene, he lobbied for additional funds for reshoots and inserts to fill the Mos Eisley watering hole with the menagerie of fantastic creatures he originally envisioned. Enter Baker, whose peculiar genius transformed the cantina sequence into a visual tour de force.

Like Muren, Baker—born December 8, 1950, in Binghamton, New York—was a lifelong fan of sci-fi and horror movies who began making 8mm films (including a version of *Frankenstein*) in high school. He also built his first gorilla costume in high school. As a teenager, he landed a job designing puppets for Clokey Productions (makers of the *Gumby* and *Davey and Goliath* TV series) and contacted makeup genius Dick Smith, who took the young Baker under his wing. In the early 1970s, unable to land a spot with a major studio, Baker began working without credit on low-budget films such as *Octaman* (1971), *The Thing with Two Heads*, and *Bone* (both 1972). In 1973, he earned his first screen credit working for his friend and frequent collaborator John Landis on *Schlock*, and he assisted Smith on *The Exorcist*. The following year he designed the monstrous baby for Larry Cohen's trashy chiller *It's Alive* (1974) and earned his first big break collaborating with makeup artist Stan Winston on the television movie *The Autobiography of Miss Jane Pittman*, about a woman who reaches age 110. The film won an Emmy for makeup. Next he created the gorilla suit and played the title character in Dino de Laurentiis' 1976 remake of *King Kong*.

During this period Baker struck up a friendship with Muren. It was Muren who suggested that Lucas hire his talented friend to beef up the cantina sequence. Baker—who was working on another low-budget horror film (*The Incredible Melting Man* [1977]) at the time—was contracted to design and build

Young Rick Baker, pictured here with an assortment of his famous monster masks, created all the most memorable creatures for the Mos Eisley cantina. He went on to revolutionize the art of makeup effects.   *Photo courtesy of Ronald V. Borst/ Hollywood Movie Posters*

thirty different alien makeups for the cantina scene, assisted by Jon Berg and Phil Tippett. Their creations included the cantina band, "Hammerhead," "Spider-Guy," "Skull-Head," and nearly all of the other most recognizable denizens of the cantina. Following *Star Wars*, like Muren, Baker went on to unparalleled esteem within his area of expertise, winning the first-ever Academy Award for makeup effects and hairstyling for *An American Werewolf in London* (1981), and eventually piling up seven Oscar wins and ten nominations (so far). Both of those are record totals for the category.

When he set out to create ILM, Lucas reasoned that owning his own visual effects house would give him total creative authority and enable him to control costs. It didn't quite work out that way. The company had great difficulty creating the footage he needed, leading to cost overruns and personality clashes (see Chapters 7 and 8). Fox wound up inserting itself into ILM when the studio fell behind schedule. And the perfectionist producer-director was never entirely satisfied with ILM's results. Lucas had many of the original visual effects redone for the 1997 *Star Wars* Special Edition.

Nevertheless, *Star Wars* emerged as a triumph for everyone involved. For ILM, the picture served as the greatest audition reel in Hollywood history.

Immediately, the fledgling company established itself as the industry's gold standard for visual effects, a spearhead for technological innovation, and a revenue engine for the nascent Lucasfilm empire. Over the next thirty-seven years (when Lucas sold ILM and the rest of Lucasfilm to the Walt Disney Co. in 2012), the company would work on nearly three hundred movies, earn fifteen Academy Awards, pioneer numerous revolutionary techniques (including further breakthroughs in CGI), and provide visual effects for ten of the fifteen highest-grossing movies of all time, and half of the top fifty. In addition to its Lucasfilm productions, ILM provided groundbreaking visuals for *E.T.: The Extra Terrestrial*, *Who Framed Roger Rabbit* (1988), *The Abyss* (1989), *Jurassic Park* (1993), and *Avatar* (2009), among many other pictures. For Lucas, arguably, founding Industrial Light & Magic remains as impressive a legacy as creating the *Star Wars* franchise itself. "They [ILM] have freed our imaginations," said Steven Spielberg, in an interview included on the *Star Wars Original Trilogy* DVD boxed set. "They have allowed us to dream and be guaranteed that our dreams will come true on the screen."

6

Your Destiny Lies with Me

Casting Call

Even before George Lucas had completed his *Star Wars* screenplay he was faced with finding actors to portray his still-evolving characters. Auditions began in late August 1975, while Lucas was finishing the fourth draft of the script. While not quite as excruciating a process as writing the film (see Chapter 4), casting soon became another protracted ordeal—both for Lucas and for the actors under consideration for major roles.

Lucas wanted to hire young, unknown performers for the picture's leading roles, as he had for *American Graffiti*. This was in part a cost-containment strategy, but he also believed that actors not already associated with other characters would be more effective in the fantasy context of *Star Wars*. It was one thing to ask viewers to accept Wookiees, lightsabers, and the Force, but something else again to ask viewers to accept someone like, say, Ron Howard as Luke Skywalker. To assist with the talent search, Lucas again relied on casting director Fred Roos, who had served marvelously on *Graffiti*. At the beginning of the process, Lucas, Roos, and several assistants worked twelve-hour days, seeing as many as 250 actors per day. After three grueling weeks of this, to save time and money Lucas joined forces with another young director, Brian De Palma, who was looking for a group of young unknowns to star in his film *Carrie* (1976). Lucas and De Palma took the unusual step of hosting joint auditions. Hundreds more actors were invited to come in and try out for both films. Lucas' demeanor during this process was so low-key that some of the would-be cast members mistook him for De Palma's assistant.

Nevertheless Lucas had definite ideas about what he wanted and placed a premium on chemistry between his leads. During callbacks (without De Palma), he screen-tested actors as ensembles to see how various would-be Leias, Lukes, and Hanses worked in concert with one another. Early on, Lucas wanted to hire legendary Japanese actor Toshiro Mifune to play

Ben Kenobi, but Mifune declined. "If I'd gotten Mifune, I would've used a Japanese princess, and then I would have probably cast a black Han Solo," said Lucas in J. W. Rinzler's *The Making of Star Wars*. One of the trios in contention for the leading roles featured newcomer Will Seltzer as Luke, former *Penthouse* centerfold Terri Nunn as Leia, and a young Christopher Walken as Han.

Jodie Foster was given serious consideration as Princess Leia. She was screen-tested but not hired because she was only thirteen years old at the time, and casting a minor would introduce restrictions on the shooting schedule. (De Palma declined to cast her in *Carrie* for the same reason.) Other performers in the running for major roles included John Travolta, Amy Irving (both eventually hired for *Carrie*), Nick Nolte, Tommy Lee Jones, and Lawrence Hilton-Jacobs (later "Boom Boom" Washington on *Welcome Back, Kotter*)—a potential Han Solo. Ultimately, of course, Lucas settled on Mark Hamill, Harrison Ford, and Carrie Fisher for the leads; a pair of distinguished British actors for key supporting parts; and four performers with specialized talents (and physiques) for the remainder of the primary cast.

None of their lives would ever be the same.

Mark Hamill

Mark Hamill, born September 25, 1951, in Oakland, California, was the son of a U.S. Navy captain who grew up on or near naval bases on both coasts and in Japan. One of seven children, he began acting while attending high school in Japan and Virginia, and majored in drama at Los Angeles City College. While still at LACC, he began landing TV guest roles and voice work. By the time he auditioned for *Star Wars*, Hamill had collected nearly thirty credits, including on-screen appearances on series such as *The Partridge Family* (1971), *Rod Serling's Night Gallery* (1972), and *Room 222* (1973), as well as voice roles in *The New Scooby Doo Movies* (1973) and animator Ralph Bakshi's postapocalyptic fantasy film *Wizards* (1977). He had a leading role in the Hanna-Barbera Saturday morning cartoon *Jeannie* (1973) and a featured supporting part on the short-lived sitcom *The Texas Wheelers* (1974-75), which also featured Jack Elam and Gary Busey.

Hamill's friend Robert Englund (the future Freddie Kreuger), after an unsuccessful audition, urged Hamill to try out for the role of the outer space "farm boy" then known as Luke Starkiller. Hamill was initially reluctant to turn up for a "cattle call" audition but needed a job following the cancellation of *The Texas Wheelers*. Lucas liked Hamill's sandy-haired All-American look, but at first the director preferred Will Seltzer as Luke. He finally chose Hamill

After an exhaustive search, fresh-faced Mark Hamill (seen here in a very early publicity still) was selected to play Luke Skywalker.

because the Hamill-Ford-Fisher ensemble displayed better chemistry than the Seltzer-Walken-Nunn triptych.

In February 1976, Hamill was finally offered the starring role in *Star Wars*. By then, he had also appeared as David Bradford in the pilot for the TV series *Eight Is Enough*. When that show was picked up by ABC, Hamill could have continued with the television series. He opted to take *Star Wars* instead, hoping to break into feature films. Hamill was paid $1,000 per week for *Star Wars*. More significantly, Lucas later rewarded all three of his lead actors with a small share of the profits (one quarter of one net percentage point—which translated into an initial payment of about $320,000). Despite his fairly extensive resume, Mark Hamill remained unknown to most viewers in early 1976. Eighteen months later, he would become one of the most recognizable people on the planet.

Harrison Ford

Harrison Ford was born July 13, 1942, in Chicago, of mixed Irish Catholic and Russian Jewish lineage. A self-described "late bloomer," Ford began taking drama classes and playing summer stock while attending tiny Ripon College in Wisconsin. Acting soon took over his life, so much so that he stopped going to class. After flunking out of school his senior year, he moved to Los Angeles to pursue a film career and in 1964 signed a studio contract with Columbia Pictures. He was among the final wave of actors to study the craft under the old studio system, as part of Columbia's New Talent program. He also appeared as an extra or a bit player in several films, usually without credit. He earned his first screen credit with a minor role in the Western *A Time for Killing* (1967), set during the Civil War and starring Glenn Ford. When his contract with Columbia ran out, Ford drifted into television, landing guest roles in more than a dozen series and TV movies before *Star Wars*—everything from *The Virginian* (1967) to *Love, American Style* (1969). It wasn't enough work to pay the bills, so Ford started a carpentry business on the side. He delivered an effective performance as hot-rodding hothead Bob Falfa in *American Graffiti*, but the film's success didn't immediately translate into more roles. Ford was forced to continue installing cabinets and taking other handyman jobs to make ends meet.

Ford badly wanted to appear in *Star Wars*, but Lucas was adamant that he didn't want any *Graffiti* cast members in his new film. For months, *Graffiti* alum Cindy Williams lobbied in vain to be considered for the role of Princess Leia. However, Fred Roos pushed Lucas to consider Ford as Han Solo and brought him in to run lines with Hamill and other actors. Perhaps because he didn't think he had a chance at landing a part in the film, Ford was frank with Lucas about the clunky, technobabble-filled dialogue of the draft screenplay, famously telling Lucas, "George, you can type this shit, but you can't *say* it." Lucas thought Ford's insolence suited the character, and he liked Ford's chemistry with Hamill and Fisher. To the surprise of everyone except Roos, Lucas eventually hired Ford. The actor's *Star Wars* contract paid him $850 per week. His small profit share would end his days in the home renovation business.

Mark Hamill (with his back turned), Carrie Fisher, and Harrison Ford goof around during an early photo session.

Carrie Fisher

Roos also suggested that Lucas consider Carrie Fisher for the role of Princess Leia. Fisher, born October 21, 1956, in Beverly Hills, was Hollywood royalty herself—the daughter of singer Eddie Fisher and actress Debbie Reynolds. Her parents divorced when Fisher was two (Eddie left Debbie to marry Elizabeth Taylor). Fisher appeared alongside her mother in the promotional short "A Visit with Debbie Reynolds" (1959) and in the TV movie *Debbie Reynolds and the Sound of Children* (1969). Beginning at age twelve, she worked in her mother's Las Vegas revue, and at sixteen she and her mother appeared together in the Broadway revival of the musical *Irene* (1972). Prior to *Star Wars*, Fisher had made just a single screen appearance, but it was an unforgettable one—as Lorna, a precocious teenager who beds Warren Beatty (minutes before her mother does the same) in director Hal Ashby's sex farce *Shampoo* (1975). Lucas liked that Fisher could believably play a bossy, intimidating character yet still seem warm and likable. Despite concerns over the actress' weight, he cast her as Leia, paying her $750 per week. With *Star Wars*, Fisher would finally step out of her mother's shadow.

Sir Alec Guinness

Even before Mifune declined to play Ben Kenobi, Lucas was formulating a backup plan. His second choice for the role was distinguished British actor Sir Alec Guinness, who Lucas knew would bring gravitas and credibility to the character and improve the profile of the entire film. Things like the Force would seem far more plausible coming from Guinness. The question was, would Guinness, who had never appeared in a science fiction film, accept the role?

Alec Guinness de Cuffe was born April 2, 1914, in London, to an unwed mother. The identity of his father was never confirmed, but Guinness suspected it was Andrew Geddes, a Scottish banker who paid for his education. Guinness studied at the Fay Compton Studio of Dramatic Art and made his professional theatrical debut at age twenty. His talent was evident from the start, and two years later, in 1936, he signed with the prestigious Old Vic Theatre in the London borough of Lambeth. For the next decade he appeared there in numerous Shakespearean and classical parts in repertory with the likes of Laurence Olivier and John Gielgud. He made an acclaimed appearance in the title role of *Hamlet* in 1938 and adapted Charles Dickens' *Great Expectations* for the stage the following year, appearing as Herbert Pocket. Guinness put his theatrical career on hold to serve in the Royal Navy during World War II, commanding landing craft during the invasions of Sicily and Elba. After the war, he returned for two more years at the Old Vic, which revived his *Hamlet*.

Guinness' first major film part arrived when director David Lean, who had seen Guinness' *Great Expectations*, decided to adapt the novel for the screen in 1946 and asked the actor to reprise his role as Pocket. For the next two decades, Guinness would remain best known for his collaborations with Lean—he appeared in six Lean films and won an Oscar for *The Bridge on the River Kwai* (1957) as the misguided Colonel Nicholson—and for his work with London's Ealing Studios. At Ealing, he starred in a series of wickedly funny comedies, including *The Lavender Hill Mob*, *The Man in the White Suit* (both 1951), and, most famously, *Kind Hearts and Coronets* (1949), in which he played eight roles (one of them female). Throughout his career, Guinness took turns appearing onstage and in films (mostly dry comedies or historical epics). Although he never became a major star in the United States, in his prime he was a top box office draw in England and was widely considered one of the finest and most versatile screen actors. He was knighted in 1959.

Fortunately for Lucas, Guinness was in Hollywood in the summer of 1975 shooting *Murder by Death*, a comedy-mystery based on a Neil Simon play. Roos had a copy of the screenplay for *Star Wars* delivered to the actor's trailer. Even though he had concerns about the script, Guinness agreed to appear in *Star Wars* because he had seen and admired *American Graffiti*. His contract paid him $1,000 per week and guaranteed him a generous 2.5 percent of the producers' 40 percent share in the movie's profits—an arrangement that would soon make him one of Britain's wealthiest actors. Despite the financial rewards, however, Guinness would be haunted by his *Star Wars* legacy (see Chapters 11 and 36).

Peter Cushing

The remaining roles were cast in England, where the majority of the film would be shot. To play the menacing Grand Moff Tarkin, Lucas hired British bogeyman Peter Cushing, then best known for playing Dr. Frankenstein in a long-running series of chillers from England's Hammer Films. Cushing was a consummate professional and one of the most skilled and subtle performers to ply his trade primarily in the peculiar oeuvre of screen terror. Lucas was delighted to add him to the cast.

Born May 26, 1913, in Surrey, Cushing earned a degree from Storeham College and worked briefly as a surveyor before enrolling in London's Guildhall School of Music and Drama. After graduating from Guildhall in 1939, he traveled to Hollywood and appeared in a few movies, including *The Man in the Iron Mask* (1939) and the Laurel & Hardy comedy *A Chump at Oxford* (1940). But unable to find steady work in America, he returned to England. After a smattering of minor film roles, including an appearance in Olivier's *Hamlet* (1948), Cushing rose to fame starring in several acclaimed BBC television productions, including a spine-tingling adaptation of George Orwell's *Nineteen Eighty-Four* (1954). Up-and-coming Hammer Films, quickly establishing itself as a world-class maker of movie horrors, cast Cushing as Dr. Frankenstein in *The Curse of Frankenstein* (1957) and as Dr. Van Helsing in *Horror of Dracula* (1958), both landmark horror shows. Cushing went on to appear in twenty-two Hammer productions, as well as dozens of other horror and science fiction films, often opposite his friend Christopher Lee (the future Count Dooku). Cushing also performed memorably as Sherlock

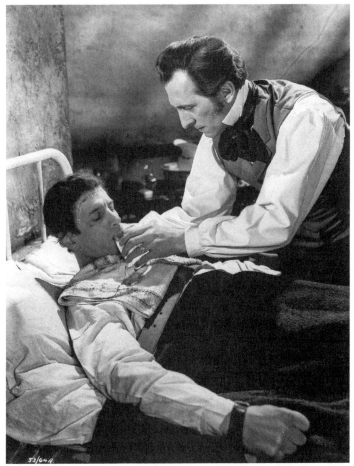

Prior to *Star Wars*, Peter Cushing was best known to moviegoers as Dr. Frankenstein, from the long-running series of chillers from England's Hammer Films. Cushing (right) tends to his new "monster," Karl (Michael Gwynn), in this scene from *The Revenge of Frankenstein.*

Holmes, first in Hammer's *The Hound of the Baskervilles* (1959) and later as the star of the eponymously titled BBC TV series in 1968.

By the mid-1970s, the kind of Gothic horror roles that were Cushing's bread and butter were rapidly disappearing. He was offered a profit share for his work on *Star Wars* but turned it down in favor of a straight salary of £2,000 per day (he worked on the film for only one week). As far as Cushing knew, *Star Wars* was just another low-budget science fiction picture—something akin to his other 1977 film, *Shock Waves*, about underwater Nazi zombies. He would rue his to decision to decline a profit share in *Star Wars*.

David Prowse and James Earl Jones

For the role of Darth Vader, Lucas needed an imposing physical presence. No performer in Britain was more physically imposing than six-foot-six former bodybuilder David Prowse. Born July 1, 1935, in Bristol, Prowse claimed the title England's Strongest Man from 1965 to 1970. He began acting in the late 1960s and had racked up more than forty film and television appearances prior to *Star Wars*. These were minor roles, ranging from *The Beverly Hillbillies* (1968) to Stanley Kubrick's *A Clockwork Orange* (1971). He played the Frankenstein monster three times—first (uncredited) in *Casino Royale* (1967), then in Hammer's *The Horror of Frankenstein* (1970) and *Frankenstein and the Monster from Hell* (1974, with Cushing). Prowse also earned fame in England as the Green Cross Code Man, a superhero character invented by the U.K.'s National Road Safety Committee to encourage children to cross streets safely. He portrayed this character from 1975 to 1990, and was honored with an M.B.E. for his efforts.

On his website, Prowse claims that he was offered the roles of either Darth Vader or Chewbacca and chose to play Vader. Prowse learned Vader's lines and delivered them during shooting; the actor also claims he didn't realize

This rare still features an unmasked David Prowse alongside Sir Alec Guinness, from the set of *Star Wars*. Lucasfilm tried to suppress photos revealing Prowse's face.

his voice would not be heard in the finished film. Yet from the beginning Lucas planned to dub Prowse's surprisingly soft, West Country voice (a rural British accent that inspired Carrie Fisher to nickname Prowse "Darth Farmer"). The director wanted a deeper, more powerful voice, and during postproduction he hired American James Earl Jones to loop Vader's dialogue.

Jones, born January 17, 1931, in Arkabutla, Mississippi, began his stage career in the early 1950s. He has worked steadily ever since both onstage and in film and television, and had compiled more than twenty-five film and TV roles prior to *Star Wars*. In 1970, he earned an Oscar nomination for his work as boxer Jack Johnson in *The Great White Hope*, adapted from a Broadway play in which he also starred. Jones was just the second black man, following Sidney Poitier, to earn an Academy Award nomination as Best Actor. In 1977, the same year as *Star Wars*, Jones played author Alex Haley in the TV miniseries sensation *Roots*. Jones spent one day rerecording Vader's dialogue for *Star Wars* and declined a screen credit. Prowse's towering and dynamic physical presence, combined with Jones' sonorous bass voice, made Darth Vader one of the preeminent screen villains of all time.

Anthony Daniels

One of the first cast members to sign a contract was Anthony Daniels, who joined *Star Wars* in early December 1975. He was hired early on in part because C-3PO's costume had to be custom built for the actor.

Born February 21, 1946, in Salisbury, England, Daniels was the son of a wealthy plastics manufacturing executive. He originally planned to pursue a legal career, but dropped out of university after two years and started taking acting lessons instead. Daniels became a trained mime and skilled voice actor, joining the BBC radio drama company in 1974 before leaving for London's Young Vic Theatre, located in London's Lambeth borough. He was touring with a Young Vic production of Tom Stoppard's *Rosencrantz and Guildenstern Are Dead* when he (and a hundred other British mimes) received an invitation to audition for *Star Wars*. Daniels' agent had to twist his arm to attend because he hated science fiction and was leery of playing a mechanical character. Daniels later told *Return of the Jedi* publicist John Phillip Peecher, "I remember being a little insulted at the time. I was doing quite well as a human being." But he warmed to the idea when Lucas showed him Ralph McQuarrie's concept painting of the beautiful, golden, art deco C-3PO. Lucas didn't provide a great deal of direction to most of his actors, but he worked closely with Daniels to fine-tune his vocal delivery, gait, and other quirks. Perhaps as a result, Daniels went on to appear in more *Star Wars* movies and related projects than any other performer (see Chapter 36). His only previous film or television experience was a guest appearance on the BBC TV series *Centre Play* (1976).

Kenny Baker

Daniels' droid partner—the Hardy to his Laurel—was three-foot-seven-inch Kenny Baker. Born August 24, 1934, in Birmingham, Baker began appearing onstage and in circuses in 1950. He worked with Burton Lester's Midgets and clowned with Billy Smart's Circus. Later, he appeared in ice shows and formed a musical comedy act known as the Mini-Tones, playing nightclubs. Prior to *Star Wars*, he had appeared in *Circus of Horrors* (1960) and on the British TV series *Man of the World* (1962). Lucas needed a performer small enough to fit into the R2-D2 suit designed by British toymaker Tony Dyson, and Baker was one of the tiniest men in England. Although mechanical versions of Artoo were used in some scenes, a human actor was required for shots where the diminutive droid hooted, blinked, waddled, or spun his head—in other words, for those moments that gave the plucky droid personality. In the early advertising for *Star Wars*, R2-D2 and C-3PO were featured more prominently than any of the human characters. Since it unfolds mainly from their point of view, *Star Wars* seemed like their story as much as Luke Skywalker's. (Vader's centrality to the narrative wouldn't become apparent until *The Empire Strikes Back* or even *Return of the Jedi*.) Daniels and Baker both made invaluable contributions to the success of the franchise.

Peter Mayhew

The downside to casting David Prowse as Darth Vader was that Chewbacca was supposed to be at least a head taller than Vader, and Vader was now being played by one of the tallest performers in England. There simply weren't any actors in the United Kingdom that much taller than Prowse. Importing an actor wasn't an option. Lucas already had to acquire a waiver from the British film board to make a film in England starring three Americans; the rest of the cast had to be British. The only remaining solution was to hire a nonactor.

Seven-foot-two-inch Peter Mayhew had acted briefly (as a Minotaur) in the Ray Harryhausen fantasy *Sinbad and the Eye of the Tiger* (1977), but was working as a hospital orderly when he received a call to come in and interview for a role in *Star Wars*. Mayhew did not provide Chewbacca's voice—sound designer Ben Burtt combined various animal growls to produce Chewie's "dialogue." Like Baker, Mayhew was hired mostly due to his physique, but he brought something unique to the character. His facial expressions and expressive blue eyes gave the Wookiee a distinct personality, complete with a sense of humor and a short temper. Chewbacca quickly emerged as one of the franchise's most enduringly popular characters. As Threepio, Artoo, and Chewbacca, Daniels, Baker, and Mayhew had struck gold. They would continue to mine that vein for the remainder of their careers.

7

Far, Far Away

Production of *Star Wars*

S *tar Wars* was, to say the least, an extraordinarily ambitious and complex production. In nearly every respect it stretched the boundaries of the possible. Delivering on time and on budget a product that met George Lucas' lofty aspirations would require the rapid development of breakthrough technology, prompt delivery of high-quality visual effects, long hours from a dedicated crew, unflinching support from Twentieth Century-Fox, and some old-fashioned good luck.

None of that happened.

Almost nothing went according to plan during the making of *Star Wars*. Failures, mishaps, personality clashes, and other woes plagued the film throughout shooting and into postproduction. As the troubles wore on and on, Lucas' expectations for the picture steadily diminished. For a while, he was certain that he was authoring an epic flop.

Century City

The problems began before the cameras ever rolled. In October 1975—while Lucas and producer Gary Kurtz were overseeing the design and construction of sets, costumes, and props in London, and in Van Nuys, California, John Dykstra, Al Miller, and Jerry Jeffress were trying to build the revolutionary Dykstraflex camera system—Fox slammed the brakes on *Star Wars*, placing the production on moratorium. Although crew members would be paid salaries during this period, work ground to a virtual halt. Fox refused to release any additional funds to the production until after a closed-door meeting of the studio's board of directors at the corporate headquarters in Century City, California, on December 13.

Executives were alarmed by the example of producer-director Stanley Donen's runaway production *Lucky Lady* (1975). When costs on that Fox-financed, independently produced film climbed to $13 million, the studio stepped in and seized control of the picture, which ultimately disappointed at the box office. Studio bosses worried that *Star Wars*—another Fox-funded independent production—was following a similar trajectory. Originally penciled in with a $3 million budget, *Star Wars*' costs had soared to $8.2 and were still rising. And, on paper at least, *Lucky Lady* had a lot more going for it than Lucas' quirky space fantasy, including an Oscar-winning director and bankable stars (Gene Hackman, Liza Minnelli, and Burt Reynolds). Hedging its bets, Fox leadership wanted *Star Wars* made for no more than $7.5 million, but Lucas (who had invested nearly a half-million dollars of his own money in *Star Wars*) insisted that was impossible.

Producer Alan Ladd Jr., who had championed *Star Wars* from the beginning, addressed the board on December 13 and earned its grudging support for the movie, but the six-week delay and ensuing belt-tightening nevertheless inflicted serious injury. Immediately, production designer John Barry's budget was slashed by 10 percent. Oscar-winning cinematographer Geoffrey Unsworth, who had shot *2001: A Space Odyssey* (1968), became fed up and walked out. He was replaced at the eleventh hour by *Dr. Strangelove* (1964) cinematographer Gilbert Taylor. Taylor was gifted and had shot the 1955 war movie *The Dam Busters*, a major influence on *Star Wars* (see Chapter 9), but he clashed with Lucas. The budget continued to be fine-tuned and haggled over, even into postproduction. Also, Lucas and the studio kept trying to hash out the final details of the production contract between Lucasfilm and Fox, which wasn't finalized until late August 1976 (it was typical for contracts to be finalized during production). This was the agreement that spelled out Lucas' ownership of sequel rights and specified a 50-50 split of merchandising profits between Fox and Lucasfilm.

Repercussions from Fox's six-week moratorium would be felt throughout production and into postproduction.

Tunisia

The financial and creative fallout from the moratorium began immediately. Because the costumes, props, and equipment, including the mechanical R2-D2 used in many shots, were completed at the last minute, they had to be flown (rather than trucked) to Tunisia, which cost an extra $17,000. But that was pocket change compared to the time lost during shooting due to mechanical failures and other problems with the robots. Production began Monday, March 22, 1976, in the salt flats at Nefta, Tunisia. The first shots on the list were exteriors of the Lars homestead on Tatooine, including the scene in which Uncle Owen and Luke purchase C-3PO and R2-D2 from the Jawas. Neither the mechanical Artoo nor the R5-D4 ("Red") robot worked properly, and both exhausted their hard-to-replace batteries much more rapidly than expected.

George Lucas (second from left) and his crew encountered troubles of all sorts—including sudden sandstorms, which necessitated the wearing of goggles—while shooting in Tunisia.

"It was purely a case of Fox not putting up the money until it was too late," said Lucas in J. W. Rinzler's *The Making of Star Wars*. "Every day we would lose an hour or two due to those robots, and we wouldn't have lost that time if we'd had another six weeks to finish them and test them and have them working before we started. Whereas before there were only about five or six people involved in the special effects, once we were on location with 150 people involved, we were paying much more in salaries."

Catastrophe struck when a truck where the robots were being stored caught fire, damaging two of them. The landspeeder prop didn't work correctly, either. Entire days of work (including nearly all the landspeeder scenes) were abandoned, or else rescheduled for "pick up" shooting during postproduction back in the United States. Rain washed out two days of shooting, and on Friday, March 26, a torrential downpour blew apart many of the sets, including the enormous sandcrawler. What was left was covered in mud and muck.

As a result of these miseries, *Star Wars* instantly fell behind schedule. The shot of Luke staring into the twin Tatooine sunsets was finally captured on Day 8; it had been slated for Day 1. To try to make up for lost time, the production split into two and sometimes three units so multiple scenes could

Mark Hamill, with binoculars, and Anthony Daniels as C-3PO were two of only four primary cast members who made the trip to Tunisia. The others were Kenny Baker and Sir Alec Guinness.

be filmed simultaneously when weather and good fortune permitted the cast and crew to work. The robots continued to be a nuisance. At one point an out-of-control Artoo strayed onto the set of director Franco Zeffirelli's *Jesus of Nazareth* (1977), which was also being shot in Tunisia at the time. There were other problems too. Living conditions for the cast and crew were less than ideal, in part because Zeffirelli's rival production had snapped up the best accommodations available (in nearby Tozeur). Anthony Daniels hated his Threepio costume, which pinched and cut him and was torturous to wear in the Tunisian heat.

Amid this chaos, Lucas was trying to finish the film's screenplay. It was at this point he decided to have Vader kill Obi-Wan Kenobi during their Death Star duel. Originally a wounded Kenobi survived the duel, but the Jedi master took no active part in the rest of the story. It would be more powerful, Lucas realized, to have Vader strike him down, and then have Kenobi's ghostly voice guide Luke the rest of the way. One evening in Tunisia, Lucas pulled Guinness aside and informed him of this script change. The esteemed actor was shocked. Not only was he being written out of the end of the film, he wasn't even being allowed to play a death scene. He stewed silently through-out the remainder of his time in North Africa.

Location shooting wrapped on Sunday, April 4, 1976. Unfortunately, Lucas (by his estimate) had only captured about two-thirds of the footage he had set out to film, and he was extremely disappointed with some of the results. He could only hope things would improve once the production moved into the studio.

That didn't happen either.

Borehamwood

Shooting began at EMI-Elstree Studios in Borehamwood, England (near London) on Wednesday, April 7, 1976. Lucas decided to film in the United Kingdom because the British studio boasted the giant soundstages *Star Wars* required, and because it was less expensive than shooting in Hollywood. Besides, it kept any potential meddlers from Fox an ocean away—or so he thought.

Among the principal cast, only Mark Hamill, Anthony Daniels, Kenny Baker, and Alec Guinness had traveled to Tunisia. For everyone else, this represented the start of shooting. If production in North Africa had been chaotic, shooting in England was just the opposite—overly regimented, due to the rigid enforcement of union rules governing the schedule of the British crew. The workday began at 8:30 a.m., included an hour-long lunch, tea breaks at 11:00 a.m. and 4:00 p.m., and ended promptly at 5:30 p.m. Although theoretically the crew could vote to work overtime, that had to be agreed upon at the beginning of the workday and required the crew to break from long-standing (and comfortable) English industry tradition. To make matters worse, the crew—most of whom were much older than Lucas and Gary Kurtz—had little respect for their unkempt-looking, neophyte American director and producer. Few of them understood the picture they were making. In the documentary *Empire of Dreams*, Kenny Baker reports that many cast and crew members, himself included, at first considered the picture "a load of rubbish."

The upshot of all this was that at 5:30 each day, even if they were in the middle of a scene, the crew would walk off the set and clock out. Scenes that could have been completed with as little as a half hour of overtime instead had to be finished the next day. This in turn meant that changes of scenery (which ordinarily occurred overnight) on the studio's massive soundstages had to be made during the workday, while the cast and crew were paid to sit idle—often for hours at a time. It was the furthest thing imaginable from the kind of guerrilla filmmaking Lucas had experienced before on *American Graffiti*, *THX-1138*, and Francis Ford Coppola's *The Rain People*. He resented

George Lucas directs Peter Mayhew (as Chewbacca) and Harrison Ford at EMI Studios in Borehamwood, England, outside London. Lucas hoped the film would make up for lost time once the production moved into the studio, but instead the picture fell even further behind schedule.

the crew's intransigence but could only watch helplessly as *Star Wars* once again fell behind schedule.

Lucas' insistence on a future universe that looked "used" and lived-in didn't endear him to costume designer John Mollo or production designer John Barry. "I wanted everything in the movie to appear very used, very beat-up looking," Lucas told publicist John Phillip Peecher in 1983. Mollo and Barry were perplexed, if not openly resentful, when Lucas took their handiwork and immediately had it torn and frayed, or else smeared with mud and sand. Mollo and Barry were happiest with the crisp imperial uniforms and gleaming Death Star interiors.

Then there was Guinness. A few days after production opened in England, having brooded over the fate of Obi-Wan Kenobi for weeks, he went to Lucas and announced that he wanted out of the picture. Guinness' departure would have been a crippling blow to the project. Not only did his presence as Kenobi lend gravitas to the character and prestige to the movie, but he had not yet filmed his Death Star or *Millennium Falcon* scenes. If Guinness left at this point, either the role would have to be hastily recast and much of the hard-won footage from Tunisia scrapped and reshot in California (returning to North Africa was impossible), or else the story would have to be radically rewritten (perhaps with Kenobi being killed during the escape from Tatooine). Neither option was palatable to Lucas. He took the actor out for a very long lunch to explain his idea of the Force and to try to convince Guinness that Kenobi would come off better sacrificing himself to save his friends than limping around uselessly for the remainder of the film. Upon reflection, Guinness reluctantly agreed to continue.

Lucas' problems weren't limited to surly grips and resentful actors. The *Millennium Falcon* had to be redesigned at the last minute because the original design was deemed too similar to that of the spaceships on a new television program, *Space: 1999*. Makeup supervisor Stuart Freeborn fell ill and had to be hospitalized. As a result, he was unable to complete his work on the monster masks and other special makeups required for the Mos Eisley cantina sequence. Although the scene was filmed successfully (around April 20, 1976), it involved fewer and less impressive creatures than Lucas had envisioned. The director was deeply disappointed.

Lucas also butted heads with editor John Jympson and director of photography Gilbert Taylor. Lucas was dismayed by Jympson's rough assembly of the Tunisian footage, dissatisfied with both the editor's selection of takes and the pacing of his cuts. Jympson, in return, complained loudly about the director to fellow crew members. He also screened rushes for the crew against Lucas' express instructions. The director clashed with Taylor over the look of the film. Lucas wanted a soft, gauzy look in the style of a classic Hollywood swash-buckler, but Taylor stopped using soft-focus lenses when Fox executives saw the rushes and complained about his footage. When Lucas (who didn't care what the studio liked or disliked) learned that Taylor had switched lenses, he felt betrayed and considered firing the cinematographer. Instead, in order to assert his authority, the director began to rearrange the lighting himself. This infuriated Taylor, who, like Jympson, began bad-mouthing Lucas to the crew.

Not everything went poorly, however. Luke and Leia's daring swing across a Death Star chasm was shot in a single take. The cast—especially Hamill, Harrison Ford, and Carrie Fisher—quickly developed a jovial rapport and seemed to roll with whatever punches circumstance threw the production. Their only serious complaint was with the clunky dialogue in Lucas' still not-quite-finished script. Fisher had one more beef: Lucas wouldn't allow her to wear a bra under her white Princess Leia gown, so her breasts were held in place with gaffer's tape.

Peter Cushing's amiable presence on the set lightened the mood during his single week on *Star Wars*. The affable screen veteran was so gentle and charming that Fisher struggled to feign disdain for Grand Moff Tarkin. Hamill requested Cushing's autograph and asked him about working with Laurel & Hardy (on *A Chump at Oxford* in 1940). Cushing loved the experience, even though his costume boots were too small for the actor's size 12 feet. Tarkin is shot mostly from the knees up because in many shots Cushing was wearing slippers.

Despite such good days, however, the production continued to slip behind schedule. On May 10 the picture was a full week behind. By early June it was nine days behind. In late June it was fifteen days behind, and Fox insisted that Lucas again split into multiple units to shoot as much footage as possible simultaneously. By then Lucas had a whole new set of headaches, this time originating half a world away.

Van Nuys

Lucas, Kurtz, and Dykstra had a clever plan intended to save time and money in both production and postproduction. The concept was for ILM to create visual effects shots (for sequences like the *Millennium Falcon*'s dogfight with the TIE fighters and the final Death Star battle) simultaneously with live-action shooting in England. The footage would be shipped to Borehamwood so that the cast could then interact with the visual effects via a front-projection process screen, eliminating the need for compositing (integrating live action and visual effects) in postproduction.

That idea didn't work either.

Lucas discovered that it was nearly impossible to synchronize, in real time, the line delivery of the actors with the movement of the visual effects. It was also hard to match the lighting on set with that used in the visual effects footage. Lucas also rejected some of the footage as substandard. And there was another, more basic problem: Most of the visual effects shots weren't available.

ILM was running even further behind schedule than the rest of the production. The reason for this differs based on who is asked. Dykstra maintains that production fell behind because development of the Dykstraflex system took longer than expected. Lucas blamed Dykstra's lax management. Fox blamed Lucas for everything. In any case, ILM was an unorthodox work environment. To help give the staff some relief in the non-air-conditioned building, where temperatures sometimes climbed to 120 degrees, a

Late in the already over-budget production, George Lucas insisted on spending several thousand dollars to construct the "white corridor" set on which the film's opening scene was shot. Originally, this sequence was to be filmed on a redressed version of the *Millennium Falcon*'s cargo hold.

swimming pool and water slide were installed on the property. The crew also blew off steam in other ways. Fox executives, including Alan Ladd Jr., were shocked to arrive at ILM one afternoon to find Dykstra seated in a forklift, raising a malfunctioning refrigerator high in the air and then letting it crash to the pavement, while his staff cheered. When the fridge stopped working, Dykstra decided to give it a grand sendoff. The bottom line was that although ILM was spending $30,000 a day, very few shots were being completed.

Even if the front-projection idea had worked, ILM wouldn't have had all the necessary footage available until well after shooting in England was scheduled to wrap. Lucas was forced to shoot these scenes the more conventional way: in front of a blue screen, with the effects composited in later. But the film wasn't budgeted for blue screen filming, which requires much more light and a larger crew.

The switch to blue screen drove the budget even higher, north of $10 million. Already skittish Fox executives were apoplectic and began scrutinizing every penny Lucas spent. Nevertheless, the director continued to push for items he believed the movie needed. This included the construction of a new set for the opening sequence in which Darth Vader and the stormtroopers board Princess Leia's ship. Originally, these scenes were supposed to be shot on a re-dressed version of the *Millennium Falcon*'s cargo hold, but this looked cramped and unconvincing. Although Fox initially balked at the expense (several thousand additional dollars), the studio ultimately approved building the additional set.

Eventually, however, Fox put its corporate foot down and insisted shooting must end by mid-July. Production wrapped on Friday, July 16, 1976, after eighty-four days (twenty over schedule). At the wrap party, as a token of their regard for their American leaders, the crew gave Gary Kurtz a Hitler mustache. Principal photography was complete, but much work remained. Nearly all the visual and sound effects were unfinished, and a large number of pickups and inserts would have to be filmed in California and elsewhere to make up for setbacks suffered in Tunisia and Borehamwood. The picture still had to be edited and scored. *Star Wars* had already taken a personal toll on Lucas, who was depressed and physically ill. The home he and his wife Marcia were renting in nearby Hampstead had been burglarized, and Marcia was briefly hospitalized with the flu.

Taking inventory of the misfortunes that had befallen the production so far, it might have seemed that everything that could go wrong already had. The law of averages dictated that matters could only improve when *Star Wars* moved home to California, right?

Wrong again.

8

I Am Here to Put You Back on Schedule

Postproduction of *Star Wars*

Bruised and dispirited after a seemingly endless series of setbacks while shooting in Tunisia and England, the *Star Wars* company limped home to California in late July 1976, behind schedule, over budget, and under pressure. The film was slated to premiere in eight months, but a tremendous amount of work remained unfinished. Extensive pickups and reshoots—far more than originally planned—waited. Even without those shots, more than six hundred hours of footage had to be sifted through and edited into a coherent form. The picture needed sound effects and a score. A marketing campaign had to be created to convince skeptical theater owners to book *Star Wars* once it was complete. But the critical path to finishing the film ran through Industrial Light & Magic, the startup visual effects house George Lucas had entrusted with creating the revolutionary imagery his story required. The original plan had been for the majority of the special effects to be completed while the movie was shooting in London. Instead, ILM (despite burning through half its budget) had completed only a handful of the ordered 360 effects shots to Lucas' satisfaction. It's little wonder that when he returned to California, the hacking cough Lucas had developed in England worsened, and he began experiencing chest pains. He was briefly hospitalized and diagnosed with hypertension and exhaustion.

ILM

Eventually, of course, ILM got back on track (otherwise, this book would end at Chapter 7). Who deserves credit for the company's turnaround depends on whose version of events you believe. Dykstra maintains that Lucas' return to the United States happened to coincide with his team resolving the final bugs in the Dykstraflex camera system. Lucas later complained to *Empire Strikes Back* publicist Alan Arnold that Dykstra "became obsessed" with developing his namesake camera technology; producing viable visual effects footage seemed to be an afterthought. Lucas insists ILM found its way only after he imposed greater managerial discipline, including more production-driven scheduling and rigorous quality control. To assist with this transition, Lucas hired the experienced George Mather to serve at ILM as a production supervisor. Mather's presence mollified anxious Fox executives but rankled Dykstra.

The culture shift at ILM was immediate. While Lucas was overseas, the entire ILM staff gathered every morning to review the previous day's footage. Now, only a few staff members reviewed the dailies; everyone else had to keep working on their own deliverables. ILM became a nearly twenty-four-hour operation. Richard Edlund and Dennis Muren were picked to lead teams that worked overlapping shifts, one from 8:00 a.m. to 6:00 p.m. and the other from 3:00 p.m. until midnight. Both shifts frequently pulled overtime. Grant McCune and Steve Gawley operated the model shop on a similar schedule. Lucas began splitting his time between Van Nuys, where ILM was located, and Lucasfilm's headquarters in San Anselmo, where the film was being edited—generally working in Southern California Monday through Wednesday and Northern California Thursday through Sunday. Every single

George Lucas personally signed off on every visual effects shot in all the original *Star Wars* movies.

visual effects shot had to receive Lucas' personal, signed approval. By mid-October, producer Gary Kurtz estimated that about 18 percent of the visual effects were complete—a low number but still a major improvement over the state of affairs three months earlier. The pace and quality of work was steadily improving as the organizational changes took hold. But the pressure being exerted by both Lucas and Fox was taking its toll on the ILM staff, and the relationship between Dykstra and Lucas became fraught with conflict and mistrust. Dykstra wanted to fire Mather, but Lucas told him he could not.

Twentieth Century-Fox mercifully postponed the premiere of *Star Wars*, pushing its launch date back a month. The studio had little choice, since ILM was still shooting footage. Harrison Ellenshaw's beautiful matte paintings (including the orbital view of Tatooine and various Death Star interiors) were filmed and composited in February and March 1977. The final ILM visuals—including the *Millennium Falcon*'s jump to hyperspace and the explosion of the Death Star—were filmed just three weeks prior to the movie's new May 25, 1977, release date.

When the space dust settled, ILM had spent about $2.5 million—25 percent over its budget (the highest cost overrun of any department). To put it in another light, according to Lucas biographer Dale Pollock, *Star Wars*' visual effects cost about $150 per frame of footage (that's $589 in inflation-adjusted terms). While the finished product wowed audiences worldwide, Lucas was never entirely satisfied with ILM's results and had many of the visual effects redone for the 1997 *Star Wars* Special Edition. One indication of his feelings was that Lucas—who typically showed his gratitude to members of his cast and crew by sharing profit points—didn't share profits with anyone at ILM, although a few staffers received cash bonuses.

Editing

Assembling the footage into a finished film was nearly as daunting a chore as finishing the visual effects. Nearly 340,000 feet of film had been shot in Tunisia and England, and new footage was arriving daily from ILM and elsewhere. Lucas had been dismayed with British editor John Jympson's work (see previous chapter), so even the Tatooine sequences, which were supposed to be nearly complete, had to be recut. Over the course of the next nine months, four more editors—including Lucas himself—labored virtually nonstop to sculpt the movie into its finished form. Richard Chew and Lucas' wife Marcia assembled a rough cut, missing most of the visual and sound effects, by Thanksgiving of 1976.

The rough cut of *Star Wars* ran 117 minutes, just four shorter than the finished (original theatrical) release. However, this version was missing many visual effects sequences, all the pickup shots, the opening narrative scroll, and closing credits. Fat had to be trimmed, and it was vital to identify as soon as possible those sequences that would be dropped or abbreviated, since so many scenes involved visual effects. Deciding to cut scenes now kept the already swamped ILM staff from wasting resources on shots that would no longer be needed. Lucas decided to delete two Tatooine sequences: Luke's exchange with his friend Biggs Darklighter at Tosche Station, in which Luke expresses his desire to join the rebellion, and Han's docking bay run-in with Jabba the Hutt. The Luke-Biggs scene (along with a later exchange between the two characters on Yavin Four, prior to the climactic Death Star battle) was omitted not only to quicken the tempo of the movie but because Lucas was unhappy with the performance of Garrock Hagon as Biggs. In the docking bay scene, Jabba had been played by actor Declan Mulholland, but Lucas intended to replace the Scottish actor with a stop-motion animated version of the character (envisioned as a sort of giant slug). ILM was running so far behind schedule that Lucas realized time-consuming stop-motion was out the question. Unwilling to put Mulholland on-screen, he was forced to cut the scene entirely.

By the time shooting wrapped in England, Industrial Light & Magic had fallen perilously behind schedule. ILM had completed only a handful of shots, most of which George Lucas considered unusable.

After helping assemble the rough cut, Marcia Griffin Lucas left *Star Wars* to work on Martin Scorsese's *New York, New York* (1977). Lucas—at the suggestion of his friend Brian De Palma—brought in editor Paul Hirsch to continue whittling away at *Star Wars*. Lucas cut the final version of the *Millennium Falcon*-TIE fighter dogfight himself. From late 1976 until the picture went into release, *Star Wars* remained in a state of perpetual revision, with new temporary cuts assembled every two weeks. The process became even more nerve-wracking when insiders including Fox executives began to see these early versions.

Reshoots and Pickups

In early 1977, second- and third units tried to recover the shots lost to poor weather and other problems in Tunisia, and to improve sequences filmed less than satisfactorily in England. In January and February, nearly all the landspeeder scenes were lensed, with Death Valley standing in for the Tunisian salt flats. Unfortunately, Mark Hamill also needed a stand-in. Speeding to the location on a Friday night in mid-January, the actor lost control of his new BMW and rolled the vehicle. Hamill required seven hours of emergency surgery and underwent three rounds of plastic surgery to reconstruct his face. Along with the landspeeder scenes, additional footage of the sandcrawler was captured in Death Valley, along with shots of a Bantha (played by an elephant in a giant, shaggy, horned costume).

Lucas was also unhappy with the Mos Eisley cantina sequence, which had been compromised when makeup artist Stuart Freeborn was hospitalized. As originally shot, the scene included few and mostly unimpressive creature makeups. Lucas—against the strenuous pleas of Fox brass—invested an additional $10,000 in shooting inserts with new creatures created by makeup wizard Rick Baker. All the most memorable aliens in the film were added at this point. (For more on Baker and his contributions, see Chapter 5.) Baker also crafted a new, more convincing version of Greedo, the green-skinned bounty hunter zapped by Han Solo in the cantina, and Harrison Ford was recalled to reshoot that part of the cantina sequence. (During reshoots, some of the dialogue from the deleted Jabba scene was moved to Han's exchange with Greedo.) Lucas' insistence on getting this sequence right would be rewarded when the Mos Eisley cantina became one of the most popular and iconic passages in the movie.

Lucas also refused to compromise regarding the last remaining second-unit assignment: the establishing shots of the jungle moon Yavin Four, which were filmed in Guatemala. Sending a second unit to the Mayan ruins in Tikal, Guatemala, had been in the budget from the beginning, but Fox tried to

During reshoots, several inserts were filmed for the Mos Eisley cantina sequence, using Rick Baker's imaginative alien costumes and makeups.

convince Lucas to film at a cheaper location in Mexico instead. Once again Lucas stuck to his blasters and wound up with breathtaking images.

Sound and Music

Throughout his career, even dating back to his earliest student films at USC, Lucas had shown an instinctive grasp of two key film disciplines. One was editing. The other was sound design, and the mating of images with music. These had been strengths of both *THX 1138* and *American Graffiti*, and they would be strengths again of *Star Wars*.

To assure this, Lucas hired his former USC classmate, the enormously talented Ben Burtt, as *Star Wars*' sound designer. Working in concert with sound editor Sam Shaw, Burtt crafted a panoramic soundscape featuring roaring spacecraft, buzzing lightsabers, and other imaginary sounds, all culled from life and manipulated into something new and distinctive. Burtt's most challenging assignment was creating the "dialogue" for R2-D2 and Chewbacca. For the droid, Burtt used a combination of electronic beeps and whistles, which he parsed into distinct words and phrases to create an electronic "language." Even though Artoo had no scripted dialogue, Burtt

George Lucas was never happy with the original version of Greedo (seen here with the director). During postproduction, he had the scene reshot with an improved Greedo designed by Rick Baker.

imagined what the droid would be saying if he could speak English and then "translated" those words using the lexicon of chirps and coos he had developed. Lucas worked closely with him on the droid's vocabulary and inflection. The director wasn't always able to provide specific suggestions, but sent Burtt back to the mixing table if Artoo's voice sounded wrong. The process was time-consuming. It took six weeks to finish R2-D2's scenes in the first ten minutes of the picture, although Burtt picked up speed once he and Lucas came to an understanding of how the droid should sound. Burtt followed a similar process in creating dialogue for Chewbacca, creating the Wookiee's voice from the sounds of growling bears, barking dogs, roaring lions, and a groaning walrus, spliced together and electronically modified.

Lucas also intended to dub the dialogue of C-3PO and Darth Vader. Originally, he planned to give C-3PO a New York accent— something along the lines of Bud Abbott (of Abbott & Costello). But as editing wore on, he grew to admire what Anthony Daniels had brought to the role of Threepio. In the end he chose to stick with the actor's conception of the droid as a prissy, nervous English butler. That did not happen with David Prowse, whose soft "Darth Farmer" voice was all wrong for Vader. Lucas hired James Earl Jones, a classically trained actor with a Tony Award and an Academy Award nomination on his resume, to loop Vader's dialogue. Jones' voice was then enhanced with sound effects by Burtt. Jones, who declined to receive screen credit, was paid $7,500 for one day's work. He completed all

Vader's dialogue in a single session lasting less than three hours, on March 1, 1977.

Four days later, at Anvil Studios in Denham, England, John Williams began recording his score for *Star Wars*, conducting the London Symphony Orchestra. Lucas admired Williams' Oscar-winning score for *Jaws* (1975) and targeted the composer from the beginning. He began meeting with Williams in the early weeks of 1977 and shared his ideas about the music of *Star Wars*. Lucas was adamantly against the use of synthesizers or anything "science fiction." Instead, he wanted an old-fashioned, sweeping, romantic sound—music in the tradition of legendary Hollywood composers such as Max Steiner and Erich Wolfgang Korngold. Williams, after viewing an early cut of the film, agreed this was the right approach and set about penning one of the most instantly recognizable scores in movie history. (For more on Williams and his contributions to the franchise, see Chapter 23.) The *Star Wars* score was recorded in fourteen three-hour sessions over seven days. For the working edits of the movie, Lucas had scored the film with selections from Igor Stravinsky, Antonin Dvorak, and Anton Bruckner. Now, as the film neared completion, Williams' stirring music added an entirely new dimension to *Star Wars*. Lucas later said that Williams' music was the only aspect of *Star Wars* that exceeded his expectations.

While investing so much time and care into the sound of *Star Wars*, Lucas made one more controversial decision: to release the film in Dolby Stereo. The hiss-reducing audio system, then in its infancy, would assure that audiences could actually hear the superb work of Burtt, Shaw, and Williams. However, again Lucas met with studio resistance. Many American theaters (and most theaters in many foreign countries) had not yet upgraded to Dolby—which was understandable since so far not many films had been released in stereo. Issuing *Star Wars* in Dolby meant creating separate stereo and mono sound mixes, again driving up production and print costs. Once more, the studio surrendered in the face of Lucas' intransigence.

Selling *Star Wars*

Eventually, of course, Lucas had to begin showing *Star Wars* to other people. At first that didn't go well. Irvin Kershner (Lucas' former USC instructor and future *Empire Strikes Back* director) said in a 2009 interview that he first saw scenes from *Star Wars* at Francis Ford Coppola's New Year's Eve party December 31, 1976. "George is standing back at the door, and we don't want to face him," Kershner said. "This is the most awful stuff we've ever seen. . . . We were really concerned for him." In mid-February 1977, Lucas screened the current work print in its entirety for the first time. The very select audience included friends and associates such as Steven Spielberg,

Brian De Palma, and screenwriters Willard and Gloria Huyck (who polished the film's dialogue), Hal Barwood, and Jay Cocks. It bombed. Most of Lucas' friends were polite in their lack of enthusiasm, or tried to offer suggestions on how to improve the picture. De Palma was openly dismissive and mocked *Star Wars* to Lucas' face. Only Spielberg saw the appeal of the film, which he predicted would be more popular than the movie he was working on, *Close Encounters of the Third Kind* (1977).

In the wake of this disastrous screening, more changes were made to the picture. The scene in which Princess Leia is interrogated aboard the Death Star was moved to later in the film, to help audiences connect with the droids and Luke. The cantina sequence and other passages were trimmed. And the clunky and verbose opening scroll was revised. De Palma, of all people, helped rewrite the text.

Soon afterward, Lucas screened the film for Alan Ladd Jr. and other Fox executives. It met a mixed reception with this crowd. Ladd couldn't make heads or tails of the picture, but his associate Gareth Wigan literally wept with joy and told Lucas *Star Wars* was the greatest film he had ever seen. Lucas took Ladd's reaction in stride but was baffled by Wigan's enthusiasm. The director continued to doubt the film's commercial viability.

The suits at Fox were worried about that too. A two-minute teaser trailer (which described the picture as "a big, sprawling space saga of rebellion and romance" and "a spectacle light years ahead of its time," from "George Lucas, the man who brought you *American Graffiti*") had been released in late 1976 but was withdrawn when audiences responded poorly. The trailer, which used unfinished visual effects and lacked Williams' music, was intriguing but failed to capture the spirit of the film. The studio's marketing department tried to convince Lucas to rename the movie after the title *Star Wars* tested badly. Women weren't interested in any film with the word "war" in the title, he was told. More troubling still, the studio's sales team was having problems convincing theater owners to book the movie under any title.

The summer of 1977 was loaded with eagerly anticipated films, including Richard Attenborough's prestigious World War II epic *A Bridge Too Far*; John Boorman's *Exorcist II: The Heretic*, a sequel to one of the highest-grossing movies in history; *Sorcerer*, director William Friedkin's first picture since *The Exorcist*; the James Bond entry *The Spy Who Loved Me*; Peter Yates' *The Deep*, based on a novel by *Jaws* author Peter Benchley; and Fox's own *Damnation Alley*, a postapocalyptic science fiction thriller from hitmaker Jack Smight (this one was eventually postponed until October). How could Lucas' quirky little space movie hold its own against such heavyweight competition? When *Star Wars* gained little traction, Fox tried twisting arms. The studio told theater owners it would allow them to book another expected summer hit—the soapy melodrama *The Other Side of Midnight*, based on a best-selling Sidney Sheldon novel—only if they also accepted *Star Wars*. This gambit, known as block booking, had been illegal since the Supreme Court's 1948 *U.S. v. Paramount Pictures* decision. The tactic not only failed but earned Fox a $25,000 fine.

The studio's marketing department gained fresh enthusiasm for *Star Wars* following another in-house screening in mid-April. In its nearly finished state, complete with Williams' score, the film generated a wildly enthusiastic response. Still, Fox was able to secure very few screens for the debut of *Star Wars*. The picture opened in just thirty-two theaters nationwide and found a slot at a Hollywood movie house (the prestigious Chinese Theatre) only when *Sorcerer* was delayed. The public saw the film for the first time May 1 at a sneak preview at San Francisco's Northpoint Theater. It was a triumph. The audience cheered from the opening shot. A subsequent screening for Fox's Board of Directors, however, proved less successful. Only a few members enjoyed the picture. Most were puzzled by it.

After the May 1 preview, Ladd lobbied the Motion Picture Association of America's Classification and Rating Administration to change the film's rating from G to PG. This was an unusual move. Typically studios lobby for softer, not harder, ratings. But Lucas believed some scenes in the film—such as Kenobi severing a man's arm in the cantina—were inappropriate for very young viewers. From Fox's perspective, it was a marketing concern. A G rating would effectively label *Star Wars* as a kids' movie, limiting its audience.

The picture finally premiered Wednesday, May 25, 1977. It ran 121 minutes and was rated PG. Hollywood—and the world—would never be quite the same.

9

Echo Base

Homages in *Star Wars*

n a column headlined "Originality," first published in the April 1986 issue of his *Isaac Asimov's Science Fiction Magazine*, the legendary SF author conceded that "total originality is just about impossible." Asimov elaborated on this point in a subsequent column, arguing that a story could be considered original even if many of its constituent parts were borrowed from earlier works—so long as those pieces were assembled in a new, inventive configuration. To prove his point he cited George Lucas' adventure serial pastiche *Raiders of the Lost Ark* (1981). Asimov might as accurately have selected *Star Wars* as his example.

Chapter 3 of this book outlined the most significant books and movies that inspired George Lucas to create *Star Wars*. While *Flash Gordon* and *The Hidden Fortress* are its two clearest cinematic ancestors, *Star Wars* reflects a wide variety of other film influences, including the classic Westerns, war films, serials, and melodramas that Lucas soaked up in his youth, as well as the art films he discovered at USC.

In many cases the similarities are purely visual. Darth Vader looks remarkably like the Lightning, a villain from the Republic Pictures serial *Fighting Devil Dogs* (1938). C-3PO could be a sibling of Maria, the feminine robot from Fritz Lang's masterpiece *Metropolis* (1927), while R2-D2 owes something to the cute, stubby robots that appeared alongside Bruce Dern in *Silent Running* (1972). Movies like *The Searchers* (1956), *Lawrence of Arabia* (1962), and *2001: A Space Odyssey* (1968) shaped Lucas' pictorial approach. He composed the Tatooine sequences, especially establishing shots of various locales on the parched planet, the same way director David Lean shot the Arabian Desert—as if it were an ocean panorama, using the endless expanse of sand to dwarf the characters. Stanley Kubrick's *2001* provided a similar model for Lucas' handling of scenes set in outer space. Director John Carpenter's *Dark Star*—the earliest movie to depict a lived-in, even drab, future universe—may also have influenced Lucas' visual style.

But *Star Wars* also contains very specific references to earlier works. Viewers with a working knowledge of classic cinema can point to *Star Wars* and say, "Hey, that (shot/line of dialogue) is straight out of (insert name of movie here)." Lucas has acknowledged some of these moments as "homages" to his cinematic inspirations. In other cases, the director may have unintentionally quoted from an earlier film. While trying to work out a given shot, perhaps an idea rose to the surface from the stew of childhood movie memories. And some of these apparent links may be purely coincidental. In any case, however, the similarities are many and often striking.

The *Tantive IV*

Lucas' homages begin at the very beginning, even before viewers meet a single character. The rolling narrative scroll that opens *Star Wars* (especially with the "Episode IV—A New Hope" subtitle, which was added in 1981) is one of Lucas' most overt tributes. It's nearly identical to the opening summaries used for Chapters 2 through 12 of the Universal Pictures serial *Flash Gordon Conquers the Universe* (1938), one of Lucas' primary inspirations.

Immediately following the scroll, an imperial Star Destroyer, chasing Princess Leia's ship, rumbles across the screen. This jaw-dropping shot ends with a close-up of the ship's giant thrusters. Then we get a reverse angle showing the front of the Destroyer firing at Leia's ship, the *Tantive IV*. This astonishing shot would be copied by many later—and lesser—sci-fi movies (see Chapter 13). Yet, as influential as this shot was, it may have been borrowed, or at least adapted, from *2001*. About fifty-four minutes into *2001*, at the beginning of the "Jupiter Mission" sequence, the massive *Discovery One* spacecraft glides across the screen. The ship is photographed from below, and the shot ends with a view of the Discovery One's giant thrusters. Kubrick then immediately cuts to a reverse angle that shows the front of the spacecraft. While the angle of the shot and the pace of the ship's movement are different in *Star Wars*, the basic idea of indicating the size of a large vessel by watching it pass in front of the camera for several seconds is the same. In both cases it's remarkably effective. At the conclusion of its opening sequence, *Star Wars* quotes a second *2001* moment. The shot of a life pod tumbling toward Tatooine rhymes with a shot of the Pan Am lunar lander falling toward the surface of the moon in *2001*'s earlier "TMA-1" sequence. Look for it at the thirty-seven-minute mark of the Kubrick film.

The Lars Homestead

In one of *Star Wars*' most searing moments, Luke Skywalker realizes that the imperial stormtroopers who have massacred Jawas in search of C-3PO and R2-D2 may have also attacked his aunt and uncle's farm. Luke climbs into his

Luke's discovery of his parents' charred bodies at the burned-out Skywalker homestead was an homage to a famous sequence from director John Ford's epic Western *The Searchers*, starring (foreground) Jeffrey Hunter, left, and John Wayne.

landspeeder and rushes home, only to find the Lars homestead a smoking ruin, and to discover the charred skeletons of his Uncle Owen and Aunt Beru. Lucas readily acknowledges drawing on director John Ford's *The Searchers* while designing this sequence. In that Western classic, Ethan Edwards (John Wayne) joins a group of Texas Rangers searching for rustled cattle. When they find that the cattle have been killed, Edwards realizes that the missing livestock was a diversion to draw the Rangers away and set the stage for an Indian attack. He climbs onto his horse and races home, only to find his brother's homestead a smoking ruin. About twenty-one minutes into the film, Ethan discovers that his brother and most of his brother's family have been wiped out by raiding Comanches. Like the Lars homestead, the Edwards' burning home was dug out of a desert hillside. Black smoke curls away from the ruined home as Edwards finds the body of his beloved sister-in-law, Martha. Both of these emotionally powerful scenes provide tremendous narrative thrust, compelling the hero (Luke/Ethan) to take up the quest that will consume the remainder of the story.

The Mos Eisley Cantina

The Mos Eisley Cantina sequence practically oozes with elements traceable to earlier works. In general terms, Lucas films the cantina the same way director Michael Curtiz shot the Rick's Café scenes from *Casablanca* (1942)—as a steamy, shadowy place full of sketchy characters, all of whom seem to be scanning the room out of the corners of their eyes. If *Casablanca* provides the setting, then Akira Kurosawa's *Yojimbo* (1961) and Sergio Leone's *The Good, the Bad, and the Ugly* (1966) supply the action.

At the bar, Luke is accosted by a drunken fugitive who brags about being marked for death in twelve systems. Ben Kenobi tries to intervene on Skywalker's behalf, but a fight ensues and Kenobi slices off the criminal's arm below the elbow. This passage ends with a shot of the thug's severed arm, still holding his blaster. About eighteen minutes into *Yojimbo*, the masterless samurai played by Toshiro Mifune demonstrates his skills by baiting a trio of unscrupulous, loud-mouthed swordsmen into a duel. One of them brags that "I'm a wanted fugitive. They'll crucify me if I'm caught." During the ensuing fight, Mifune's character slices off one of the bandits' arms. The sequence concludes with a shot of the thug's severed arm, still holding a katana sword.

Later, Jabba's henchman Greedo confronts Han over a table in his booth. Greedo demands the money Solo owes Jabba. When Han tells him he has a profitable new fare lined up, Greedo tries to extort money from Solo. Ultimately Han blasts Greedo, firing his hidden blaster from under the table. (For now, we will set aside the sticky issue of who shoots first.) In *The Good, the Bad, and the Ugly* (at about the ten-minute mark) the roles are reversed but the action is similar. Across a dinner table, a man Angel Eyes (Lee Van Cleef) has been hired to kill tries to bribe the bounty hunter to set him free, but Angel Eyes blasts him with a pistol hidden beneath the table. For the record, Angel Eyes—aka "the Bad"—shoots first. The cantina sequence concludes with Han dropping a coin onto the bar and apologizing to the bartender for the mess. In the classic Western *The Magnificent Seven* (1960, adapted from a Kurosawa film), a barroom confrontation concludes (about thirty-nine minutes into the film) with star Yul Brynner flinging a coin onto the bar and issuing a similar apology to the barkeep.

The Death Star

Lucas' tributes to Kurosawa and others continue when Luke, Han, Kenobi, and the droids are taken aboard the Death Star. In one memorable scene, stormtroopers search the captured *Millennium Falcon* but find no sign of the crew. Once they leave, the camera pans down to the ship's deck plates, which move aside and reveal our heroes, hidden underneath in secret compartments. Their heads pop into view from below. This moment is staged almost identically to a scene from Kurosawa's *Sanjuro* (1962, a sequel to *Yojimbo*). Mifune's ronin helps a group of rebel samurai hide to evade capture. Once the enemy leaves (at about the twelve-minute mark of the film), the camera pans down the floorboards of the house, which move aside to reveal the conspirators hidden underneath. Their heads pop into view from below.

When Kenobi disables the Death Star's tractor beam, he traverses a narrow catwalk across a metallic abyss. This scene strongly recalls a sequence

Luke and Leia's breathless swing to safety across a chasm in the Death Star recalls a similar sequence from the classic fantasy film *The Seventh Voyage of Sinbad*, which featured stop-motion animation by the legendary Ray Harryhausen (including a climactic battle between a dragon and a Cyclops).

from *Forbidden Planet* (1956) in which Dr. Morbius (Walter Pidgeon) leads Commander Adams (Leslie Nielsen) and Dr. Ostrow (Warren Stevens) on a tour of the massive underground facilities left behind by the extinct Krell species on planet Altair 4. The Death Star power terminal closely resembles the miles-deep Krell ventilator shaft seen at the sixty-minute mark of *Forbidden Planet.*

Perhaps the most iconic moment of our heroes' adventures aboard the Death Star arrives when Luke and Leia, trapped by stormtroopers at the edge of another cavernous gulf, use a rope and grappling hook to swing across the chasm. This may have derived from an unforgettable sequence in *The Seventh Voyage of Sinbad* (1958). Near the climax of that film (eighty minutes along), while fleeing the cave of the evil sorcerer Sokurah (Torin Thatcher), Sinbad (Kerwin Matthews) and Princess Parisa (Kathryn Grant) are trapped by a broken rock bridge at the edge of a stony crevasse with flowing lava at the bottom. With the help of a friendly genie (Richard Eyer), who produces a magic rope, Sinbad and the princess swing across the abyss.

Space Battles

Lucas' cinematic inspirations are most obvious in *Star Wars*' space battles. He used footage from old war movies to demonstrate to the staff at Industrial Light & Magic the kind of movements he wanted to see executed by X-wings, TIE fighters, and other spacecraft. In the rough cut of *Star Wars*, he used this same footage to substitute for unfinished visual effects. In numerous interviews, Lucas has stated that these scenes provided much of the impetus behind the entire movie. The fact that he personally edited the *Millennium Falcon*'s battle with attacking TIE fighters also demonstrates the importance the director placed on these scenes. This interlude was clearly modeled on a similar sequence from director Howard Hawks' classic World War II film *Air Force* (1943), in which turret gunners aboard an American B-17 "Flying Fortress" fend off an attack by Japanese A6M "Zero" fighter planes. This pulse-quickening scene begins at the eighty-minute mark of *Air Force* and will seem uncannily familiar to anyone who has seen *Star Wars*.

For the climactic attack on the Death Star, Lucas appropriated shots from numerous other classic WWII films. The preflight briefing, in which General Dodonna explains the tricky plan to attack the space station, recalls a similar scene in *633 Squadron* (1964), a British film about an airstrike on a German V-2 rocket fuel refinery. Shots of imperial troops manning the Death Star's giant laser resemble the Nazis manning the titular weapons from *The Guns of Navarone* (1961). The battle itself is shot in the same fashion as the aerial conflicts depicted in *633 Squadron*, *The Bridges at Toko-Ri* (1954), *Battle of Britain*

Associated British Presents

RICHARD   MICHAEL
TODD · REDGRAVE

The DAM
BUSTERS

The thrilling space battle finale of *Star Wars* was patterned after the climax of the British World War II drama *The Dam Busters.*

(1969), and especially *The Dam Busters,* a 1955 British film based on an actual mission to destroy three German dams that provided the hydroelectric power behind the Nazi war industry. *The Dam Busters* connection is another one that Lucas has readily acknowledged. He could hardly do otherwise. Not only are individual shots duplicated from the earlier film, but so is the general plan of attack, with craft flying low along a narrow trench guarded by heavy weapons. In both films, an initial attempt to destroy the target fails, and a second attack run must be undertaken. Some of the chatter between pilots is almost identical. And both films climax with a massive explosion.

The Medal Ceremony

One possible homage Lucas has always denied—for obvious reasons—is to Leni Riefenstahl's infamous Nazi propaganda film *Triumph of the Will* (1935). The triumphant medal ceremony that concludes *Star Wars* is staged and photographed in a manner eerily similar to the way Riefenstahl filmed the 1934 Nuremberg rallies. Lucas has always insisted the similarity is coincidental. His argument is, basically, how many ways are there to film such an event? However, in his book *Star Wars: The Art of Ralph McQuarrie*, the production illustrator recalls that Lucas instructed him to paint "something akin to a Nazi rally with hundreds of troops lined up and huge banners on display." In any event, when viewed side by side, Luke, Han, and Chewie's walk through the assembled troops toward the medal dais and Hitler's march through the assembled, cheering brownshirts on his way to his speaking platform (about ninety minutes into *Triumph of the Will*) are so much alike that it's squirm-inducing.

> "Those who do not want to imitate anything produce nothing."
> —Salvador Dali

None of these similarities, as Dali (or Asimov) might argue, should suggest that *Star Wars* was unoriginal. Even if you string together clips from *Flash Gordon*, *2001*, *Casablanca*, *Air Force*, *The Dam Busters*, and all the other movies Lucas borrowed from while making *Star Wars*, you still wouldn't have *Star Wars*. (It's been tried; check YouTube.) Lucas' love of vintage war movies, Westerns, serials, and other classic films was creative fuel that provided the imaginative thrust for *Star Wars*. It was only natural for him to tip his hat to those pictures. More importantly, while some of the individual building blocks were derived from earlier works, Lucas rearranged those pieces to construct something very different from anything viewers had seen before—a mash-up of cowboys, pirates, princesses, sorcerers, and Nazis splashed across a galaxy-wide canvas. The components that were recognizable to audiences only served to make a scenario unlike anything audiences had experienced before, and which was in some respects bizarre, somehow seem relatable, even comforting. Lucas had taken a different course with his first foray into science fiction, *THX 1138*. Although intended as a commentary on the state of American culture, viewers rejected that film's sterile dystopia. *THX 1138* remained icy and aloof. With *Star Wars*, Lucas was able to create something paradoxically fresh yet familiar, innovative but approachable.

10

New Hope

Assessing Episode IV (1977)

F ew films are as venerated—or as vilified—as *Star Wars*. Its supporters revere it as a model of escapist filmmaking and an exhilarating, inspirational reframing of ancient myth. Writing for *The Atlantic* in 2011, critic Colin Fleming called *Star Wars* "the galactic gold standard" and argued that "you can put [it] alongside *The Searchers*, *Bride of Frankenstein*, or *The Wizard of Oz* as an American film masterpiece." *Star Wars* regularly finishes at or near the top of the poll when fans are asked to name the greatest movies ever made. On the other hand, *Star Wars*' detractors revile the picture, arguing that it served as a catalyst for the dumbing down of popular culture in general and Hollywood in particular. John Simon, film critic for the *National Review*, summed up the complaints of many *Star Wars* haters during an appearance on ABC's *Nightline* following the release of *Return of the Jedi* in 1983. "Obviously, let's face it, they [the *Star Wars* films] are for children, or for childish adults," Simon said. "They are not for adult mentalities." He bemoaned the films' reliance on special effects, dismissing the series as "a technological whirligig" with "lousy actors," "ghastly dialogue," "terrible plotting," and "miserable characterization." Opinions between these two camps are so sharply divided that it's hard to believe these people watched the same movie. Yet the qualities that made *Star Wars* such a popular sensation are, in large part, the same ones that invited vehement critical backlash.

Images in Motion

They call them motion pictures for a reason. First and foremost among the reasons why *Star Wars* enchanted moviegoers in 1977 was that it put spectacular pictures in thrilling motion. The film played to all of director George Lucas' strengths: pictorial composition, rhythmic film editing, innovative sound design, and the wedding of images with music. His dexterity in these areas had been apparent as far back as his student films at USC and was displayed in *THX 1138* and *American Graffiti*. But *Star Wars* enabled Lucas to apply these skills in conjunction with the next-generation visual artistry of

Industrial Light & Magic and the stirring music of John Williams. The results were extraordinary. Nothing had ever looked or moved quite like it.

The film has become so iconic, and has been so frequently copied, that it may be difficult at this distance to appreciate how dazzling a visual experience *Star Wars* was when it premiered. When the massive Star Destroyer rumbled across the screen, jaws literally dropped—not only because the shot was beautifully rendered but because it immediately drew viewers into the story. The Destroyer roared past with blasters flaring in hot pursuit of Princess Leia's spaceship, instilling a sense of urgency and establishing that (unlike, say, *2001: A Space Odyssey*) *Star Wars* would value action as much as image. Crisp editing—the picture cuts almost mercilessly from one eye-popping scene to the next—kept the picture crackling with energy. Although not particularly fast by today's standards, *Star Wars* was edited at a breakneck pace for a 1977 film. Viewers were held in thrall by a succession of spellbinding and visually arresting sequences, including the Mos Eisley cantina interlude, Leia's rescue from the Death Star, and the epic space battles. Beyond these showpieces, however, the narrative is punctuated with still more lovely shots— for example, Luke posed against the rugged landscape of Tatooine as the planet's twin suns sink into the horizon. This moment, like most of the film's other most powerful scenes, is greatly enhanced by Williams' evocative score.

The sheer visual power of *Star Wars*, in and of itself, would have made the film a can't-miss event for many moviegoers. Some critics looked askance at

Audiences in 1977 had never seen anything quite like the dogfighting spaceships in *Star Wars*.

ILM's technical wizardry, or at least at the way Lucas so thoroughly integrated it into the film. "Special effects are like the tail of the dog, which should not wag the whole animal," Simon groused. "When you have a film that's 90 percent special effects you might just as well be watching an animated cartoon." But what the detractors failed to appreciate was the virtuosity with which those effects were employed—how seamlessly integrated and fluidly edited they were, and how beautifully they were mated with Williams' music. Later filmmakers would find it simpler to match ILM's work than Lucas'. Take, for instance, *Star Trek: The Motion Picture* (1979), which offered equally impressive visuals but remained a turgid, tedious misfire.

Story and Performance

In other respects, as Lucas readily admits, *Star Wars* was less successful. "From a technical point of view—my own point of view—I don't think it's altogether that well-made a movie," the director told *Starlog* magazine in 1981. The skeptics are correct that *Star Wars* is not a work of sublime artistry, subtlety, or depth. But it wasn't meant to be. It's the grandchild of *Flash Gordon*, not *Citizen Kane*. Judged apples-to-apples with its forebears, *Star Wars* looks very good indeed. "One of Mr. Lucas' particular achievements is the manner in which he is able to recall the tackiness of the old comic strips and serials he loves without making a movie that is, itself, tacky," wrote Vincent Canby, film critic for the *New York Times*, in his review of the film.

Star Wars instantly became the new standard-bearer for spacefaring action-adventure. Lucas took the muscle from vintage sci-fi serials and discarded the fat and connective tissues. *Star Wars* plays like a highlight reel, rushing headlong from one thrilling incident to the next, devil take the exposition. Niceties like scientific plausibility were beside the point. Devising a clever plot and sketching fully realized characters wasn't part of the calculus either, which is why Lucas had such difficulty writing the screenplay. His script is lumpy, with holes in story logic, thinly sketched characters, and tin-eared dialogue. But the story merely serves as a framework on which to hang the picture's breathtaking set pieces. The *Millennium Falcon*'s battle with the TIE fighters, for instance, was one of Lucas' primary inspirations for the entire project. While atypical, this manner of constructing a screenplay was hardly unprecedented or invalid. Alfred Hitchcock often worked the same way. Hitch constructed the rest of *North by Northwest* (1959) around two showstopping scenes—the crop duster attack and the Mount Rushmore finale.

Critics also overstate the deficiencies of the film's cast. Mark Hamill, Harrison Ford, and Carrie Fisher may not deliver finely nuanced portrayals, but they fully inhabit their characters, which is an accomplishment given

A long time ago in a galaxy far, far away...

TWENTIETH CENTURY-FOX Presents
A LUCASFILM LTD. PRODUCTION
STAR WARS

This newspaper ad slick was based on the original, now-iconic, one-sheet movie poster that announced *Star Wars*.

Lucas' frequently awkward dialogue. It may represent a triumph of casting more than performance, but Hamill the earnest naïf, Ford the skeptic, and Fisher the Hollywood princess serve the film well and have wonderful chemistry as an ensemble. It's impossible to imagine anyone else playing Luke Skywalker, Han Solo, or Leia Organa.

As Obi-Wan Kenobi, Sir Alec Guinness doesn't approach his finest work, but he easily tosses off the movie's best performance. Guinness anchors *Star Wars*, lending dignity and credibility to the universe Lucas is creating, and his presence enhances the work of all his cast mates. His matter-of-fact interactions with C-3PO, R2-D2, and Chewbacca help sell the idea that Laurel & Hardy robots and giant "walking carpets" are commonplace things. As Threepio, Anthony Daniels delivers another of the film's best performances, remarkable for both its distinctive physicality and his delightful comedic delivery. The actor's work is even more impressive because it was accomplished under almost unendurable circumstances, especially in Tunisia. The composite performance of David Prowse and James Earl Jones as Darth Vader is also startlingly effective. Vader became the breakout character of the film, even though he was on-screen for just 12 of the movie's (original) 121 minutes. Peter Cushing shines in his brief appearance as Grand Moff Tarkin, playing against type as an icy, pitiless villain. (In his horror films, Cushing was most often cast in sympathetic roles.) Even Peter Mayhew, buried under fur and makeup as Chewbacca, brings vitality and personality to what could have been a thankless part, through his body language and wonderfully expressive eyes.

The Future of the Future

Heading into the summer of 1977, Twentieth Century-Fox executives figured they had a sure-fire science fiction blockbuster in the bag—but it wasn't *Star Wars*. It was *Damnation Alley*, a postapocalyptic thriller based on an acclaimed novel by Hugo- and Nebula-winning author Roger Zelazny, starring rising heartthrob Jan-Michael Vincent and the stalwart George Peppard. Helming the production was Jack Smight, a reliable hitmaker whose previous two films—*Airport 1975* (1975) and *Midway* (1976)—had earned a combined $90 million, both ranking among the ten highest-grossing films of their year. Yet, while *Star Wars* did record business, *Damnation Alley*, which cost $17 million ($6 million more than *Star Wars*) failed to recover its production expenses. *Damnation Alley* failed, primarily, because it simply isn't a very good movie. Its screenplay, which veered away from the source material, is inane (Zelazny disowned the film), and its visual effects are clumsy. But there was something larger working against the picture.

The release of *Damnation Alley*, originally slated for a month after *Star Wars*, was postponed so it wouldn't compete with Fox's surprise smash. By the time *Damnation Alley* finally appeared in late October, however, audience tastes had changed. Following *Star Wars*, *Damnation Alley* seemed hopelessly out of date—and not just because its visual effects were laughable. *Damnation Alley* belonged to an earlier era of screen SF, one that had reached an abrupt end.

The renowned *2001* had earned the genre new critical acceptance, but with respectability came a desire by filmmakers and an expectation from audiences that sci-fi cinema would approach serious issues (nuclear proliferation, pollution, overpopulation, rising violence, etc.) in serious ways. As a result, the major science fiction films of the early and middle 1970s were relentlessly downbeat and usually dystopian. These included *No Blade of Grass* (1970), *A Clockwork Orange*, *The Omega Man*, *Silent Running* (all 1971), *Soylent Green* (1973), and *Rollerball* (1975). Lucas' *THX 1138* (1971) was among the many smaller-budget films of the period to depict a grim future for humankind, along with pictures like *Death Race 2000*, *A Boy and His Dog* (both 1975), and others. Fox issued its fatalistic *Planet of the Apes* sequels and Andrei

Tarkovsky made his dour *Solaris* (1971) during this era. *Logan's Run* (1976), although presented as a lighthearted adventure, took place in a future where people are sentenced to die when they reach age thirty. Hollywood had seen the future, and it sucked. It was taken as a given in these films that life would only worsen as the decades and centuries wore on, and that some sort of apocalypse— nuclear, environmental, or political—was inevitable.

Star Wars changed the orbit of mainstream sci-fi. The major SF films released between *Star Wars* and *Return of the Jedi* (1978–83) were lighter in tone, with less emphasis on social messaging and greater investment in action-packed or horror-tinged thrills:

Jan-Michael Vincent, left (with rock), and George Peppard, right (with pistol), costarred with Dominique Sanda (background) in *Damnation Alley*, a postapocalyptic thriller that Twentieth Century-Fox expected to be a summer blockbuster. Released in the wake of *Star Wars*, *Damnation Alley* flopped.

Invasion of the Body Snatchers (1978), *Superman: The Movie* (1978), *Superman II* (1980), *Superman III* (1983), *Alien* (1979), *Star Trek: The Motion Picture* (1979), *Star Trek II: The Wrath of Khan* (1982), *E.T. The Extra-Terrestrial* (1982), and *The Thing* (1982). And that list omits the torrent of blatant *Star Wars* knockoffs that flooded theaters during those years (see Chapter 13). Even the dystopian pictures released during this era—such as *Mad Max* (1980), *Escape from New York* (1981), and *Blade Runner* (1982)—were less preachy and more adventure oriented. Issue-based "pure science fiction" films like those of the early 1970s grew increasingly rare. This stuck in the craw of some hardcore SF fans, who appreciated the more erudite, literary turn the genre had taken earlier in the decade. They resented *Star Wars*—which Lucas never claimed as true science fiction, usually referring to the movie as a "space fantasy"—for setting the genre back, intellectually.

It's true enough *Star Wars* shoulders much of the responsibility for this radical shift in the tone and style of science fiction movies. Its unprecedented financial success—not only in terms of box office returns, but also in ancillary revenue streams such as merchandising and publishing—put dollar signs in the eyes of every executive in Hollywood. Rival studios immediately launched a frantic search for similarly exploitable properties. Pictures like *Soylent Green* weren't what they were looking for. However, the extraordinary profitability of *Star Wars* didn't create a change in moviegoers' appetites; a change in moviegoers' appetites enabled *Star Wars* to achieve its extraordinary profitability. It was simply the right film for its moment.

New Hope

The science fiction films of the early 1970s reflected their times, an era scarred by war, race riots, terrorism, a global energy crisis, and social and political upheavals of all sorts. In America, economic inflation, ongoing anti-war protests, more strident civil rights and "women's liberation" movements, and growing ecological activism roiled the country, while the "credibility gap" of the Vietnam War years, followed by the Watergate scandal, created lingering mistrust of government and skepticism that the United States, as a nation, retained any sort of moral compass. Cynical films like *M*A*S*H* (1970), *Chinatown* (1974), *Dog Day Afternoon* (1975), and *Network* (1976) became major hits. Even the escapist entertainments of the era were relatively grim—disaster movies like *Airport* (1970) and *The Poseidon Adventure* (1972), and rogue cop films like *Dirty Harry* and *The French Connection* (both 1971).

By the late '70s, however, audiences were growing weary of misery and cynicism. They wanted more upbeat fare, as the popular and critical success of Sylvester Stallone's feel-good boxing drama *Rocky* signaled in 1976. All four of the 1977 blockbusters (*Star Wars*, *Saturday Night Fever*, *Smokey and the Bandit*, and *Close Encounters of the Third Kind*), like many earlier 1970s movies, featured corrupt, absent, ineffectual, or conspiratorial authority figures. But they also featured underdog everymen (and everywomen) who triumphed in the end. They were various types of escapist fantasy. *Star Wars* outdid the others because it offered something in addition to escape: reassurance.

Star Wars didn't acquire the retronym *A New Hope* until its 1981 rerelease, when the *Episode IV* subtitle was added to the film. But it was a perfect name for the picture, since the new hope of the title could refer both to the triumph of the heretofore downtrodden rebels in the film and to the emotional invigoration the movie provided audiences. In an era (and a genre) rife with doom and gloom, *Star Wars* shined like a beacon of positivity. But this wasn't the optimism of some literary science fiction, reflecting the conviction that new technologies could solve society's problems. Nor was it anything like *Star Trek* creator Gene Roddenberry's belief in the perfectibility of the human species. In fact, it wasn't anything new or forward-looking at all.

Although on the surface, the two films could hardly seem more different, *Star Wars* stemmed from the same impulse that led Lucas to create *American Graffiti*. "This is my next movie after *American Graffiti* and, in a way, the subject and everything . . . is the very same subject that *American Graffiti* is about," Lucas said in his audio commentary for *Star Wars*.

In 1974, Lucas told *Film Quarterly* interviewer Stephen Farber that the defeatist attitude of *THX* had been a mistake. "All that movie did was make people more pessimistic, more depressed, and less willing to get involved in trying to make the world better," Lucas said. "So I decided that this time [with *Graffiti*] I would make a more optimistic film that makes people feel positive about their fellow human beings." *Graffiti* transported viewers back to 1962. It was the year America became involved in the Vietnamese civil war, and the beginning of the end for America's postwar economic boom, although few people recognized those things at the time. From a mid-'70s perspective, 1962 could be remembered as the last gasp of the Good Old Days, before President John F. Kennedy was assassinated, before America began to rip itself apart. *Star Wars* reflected the same 1962 worldview as *American Graffiti*, inspired

Tender character moments generally aren't a strength of *Star Wars*, but the movie features one when Princess Leia (Carrie Fisher) comforts Luke Skywalker (Mark Hamill) following the death of Ben Kenobi.

as it was by the kinds of movies that the kids in *American Graffiti* would have watched in movie theaters or on television, the kinds of movies Lucas watched when he was one of those *Graffiti* kids.

In '62, straightforward, good-guys-versus-bad-guys Westerns, war movies, and adventure stories didn't seem corny or ironic. "My main reason for making it [*Star Wars*] was to give young people an honest, wholesome fantasy life, the kind my generation had," Lucas told *Time* magazine in 1977. "We had Westerns, pirate movies, all kinds of great things. Now they have *The Six Million Dollar Man* and *Kojak*. Where are the romance, the adventure, and the fun that used to be in practically every movie made?" Indeed, if *Star Wars* had existed in 1962, it would have fit nicely at movie theaters alongside fare like *The Longest Day*, *The Man Who Shot Liberty Valance*, and *Dr. No*.

Star Wars moved beyond the bittersweet nostalgia of *American Graffiti* by undergirding the picture's moral outlook with a mythic story structure and classically archetypal characters. This made the story and its message seem timeless, like the expression of some eternal truth. Lucas, in his interview with Farber, described his values as "all that hokey stuff about being a good neighbor, and the American spirit and all that crap. There *is* something in it." *Star Wars* offered affirmation that such old-fashioned ideals still held meaning and relevance.

A pivotal yet sometimes overlooked factor in Lucas' treatment of this material is that, unlike many of the copycat space operas that followed it—including, ironically, the 1980 remake of *Flash Gordon*—*Star Wars* never condescends to its inspirations. The snobby critics who lambasted *Star Wars* might have gone for the picture if Lucas had treated it as some sort of smirking inside joke. But there is nothing spoofy or tongue-in-cheek about it. It is a straightforward, heartfelt story that could be taken at face value. This appealed to viewers, if not reviewers.

Although its ethics can't be categorized as entirely conservative (see Chapter 29) or even overtly political, *Star Wars* struck a chord with the American public by harkening back to the sincere and uncomplicated outlook of a bygone era. Ronald Reagan's 1980 presidential campaign struck many of these same notes. Reagan, calling for a return to the kind of fundamental morals and simplistic policies that guided America during what might be thought of as the *American Graffiti* era, captured the White House. Once in office, his administration mined the *Star Wars* phenomenon in more overt ways. Reagan, a Cold War hard-liner, referred to the Soviet Union as "the Evil Empire" in a 1983 speech. That same year, Reagan unveiled the Strategic Defense Initiative—a proposed system to protect the United States from nuclear attack by placing interceptor missiles on orbital satellites—which Senator Ted Kennedy labeled "Star Wars." Although this sobriquet was intended derisively, Reagan's supporters loved it, and the moniker stuck. Defending his "Star Wars" idea in 1985, Regan quipped, "If you will pardon me stealing a film line, the Force is with us." An irritated George Lucas attempted to sue two conservative advocacy groups who were promoting SDI using the "Star Wars" nickname. The lawsuit failed. By then, Reagan had been reelected in a historic 1984 landslide, the ballot equivalent of *Star Wars*' box office returns.

All of which disproves the final complaint frequently lodged against *Star Wars* by its critics during the late 1970s: that the movie is childish and vacuous. In their 1979 book *The Movie Brats: How the Film Generation Took over Hollywood*, authors Michael Pye and Linda Myles followed a lengthy interview

Conservative politicians including Margaret Thatcher (center) took the public's embrace of *Star Wars* as a signal that voters wanted a return to old-fashioned, black-and-white ideas and policies.

with Lucas with a dismissive appraisal of the director's most famous work: "*Star Wars* has been taken with ominous seriousness. It should not be. The single strongest impression it leaves is of another great American tradition that involves lights, bells, obstacles, menace, action, technology and thrills. It is pinball on a cosmic scale."

Pye, Myles, and many other critics accused *Star Wars* of being a movie with nothing to say. In actuality, *Star Wars* simply wasn't saying what its detractors wanted to hear. It was, however, delivering a message that a growing percentage of the American public wanted to believe.

Star Wars, Nothing but *Star Wars*

Popular Impact, 1977–79

tar Wars wasn't the only trend-setting blockbuster hit of 1977. *Smokey and the Bandit* earned $127 million in the United States and sparked a short-lived craze for citizens band radios. *Saturday Night Fever* grossed $282 million worldwide and popularized the previously underground disco culture. *Close Encounters of the Third Kind* raked in nearly $338 million worldwide and brought UFO conspiracy theorists out of the woodwork. But *Star Wars* outdid them all, racking up a then-record $775 million in worldwide box office receipts (that's over $3 billion in inflation-adjusted terms). Yet, as impressive as it is, the film's box office tally tells only part of the story.

Unless you lived through it, it's difficult to imagine the impact *Star Wars* had in the late 1970s. The movie struck popular culture like a blast from the Death Star. The audience response was unlike anything generated by any movie before or since. Some writers have compared *Star Wars* to Beatlemania, but even that comparison doesn't fit. During the mid-'60s peak of Beatlemania, the Beatles' appeal was strongest with teenagers, especially teenage girls. It took a while for the group to be taken seriously as musicians. Many of the most intense *Star Wars* fans were young too, but—as the box office figures indicate—the movie's appeal was broad and inclusive. And while some critics were dismissive (see previous chapter), *Star Wars* earned mostly favorable reviews and was generally considered a significant work, as its haul of Academy Awards and other honors demonstrates.

To come up with an apt parallel for *Star Wars*, students of popular culture must look back to the early nineteenth century, when patrons queued up near London newsstands for the latest installment of *The Pickwick Papers*, the first novel by author Charles Dickens (whose work was published in serial form before being collected in single volumes). Demand for *The Pickwick Papers* far outstripped supply, even though publisher Chapman & Hall increased print runs with each new installment, beginning in March 1836 at 500 copies and

Darth Vader puts his boot prints and signature in the cement outside the Chinese Theater in Los Angeles, summer of 1977. The actor in the Vader suit was an anonymous substitute, not David Prowse.

concluding in October 1837 at 40,000. This was the emergence of one of the most enduringly popular authors of all time.

In the summer and fall of 1977 there didn't seem to be enough *Star Wars* to satisfy the masses either. Theaters were sold out. Stores had difficulty stocking enough T-shirts, posters, toys, and other merchandise to meet the demand. The movie's double-album soundtrack recording went platinum (selling over a million copies), and a disco version of the theme song hit No. 1 on the *Billboard* Hot 100 chart on October 1, 1977. The novelization of the movie topped the *New York Times* bestseller list. The movie and the public's fascination with it became the subject of both conversation and stories for

Time, Newsweek, and *Rolling Stone.* See Threepio appeared on the cover of *People* magazine. On September 16, ABC broadcast *The Making of Star Wars,* an hour-long television special written by critic Richard Schickel, produced by Fox, and "hosted" by C-3PO and R2-D2. (George Lucas, producer Gary Kurtz, and stars Mark Hamill, Harrison Ford, Carrie Fisher, and Sir Alec Guinness also appeared.) All this made *Star Wars,* for a while, inescapable. It was virtually impossible to be unaware of the film, even if you hadn't seen it. *Saturday Night Live's* Bill Murray lampooned the phenomenon by crooning, to the tune of John Williams' *Star Wars* theme, "*Star Wars,* nothing but *Star Wars*/Give me those *Star Wars*/Don't let them end. . . . "

The reality was, millions of fans felt exactly that way.

Box Office Domination

Star Wars finished so far behind schedule that George Lucas was still working on the picture after it went into release. He was in Los Angeles on May 25, 1977, overseeing the final mono audio mix of the film with editor Paul Hirsch and consulting on advertising materials. Marcia Lucas was in town to finish editing director Martin Scorsese's *New York, New York.* The Lucases decided to meet for dinner at the Hamburger Hamlet on Hollywood Boulevard, near Mann's Chinese Theatre—coincidentally, the only cinema in town showing *Star Wars.* They were shocked to discover Chinese Theatre patrons lined up out the door and around the block.

After lunch, Lucas immediately called Alan Ladd Jr. at Fox, who informed the director that *Star Wars* was playing to sellout houses in every market. The news was encouraging, but Lucas remained skeptical of the film's long-term prospects. Many previous science fiction movies had opened well only to fade quickly, because at the time the genre's audience was devoted but relatively small. Besides, the Fox marketing department had convinced him the film wouldn't appeal to women. To Lucas' surprise, however, the returns didn't quickly tail off. Just the opposite happened. As word of mouth spread, *Star Wars* became an even hotter ticket. Within weeks, Harrison Ford discovered how popular the film had become when he walked into a Tower Records store to buy an album and was besieged by fans, who tore off his shirt.

Star Wars earned $3 million in its first week of release (during an era when movie tickets cost $4 or less). Newspapers and TV news broadcasts across the country ran pictures of fans lined up to see this quirky little space movie. On August 3, C-3PO, R2-D2, and Darth Vader had their footprints and signatures immortalized in concrete on the sidewalk in front of the Chinese Theatre. Eventually, the box office lines went away, but the movie did not. *Star Wars* remained in first-run movie theaters for over six months (an achievement

Star Wars opened on fewer than forty screens nationwide, but attracted long lines of patrons everywhere it played. The movie's gradual rollout enabled Twentieth Century-Fox to use the sensational early response as a selling point when *Star Wars* began expanding to additional markets.

marked by a special advertising campaign featuring holiday greetings from the movie's primary characters). Fox had to strike new prints because the original batch was literally worn out. By that time, *Star Wars* had eclipsed *Jaws* to become the highest-grossing movie in history, and it was far from finished. Eventually *Star Wars* moved to second-run houses. In some cities it played—in one venue or another—for more than a year. This anniversary was marked by another special advertisement, this time featuring a birthday cake surrounded by *Star Wars* action figures. In other cities, the film was rereleased in 1978, returning to first-run theaters for another very successful engagement. The movie's staying power derived primarily from loyal fans who (before the dawn of home video) paid to see it over and over again, another phenomenon that also became fodder for newspaper and television reporters across the country.

Along the way, *Star Wars* pulverized most of the summer's expected hits. *A Bridge Too Far* earned $50 million in the United States, a disappointing number given the film's $26 million budget. *The Other Side of Midnight*—the movie Fox salesmen tried to use to strong-arm theater owners into booking *Star Wars*—drew an anemic $24 million worldwide. John Boorman's *Exorcist II: The Heretic*, made for $14 million, returned only $25 million. But that looked good next to William Friedkin's *Sorcerer*, which cost nearly $22 million and earned only $12 million. *The Spy Who Loved Me* turned a respectable $47 million in the United States and a laudable $185 million worldwide. Despite mixed reviews (but with help from Jacqueline Bisset's wet T-shirt), *The Deep* racked up $50 million in the United States. During the summer of 1977, *Star Wars*' biggest box office competition came from Hal Needham's *Smokey and the Bandit*, another out-of-left-field overachiever, made for about $3 million and released two days after *Star Wars*. *Close Encounters* was issued November 16, and *Saturday Night Fever* December 14, in the waning days of *Star Wars*' assault on first-run theaters.

Studio Resurrection

The jaw-dropping returns for *Star Wars* were met with a curious mix of elation and recrimination by Twentieth Century-Fox executives. One of the reasons Fox had been so guarded in its support of the picture during production was that the studio was on shaky financial footing. President Dennis Corothers Stanfill had inherited a doddering company from Richard Zanuck, son of legendary mogul Darryl F. Zanuck, in 1971. Stanfill had brought the company back from the brink of bankruptcy, but its fortunes remained tenuous. The studio had suffered recent big-budget flops and might not withstand another high-priced turkey. In early May 1977, less than a month before *Star Wars* premiered, the studio was so desperate for cash and so unsure about the picture's prospects that Fox attempted to sell the rights to *Star Wars* and two other upcoming releases to Bel-Aire Associates, a California investment group. Fortunately for Fox, its offer was declined, and soon *Star Wars* profits began gushing into the studio's coffers. *Washington Post* movie critic Gary Arnold did not overstate the case when he wrote, "In *Star Wars* George Lucas has supplied Twentieth Century-Fox with a new lease on life."

Fox stock leaped from six dollars per share to twenty-seven dollars per share following the movie's release. Production chief Alan Ladd Jr., at times the lone champion of *Star Wars* at Fox, received a nearly $400,000 per year pay hike and was promoted to president. *Star Wars* not only stabilized the studio's finances but set the table for a lucrative sale of the company that netted shareholders millions more. That happened in 1978, when investors Marc Rich and Marvin Davis purchased Twentieth Century-Fox for $116 million (six years later Davis sold his share of the studio to media magnate Rupert Murdoch for $250 million).

Yet the same cash bonanza that elicited such joy also brought regret. Suddenly executives realized the mistake they had made by ceding all the sequel rights and half the merchandising revenue to Lucasfilm. Finger-pointing and hand-wringing ensued, even though no one—not even Ladd or Lucas—could have anticipated a response anything like the one *Star Wars* generated. It was unprecedented. However, the result was that Lucas now held all the leverage and would soon negotiate an even more favorable deal with the studio for *The Empire Strikes Back* (see Chapter 12).

Star Wars also helped revive the previously declining EMI-Elstree Studios in Borehamwood, which was so little used in the mid-1970s that two of its soundstages were demolished (apartment buildings were constructed in their place). Lucasfilm booked all available space at EMI (eight total soundstages) for *Star Wars* (and later for *The Empire Strikes Back*, *Return of the Jedi*, three Indiana Jones movies, and *Willow*) and, for *Empire*, helped fund construction of a huge new soundstage that attracted still more productions to the facility. EMI could have made out much better on the deal, however. According to Gary Kurtz, he and Lucas offered EMI a share of the profits from *Star Wars* in lieu of rental fees, but the studio declined.

Critical Reception

Star Wars also drew enthusiastic reviews—at first. *Time* magazine called it "the year's best movie," a line touted in print ads for months. Roger Ebert and Gene Siskel gave it two thumbs up on their PBS review show *Sneak Previews*. Critics from across the country concurred. Arnold of the *Washington Post* called it "a new classic" and "a spectacular intergalactic joyride." "*Star Wars* is a magnificent film," wrote *Variety*'s A. D. Murphy. "George Lucas set out to make the biggest possible adventure fantasy out of his memories of serials and older action epics, and he succeeded brilliantly. . . . The results equal the genius of Walt Disney, Willis O'Brien and other justifiably famous practitioners of what Irwin Allen calls 'movie magic.'" Vincent Canby of the *New York Times* opined that "*Star Wars* is good enough to convince the most skeptical 8-year-old sci-fi buff, who is the toughest critic." *Time* magazine's Gerald Clarke—the critic who called *Star Wars* "the year's best movie" in his May 30, 1977, story—ventured that the film was "aimed at kids—the kid in everybody." But not all critics were in touch with their inner child.

The earliest reviews for *Star Wars* were uniformly favorable. But it's important to keep in mind that the film originally opened midweek in just thirty-two theaters across the country (expanding to forty-three screens on Friday) and rolled out to other cities over a period of weeks and months. As the summer of *Star Wars* continued, a minority of dismissive reviews appeared. These later critics were reacting not only to the film itself but to the popular frenzy that accompanied it. Chief among the naysayers was Pauline Kael of the *New Yorker*, who went out of her way to denigrate *Star Wars* in her September column, even though the *New Yorker* had previously published a glowing review of the film by critic Penelope Gilliatt. Kael (who couldn't be bothered to see *Star Wars* during its first week) called the picture "an epic without a dream" and compared it to "a box of Cracker Jacks which is all prizes." The movie was also panned by the *Village Voice* and other outposts of the intelligentsia. In general, the film's detractors seemed dismayed that anything as simplistic and old-fashioned as *Star Wars* should become so popular. That was the attitude of notoriously irascible science fiction author Harlan Ellison, who wrote a *Los Angeles* magazine article titled "Luke Skywalker Is a Nerd and Darth Vader Sucks Runny Eggs."

Despite increasing critical headwinds, *Star Wars* earned ten Academy Award nominations, including Best Picture, Best Director, and Best Original Screenplay. It was shut out of the major categories but took home six Oscars in various technical disciplines. It was also nominated for five Golden Globe Awards and six BAFTA Awards (British

When Christmas 1977 arrived, *Star Wars* was still playing at first-run cinemas in most cities. Twentieth Century-Fox celebrated with this newspaper advertisement, featuring holiday wishes from the film's primary characters.

Oscars). For a complete rundown of the film's many awards and honors, see Chapter 35.

Fashion, Fortune, and Fame

The reverberations of *Star Wars* were felt in numerous other places, most of which are covered at length elsewhere in this book. The film wrought changes to Hollywood filmmaking (Chapter 1) and merchandising (Chapter 12), and spawned a plethora of rip-offs (Chapter 13) and parodies (Chapter 32). The final chapter of *Star Wars FAQ* considers the indelible thumbprint the franchise has left on popular culture and our collective imagination. And even that isn't a comprehensive inventory of the film's popular impact.

Star Wars also influenced fashion and women's hairstyles—although, thankfully, the double-bun look never caught on. Fashion writer Jian Deleon points out that the Oscar-winning costumes John Mollo created for *Star Wars* (based on drawings by production artist Ralph McQuarrie) mirrored ideas introduced at the same time by Asian designers such as Yohji Yamamoto, Issey Miyake, and Rei Kawakubo. Later, *The Empire Strikes Back* integrated concepts similar to those promulgated by European stylemakers, including Jil Sander and the cadre of avant-garde fashionistas known as "the Antwerp Six." "The evolution of *Star Wars*' sartorial identity inadvertently paralleled fashion designs that remain highly influential today," Deleon wrote. Inevitably, if unintentionally, *Star Wars* helped popularize these then-edgy styles. In 1977, *Vogue* magazine winked at the film's fashion influence with a photo spread extolling "The 'Force' of Fur." It featured C-3PO, Darth Vader, a Jawa, storm-troopers, and a cantina alien photographed alongside supermodel Jerry Hall and other models dressed in mink, sable, and other fur coats. Chewbacca was conspicuous in his absence.

Star Wars also left a permanent mark in at least one more area: the careers and personal lives of the movie's cast and crew. Personnel whom Lucas rewarded with a partial profit percentage or a cash bonus received a financial windfall. Perhaps as importantly, association with the picture became a prestigious calling card for technicians and artisans who worked on it, even in low-profile roles. Model builders and sound technicians were sometimes asked for autographs if they revealed they had helped make *Star Wars*.

Still, like the Force, *Star Wars*' sensational success had a dark side. In late 1977, a man carrying a large knife walked into the Lucasfilm offices and demanded to see George Lucas. This individual, who claimed that he had written *Star Wars* and that the *Millennium Falcon* was parked outside, had to be removed by police. The always-shy Lucas grew increasingly wary and reclusive.

Star Wars also proved to be a mixed blessing for the picture's stars. Hamill, Ford, and Fisher were instantly and eternally imprinted on the imaginations of moviegoers as Luke Skywalker, Han Solo, and Princess Leia, making it difficult for them to translate their sudden stardom into other roles. Hamill, whose prospects were temporarily compromised by the severe facial injuries he suffered during postproduction (see Chapter 8), landed just three other major roles—in *Corvette Summer* (1978), *The Big Red One* (1980), and *The Night the Lights Went Out in Georgia* (1981)—during the making of the *Star Wars* trilogy. He lost potentially career-expanding roles in the dramas *Midnight Express* (1978) and *Breaking Away* (1979), in part because directors Alan Parker and Peter Yates didn't want "Luke Skywalker" headlining their casts. To distance himself from *Star Wars*, Hamill appeared on Broadway in the title role of *The Elephant Man* during the play's final three weeks in 1981. "Instead of being a real breakthrough in my career, the film [*Star Wars*] increased my struggle in a way," Mark Hamill told publicist John Phillip Peecher, for his 1983 book *The Making of Return of the Jedi.*

Ford appeared in seven movies, but his career didn't really take off until after *Raiders of the Lost Ark* (1981) proved the public would embrace him as someone other than Han Solo. Fisher found work primarily onstage and in television for the next six years, although she also costarred with Chevy Chase in the comedy flop *Under the Rainbow* (1981). Lucas recommended her for a costarring role in *Grease* (1978), but director Randal Kleiser instead cast Australian singer Olivia Newton-John as All-American girl Sandy Olsson. "I function exclu-

To celebrate *Star Wars*' one-year anniversary—the film was still playing in theaters in many markets—Twentieth Century-Fox took out this trade ad.

sively in space, it seems," Fisher would later bemoan to publicist Alan Arnold. *Star Wars* also had an even darker legacy for the actress. Fisher, constantly hounded about her weight, discovered during production that cocaine was an effective appetite suppressant. This had unfortunate repercussions, which the actress has addressed in interviews and her memoirs.

The legacy of *Star Wars* was also bittersweet for Sir Alec Guinness. His generous two and a half profit points (taken from the producer's 40 percent) made him one of the wealthiest actors in England, but the global craze for the film seemed to all but obliterate, in the public mind, the rest of his distinguished, thirty-year career in film. Millions of new fans knew him only as Ben Kenobi. (When he died in 2000, most newspapers printed a photo of Kenobi alongside Guinness' obituary.) The actor was puzzled and disturbed by the movie's enormous popularity. Everywhere he went, all everyone wanted to talk with him about was *Star Wars*. He stopped giving interviews on the subject and reportedly threw away the mail he received from *Star Wars* fans. In his memoir *A Positively Final Appearance*, Guinness recalls signing an autograph for a young fan who—as the actor scribbled his signature—proudly reported that he had seen *Star Wars* more than a hundred times. Appalled, Guinness asked the boy, "Do you think you could promise never to see *Star Wars* again?" The child burst into tears.

History does not record whether or not the young man took Guinness' advice. But, like most of the rest of the world, he probably found *Star Wars* difficult to let go.

Collect 'em All!

A Merchandising Revolution

The unprecedented box office returns reaped by *Star Wars* were only the beginning of the film's staggering earning power. In the months and years that followed its release, *Star Wars* raked in hundreds of millions (and eventually billions) of dollars through the sale of T-shirts, posters, action figures, novels, comic books, record albums, trading cards, board games, bumper stickers, bed linens, fan club memberships, and just about everything else in the galaxy—including, finally, the movie itself, once it became available on home video (see Chapter 34). The merchandising power of *Star Wars* made—and sometimes broke—the fortunes of companies. But the enterprise that benefitted the most was *Star Wars* itself. Profits from the sale of *Star Wars* memorabilia kept Lucasfilm afloat during the making of *The Empire Strikes Back.*

Black Falcon

Since he and not the studio owned the sequel rights to *Star Wars*, George Lucas was at a major advantage when he began contract negotiations with Twentieth Century-Fox for the movie eventually known as *The Empire Strikes Back.* To gain even greater leverage, Lucas decided to fund the picture himself. This gave him near-total creative control, since the studio wouldn't control the project's purse strings. Lucas took out a bank loan to cover production costs, using his pending *Star Wars* residuals as collateral. Fox, which had received $15 million in guarantees from exhibitors for the picture, also gave Lucas a $10 million advance, which was applied toward the picture's projected $15.5 million budget.

On September 21, 1977, Fox and Lucasfilm (specifically, a new Lucasfilm subsidiary called the Chapter II Company, which served as the production company for the sequel) entered into an agreement that gave even more money and power to Lucas than his original *Star Wars* pact. Lucas was so secure in his footing that he fired his talent agency, ICM Partners, and negotiated the deal himself, with the assistance of attorney Tom Pollock. This time around, Lucasfilm would garner a higher percentage of the gross receipts (a sliding scale ranging from 52.5 to 77.5 percent, topping out once the film reached the $100 million mark). The contract was unequivocal in granting Lucasfilm total creative authority over the finished product; Fox would serve merely as the picture's distributor. Lucas retained all sequel rights. Also, effective July 1, 1978, the management of all *Star Wars* merchandising would revert to another new Lucasfilm subsidiary, Black Falcon. On that same date, Lucasfilm's cut of the proceeds from these ventures would increase from 50 to 80 percent. They would increase again to 90 percent in 1981.

With his *Star Wars* revenue tied up in *The Empire Strikes Back*, merchandising proceeds funded the rest of the incipient Lucasfilm empire, underwriting employee paychecks as well as the relocation of Industrial Light & Magic to Northern California and preliminary development of the company's earliest non-*Star Wars* ventures, which included *More American Graffiti* (1979), *Raiders of the Lost Ark* (1981), and the long-delayed comedy *Radioland Murders* (1994). San Francisco attorney Douglas Ferguson, a film industry outsider, was hired to oversee Black Falcon, which was officially incorporated on February 27, 1978. Following the release of *The Empire Strikes Back*, the subsidiary was merged back into Lucasfilm and later renamed Lucas Licensing.

In 1977, however, the biggest issue facing Lucasfilm was simply bringing enough merchandise to market to meet the public's insatiable appetite for everything *Star Wars*. While T-shirts and posters were in production (Lucasfilm sold $100,000 worth of T-shirts during the film's first month of release), a novelization and comic books were in print, and an official fan club had been established, very few other authorized products were available. Bootleggers took advantage, hawking cut-rate substitutes for other badly desired items. These included the most aching vacancy among the official *Star Wars* tie-ins: toys, specifically action figures. Lucas told French reporter Claire Clouzot in 1977 that tie-ins like toys and comic books were an integral component of his plan from the beginning. "All of this was a part of the film, the intention of launching toys in supermarkets, creating books and stuff," he said. But who would make those toys?

Kenner

Cincinnati-based Kenner Products was founded in 1947 by brothers Albert, Philip, and Joseph Steiner. The toy company's first big seller was the Bubble-Matic Gun, a pistol that "fired" bubbles. In 1949, the company upped the ante with the Bubble Rocket, which sold more than one million units. Nine years later, Kenner sponsored the Captain Kangaroo Show, becoming one of the first toy companies to advertise its products nationally. Cereal maker

Kenner's initial batch of *Star Wars* action figures finally became available in early 1978, after an eight-month wait.

General Mills purchased Kenner in 1967 and later merged it with Rainbow Crafts, makers of Play-Doh. Kenner greatly expanded the Play-Doh product line and introduced other best-selling toys, including the Easy Bake Oven, the Close n' Play record player, the cooing Baby Alive doll, and the Spirograph.

Kenner began manufacturing action figures in 1975 after acquiring the rights to produce articulated twelve-inch-tall dolls based on the popular *Six Million Dollar Man* TV series. That year the company's lifetime sales topped $100 million for the first time. The next year, Kenner introduced Stretch Armstrong, a bendable thirteen-inch figure that could be "stretched" to nearly four feet in length. It was another huge seller and encouraged Kenner executives to become more aggressive in the action figure segment of the toy market, which was then dominated by rival Mego Corporation. Mego manufactured popular lines of eight-inch poseable figures based on Marvel and DC Comics superheroes; characters from *Star Trek*, *Planet of the Apes*, and other movies and TV shows; and celebrities such as Farrah Fawcett, Muhammad Ali, and Kiss. The secret to Mego's success was the ingenious design of its plastic figures, which had interchangeable heads. This enabled the company to stockpile standard body types that, by changing only the

The author's somewhat battered collection of the original twelve *Star Wars* action figures, vintage 1978. From left: A Tusken Raider, a Death Star commander, a stormtrooper, Darth Vader, Luke Skywalker, Ben Kenobi, Princess Leia, Han Solo, C-3PO, R2-D2, Luke
continued →

figures' cloth costumes and the removable head, could be refitted to resemble many different characters.

Star Wars changed the fortunes of both Kenner and Mego. Kenner outbid Mego Toys for the license to produce *Star Wars* action figures in April 1977—about a month before the movie was released. According to some reports, Mego executives, skeptical of the sales potential for figures based on characters no one had yet heard of, and confident in the ongoing appeal of its superheroes and other figure lines, didn't place an aggressive bid. Kenner president Bernie Loomis, looking to strengthen his company's foothold in the action figure world, gambled that *Star Wars* would be a hit. Kenner won the exclusive license to produce *Star Wars* action figures and playsets from 1977 to 1985. No one knew it yet, but Loomis had just destroyed Mego.

In an effort to differentiate its product from Mego's, Kenner decided to produce articulated *Star Wars* figures in 3.75-inch molded plastic. This format became the new industry standard for action figures. However, it took longer to design and produce figures of this type (you couldn't just manufacture heads and sew together costumes to fit premade bodies). As a result, *Star Wars* action figures were not yet available during the holiday season of 1977. Instead, Kenner sold "Early Bird Certificate Packages"—essentially empty boxes, which were redeemable for four action figures (Luke, Leia,

Skywalker in his X-wing pilot gear, and Chewbacca. Please note that the author also has all the original weapons and accessories for these figures, which he stored in a safe place so his six-year-old son wouldn't lose them. Sometime after this book is published, the author is confident he will remember the location of that safe place.   *Photography by Preston Hewis/East Bank Images*

Chewbacca, and R2-D2) planned for release early the following year. Kenner sold hundreds of thousands of these Early Bird packages, which also included a display stand, stickers, and a *Star Wars* fan club membership card. By the time the first wave of Kenner *Star Wars* figures premiered in 1978, the line had been expanded from four to twelve, also including Han Solo, Darth Vader, C-3PO, Chewbacca, Obi-Wan Kenobi, a stormtrooper, a Jawa, a Tusken Raider, and a Death Star Commander (one of the gunners, wearing a gray uniform with a black, samurai-like helmet). These figures sold for $1.97 each. Some of them (in unopened, mint condition) now fetch hundreds. Rare and discontinued variant editions (e.g., early models of the Darth Vader figure, which included a telescoping lightsaber) are worth thousands.

Kenner issued a second wave with eight more figures—including Greedo and three other aliens from the Mos Eisley cantina, three additional droids, and Luke in his X-Wing flight suit—later in 1978, but had difficulty producing enough of them to meet demand, so *Star Wars* toys were scarce again during the 1978 Christmas rush. Eventually Kenner issued nearly one hundred different *Star Wars* figures (featuring characters from all three original films), along with numerous playsets (including the Death Star and Mos Eisley Cantina), vehicles (including an X-Wing, TIE Fighter, and the *Millennium Falcon*), and other accessories.

Along the way, *Star Wars* toys revolutionized the action figure market. "It was *Star Wars* that jump-started the idea of collecting modern toys," author Stephen J. Sansweet writes in the introduction to his book *Star Wars: The Ultimate Action Figure Collection.* "A key part of that was wave after wave of *Star Wars* action figure releases that got kids and their parents to return to stores looking for the next characters—and maybe picking up a vehicle or playset to use with the figures. With home video still half a decade away, *Star Wars* toys became a way for children to bring home a piece of the fantasy and experience it over and over again in their imaginations." Being forced to reenact the film, or make up their own stories, with figures—actively engaging their imaginations, rather than passively sitting and rewatching the movie on video—may account in part for the ferocious devotion many young *Star Wars* fans developed for the franchise.

The *Star Wars* line was easily the greatest success in Kenner's history, selling nearly a quarter of a billion total units and earning $300 million for Kenner between 1977 and 1983. The stock price for General Mills, the parent company of Kenner, skyrocketed. Meanwhile, Mego saw sales of its toys dwindle. The onetime master of the action figure world folded in 1983. Kenner went on to other successes, introducing the Care Bears in 1983 and, with Mego out of the way, launching the popular DC Super Powers action figure line a year later. When its original *Star Wars* license expired, Kenner won new licenses to produce toys based on the *Droids* and *Ewoks* Saturday morning cartoon series, as well as a new line of *Star Wars* toys marketed under the name "Power of the Force." General Mills spun off Kenner in 1985. The company was purchased by toymaker Tonka in 1987 and sold again in 1991, when it was absorbed into the Hasbro Toy Group. Today Hasbro makes, among other things, *Star Wars* toys.

Marvel

Marvel Comics remains best known as the home of Spider-Man, the Avengers, and the X-Men, superheroes who have saved the world countless times. But in the late 1970s, Marvel itself needed saving. Luke Skywalker came to the rescue.

Marvel was founded in 1939 as Timely Publications and changed its name to Atlas Comics in the 1950s before settling on its current moniker in 1961. During the 1940s, the company introduced characters such as Captain America and the Sub-Mariner, but Marvel didn't make much impact on popular culture until the early 1960s, when young editor in chief Stan Lee partnered with artists Jack Kirby and Steve Ditko to introduce the Fantastic Four, the Hulk, Spider-Man, the X-Men, and other characters. Marvel's sometimes ill-tempered super-heroes seemed to spend as much time fighting each other as battling supervillains, and were the first to grapple with everyday problems like paying the rent. This fresh approach catapulted Marvel from also-ran to front-runner in the comic book marketplace, out-pacing rival DC Comics (home of Superman and Batman) throughout much of the 1960s and early 1970s.

By the mid-'70s, however, due to slumping sales and skyrocketing printing costs, Marvel was losing "several millions of dollars a year." That's according to Jim Shooter, who served as Marvel's editor in chief from 1978 to '87. "If we hadn't done *Star Wars* . . . well, we would have gone out of business. *Star Wars* single-handedly saved Marvel," Shooter told Michael David Thomas, in an interview published on

This comic book ad offered fans a chance to order *Star Wars* posters, T-shirts, posters, and backpacks—just a handful of the countless *Star Wars*–branded items available in the late 1970s and early 1980s.

the Comic Book Resources website in 2000. "A lot of credit should go to [Shooter's predecessor] Roy Thomas, who—kicking and screaming—had dragged Marvel into doing *Star Wars*."

George Lucas was convinced that a tie-in with a major comic book company would benefit *Star Wars*, since many young science fiction fans read comics. But DC wasn't interested, and at first Marvel wasn't either. Like the toy deal with Kenner, the *Star Wars* comic book license was sold prior to the film's release. At that time most Marvel executives, including circulation chief Ed Shukin, were leery. Few people expected great things of *Star Wars*, and Marvel's previous attempts at comics based on science fiction movies— including *Planet of the Apes* (1974–77), *2001: A Space Odyssey* (1976–77), and *Logan's Run* (1977)—garnered mixed results at best. But Thomas eventually convinced the powers that were to gamble on another licensed property. It was a wise decision.

Marvel's *Star Wars* comics were a smash, continuing for 114 issues (counting annuals, specials, and a mini-series) from July 1977 through September 1986. (For details on the content of these comics, see Chapter 30.) This remains the longest-running *Star Wars* comic series. Additional stories were created for British readers, where *Star Wars* comics appeared in a weekly instead of monthly format. Marvel also published *Droids* and *Ewoks* comics based on the Saturday morning cartoon series. The company stopped producing *Star Wars* comics only because its license expired and the rights reverted back to Lucasfilm. In the wake of its *Star Wars* success, Marvel licensed several more sci-fi properties that became hit comics, including *Godzilla* and the *Star Wars* imitator *Battlestar Galactica*, as well as *Rom: Spaceknight*, *The Micronauts*, and *Shogun Warriors*, all based on toys.

In 1991, Lucasfilm licensed *Star Wars* to Dark Horse Comics. In 2009, the Walt Disney Company purchased Marvel Entertainment, the parent company of Marvel Comics. Three years later, Disney acquired Lucasfilm. Finally, on January 3, 2014, Disney announced that it would end the licensing arrangement with Dark Horse and bring *Star Wars* back to Marvel Comics. Marvel plans to launch two new ongoing *Star Wars* titles and a limited series in 2015, once again placing Spider-Man and Luke Skywalker on the same team.

Topps, the dominant maker of sports and nonsports trading cards during the 1970s, produced hundreds of *Star Wars* cards, including this one.

Topps

The Topps Company was formed in New York City in 1938 as an outgrowth of American Leaf Tobacco, which imported tobacco from countries like Turkey to sell to American cigarette makers. Topps was founded to sell a more kid-friendly product: chewing gum. Initially the company's big seller was Bazooka bubble gum, which came with a short comic on the inside of the wrapper. In 1950, Topps tried to improve bubble gum sales by marketing gum in packets along with cards featuring photographs of popular Western star Hopalong Cassidy. Two years later, it introduced the first modern baseball card. Designed by Topps employee Sy Berger, the cards featured a player's name and photograph on the front and statistics on the back. The collectible cards proved wildly popular, and bubble gum quickly became an afterthought. For the next thirty years Topps virtually monopolized the market it had created for trading cards. In addition to baseball and football cards, Topps issued card sets devoted to the space program, President John F. Kennedy, and the Beatles, among other subjects, and had a long-standing association with science fiction. In 1962, the company released its now-legendary (and ultra-collectible) *Mars Attacks* cards, and later it also issued cards based on TV series such as *The Outer Limits*, *Lost in Space*, and *Star Trek*, and the *Planet of the Apes* movies.

Acquiring the license for *Star Wars* trading cards helped Topps extend its hegemony over the trading card world. Beginning in 1977, Topps released 330 *Star Wars* trading cards and fifty-five stickers (in five individual series of sixty-six cards and eleven stickers apiece). Wax packs of cards, which sold for fifteen cents, contained seven cards, one sticker, and a stick of gum. Each full-color card featured a scene from the film on the front. The backs of the cards in the first series could be assembled like a puzzle to create a replica of the famous one-sheet poster created by artists Greg and Tim Hildebrandt. The various series featured color-coded borders (blue for Series 1, red, yellow, green, and orange for the subsequent waves of cards). By the time the final series appeared, Topps was running out of scenes and began using promotional stills and other photographs. For *The Empire Strikes Back* the company released 352 cards and eighty-eight stickers across three color-coded series, and for *Return of the Jedi* Topps produced 220 cards and fifty-five stickers in two (red- and blue-bordered) waves. These cards ranked among the company's all-time best-selling non-sports products. Topps remains the primary producer of *Star Wars* trading cards—although other cardmakers, such as Panini Group and Metallic Images, have also issued card sets over the years. Additionally, through separate agreements, General Mills produced *Star Wars* cards available exclusively in various breakfast cereal boxes from 1977 to '79, and Burger

King and Coca-Cola issued a thirty-six-card set devoted to *Star Wars* and *The Empire Strikes Back* in 1981, available only in fast food restaurants.

In the late 1980s, Topps' stranglehold on the trading card market loosened, and since then it has faced stiff competition in the sports card arena from other makers such as Fleer, Donruss, and Upper Deck (although it has outlived both Fleer and Donruss), and in the non-sports market from companies like Cryptozoic Entertainment. Sales in the non-sports card market have generally declined since the rise of collectible card games like *Magic: The Gathering*, published by Wizards of the West Coast, and Nintendo's *Pokemon*. There are, of course, *Star Wars* card games (see Chapter 31), but Topps does not produce those. Perhaps the upcoming new cycle of *Star Wars* films will help the company reclaim its mastery of the non-sports card market.

Other

While *Star Wars* altered the fortunes of individual companies (including Twentieth Century-Fox, as noted in the previous chapter), the franchise's economic power was felt most powerfully in the aggregate, exerting a sort of gravitational pull over the collectibles market and other industries. According to figures published in January 2014 on the website Statistic Brain, *Star Wars*, as of that date, had generated $27 billion in total revenue, with the sale of toys ($12 billion) surpassing the franchise's lifetime box office ($4.3 billion) and home video ($3.8 billion) sales *combined*. *Star Wars* video games had earned $2.9 billion, books $1.8 billion, and the franchise had generated $1.3 billion in sales of miscellaneous items, identified simply as "Other."

Some of these "Other" products are fascinating in their own way. In the late 1970s, Clarks Shoes released a curious line of officially licensed *Star Wars* footwear that, while marketed under names such as the Skywalker and the Tusken Raider, were simply leather oxfords and moccasins without the franchise logo or any character images on the outside of the shoe. (The logo was stamped on the insole, where it quickly wore off.) The shoes became hot sellers anyway. Eventually Clarks issued *Star Wars* canvas sneakers, some (but not all) of which featured likenesses of characters such as C-3PO and Darth Vader emblazoned on the side, the toe, and/or the sole. Meanwhile, Fruit of the Loom produced Princess Leia Underoos—thankfully, based on Leia's quilted Hoth body suit from *The Empire Strikes Back* rather than her metal bikini from *Return of the Jedi*. Underoos featuring C-3PO and R2-D2 were also marketed to girls, while boys could choose from Luke Skywalker, Yoda, and Boba Fett. And Kellogg's sold C-3POs cereal, with the golden droid pictured on the front of the box. The cereal itself was sugarcoated puffs of oats, wheat, and corn shaped like chain links. Reportedly, Kellogg's paid $3 million for the rights to make C-3POs.

In the early 1980s, the young *Star Wars* fanatic could suit up in his Luke Skywalker Underoos, a *Star Wars* T-shirt, and a pair of jeans supported by his *Star Wars* belt (made by Lee Co.), slip into his Clarks sneakers, and strap on his *Star Wars* wristwatch (by Bradley). Then he could eat C-3POs cereal for breakfast and carry his lunch to school in a *Star Wars* lunch box (courtesy of King-Seeley Thermos Co.). At school, thanks to Helix Stationary, he could write or draw using pencils branded with the *Star Wars* logo and the slogan "May the Force Be with You." When he was finished, he could tuck the pencils away in a Helix pencil pouch decorated with Luke Skywalker, Han Solo, Princess Leia, C-3PO,

This comic book advertisement invited fans to join the Official Star Wars Fan Club, founded in the summer of 1977.

or Darth Vader. (The company also made pencil-top erasers featuring the same assortment of characters, rulers, and a pencil sharpener that looked like the Death Star.) After school, he might check the mailbox for the latest issue of *Bantha Tracks*, the bimonthly newsletter from the Official Star Wars Fan Club (naturally he would be a member). Then he could go to his room—decorated with *Star Wars* posters and Bibb Co. *Star Wars* curtains— remove the plastic stopper from the bottom of his Roman Ceramics brand *Star Wars* bank (shaped like Artoo, Threepio, or Vader), withdraw some of his allowance, hop on his Huffy brand *Star Wars* bicycle, and pedal to the neighborhood pharmacy or grocery to buy a Marvel *Star Wars* comic or a pack of Topps trading cards, then return home to play with his action figures, color in a Kenner *Star Wars* coloring book, assemble an MPC model kit (an X-Wing, TIE fighter, the *Millennium Falcon,* or even R2-D2), or maybe play Kenner's *Star Wars: Escape from the Death Star* board game with friends. Later, he could eat dinner using a Deka brand *Star Wars* plate, bowl, and cup. Then he could brush his teeth with a Kenner *Star Wars* electric toothbrush (designed to resemble a lightsaber) and bathe with Addis brand *Star Wars* bubble bath, Addis character-shaped soap, and Cliro brand *Star Wars* shampoo. Then it would be time to put on his Wilker Brothers *Star Wars* pajamas, snuggle into his Bibb Co. *Star Wars* sheets, and drift off to sleep dreaming of a galaxy far, far away.

Attack of the Clones

Star Wars Imitators

n Hollywood, one measure of a movie's success is how many copycats it spawns. By that yardstick, as by more traditional accountings, *Star Wars* ranks among cinema's greatest triumphs. In the late 1970s and 1980s, producers around the world cranked out droves of ersatz *Star Warses*—action-oriented sci-fi adventure yarns featuring comedy relief robots, princesses in distress, dogfights in space, laser swordfights, and other highly imitative derring-do. While these pictures included a few large-scale productions from major studios, most were low-budget rip-offs. No one has yet assembled a comprehensive survey of these movies, but they numbered in the dozens at the very least. Looking back, many of these pictures seem notable or amusing for one reason or another. Please note that, while some of the films in this chapter will provide big laughs, those that actually *try* to be funny (such as *Galaxina* [1980] and *Spaceballs* [1987]) are covered in Chapter 32.

Starcrash (1978)

Producers were not slow in responding to the sudden public demand for sci-fi. Tiny Monarch Releasing dug up a low-budget Italian science fiction film made in 1965, *2 + 5: Missione Hydra* (which reused footage from two even earlier Japanese SF films), hastily dubbed it into English, and rushed to American theaters under the new name *Star Pilot*. It premiered Stateside in October 1977. That same month, a cheap Canadian alien invasion movie produced under the title *Starship Invasions* was released under the new, more *Star Wars*-y name *War of the Aliens*. (Later, when *Close Encounters* became a hit, *Starship Invasions* was reissued as *Alien Encounters*.)

The earliest film to be specifically created in the image of *Star Wars* was another low-budget Italian sci-fi romp, *Starcrash*. The picture tips its hand immediately by mimicking the opening shot of *Star Wars*: the belly of a giant spaceship emerges from the top of the screen and rumbles slowly across a blue-black starfield. Other *Star Wars*-isms abound. A narrative scroll explains the setting and backstory. There are scared but loyal robots, ray gun battles, laser sword fights, jumps to hyperspace, a caped villain in a metallic black costume, and a climactic attack against the villain's star base. The harebrained plot involves a conflict between the wise and benevolent Emperor of the Universe (played by a slumming, uninterested Christopher Plummer) and his would-be usurper, the evil Count Zarth Arn (Joe Spinell), who has developed a superweapon. Our heroes are a space smuggler named Stella Star (former Hammer Films glamour girl Caroline Munro); her sidekick Akton (Marjoe Gortner), who possesses mystical, Jedi-like powers; a robot named El (Judd Hamilton), who speaks with a Southern twang; and Simon, the emperor's son and Stella's romantic interest (played by future *Knight Rider*, *Baywatch* hunk, and German pop music sensation David Hasselhoff).

The film was written and directed by exploitation specialist Luigi Cozzi (credited here as Lewis Coates), who wanted to create a science fiction epic with the feel of a Ray Harryhausen Sinbad picture. Cozzi works in a sequence involving a giant robot closely resembling Talos from Harryhausen's *Jason and the Argonauts* (1963) and a laser sword fight against skeletal-looking robots, which recalls another famous scene from *Jason*. He also hired Munro, who had costarred in *The Golden Voyage of Sinbad* (1973), to play Stella Star. In addition to robots of various sizes, Stella, Akton, and El battle amazons and jabbering cannibal cavemen, not to mention Count Zarth Arn and his minions. With its hokey special effects and cut-rate sets and costumes, *Starcrash* never approaches the level of either *Star Wars* or a Ray Harryhausen feature, but it moves quickly and contains some kooky-fun ideas. (For instance, Count Zarth Arn's spaceship is shaped like a giant hand, which balls itself into a fist when it prepares for battle.) Two years before *The Empire Strikes Back*, Stella and company visit a Hoth-like ice planet.

American International Pictures initially agreed to distribute this movie in the United States but dropped out when they saw the finished picture. Roger Corman's New World Pictures stepped in and scooped it up. Originally titled *Scontri stellari oltre la terza dimensione* ("Stellar clashes beyond the third dimension"), it was issued in the United States as both *Starcrash* and *The Adventures of Stella Star*. By any name, it earned scathing reviews, but in recent years has developed a cult following. Although certainly terrible, *Starcrash* will amuse indulgent viewers. (Beer helps.)

Message from Space (1978)

If *Starcrash* was Italy's answer to *Star Wars*, Japan's response was *Message from Space* (in Japanese *Uchu kara no messeji*). Rather than a cheap knockoff, this was a prestige production (its $6 million budget was extravagant by Japanese standards) and an unusually ambitious one for modest Toei Studios. It was

The Italian-made *Starcrash* features former Hammer Films starlet Caroline Munro and the Darth Vader-like Count Zarth Arn (Joe Spinell). The unintentionally hilarious picture ranks among the more entertaining *Star Wars* knockoffs.

Photo courtesy of Ronald V. Borst/ Hollywood Movie Posters

directed by Kinji Fukusaku, who had codirected the big-ticket Pearl Harbor epic *Tora! Tora! Tora!* (1970), and costarred Japanese action hero Sonny Chiba and American Vic Morrow, imported to provide international appeal. *Star Wars*y elements abound. There's a sawed-off, beeping comedy relief robot named Beba-2; the inevitable caped black-armored villain; a princess; a rowdy cantina; and a *Millennium Falcon* look-alike spaceship. Fukusaku borrows several shots from *Star Wars*, and composer Ken-Ichiro Morioka apes musical cues from John Williams' *Star Wars* score. In *Message from Space*'s climactic sequence our heroes must fly their spaceships through a narrow tunnel and destroy the enemy's power source by hitting a tiny ten-meter-wide target (sound familiar?).

Where *Star Wars* borrowed heavily from Akira Kurosawa's *The Hidden Fortress*, *Message from Space* co-opts the premise of Kurosawa's *Seven Samurai*. (Coincidentally, the *Star Wars* comic book had offered a *Seven Samurai*-in-outer-space yarn earlier in 1978.) Princess Emeralida (Etsuko Shihomi) sets out to find eight warriors to help the subjugated Jellucian people throw off the yoke of the evil Gavanas Empire and rounds up a motley assortment of

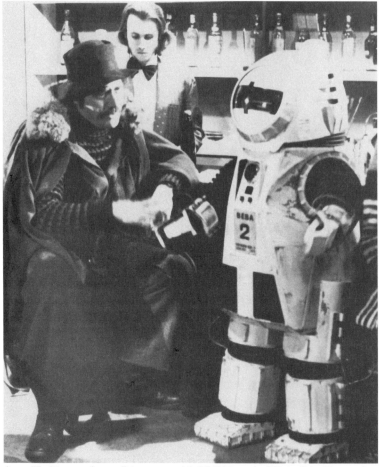

Actor Vic Morrow (seated) interacts with R2-D2 knockoff Beba-2 in *Message from Space*, Japan's answer to *Star Wars*.

Photo courtesy of Ronald V. Borst/Hollywood Movie Posters

layabouts and petty criminals, a bitter retired general (Morrow), and the outcast son of the Gavanas emperor (Chiba). The film has some charming ideas—for instance, the Jellicians' spaceship, rigged with sails, resembles a spacefaring *Flying Dutchman*—but also some glaring lapses (at one point two characters take a spacewalk without benefit of space suits!). The script is slow-moving and repetitive. Much of the first act plays like a sci-fi version of a beach movie, with teenage delinquents drag-racing through an asteroid belt and go-go dancing at the local space cantina. Despite the money lavished on it, the picture's production values and visual effects fall far below the *Star Wars* standard, although they remain acceptable for a Japanese fantasy film of this vintage. Morrow seems out of place—his laconic, naturalistic delivery clashes with the higher-pitched performances of the Japanese cast. Still, *Message from Space* isn't all bad—and that's its biggest problem. Although certainly not a good film, and often risible, it's never as entertainingly inept as, say, *Starcrash*. *Message from Space* was released by United Artists in the United States, where it sank like a stone. However, it proved very successful in Japan and spawned a follow-up TV series, *Message from Space: Galactic Wars* (1978–79).

War of the Planets (1977), Battle of the Stars (1978), War of the Robots (1978), and Star Odyssey (1979)

You have to hand it to Italian grindhouse director Alfonso Brescia, who cranked out an entire quadrilogy in less time than it took George Lucas to make a single installment of the *Star Wars* saga. Brescia's adventures in outer space began with *War of the Planets* (*Anno zero: Guerra nello spazio,* 1977) and continued with *Battle of the Stars* (*Battaglie negli spazi stellari,* 1978), *War of the Robots* (*La guerra dei robot,* 1978), and *Star Odyssey* (*Sette uomini d'oro nello spazio,* 1979)—not to mention *Beast in Space* (*La bestia nello spazio,* 1980), a sci-fi-themed porn film. These were among a total of thirteen movies Brescia directed from 1977 through 1980, often credited to his Americanized pseud-onym, Al Bradley. Brescia's shoestring space operas were each shot in about three weeks, with a couple of weeks for postproduction (including visual effects, editing, and scoring), proving the axiom that haste makes waste. Production values and visual effects, perhaps understandably, are laughably weak. The derivative and slow-moving scripts are even worse.

Even though it was marketed as such in the United States, *War of the Planets* isn't a *Star Wars* clone. It was released in Italy in September 1977, a month *earlier* than *Star Wars.* Although issued May 25, 1977, in the United States, *Star Wars* didn't reach many European markets until October. *War of the Planets* is generic, Z-grade sci-fi that borrows primarily from *2001: A Space Odyssey,* with touches of *Barbarella* (1968): In a future where Earthmen are growing ever more reliant on computers to make decisions, astronauts discover a planet where a once-mighty civilization is now ruled by a malevolent super-robot. Brescia had *War of the Planets* in the can when *Star Wars,* by happy accident, greatly expanded the market for the picture. *War of the Planets* eventually reached America in 1979.

Brescia's later SF entries bear the imprint of *Star Wars* to varying degrees. The *Star Wars*-iest of the lot is *War of the Robots,* in which aliens kidnap an eminent Earth scientist and whisk him away in a flying saucer. A team of astronauts investigate and discover that the professor has fallen under the sway of an evil galactic empire. Desultory laser sword fights, blaster shoot-outs, and space dogfights ensue. In *Star Odyssey,* maverick scientist (and Obi-Wan substitute) Professor Mauri (Ennio Balbo) and Han Solo-like adventurer Oliver "Hollywood" Carrera (Nino Castelnuovo) lead a motley band of rebels and robots to overturn an alien conqueror and free Sol-3 (aka Earth). One of Mauri's robots looks like a cross between R2-D2 and a rubbish bin, which is an apt metaphor for the entire film.

The Black Hole (1979)

Walt Disney Pictures surveyed the rising tide of science fiction movies flooding the market in the wake of *Star Wars* and responded as only it could: with *The Cat from Outer Space* (1978), starring Ken Berry, Sandy Duncan, and a telepathic ginger tabby. A year later, it issued *Unidentified Flying Oddball*, about an astronaut and his robot friend who accidentally travel back to the time of King Arthur (the screenplay was an update of Mark Twain's *A Connecticut Yankee in King Arthur's Court*). When neither of these efforts made much of a splash, Disney decided to mount a bona fide sci-fi epic, investing $20 million in *The Black Hole*.

Intended as a mature, serious-minded action-adventure, *The Black Hole* was the first Disney film to include (mild) profanity, the first live-action Disney movie in which people were killed, and the first film produced by the studio to earn a PG rating. Although it contains nods to *Star Wars*—including a pair of lovable, rotund, R2-D2-ish robots voiced by Roddy McDowall and Slim Pickens—*The Black Hole* owes more to Disney's 1954 SF-adventure yarn *20,000 Leagues Under the Sea*. It involves a team of astronauts exploring deep space who discover a giant spacecraft teetering on the event horizon of an enormous black hole. The ship is under the control of the reclusive, Captain Nemo-like Dr. Hans Reinhardt (Maximilian Schell), who has turned his crew into cybernetic zombies and is obsessed with traveling through the black hole into a new universe where known scientific laws no longer apply.

The Black Hole has a great deal going for it, beginning with strikingly beautiful visual effects and imaginative production design, both overseen by Peter Ellenshaw; an intriguing cast of Hollywood veterans (Anthony Perkins, Yvette Mimieux, Ernest Borgnine, Robert Forster, Schell, McDowall, and Pickens); and an evocative score by John Barry. If the viewer can set aside its laughable physics, the scenario includes some potentially exciting action sequences. Alas, most of those scenes are bungled by director Gary Nelson and editor Gregg McLaughlin. Nelson shoots everything in the most banal, predictable manner, and McLaughlin lingers on many visual effects shots, more concerned with showing off Ellenshaw's work than with the pace of the story. *The Black Hole* sorely lacks the dynamic compositions and crisp editing that created *Star Wars*' heart-quickening tempo. Tellingly, Alan Dean Foster's novelization of *The Black Hole* is far more effective than the finished film; what reads great on paper is poorly realized on-screen.

The Black Hole also suffers from a weak ending—or rather from the lack of one. The picture went into production without a scripted conclusion. The one Nelson and company eventually devised attempts to evoke both the stargate sequence from *2001: A Space Odyssey* and Dante's *Inferno*, without doing justice to either. Foster's novelization and the Whitman Comics adaptation of the film featured two entirely different endings, both of them superior to the movie's resolution. *The Black Hole* was Disney's most ambitious and expensive production to date, but it returned only a middling $36 million in the United States. While it has its moments, it remains a wasted opportunity. On the whole, *The Cat from Outer Space* is more enjoyable.

H. G. Wells' The Shape of Things to Come (1979)

Despite the title, there is no real connection between H. G. Wells and this drab misfire, except perhaps the calisthenics this picture inspired the author to perform in his grave. Although supposedly "inspired by" Wells' future history of the same name, the story bears no meaningful similarity to that work, nor to the 1936 film *Things to Come*, which Wells personally adapted from the book. Instead, the dunderheaded scenario concocted by writers Mike Cheda, Joseph Lazner, and Martin Lager combines elements purloined from both *Star Wars* and TV's *Space: 1999* (1975–77).

In a vague future ("the tomorrow after tomorrow," per the inevitable precredit scroll), Earth has been reduced to an irradiated wasteland by the Robot Wars. Most of the survivors fled to the moon, where they built a colony apparently composed entirely of geodesic domes and underground tunnels, and have grown dependent on Raddic-Q-2, an antiradiation drug made only on the distant planet Delta Three. Then a caped supervillain named Omus (Jack Palance) seizes control of Delta Three and declares himself emperor of the solar system. Four heroes from the moon colony—the aged Professor Caball (Barry Morse), his son Jason (Nicholas Campbell), Jason's girlfriend Kim (Anne-Marie Martin, credited as Eddie Benton), and Sparks, a comedy relief robot who looks like a cross between R2-D2 and the wisecracking robot from *Lost in Space*—set out to aid the Princess Leia-like Governor Niki (Carol Lynley), whose outgunned rebel forces are battling the tyranny of Omus and his robot minions on Delta Three.

H. G. Wells' The Shape of Things to Come was produced in Canada by notorious schlockmeister Harry Alan Towers. It is cheap, colorless, and scatterbrained, with plot holes you could fly a Star Destroyer through. In one particularly maddening sequence, Jason and Kim land on Earth to find parts

Look familiar? Roger Corman's *Battle Beyond the Stars* was one of many films to ape the opening shot of *Star Wars* (which was itself adapted from *2001: A Space Odyssey*).

Photo courtesy of Ronald V. Borst/ Hollywood Movie Posters

needed to repair their spaceship. They meet a group of radiation-scarred children and pledge to return and save them, but fail to locate the replacement parts they were searching for. Somehow the ship is repaired anyway, and the boil-faced urchins are never seen again. The performances are uniformly terrible, but in all fairness it would be difficult to do much with the film's absurd scenario and wretched dialogue. The visual effects are widely variable but never good; some (like the footage of Jason and Kim's craft landing on Earth) function on a level barely higher than *Plan 9 from Outer Space*. The amateurish musical score, by Paul Hoffert, is even worse. Reserve this one for only the most committed cinema masochists.

Battle Beyond the Stars (1980)

Like *Message from Space*, *Battle Beyond the Stars* takes Kurosawa's *Seven Samurai* and transplants it to a *Star Wars*-like setting. As a result, it plays like an imitation of an imitation—and, as with photocopies of photocopies, the quality decreases with each generation.

Executive produced by legendary B-movie maker Roger Corman (whose New World Pictures issued *Starcrash* in 1978), the film boasts an interesting cast (including Richard Thomas, George Peppard, Robert Vaughn, John Saxon, and Sybil Danning) and widely variable but sometimes impressive visual effects (overseen by a young James Cameron). Thomas plays Shad, a young farmer who sets out to find mercenaries to help residents of the planet Akir (a pacifist, agrarian world) resist a coming invasion from the planet Malmor and its malevolent, scar-faced ruler, Sador (Saxon).

Battle Beyond the Stars, written by John Sayles, moves quickly but is riddled with hackneyed and silly ideas. For instance, Shad's first stop after leaving Akir is to a space station inhabited only by an aging scientist, his nubile daughter, and dozens of androids; the scientist (now a severed head connected to a robotic body) tries to force Shad to give up his mission and remain as a mate for his daughter. Later, Shad meets Space Cowboy (Peppard), an Earthman who loves whiskey and Westerns, and has a Confederate flag painted on the side of his spaceship; Gelt (Vaughn), a jaded assassin wanted on every planet in the galaxy; an oversexed warrior-woman out to prove her mettle (Danning); a lizard-like alien with a grudge against Sador; and five members of a species that share a common consciousness. He's also aided by Nell, the talking computer of his starship. Together, this mismatched assortment of rejects and goofballs must vanquish the mighty Sador, whose giant flagship carries (you guessed it) a planet-destroying superweapon.

While its special effects are mostly adequate and sometimes surprisingly good, the picture's costumes, sets, and makeup are comically chintzy. Many items are poorly designed—such as Shad's absurd-looking spaceship, which seems to have breasts. Director Jimmy Murakami, who worked primarily in animation, swipes from *Star Wars*, *Alien*, and *2001: A Space Odyssey*, but offers nothing unfamiliar—which is a problem since the story is entirely predictable for anyone who's seen *Seven Samurai*, or John Sturges' Western remake *The Magnificent Seven* (1960), or, for that matter, *Message from Space*. Murakami also apparently let the cast have its way; there is no continuity between the performances. Thomas plays Shad with the same earnest reserve he brought to John-Boy Walton, while Peppard and Saxon leave teeth marks in the scenery, and Vaughn seems embarrassed and uncomfortable. Made for $2 million (most of which reportedly went to the salaries of Peppard and Vaughn), *Battle Beyond the Stars* grossed $11 million, despite dismissive reviews. While, overall, it's not the weakest *Star Wars* imitator, it may be the most pointless.

Flash Gordon (1980)

George Lucas' original dream of reviving Flash Gordon was thwarted, but the phenomenal success of *Star Wars* made it inevitable that someone else would resurrect Alex Raymond's sci-fi hero. That someone turned out to be producer Dino de Laurentiis, who sank $20 million into the stylish, campy 1980 *Flash Gordon*. When Federico Fellini (!) declined de Laurentiis' offer to direct, the producer turned to British action specialist Mike Hodges, who had

The iron-faced General Klytus (Peter Wyngarde), a Darth Vader wannabe, was added as a henchman for Ming the Merciless (Max von Sydow, in the background) for producer Dino de Laurentiis' remake of *Flash Gordon*.

Photo courtesy of Ronald V. Borst/Hollywood Movie Posters

helmed *Get Carter* (1971) and *The Terminal Man* (1974). Perhaps more impor-tant than Hodges, however, were designer Danilo Donati and the rock band Queen. Donati designed gorgeous art deco–influenced sets and costumes, most in vibrant reds and golds, while Queen provided a pulsing, energetic musical score. The picture's highly stylized visual effects, supervised by George Gibbs (who later worked on the Indiana Jones series), are eye-catch-ing—a four-color comic strip come to life. No other movie looks or sounds quite like the cartoonish, rocking *Flash Gordon*.

Lorenzo Semple Jr.'s screenplay touches on all the key plot points of the early Alex Raymond comic strips, previously adapted for the original 1936 *Flash Gordon* serial: Hunky athlete Flash Gordon (here a football hero rather than a polo player) and lovely Dale Arden accompany crackpot scientist Hans Zarkov on a desperate mission to save the Earth from the evil Ming the Merciless, an interstellar tyrant who has decided to destroy our planet (by crashing the moon into it) for his own amusement. They travel to Ming's homeworld, Mongo, and try to incite a revolt against Ming among the subjugated tribes there, including the winged hawkmen. The similarities between *Star Wars* and *Flash Gordon* arise mostly through their common inspiration, although Semple invents a Vader-like henchmen for Ming in the person of General Klytus, who wears black robes and a metallic mask. Hodges lifts a few camera angles from *Star Wars* but also pays homage to *The Wizard of Oz* (among other lifts, in some shots the hawkmen look remarkably like flying monkeys), which underscores *Flash Gordon*'s light fantasy ambitions.

Where the production faltered was in casting. Max Von Sydow delivers a zesty performance as Ming, and the supporting cast—including Topol as Zarkov, Timothy Dalton as Prince Barin, and Brian Blessed as Vultan of the hawkmen—also give a good accounting. However, newcomers Sam J. Jones as Flash and Melody Anderson as Dale seem out of their depth and display little chemistry together. Jones was "honored" with a Golden Raspberry nomination for Worst Actor of the Year. *Flash Gordon* met with mixed box office results, earning a disappointing $27 million in the United States but faring far better worldwide. Despite its creaky lead performances, the picture remains a breezy, colorful romp, executed in bravura, tongue-in-cheek style. It's the most enjoyable *Star Wars* wannabe of the era and has gathered an enthusiastic cult audience.

Saturn 3 (1980)

Although sometimes described as a *Star Wars* rip-off, the British-made *Saturn 3* is actually an *Alien* rip-off. It lifts some shots and costuming ideas from *Star Wars* but borrows more extensively from director Ridley Scott's creepy 1979 SF-horror hybrid with its tale of two scientists on a remote research installation (on a moon of Saturn) menaced by a creepy corporate interloper and a homicidal robot. *Saturn 3* was one of the more notorious bombs of the early 1980s, especially given the talent involved—director Stanley (*Singin' in the Rain*) Donen; stars Kirk Douglas, Harvey Keitel, and Farrah Fawcett; and Oscar-winning composer Elmer Bernstein. The dull, formulaic film earned a meager $9 million, failing to recover its production costs. It lives down to its reputation.

Other Imitators

The attack of *Star Wars* clones continued well into the 1980s, even after the release of *Return of the Jedi* in 1983. Others include *Spacehunter: Adventures in the Forbidden Zone, Space Raiders* (both 1983), *The Last Starfighter* (1984), and the animated feature *Starchaser: The Legend of Orin* (1985). A pair of cut-rate sword-and-sorcery epics from this era, *Hawk the Slayer* (1980) and *Krull* (1983), also borrowed extensively from *Star Wars*. There were also curious hybrids like *Metalstorm: The Destruction of Jared-Syn* (1983), which tried to combine the approaches of *Star Wars* and *Mad Max 2: The Road Warrior* (1981); and *Yor, the Hunter from the Future* (1983), a sort of prehistoric *Star Wars*.

But for sheer audacity and jaw-dropping shoddiness, nothing tops *Dünyayı Kurtaran Adam* (1983). Its title translates as *The Man Who Saved the World*, but this notorious production is better known as the Turkish *Star Wars*. In total disregard of copyright law, the film combines amateurish new footage with visual effects shots lifted directly from a print of *Star Wars*, as well as musical cues from John Williams' *Star Wars* and *Raiders of the Lost Ark* scores. The contrast between these disparate elements only makes the puerile Turkish copycat more laughable. Nearly all the movies mentioned in this chapter are readily available on DVD or Blu-ray, or on YouTube. If nothing else, these pictures help viewers fully appreciate just how far ahead of the field *Star Wars* was.

Television also saw its share of *Star Wars* imitators, with prime-time series such as *Battlestar Galactica* (1978–79) and *Buck Rogers in the 25th Century* (1979–1981), to say nothing of the SF-themed sitcom *Mork & Mindy* (1978–1983), and Saturday morning fare like *Space Academy* (1977) and *Jason of Star Command* (1978–1981).

In addition to these blatant copycats, Hollywood studios rushed to release similar action-oriented sci-fi properties with merchandising potential. Warner Brothers launched its Christopher Reeve *Superman* series with *Superman: The Movie* (1978), Paramount moved *Star Trek* to the big screen with *Star Trek: The Motion Picture* (1979), and United Artists sent superspy James Bond into orbit for *Moonraker* (1979). For the next several years, science fiction enjoyed a Hollywood vogue on par with the genre's 1950s heyday, resulting in other films as varied as *Invasion of the Body Snatchers* (1978), *Alien, Time After Time* (both 1979), *Altered States, Scanners* (both 1980), *Escape from New York, Heavy Metal, Outland, The Road Warrior* (all 1981), *Blade Runner, E.T.: The Extra-Terrestrial, The Thing, Tron, Star Trek II: The Wrath of Khan* (all 1982), and David Lynch's *Dune* (1984). Although its popularity has waxed and waned in the years since, science fiction has never again been considered a niche genre.

14

New Recruits

F ollowing the blockbuster success of *American Graffiti* and the history-making triumph of *Star Wars*, George Lucas had carte blanche. Just six years into his career as a feature film director, Lucas could have received a blank check from any studio in Hollywood for any project he could imagine. It was a position most filmmakers can only dream about. Yet Lucas chose to stop directing.

This decision shocked many in the industry but was understandable to those who knew Lucas well. In interviews, he typically referred to himself as a "filmmaker" rather than a director, naming editing and cinematography as his primary strengths and repeatedly downplaying his skills at writing and directing. In 1977, he told French journalist Claire Clouzot that writing *Star Wars* was "painful, atrocious." Shortly before the film's release, he told Stephen Zito of *American Film* that directing a movie "when it goes on for over a year, really gets to be a drag." Indeed, directing *Star Wars* had been so traumatic that Lucas felt no desire to undertake such an ordeal again. Besides, he was busy overseeing Lucasfilm, Industrial Light & Magic, and the other outposts of his burgeoning Hollywood empire. Twenty-two years elapsed before another film directed by George Lucas reached movie screens. He returned to helm *Star Wars Episode I: The Phantom Menace* (1999).

In the meantime, Lucas continued to make movies, of course, but he did so as an executive producer, happily turning over the writing and directing responsibilities, and the line production tasks, to others. He was not a typical Hollywood executive, however. Rather than ceding primary creative control to the director, Lucas operated along the lines of old-time Hollywood moguls like David O. Selznick, who retained ultimate authority on all his films, even when working with strong-willed and idiosyncratic directors such as Alfred Hitchcock, George Cukor, and William Wellman.

Lucas had to find talented writers, directors, and producers who were willing work with him on this basis, with their own creativity subservient to the executive producer's vision. While that arrangement was typical during the days of the old Hollywood studio system, it was anathema to the New Hollywood ethos of the 1970s. This must have been a tough sell, but Lucas nevertheless found gifted personnel who were able to bring depths and subtleties to his projects that aren't present in most of the movies he developed and directed on his own. For his later non-*Star Wars* projects, his collaborators would include Steven Spielberg (the Indiana Jones movies) and Ron Howard (*Willow*), both future Oscar winners. But in late 1977, Lucas was concerned only with finding the talent to help him get his next *Star Wars* movie off the ground. Since it had taken him four grueling years to write the original film, his first priority was recruiting a screenwriter.

Leigh Brackett

Leigh Brackett, born December 7, 1915, in Los Angeles, was one of the few women to break into the male-dominated world of science fiction during the genre's Golden Age. Her father, an accountant, died of the flu when she was three, leaving her and her mother in difficult financial straits. Brackett finished high school but, despite her obvious intelligence, could not afford to attend college. In 1939, she joined the Los Angeles Science Fiction Society, where she befriended authors such as Ray Bradbury and Robert Heinlein, who helped her connect with editors and other industry insiders. Brackett published eleven novels and dozens of short stories between 1940 and 1976, including the acclaimed novel *The Long Tomorrow* (1955) and the popular Skaith Trilogy, which melded elements of science fiction and "sword-and-sandal" fantasy.

While Brackett's sci-fi bona fides were impeccable, what attracted Lucas to the author was her second vocation, as a Hollywood screenwriter. Early in her career Brackett also wrote hard-boiled detective stories and novels, one of which (*No Good from a Corpse*, 1944) impressed director Howard Hawks, who hired her to collaborate with William Faulkner and screenwriter Jules Furthman in adapting Raymond Chandler's convoluted novel *The Big Sleep*. The film, directed by Hawks and starring Humphrey Bogart and Lauren Bacall, was released in 1946 and became a noir classic. Hawks placed Brackett under contract. In addition to her novels and short stories, Brackett wrote or cowrote eleven screenplays, including the scripts for Hawks' *Hatari!* (1962), *El Dorado* (1967), and *Rio Lobo* (1970), all starring John Wayne, as well as director Robert Altman's *The Long Goodbye* (1973), which was based on another Chandler novel. Brackett often took long breaks from screenwriting to focus on her novels and short stories, which she considered her more important work.

Lucas admired Brackett's screenplays for Hawks and loved the idea of working with someone who could bring an authentic classic Hollywood approach to *Star Wars*. In November 1977, he began meeting with Brackett to discuss his ideas for the film then known as *Star Wars Chapter II* but eventually renamed *The Empire Strikes Back*. In late February 1978, Brackett delivered a first draft, but her screenplay failed to meet Lucas' expectations (see Chapter 16). By then the sixty-two-year-old author's health was failing. When Lucas contacted her about undertaking a rewrite, Brackett had been hospitalized. She died of cancer March 18, 1978. Although little of her work survives in the final version of the script, Lucas insisted that she receive a screenplay credit. In 1980, *The Empire Strikes Back* won a Hugo Award, a major honor in the world of literary science fiction and a distinction that had eluded Brackett during her "legitimate" SF career. She was inducted into the Science Fiction Hall of Fame in 2014.

Lawrence Kasdan

Lawrence Kasdan was born January 14, 1949, in Miami, but was raised in Morgantown, West Virginia, where his father managed a chain of retail electronics stores and his mother worked as an employment counselor. He graduated from Morgantown High School in 1966 and attended the University of Michigan with the intent of becoming an English teacher. Unable to land a teaching job, however, Kasdan accepted work as an advertising copywriter in Chicago and promptly won a Clio Award. He relocated to Los Angeles in the mid-1970s, paying the bills by writing television commercials while moonlighting writing screenplays.

By his own accounting, Kasdan was turned down sixty-seven times before he finally sold a script. Unfortunately, his movie *The Bodyguard*, originally envisioned as a vehicle for Steve McQueen and Diana Ross, became trapped in development purgatory for over a decade, eventually reaching screens in 1992, starring Kevin Costner and Whitney Houston. His next sale, *Continental Divide*, was produced in 1981 as a seriocomic vehicle for John Belushi, directed by Michael Apted. Although he had no produced screenplays on his resume at the time, Kasdan's unsold works were highly regarded in Hollywood. Lucas, at the suggestion of Steven Spielberg, hired him to write *Raiders of the Lost Ark* (1981). In June 1978, Kasdan delivered his *Raiders* screenplay, which delighted everyone, and Lucas asked him to finish the script for *The Empire Strikes Back*. Lucas had rewritten Brackett's screenplay himself; Lucas and Kasdan both report that Kasdan never even saw Brackett's draft. Nevertheless, Kasdan and Brackett would share the film's screenplay credit. (Lucas declined a credit.) Three years later, Kasdan returned to pen *Return of the Jedi*.

By then, Kasdan's career was taking flight. In 1981, the year following *The Empire Strikes Back*, three impressive movies written by Kasdan were released: *Raiders, Continental Divide*, and the sexy neo-noir thriller *Body Heat*. On the strength of this cinematic hat trick, Kasdan ascended to the rarefied ranks of Hollywood filmmakers who serve as writer, director, and producer of their own projects. He remains best known for mature, character-driven movies that tap into Baby Boomer angst, such as *The Big Chill* (1983), *The Accidental Tourist* (1988), *Grand Canyon* (1991), and *Darling Companion* (2012). But Kasdan also wrote and directed the Westerns *Silverado* (1985) and *Wyatt Earp* (1994); helmed the comedies *I Love You to Death* (1990), *French Kiss* (1995), and *Mumford* (1999); and even made a horror film (Stephen King's

Dreamcatcher, 2003). His screenplays for *Grand Canyon*, *The Accidental Tourist*, and *The Big Chill* all earned Academy Award nominations.

Kasdan's facility for creating rich, lifelike characters and natural-sounding dialogue greatly enhanced both *The Empire Strikes Back* and *Return of the Jedi*. He fleshed out the personalities of Luke, Leia, and Han, and helped introduce Lando Calrissian and Yoda, two of the series' most memorable dramatis personae. He also brought vitality and believability to the often prickly but ultimately warm relationships between the characters, particularly the Han-Leia romance in *Empire*. These qualities were glaringly absent from the screenplays for the *Star Wars* Prequel Trilogy, which Lucas penned himself. It was not

Writer-director Lawrence Kasdan, pictured here on the set of his film *I Love You to Death*, received his big break when George Lucas and Steven Spielberg asked him to write *Raiders of the Lost Ark*. He later cowrote *The Empire Strikes Back* and *Return of the Jedi*.

surprising that writer-director J. J. Abrams, after signing on to helm the upcoming *Episode VII: The Force Awakens*, hired Kasdan to cowrite and coproduce. "Working with Larry Kasdan, especially on a *Star Wars* movie, is kind of unbeatable," Abrams told reporters. Abrams' stated aspiration is to return to the franchise all the strengths of the Original Trilogy, and one of those strengths is Kasdan's writing.

Irvin Kershner

Lucas may have been willing to relinquish the director's chair, but not to just anyone. "Following *Star Wars*, I knew one thing for sure: I didn't want to direct the second movie myself," Lucas told a reporter from the *New York Daily News* in 2010. "I needed someone I could trust, someone I really admired and whose work had maturity and humor. That was Kersh all over." "Kersh," of course, was director Irvin Kershner.

Born April 29, 1923, in Philadelphia, Kershner was a polymath who began playing violin in elementary school and majored in music composition at Temple University's Tyler School of Fine Arts. His studies were interrupted by the Second World War. Kershner served two and a half years as a member of the Army Air Corps, stationed in England. After returning to the States, he studied painting with famed instructor Hans Hofmann in New York and then moved to Los Angeles, where he took photography classes at the Art Center College of Design. Finally, he enrolled in the film program at USC, discovering a medium that combined his interests and abilities in all the arts he had studied previously, and integrated new disciplines. After USC, Kershner worked for the U.S. State Department directing documentaries in Iran, Greece, and Turkey. He returned to the United States and developed the KTTV Los Angeles television show *Confidential File* (1953–58), a thirty-minute topical documentary series hosted by *Los Angeles Times* columnist Paul Coates. In 1958, Kershner made his first fiction movie, *Stakeout on Dope Street*, a low-budget melodrama about two teenage boys who decide to go into the drug business when they accidentally come to possess a coffee can full of uncut heroin. More low-budget films and television episodes followed, including *The Rebel* (1959–1961), a Western series starring Nick Adams that Kershner developed and sold. His most recent pre-*Empire* credits included *Return of a Man Called Horse* (1976) with Richard Harris, the Emmy-nominated telefilm *Raid on Entebbe* (1976), and the hit paranormal thriller *Eyes of Laura Mars* (1978) starring Faye Dunaway.

For Lucas, however, Kershner's most important credential was that he had briefly taught film at USC. One of his students was George Lucas, who studied under Kershner for two terms. Kershner was one of the judges that awarded

This rare publicity still unites all three Original Trilogy directors. From left: Irvin Kershner, George Lucas, and Richard Marquand.

a national student film award to Lucas' *THX 1138 4EB*. "Even then I could tell he was a very special student," Kershner said in a 2009 interview at the Colorado Film School. Lucas "had vision. . . . He saw things that others didn't see in terms of film." Lucas trusted Kershner's insights, and his former instructor became part of his inner circle, along with people like Spielberg, Francis Ford Coppola, Brian De Palma, cinematographer Haskell Wexler, screenwriters Willard Huyck and Gloria Katz, and sound editor Walter Murch. Lucas considered Kershner a mentor.

Nevertheless, Kershner was flabbergasted when Lucas asked him to direct the sequel to *Star Wars*. "I was surprised when he asked me to do it, and I turned him down," said Kershner, in an interview on the public television program *Artsmash*. "I turned him down for about six weeks. I said, 'You've just made a film that's made a fortune. Everybody loves it. All I can do is make the second best.' He said, 'No, that's not the point. The point is you have to make a *better* picture than *Star Wars*, because if the second one is successful then I can continue making them. If it was a one-picture phenomenon, then it's over.' And I thought, 'Boy that's pretty good.'" Kershner was even more impressed when Lucas told him he intended to finance the picture himself. This meant that Lucas was betting his own financial security—"mortgaging everything," as Kershner put it—on the project, and on Kershner's ability to do the seemingly impossible and top *Star Wars*. Lucas also promised Kershner that he wouldn't interfere with the production, a vow that he kept for the most part (see Chapter 17). Finally, Kershner signed on.

"We hoped to find someone who not only had the right attitude toward fantasy, but who would develop the characters without losing sight of the inherent humor or slow down the action of what is essentially an adventure story," producer Gary Kurtz told publicist Alan Arnold, as quoted in Arnold's book *Once Upon a Galaxy: A Journal of the Making of The Empire Strikes Back*. Kershner was just what the producer ordered.

Although his efforts weren't immediately appreciated (see Chapter 18), today *The Empire Strikes Back* is widely regarded as the most polished *Star Wars* movie so far released. This is a testament to the consummate craftsmanship of Kershner, who had never helmed a blockbuster before but remained unfazed by the film's many technical challenges (in some respects, *Empire* was an even more complex shoot than *Star Wars*). More importantly, Kershner brought subtlety and humor to the picture, eliciting series-best performances from Hamill, Fisher, and Ford, and handling the difficult character of Yoda brilliantly. With his fine arts background, he also brought a painterly visual style to the film. No *Star Wars* picture is as handsomely composed and photographed.

After *The Empire Strikes Back*, Kershner helmed the James Bond film *Never Say Never Again* (1983) with Sean Connery, *Robocop 2* (1990), and several more TV movies and episodes. He also acted in five pictures, beginning with Martin Scorsese's *The Last Temptation of Christ* (1988), in which he played Zebedee, the father of apostles James and John. Kershner retired in 1994 and died in 2010, following a long battle with lung cancer.

Richard Marquand

Like Lucas before him, Kershner (then fifty-seven years old) found directing a *Star Wars* film physically and mentally exhausting. Kershner spent a year storyboarding the picture and then six months shooting it, and remained involved throughout the lengthy postproduction. "After working for two years and nine months doing *Empire*, and having it take so much out of my life . . . I felt that it was . . . time to move on," Kershner told *Vanity Fair* in 2010. Besides, Kershner had badly overrun his schedule and budget on *Empire* (see Chapter 17). To helm his third *Star Wars* film, Lucas wanted a director more pliable than his strong-willed mentor. After seriously pursuing other options (see Chapter 20), Lucas eventually settled on Richard Marquand.

Born September 22, 1937, in Cardiff, Wales, Marquand was the son of a member of the British parliament and the brother of author and political activist David Marquand. He was educated at private schools in London and

Provence, France, and attended college at Cambridge. During his eighteen months of conscripted national service, Marquand served as a newsreader on English television broadcasts in Hong Kong. This led to a postservice career writing and directing television documentaries for the BBC. His first fiction film was *The Legacy* (1978), a low-rent horror film starring Katharine Ross, Sam Elliott, and singer/sometime actor Roger Daltrey of the Who. That picture didn't leave much of an impression, but Marquand's next feature, the made-for-TV biopic *Birth of the Beatles* (1979), earned enthusiastic reviews and high ratings. Next Marquand helmed the Word War II espionage thriller *Eye of the Needle* (1981), based on a best-selling Ken Follett novel and starring Donald Sutherland and Kate Nelligan. The film earned a modest $17 million but was warmly received by most critics—and, more importantly, by George Lucas. "*Eye of the Needle* was the film I'd seen that he had done that impressed me the most," Lucas said in the audio commentary on *Return of the Jedi* DVD. "It was really nicely done and had a lot of energy and suspense."

While Kershner was reluctant to take the reins of the *Star Wars* franchise, Marquand jumped at the chance. "I'm a tremendous *Star Wars* fan," Marquand said in a 1984 interview posted on the Den of Geek website. "I felt like a young man who knows the music of Beethoven extremely well, and who is finally asked to play it with the London Symphony Orchestra." Marquand went on to compare himself to his predecessor. "Kershner was absolutely perfect for the middle film, which is a dark, troubled, and anguished film. That's the kind of character Kershner is himself; he's very amusing socially, but his mind is full of dark torments and worries. . . . But I think I was probably the right guy for the third film, because I like the great virtues: I love loyalty, friendship, love. . . . And I love happy endings."

Marquand had a reputation as an "actor's director," and, like Kershner, he elicited good work from the cast, especially during the film's Han-Leia and Luke-Vader exchanges. At the time he made *Jedi*, Marquand had a young son who shared his love of the franchise, and (for better or worse) he supported Lucas' idea of turning the film into more of a children's movie. Because Lucas was more directly involved in the production of *Jedi* than he was in the making of *Empire* (see Chapter 20), it's difficult to fairly assess the director's contributions. Marquand also made a cameo in *Return of the Jedi*, appearing as an AT-AT driver.

After *Jedi*, Marquand directed three more movies, including the hit thriller *Jagged Edge* (1985) starring Jeff Bridges and Glenn Close. His career was cut short when he died of a stroke September 4, 1987, at age forty-nine. His final film—*Hearts of Fire* (1987), a poorly received music industry drama starring Bob Dylan—was released posthumously. George Lucas was one of the few Hollywood figures to attend Marquand's funeral.

Howard Kazanjian

As production of *Empire* dragged on and on, and costs tripled original estimates, George Lucas grew increasingly frustrated with producer Gary Kurtz, who had served at his right hand since *American Graffiti*. In late August 1979, with the end of shooting still a few weeks away, Lucas quietly removed Kurtz (see Chapter 17). Howard Kazanjian took over line production duties and remained aboard for *Return of the Jedi*.

Kazanjian, an Armenian American, was born in 1942 in Pasadena, California, and attended film school at USC, where he was a classmate of Lucas. In a 2010 interview, Kazanjian claimed that he introduced Lucas to Francis Ford Coppola while working as an assistant director on *Finian's Rainbow* (1968). Early in his career, Kazanjian worked as an AD under a laundry list of legendary filmmakers, including Sam Peckinpah on *The Wild Bunch* (1969), Billy Wilder on *The Front Page* (1974), Robert Wise on *The Hindenburg* (1975), and Alfred Hitchcock on *Family Plot* (1976).

Kazanjian joined Lucasfilm in early 1978 as the producer of *More American Graffiti* (1979). He later worked as an executive producer on *Raiders of the Lost Ark* (1981). Kazanjian pushed for the casting of Harrison Ford as Indiana Jones and was instrumental in luring Ford, who was not under contract for another *Star Wars* film following *Empire*, back for *Return of the Jedi*. As producer, Kazanjian participated in story conferences for *Jedi* along with Lucas, Kasdan, and Marquand. Among other things, Kazanjian suggested that the redeemed Anakin Skywalker should appear alongside Ben Kenobi and Yoda at the end of the film. Kazanjian has a reputation as an efficient, no-nonsense professional. Lucas biographer John Baxter called him "the iron hand within the velvet glove of Lucasfilm."

George Lucas tapped no-nonsense producer Howard Kazanjian, who had worked on *More American Graffiti* and *Raiders of the Lost Ark*, to replace Gary Kurtz as the producer of the *Star Wars* films.

Kazanjian eventually rose to the position of vice president of Lucasfilm but left the company in the late 1980s to strike out on his own. Since then, he has produced fifteen film and television projects, including *The Rookie* (1990) with Clint Eastwood and Charlie Sheen, and *Demolition Man* (1993) with Sylvester Stallone and Wesley Snipes. A devout Christian, Kazanjian has taught at Act One, a workshop for Christian filmmakers. He is currently producing a trilogy of films titled *The Truth About the War in Heaven,* slated for release in 2014, 2016, and 2018. A Western enthusiast, Kazanjian also coauthored two books on the life and career of cowboy stars Roy Rogers and Dale Evans. Kazanjian lives in San Marino, California, with his wife and three children, and he remains close friends with George Lucas.

15

I Have a Bad Feeling About This

The *Star Wars Holiday Special* (1978)

It must have seemed like a good idea at the time.

A *Star Wars* television special, arriving in late 1978 (about halfway between the releases of the original film and the upcoming sequel) would keep the franchise in the public eye and build anticipation for *The Empire Strikes Back*. The show could be used to introduce new characters and to create additional merchandising opportunities. It would serve as a thank-you to loyal fans, who were eager for new *Star Wars* product after paying to see the original over and over again. And the special could give the franchise—which had already conquered the motion picture, merchandising, and publishing realms—a toehold in the domain of television. If successful, it might pave the way for an ongoing *Star Wars* spin-off TV series.

The fact that the proposed *Star Wars Holiday Special* would be a variety show, with musical interludes and comedy skits, doesn't seem to have given anyone pause. Confidence was sky-high at Lucasfilm and Twentieth Century-Fox. So far everything *Star Wars* touched had turned to piles of cash. "We should have realized that there was no way that we could fit the characters into this kind of format," said producer Gary Kurtz in a 2008 interview with *Vanity Fair*. In the late 1970s, however, the concept wasn't as obviously crazy as it sounds today.

The Format

Variety was not just the spice, but a staple of television programming in the 1970s. Like today's ubiquitous reality series, variety shows were inexpensive to produce and extremely popular. Ed Sullivan, Milton Berle, and Sid Caesar had pioneered the format during television's infancy with programs that featured a mix of stand-up routines, musical performances, comedy skits, dance numbers, and everything else imaginable. But the format peaked in popularity in the late 1960s and early '70s with series hosted by performers such as Carol Burnett, Red Skelton, Dean Martin, Flip Wilson, and Sonny and Cher.

The hosts of these series were major draws, but viewers also tuned in to watch each week's guest stars, who often were allowed to demonstrate previously hidden talents. If you wanted to see Jim "Gomer Pyle" Nabors sing, or Helen "I Am Woman" Reddy do sketch comedy, variety shows were your ticket. There was a variety show to suit every taste, from the homespun *Hee Haw* to the confrontational *Smothers Brothers Comedy Hour.* During the 1969–1970 broadcast season, nine of the twenty highest-rated TV programs were variety shows. This quickly led to a glut of variety series and "specials," semiregular programs hosted by stars such as Bob Hope, Bing Crosby, and Perry Como, among many others. All three networks ran multiple variety series, sometimes on the same night. During the 1970–71 season CBS ran an all-variety lineup on Sundays: *The Ed Sullivan Show* at 8:00 p.m., followed by *The Glen Campbell Goodtime Hour* at 9:00, and *The Tim Conway Show* at 10:00. A successful appearance on any one of these shows could easily lead to a performer getting his or her own series, which is how people like Don Ho, Shields and Yarnell, Howard Cosell, and the Starland Vocal Band wound up hosting their own self-named variety programs.

By the late 1970s, the appeal of the format was beginning to fade, but seasonal variety specials, like the annual Christmas shows hosted by Hope, Crosby, Como, and Andy Williams continued to garner high ratings. The calculus behind the *Star Wars Holiday Special* was simple: People loved holiday variety shows and people loved *Star Wars.* Why not combine the two? How could it miss?

The Production

Detailed information about the creation of the *Star Wars Holiday Special* is hard to come by, mostly because everyone involved would like to forget the thing ever happened. "The special from 1978 really didn't have much to do with us, you know," George Lucas said in a 2005 interview with the website StaticMedia.com. "I can't remember what network it was on, but it was a thing that they did. We kind of let them do it. . . . We let them use the characters and stuff, and that probably wasn't the smartest thing to do, but you learn from those experiences."

It isn't clear, at this distance, where the proposal for a *Star Wars* television special originated. Gary Smith, one of the show's executive producers, claims that Twentieth Century-Fox dreamed up the idea, while Leonard Ripps, who cowrote the special, remembers that the project came from Lucasfilm.

Although Lucas gave the show a green light, he was not actively involved in its development. Instead, the making of the show was farmed out to Smith-Hemion Productions, which to date had created twenty-two mostly successful television specials, working with such luminaries as Sammy Davis Jr., John Wayne, Dorothy Hamill, and Elvis Presley.

Screenwriters Pat Proft, Bruce Vilanch, and Ripps spent a day at Lucasfilm and were provided with a thumbnail story idea from Lucas: Luke, Leia, and Han are harassed by the Empire while taking Chewbacca to his homeworld to spend "Life Day" with his family. Based on this brief sketch, Proft, Vilanch, and Ripps worked up a short treatment, which they turned over to producers Ken and Mitzie Welch, who tailored the wafer-thin scenario to suit the particular talents of the guest stars who had been hired for the show: comedians Bea Arthur, Art Carney, and Harvey Korman; singer Diahann Carroll; rock band Jefferson Starship (signed, no doubt, because of their name); juggling duo the Mumm Brothers; and a quintet of acrobats known as the Wazzan Troupe. Writer Rod Warren contributed special material for specific

Bea Arthur poses with the denizens of the Mos Eisley cantina in this publicity shot. In the *Star Wars Holiday Special*, she plays a singing bartender.

segments, and the Welches composed original songs, two of them sung to the tune of composer John Williams' *Star Wars* themes.

The project was assigned a relatively generous $1 million budget, which covered the construction of an elaborate Wookiee treehouse set. In addition, many sets, props, costumes, and makeups (including most of Rick Baker's cantina creatures) from *Star Wars* were reused. As a bonus, Canadian animation studio Nelvana was engaged to create a short animated segment. Although Lucas was not directly involved with the special—he had his hands full developing *The Empire Strikes Back*—he did what he could to assure the product's quality, insisting that Oscar winner Ben Burtt create the Wookiee "dialogue" and that celebrated makeup artist Stan Winston assist with the Wookiees. Lucas also suggested that Smith-Hemion hire USC alum David Acomba to direct the special. In a *Vanity Fair* article about the show, Ripps defended the talent and professionalism of everyone involved in making the *Star Wars Holiday Special*, but added, "I'm sure there wasn't a bad welder on the *Titanic*."

The Holiday Special was furiously promoted by CBS, including this *TV Guide* advertisement.

Mark Hamill, Carrie Fisher, and especially Harrison Ford had to be pressured and cajoled into participating in the project. Anthony Daniels and Peter Mayhew also reprised their roles as C-3PO and Chewbacca. Fisher reportedly agreed to appear on the condition that she be allowed to sing. None of the stars enjoyed the shoot. Someone took a snapshot of the weight-conscious Fisher sitting in her Princess Leia costume—white dress and double-bun hairdo—drinking a can of sugar-free Tab cola and looking depressed.

Acomba began the project but clashed with the Welches and was replaced midway through production (he helmed the Bea Arthur and Jefferson Starship segments). Veteran variety director Steve Binder took over and received sole credit—or blame—for the program. Miki Herman, who had worked on *Star Wars* as a production assistant and was rising quickly through the ranks at Lucasfilm (she would eventually become co-executive producer of the *Droids* and *Ewoks* animated series), was assigned as a liaison to the project and is credited as a "*Star Wars* consultant." Patty Maloney, who played Chewie's son "Lumpy" in the show, told an interviewer from the StarWarsHolidaySpecial.com fan site that Lucas received dailies from the special during production, but it's possible Lucas delegated reviewing the footage to Herman.

The *Star Wars Holiday Special* aired just once, 8:00 p.m. Friday, November 17, 1978, on CBS, preempting episodes of *The New Adventures of Wonder Woman* and *The Incredible Hulk*. It was also shown the same day and time on Canada's CTV network. In the United States it attracted an estimated 13 million viewers.

The Broadcast

I was one of those 13 million. I was twelve years old at the time and watched the *Holiday Special* sitting cross-legged in the floor in front of my parents' big, wooden console TV. My eight-year-old brother sat next to me, with my parents on the couch a few feet behind us, on the other side of the coffee table. I had read about the upcoming special in *Bantha Tracks*, the newsletter of the Official Star Wars Fan Club, and had seen the promos on our local CBS affiliate (WHAS-11 in Louisville, Kentucky). Christmas was a little over a month away, and my birthday a couple of weeks after that, but I was more excited about this TV broadcast than either of those milestones. It was *new Star Wars*! I was literally tingling with excitement when the show began. Han and Chewbacca were at the helm of the *Millennium Falcon*, being pursued by a (stock footage) Star Destroyer. "That's the spirit," Han assured Chewie, as they dodged blaster fire. "You'll be celebrating Life Day before you know it." Then the *Falcon* jumped to hyperspace, barely avoiding destruction. *Wow*, I thought. *This is going to be great!*

My enthusiasm soon waned.

The fundamental problem with the screenplay that Proft, Ripp, Vilanch, and the Welches had written for the *Holiday Special* was that their scenario inverted Lucas' simple concept. Rather than following Han and Chewie as they fought their way to the Wookiee homeworld of Kashyyyk, the show spends most of its running time with Chewie's family and friends—wife Malla (Mickey Morton), son Lumpy (Patty Maloney), father Itchy (Paul Gale), and kindly human trader Saun Dann (Art Carney)—as they fret over Chewbacca's absence. These characters spend most of their time watching viewscreens or holograms, the venues through which most of the guest performers appear.

Carrie Fisher agreed to appear in the *Holiday Special* on the condition that she was allowed to sing. Unfortunately, the song written for her—like nearly everything else in the show—was terrible.

As a result, during nearly the entirety of the two-hour *Star Wars Holiday Special*, viewers sat in front of TV screens watching other people sit in front of TV screens. Stars Harrison Ford, Mark Hamill, and Carrie Fisher had extremely limited screen time—just five minutes and fifteen seconds for Ford, and four-and-a-half apiece for Hamill and Fisher, including a two-minute-thirty-second passage in which all three appear together.

The hallmark of *Star Wars* had been fleet-footed, thrill-packed action-adventure, but the *Holiday Special* was glacially paced. After the opening credits and a commercial break, the show continued with an unbroken ten-minute sequence in which Chewie's relatives go about the mundane preparations for their Life Day celebration. The dialogue for this tedious sequence consists entirely of untranslated Wookiee growls and groans. The grunting and howling abates momentarily when Malla calls Luke Skywalker on her video screen. Luke can't talk long—he and Artoo are busy repairing an engine—but he assures her Han and Chewbacca will arrive soon. This scene, the only one featuring Luke until the climax of the show, lasts two minutes. Afterward, Lumpy watches a team of holographic tumblers and jugglers perform. Next Saun Dann is introduced, nervously dealing with an imperial officer who walks into his trading post in what is, at least theoretically, a comedic interlude. Then we cut back to Chewie's house, where Malla makes "Bantha Surprise" for the holiday meal, with instructions from a bumbling holographic chef (played by Harvey Korman—in drag).

By now, I was beginning to fidget restlessly. *What's that old guy from the Honeymooners doing here?* I wondered. *When are we going to get back to Han and Chewie?*

They finally reappear, after being offscreen for nearly half an hour, battling (stock footage) TIE fighters, still trying to reach Kashyyyk. This scene also lasts two minutes. Then it's back to Chewie's treehouse, where an imperial broadcast informs all residents of Kashyyyk that the planet is being blockaded by the Empire due to "suspected rebel activity." Soon, Saun Dann arrives with Life Day presents for the family. Itchy's gift is a pseudo-pornographic hologram of a scantily clad young woman (Carroll) who informs the gray-furred Wookiee "I am your pleasure, enjoy me!" and sings "This Minute Now," a cheesy romantic ballad.

About this time, I realized that my parents had left the room and that my brother was playing with his Hot Wheels. I stuck with the show, figuring it had to get better. And it did—briefly.

Leia and Threepio finally appear, via a two-minute videophone call to Malla. Han and Chewie finally reach Kashyyyk, but are forced to land several miles away from the Chewbaccas' home to avoid imperial troops. Before they can reach Chewie's family, stormtroopers and imperial officers arrive, on a treehouse-to-treehouse search for signs of rebel activity. Just when it seems something exciting might happen, however, more attempted comedy ensues as Carney tries to distract the soldiers. Then one of the officers watches a holographic Jefferson Starship lip-synch to their new single "Light the Sky on Fire."

The unquestioned highlight of the special comes next: the ten-minute animated sequence, which Lumpy watches on a small video screen. In this story-within-a-story, the Alliance has lost contact with Han and Chewbacca, who were out searching for a "magic talisman" in the *Millennium Falcon*. Luke, Threepio, and Artoo go after them in a Y-Wing fighter, but both ships crash on a water planet. Luke and the droids are rescued by Boba Fett, who convinces Luke he's a friend of the rebellion by helping him locate the *Falcon*. But the droids intercept a transmission from Darth Vader to Fett, which reveals the bounty hunter is on a secret mission to gain the trust of the rebels in order to learn the location of their new hidden base. The exposed Fett escapes.

My brother looked up from his toy cars to watch this part of the show.

Following the cartoon, Lumpy assembles his Life Day present—a transmitter—with the "help" of a malfunctioning robot (also played by Korman). Next, Chewie's family and the imperials watch "Life on Tatooine," a thirteen-minute segment set in the Mos Eisley Cantina in which bartender Bea Arthur fends off advances by a lovestruck alien (Korman yet again) who drinks

The undisputed highlight of the *Star Wars Holiday Special* was a short cartoon segment that featured the debut of Boba Fett (seen here riding a dinosaur).

through a blowhole on top of his head. Then the barkeep sings the Welch-penned number "Goodnight, but Not Goodbye" (to the tune of the *Star Wars* cantina band theme) as she closes down the place.

When this sequence ends, Lumpy uses his transmitter to trick the soldiers into returning to base. But they leave a trooper behind. Han and Chewie finally arrive and rescue Lumpy from the trooper, who discovers the young Wookiee's trick. Han embraces Chewbacca's family but tells his friend he must return to the *Falcon* before it's discovered. Soon Chewie and his family don red ceremonial robes and shuffle off to the Tree of Life for the big Life Day celebration. Inexplicably, Han, Luke, Leia, and the droids appear at the event to wish the Wookiees a happy Life Day, and Leia sings a song (lyrics set to the tune of the *Star Wars* title theme). A time-filling montage of clips from the movie plays.

The montage only underscored for me how great the movie was and how far short of that mark the *Holiday Special* had fallen. It was almost unendurable, like pouring salt on an open wound.

Finally, Chewie and his family bow their heads in prayer and begin eating their Life Day dinner (Bantha Surprise). Roll credits.

"How was it?" My mother asked, wandering into the living room from the kitchen. "Good," I said, feeling crestfallen but keeping a brave face. As the months and years wore on, however, the *Holiday Special* improved, at least in my recollection. Since I was unable to rewatch it, my imagination began to polish the show, editing out memories of Bea Arthur and Harvey Korman while clinging to those of the animated segment with Boba Fett. As I entered high school, the show became a point of connection with fellow *Star Wars* fans. "Hey, do you remember that Christmas special with the Wookiees and that cool little cartoon?"

Shortly after I graduated from college, and a little over a decade since its initial broadcast, I acquired a videotape of the *Holiday Special*. I wasn't as eager to see it then as I had been in 1978, but I was more than curious. I was hopeful. I really wanted to enjoy it. *Come on*, I thought to myself, *it can't be as bad as I remember, can it?* It wasn't.

It was worse.

The Fallout

When they began work on the *Star Wars Holiday Special*, the show's writers envisioned a lifelong string of fat residual checks. "We were really excited, because, 'My God, this is an annuity—*Star Wars!*'" screenwriter Ripps told *Vanity Fair*. It didn't work out that way. The *Star Wars Holiday Special* was heavily promoted by CBS and earned good ratings (it finished as the third most-watched program of the week, behind *The Love Boat* and an episode of *Pearl*, a miniseries about the Japanese attack on Pearl Harbor). But it was excoriated by critics and disowned by Lucas. A special line of Kenner action figures planned to tie with the show was canceled. The only officially sanctioned merchandise released in conjunction with the program was a children's book featuring characters from the special—*Star Wars: The Wookiee Storybook*, published in 1979. There were no residuals.

In an online interview with fans, Lucas declared that the *Holiday Special* "does not represent my vision." Co-executive producer Dwight Hemion, in an interview with National Public Radio, was more direct, calling the show "the worst piece of crap I've ever done."

Nowadays, interviewers who raise the topic of the *Holiday Special* while speaking with Lucas or the stars of the show do so at their own risk. In a 2005 interview with *Maxim* magazine, Lucas said of the special: "That's one of those things that happened, and I just have to live with it." During a 2006 appearance on *Late Night with Conan O'Brien*, Harrison Ford claimed to have never seen the special. (O'Brien helpfully ran a short clip for Ford.) And in 2010, Carrie Fisher told *New York Times* columnist David Carr that she owns a copy of the special, which she shows at parties, "mainly at the end of the night, when I want people to leave."

Surprisingly, considering what a fiasco it was, some story elements and characters introduced in the *Holiday Special* have been accepted as "canon" within the mythology of *Star Wars*. For instance, the Wookiee homeworld Kashyyyk later appeared in numerous authorized *Star Wars* novels and comic books, and was eventually shown in *Episode II: Attack of the Clones* (2002). Chewbacca's family have occasionally reappeared in *Star Wars* novels, comics, and video games. And, of course, Boba Fett became a major figure in the franchise.

The special has never been officially released on home video in any format, although the animated Boba Fett sequence showed up as an "Easter egg" bonus feature on the *Star Wars: The Complete Saga* Blu-ray boxed set in 2011. In the late 1970s and early '80s, the full special was rebroadcast—apparently without permission—on Swedish, Australian, Venezuelan, and Brazilian television. The night of its original broadcast it was taped by a handful of fans (home video recording was in its infancy at the time) and later widely bootlegged. It is now available (unofficially) at various locations online. Lucas once reportedly vowed that "If I had the time and a sledgehammer, I would track down every copy of that show and smash it." The *Holiday Special* has seen rare authorized screenings at archival events, including a showing at the Library of Congress in the 1990s.

Perhaps because in the right frame of mind it can be fun to watch really awful programming, or possibly because people are naturally curious to taste forbidden fruit, or maybe simply because it's *Star Wars*, the *Holiday Special* has developed a clandestine cult following. An online petition urging Lucasfilm to release the show on DVD gathered thousands of signatures. While George Lucas was in charge of Lucasfilm, however, the *Holiday Special* was under permanent embargo. It was seldom even mentioned in authorized *Star Wars* books and websites. A segment on the special was redacted from director Kevin Burns and Edith Becker's 2004 documentary about the franchise, *Empire of Dreams*. Now that Disney controls Lucasfilm, it's (barely) conceivable that the *Star Wars Holiday Special* may someday escape the vaults, perhaps as part of a revised, truly *Complete Saga* type of collection. This would, doubtless, excite those hardcore fans who have been clamoring for such a release. The special, however, would also certainly perplex and dismay most casual viewers. Some genies are best left in the bottle.

16

You'll Find I'm Full of Surprises

Preproduction of *The Empire Strikes Back*

In September 1977, after reaching an advantageous deal with Twentieth Century-Fox, George Lucas had everything he needed to make his second *Star Wars* film—except time. The one caveat in Lucas' original *Star Wars* contract, which granted the director the sequel rights to the property, was that shooting of the second picture had to begin no later than the first quarter of 1979. Otherwise, ownership of any sequels would revert back to Fox. This meant that Lucas had, at most, eighteen months to write a screenplay, hire a cast and crew, re-form Industrial Light & Magic, secure studio space, scout locations, and accomplish all the other preproduction chores that had taken four years with *Star Wars*. If he missed this deadline, he would lose the most sensational property the movies had ever seen.

From "The Adventures of Luke Skywalker" to "The Tragedy of Darth Vader"

For Lucas, who found writing excruciating, the most daunting deliverable was the screenplay. In later years, Lucas would claim that even before *Star Wars* premiered, he had written a complete outline for a multipart space saga as well as finished treatments for each installment. However, the surviving scripts, summaries, and other documentation, along with interviews with Lucas and other insiders from the late 1970s, indicate this was not the case. Gary Kurtz bluntly told author Chris Taylor, for his book *How Star Wars Conquered the Universe*, that Lucas' version of events "is not true."

Rather than a fully developed, preplanned saga, Lucas appears to have had several sequences and ideas that had to be trimmed from the first film (including a scene set in an asteroid belt and another in a city floating in the clouds), as well as the tent poles of a narrative: Luke Skywalker finds a new teacher, becomes more powerful with the Force, and confronts Darth Vader; the rebels cope with the consequences of destroying the Death Star; the romantic triangle between Luke, Princess Leia, and Han Solo is resolved. Perhaps as a result, the sequel did not endure the kind of radical draft-to-draft reimagining (outlined in Chapter 4) that dogged the first picture. Previously, Lucas had commissioned science fiction author Alan Dean Foster to create a possible low-budget sequel to *Star Wars*, which was published as a novel under the title *Splinter of the Mind's Eye* in 1978 (see Chapter 30). But he now scrapped the idea and began imagining a more ambitious story.

Working as usual in longhand, Lucas jotted down additional ideas. He envisioned a battle on an ice planet, Threepio being blown apart and reassembled, and a cliff-hanger ending with Han Solo missing in action. He also imagined sequences set on a swamp planet, a city planet, a forest planet (perhaps the Wookiee homeworld), and in an underwater city. These concepts would be realized eventually, but not all in the movie then known as *Star Wars Chapter II*. On November 28, 1977, Lucas carried his notes into the first in a series of story conferences with science fiction author and screenwriter Leigh Brackett (see Chapter 14). During these meetings, it was decided that the film would open on the ice planet, where Luke would be slashed across the face by a snow monster to account for the change in actor Mark Hamill's appearance following his automobile accident (described in Chapter 8). This sequence would conclude with the imperials attacking a rebel base on the ice planet, which Lucas named Hoth. Lucas and Brackett also planned to introduce three important new characters: the evil Emperor, an alien Jedi master, and a smooth-talking riverboat gambler type from Han Solo's past. Also at this time, the project was retitled *Star Wars Chapter II: The Empire Strikes Back*.

Afterward, Lucas crafted a treatment. The plot was essentially the same as the finished film: The rebels flee Hoth following an imperial attack, separating into two groups. Luke trains on a swampy planet called Dagobah with an elfin Jedi Master referred to simply as the Critter, while Han and Leia evade the imperial fleet and travel to a floating city above a giant gas planet. There they meet Han's old gambler friend, but they are betrayed and taken hostage by Vader, who uses Leia to bait Luke into a showdown. At this stage, however, the story included additional elements that were later discarded. Originally, the beginning of the film played like an homage to producer Howard Hawks' sci-fi/horror classic *The Thing (from Another World)* (1951), with the rebels being stalked by mysterious snow creatures. The imperials attacked in tank-like giant landspeeders, not AT-AT "walkers." The gas giant was home to two civilizations—one primitive and (in a separate floating city) one advanced. The treatment also provided a Tarzan-like backstory for Solo: He was an orphan raised by Wookiees following a starship crash. As a young man he had been the protégé of a notorious space pirate, who he hasn't seen in years. Han vanishes while on a secret mission to reconnect with his old mentor.

Brackett's ensuing first-draft screenplay, delivered February 21, 1978, did not meet Lucas' expectations. She had followed the agreed-upon outline for the story, the broad contours of which would remain unchanged throughout development. But the tone was wrong, and the dialogue, especially Vader's, was corny. It simply didn't read like a *Star Wars* film. Also, Lucas was having second thoughts about some of the ideas from the treatment, particularly the Han Solo backstory. In this first draft, Luke's new Jedi teacher was named Minch Yoda and described as a froglike alien about three feet tall. Han's gambler friend, now named Lando Calrissian, was a clone. Finally, in this first draft, Vader was not Luke's father. The deceased Anakin Skywalker appeared in spectral form to encourage his son during Luke's training on the swamp planet. The ghostly Anakin led Luke in reciting a Jedi Oath.

Under intense deadline pressure, and with Brackett in failing health (see Chapter 14), Lucas was forced to rewrite the screenplay himself. Working with astonishing (for Lucas) speed, he turned in a finished second draft April 1, completing the script in less than six weeks. His version streamlined Brackett's draft, paring the story back to something very close to its finished form, while also integrating critical new elements. The second draft discarded the Han Solo backstory but revived the plot point of Han's debt to Jabba the Hutt. It also added the interlude in which Han saves Luke's life during a snowstorm, a sequence remarkably similar to one from Akira Kurosawa's *Dersu Uzala* (1975). Lucas' draft

Bounty hunter Boba Fett (played by Jeremy Bulloch) received a major buildup *in The Empire Strikes Back*, but would be summarily dispatched in the next film.

also introduced the bounty hunter Boba Fett, who eventually carts away Solo in "carbon freeze." This provided the requisite cliff-hanger ending since Solo's pirate mentor and secret mission had been eliminated. The business of Lando being a clone was also dropped, as was the second Bespin civilization. In general, the focus of the story shifted to the developing romance between Han and Leia, and to Luke learning about the Force and being tempted by its Dark Side. Luke's teacher, now named simply Yoda, was given his distinctive backward-syntax speech pattern. The Force itself—a nebulous spiritual discipline in the original film—here became a full-blown telekinetic superpower.

By far the most significant development in Lucas' draft, however, was that for the first time Vader was revealed as Luke's father. Lucas probably hit on this idea in his efforts to pare back unnecessary story threads and characters. Luke didn't need three mentors—Yoda, the spectral Ben Kenobi, *and* his dead father as well. Making Vader Luke's father not only tightened the script, it brought new and truly mythic dimensions to the overarching narrative. It was a stroke of genius. The importance of this revision within the overall framework of the franchise cannot be overstated. "With this change in character and story, the *Star Wars* series would irrevocably shift . . . from a storybook-like tale of good versus evil to a complicated chronicle of temptation and redemption," author Michael Kaminsky observes in his book *The Secret History of Star Wars*. "With the second draft of *The Empire Strikes Back*, George Lucas had created the basis for the *Star Wars* saga."

There was one other telling revision. The film was retitled *Star Wars Episode V: The Empire Strikes Back*. About this time Lucas stopped referring to *Star Wars* as a series of twelve films (the same number of chapters as most Hollywood serials) and as a trilogy of trilogies—the current story arc, dealing with the rebellion of the Empire, a prequel trilogy about the rise of the Empire, and a sequel trilogy dealing with the establishment of the New Galactic Republic. Ultimately, Lucas would pare his saga back to six episodes, which he sometimes referred to collectively as "The Tragedy of Darth Vader." The phrase "From the Adventures of Luke Skywalker," which had been attached to the early *Star Wars* novels and comics, was quietly dropped.

The implications of this plot point, and the shift in focus it represented, were so great that Lucas instructed his secretary (whose duties including typing his handwritten manuscripts) to omit the passage where the Vader-Skywalker relationship was revealed. It was absent from most working copies of the script—including the version provided to Fox executives. At first, Lucas didn't even inform director Irvin Kershner. Secrecy was maintained as long as possible.

Although Lucas' second draft was pivotal, it was not a finished product. His dialogue, while less arch than Brackett's, remained clunky, and the Han and Leia romantic scenes were wince-inducing. So Lucas engaged screen-writer Lawrence Kasdan, fresh from penning *Raiders of the Lost Ark* (1981), to undertake a rewrite (see Chapter 14). Kasdan wrote all the subsequent drafts of the screenplay, smoothing over the rough spots in Lucas' version and punching up the romantic and character moments. In the screenplay's third draft, delivered in August 1978, Kasdan brought in the idea of Luke losing a hand during his climactic battle with Vader (originally, his arm was sliced off below the elbow) and having it replaced with a mechanical one to signify his possible transformation into a being like his father. Kasdan also wrote some of Yoda's most famous dialogue, including "There is no try." Kasdan delivered fourth and fifth drafts, which honed the character material still further and incorporated—at Kershner's suggestion—a race of alien grunt workers on Bespin. Kershner had called them "hogmen," but they were renamed Ugnaughts. The fifth draft, finalized February 20, 1979, served as the shooting script.

From Van Nuys to San Rafael

While the screenplay passed through its many iterations, Lucas had his hands full with other vital tasks, none more essential than the resurrection of Industrial Light & Magic. Although ILM had persisted as a corporate entity, the upstart visual effects studio had been on hiatus since the completion of *Star Wars*. With no other projects to work on, the staff had disbanded. Some joined John Dykstra's breakaway studio, Apogee, which was operating out of ILM's space on Valjean Avenue in Van Nuys, California, and even using ILM's equipment (which it had leased). Others—such as Dennis Muren, who joined the visual effects team working on Steven Spielberg's *Close Encounters of the Third Kind*—had moved on to other projects. Now Lucas and producer Gary Kurtz had to round them up again—those they wanted back in the fold, that is.

It was a given that the re-formed Industrial Light & Magic staff would not include its former chief, Dykstra. Not only had Lucas and Dykstra suffered an acrimonious falling-out, but Lucasfilm was currently suing Dykstra and the rest of the producers behind TV's *Battlestar Galactica*, which Lucas considered a blatant *Star Wars* rip-off. In his stead, Lucas and Kurtz lured back Richard Edlund, who would soon win an Oscar for his contributions to *Star Wars*, and recruited British visual effects artist Brian Johnson. Lucas and Kurtz had tried to hire Johnson for the first film, but at the time he was unwilling to relocate to California. Johnson had worked on *2001: A Space Odyssey*, TV's *Space: 1999*, and, perhaps more importantly, on the BBC sci-fi series *Thunderbirds*, which featured puppet characters and miniature effects, and was a childhood favorite of Lucas'. Along with Edlund, Dennis Muren, who had proven his mettle during the troubled postproduction of *Star Wars*, agreed to return to ILM, as did ace model builder Lorne Peterson, who left Dykstra's Apogee team to rejoin Lucas and Kurtz.

Among the inducements Lucas and Kurtz used to lure potential ILMers was the prospect of moving out of the old, non-air-conditioned warehouse in Van Nuys where *Star Wars* had been made and into a posh, new, custom-built effects studio located at 3210 Kerner Boulevard in San Rafael, California, near San Francisco. In July 1978, all the equipment from the old ILM location in Van Nuys—previously leased to Apogee—was moved, lock, stock, and barrel, to the new facility in San Rafael. By then, Lucas and Kurtz had assembled a core group of a dozen visual effects artists, also including *Star Wars* alumni Phil Tippett, Joe Johnston, and Ken Ralston. Even earlier—almost as soon as the ink was dry on the contract for the sequel—they welcomed back another key contributor, production artist Ralph McQuarrie. As they had on the first film, McQuarrie's sketches and paintings would not only help provide a visual guide for the work of the ILM staff, but would help Lucas focus his own ideas about the universe he was continuing to create.

The re-formed ILM staff faced a major challenge. Everyone realized that duplicating the work they had done on the first film would not suffice; to deliver the same visual "wow" factor, they would have to top their previous efforts and break even more new ground. Among the more difficult assignments was figuring out how to create the All Terrain Armored Transport (AT-AT) "walkers," which had replaced the Empire's tank-like landspeeders in later drafts of the screenplay, and Hoth's beasts of burden, the Tauntauns. In both cases the ILM team decided to employ old-fashioned stop-motion animation—the same process that had been used in the making of *King Kong* back in 1933. Tippett had created a brief stop-motion sequence for the first *Star Wars* film, for the holographic chess game played by Threepio and Chewbacca. But *Empire*'s AT-AT and Tauntaun sequences were far more extensive and would be shot in unforgiving snowy daylight. For guidance, Lucas and Kurtz consulted with visual effects legend Ray Harryhausen, who had created iconic stop-motion animated sequences for pictures like *The Seventh Voyage of Sinbad* (1958) and *Jason and the Argonauts* (1963). In the end, it was decided that the herky-jerky look of stop-motion would be ideal for the mechanical Walkers, while motion-control photography could be used to supplement some of the Tauntaun shots for a more fluid, animal-like movement. Muren filmed test footage of an Indian elephant, and a horse and rider, to provide a model for the gait of the walkers and the Tauntauns, respectively.

From Lucas to Kershner

Beyond ILM, Lucas and Kurtz had to recruit the rest of the film's cast and crew, beginning with its director. Lucas never intended to helm the second *Star Wars* movie and eventually settled on his former instructor, Irvin Kershner, as his replacement (see Chapter 14). But he considered a wide range of other filmmakers before approaching Kershner. Kurtz compiled a list of one hundred directors who might be right for *The Empire Strikes Back*. Many of those were eliminated immediately because they were unavailable or for other reasons, but Lucas reached out to Alan Parker (whose later works include *Mississippi Burning* [1988] and *The Commitments* [1991]) and *Saturday Night Fever*'s John Badham. Neither was willing to set aside upcoming projects—Parker was preparing *Midnight Express* (1978), while Badham's next film would be a remake of *Dracula* (1979)—and devote two years of their careers to *Star Wars*. Both men figured directing a *Star Wars* sequel was a no-win proposition: If the film failed, the director would be blamed; if it succeeded, credit would go to Lucas, not the director. Sadly, this proved to be true (see Chapter 18).

Lucas also considered replacing another key member of the team: Kurtz. He was disappointed that Kurtz hadn't taken a stronger hand in dealing with troublesome crew members in England, particularly director of photography Gil Taylor, and believed Kurtz had left too many other issues for him to resolve. Kurtz, who had been with Lucas since *American Graffiti*, appealed to the director's sense of loyalty and retained his position. To replace Taylor, Lucas and Kurtz selected Peter Suschitzky, who had photographed *The Rocky Horror Picture Show* (1975), among many other films. For other key posts, Lucas rehired costume designer John Mollo and makeup supervisor Stuart Freeborn, both *Star Wars* veterans, and promoted Norman Reynolds, who served as art director on the first film, to production designer. Originally, Lucas wanted to bring back production designer John Barry, but Barry was unavailable. He had capitalized on his *Star Wars* acclaim by landing a gig directing the sci-fi adventure *Saturn 3*, which was based on a story he had written. As it turned out, Barry would be back sooner than anyone expected.

From Guinness to Oz

Securing a cast was comparatively straightforward. Most of the principal players had signed multipicture deals in the first place. The notable exceptions were Sir Alec Guinness and Harrison Ford. Guinness, despite his discomfort with the popular frenzy generated by *Star Wars*, was grateful for the financial rewards the film had brought him and was willing to return as Obi-Wan Kenobi. However, he had developed a serious infection that degraded the vision in his left eye, a condition exacerbated by exposure to bright lights (like those used on a film set). It was unclear, throughout most of the time *Empire* was shooting, whether or not Guinness would be able to participate in the sequel. Ford indicated his willingness to return as Han Solo early on but refused to sign for more than one picture at a time. Ford's reluctance to commit to a third *Star Wars* film was the primary reason for the Han Solo cliff-hanger at the end of *The Empire Strikes Back*. The picture had to be written so that the story could continue with or without Ford's participation in a third film.

There were few major new characters in the film, but one of those—Lando Calrissian—was particularly important. If Han Solo didn't return, Lando would serve as a substitute. Although the character was written without

any specific ethnicity, Lucas decided to hire an African American actor for the role, in response to critics who had accused *Star Wars* of being racist since it featured no black cast members (aside from the uncredited James Earl Jones as the voice of Darth Vader). Kurtz, Lucas, and the film's casting team considered African American performers Howard E. Rollins Jr., Terry Alexander, Robert Christian, and Thurman Scott for the part, but ultimately chose Billy Dee Williams, who had the most experience and highest profile of the candidates. Among the thirty credits on Williams' resume were costarring roles with James Caan in *Brian's Song* (1971), with

Stung by accusations of racism, since *Star Wars* had featured an all-white leading cast, George Lucas cast Billy Dee Williams as "river boat gambler" Lando Calrissian.

Diana Ross in *Lady Sings the Blues* (1972), and with Richard Pryor and James Earl Jones in *The Bingo Long Traveling All-Stars and Motor Kings* (1976). Williams was a versatile actor whose suave screen presence was perfect for Lucas' smooth-talking riverboat gambler.

Jeremy Bulloch, a former British soap opera star, was hired to play Boba Fett. Kenny Baker's cabaret partner, Jack Purvis, who had played the lead Jawa in *Star Wars*, was asked to play the lead Ugnaught in *The Empire Strikes Back*. Clive Reville, a veteran British stage and screen character player, was hired to make a cameo as the emperor. (In the Special Edition version of *The Empire Strikes Back*, Reville was replaced by actor Ian McDiarmid, who assumed the role in *Return of the Jedi*.)

By far the most difficult role to cast was Yoda. In those pre-CGI days, there was great consternation and debate over how the character should be realized. Numerous options were considered. Stop-motion animation was

The most important new character in *The Empire Strikes Back* was Yoda, a puppet operated by Frank Oz. Before hitting on this method for creating the elfin Jedi master, George Lucas and his ILM team considered numerous other possibilities, including using a trained monkey.

ruled out because no one believed the process would be feasible for such a prominent character. Hiring a midget or child actor was considered, but no one could think of a performer with the acting chops the role required, especially given the difficulty of appearing under heavy makeup. The production's brain trust even floated the idea of using a trained monkey in a costume. Finally, it was decided that the best solution was to use a puppet—or, more specifically, a Muppet. Henson Studio loaned Lucas the services of puppet-maker Wendy Midener, who assisted Stuart Freeborn in designing the pint-sized, green, eight-hundred-year-old Jedi master. Yoda's features emulated both Albert Einstein and *Seven Samurai* star Takashi Shimura, but he most closely resembled Freeborn. To operate the puppet and provide the voice for the character, Lucas and Kurtz signed Henson Studio mainstay Frank Oz, whose Muppet characters included Miss Piggy, Fozzie Bear, and Animal. It was probably the wisest decision Kurtz and Lucas made while casting the film. Oz was a unique talent whose subtle, multifaceted work brought not only believability but a surprising emotional richness to the character.

From Finse to Borehamwood

The other major decision to be made was where to shoot the film. Despite the difficulties he had encountered while making *Star Wars*, Lucas decided to return to EMI-Elstree Studios in Borehamwood, outside London, for principal photography. The devaluation of the British pound had taken some of the sting out of the cost overruns on the first film, saving the production $500,000. It was hoped that exchange rates would remain favorable, making it more cost-effective to shoot in England than in Hollywood. Since Lucas was self-funding, controlling costs was essential; by December 1978, the film's budget already had swollen from $15.5 million to $18 million to $21.5 million. Black Falcon, the Lucasfilm licensing subsidiary and cash cow, had already loaned the production $400,000 (and ILM another $100,000) to cover some of these increases and would continue to pump money into *Empire*.

No studio in Hollywood had enough available studio space to accommodate *Empire* anyway. Actually, EMI didn't either. However, Lucas and company struck a complicated agreement with the studio whereby Lucasfilm funded construction of a new oversized soundstage, built to customized specifications. EMI owned and maintained the space, and eventually repaid Lucasfilm the construction costs as the stage was rented out to later productions.

Unfortunately, not everything could be shot at Borehamwood. The opening Hoth sequence would require an actual snowy location. Since the script described a terrain without trees (rather than, say, an Alpine forest), production designer Norman Reynolds and John Barry (Reynolds' former boss, working as a consultant) spent the early part of 1978 scouting locations in Northern Europe, including places in Finland, Lapland, and Sweden. The most promising location was atop a magnificent six-thousand-foot-elevation blue ice glacier in Finse, Norway. It was a popular site for cross-country skiing, with a lodge and other infrastructure nearby. Later, Lucas, Kurtz, Kershner, and other insiders visited and approved the site. An advance crew arrived and began preparing the site for filming in late January, about six weeks ahead of shooting. Barry and associate producer Robert Watts scouted locations in central Africa for the Dagobah scenes. But, in another cost-containment measure, those scenes were moved to one of EMI's enormous soundstages. This was probably just as well, since McQuarrie's production paintings looked more like Louisiana than the Congo.

Everything seemed to be in order as the start of production approached. Then disaster struck. A fire broke out during production of director Stanley Kubrick's *The Shining* (1980), which was also being filmed at EMI. The studio's Stage 3—home of *The Shining*'s Overlook Hotel set—burned to the ground. In the aftermath, Kubrick's picture took over several other stages, which were slated for use by *Empire*. And Kubrick, as usual, was running behind schedule; principal photography on *The Shining* ran on for almost a year. As a result, *Empire* was pressed for studio space, and set construction ran behind schedule throughout the shoot.

Still, Lucas had met his deadline. *The Empire Strikes Back* went into production March 5, 1979, in Norway. That's when the real problems began.

17

Our Most Desperate Hour

Production of *The Empire Strikes Back*

eorge Lucas literally bet the farm on *The Empire Strikes Back*.
In September 1978, working through a corporate intermediary, Lucas acquired the seventeen-hundred-acre Bulltail Ranch in rural Marin County, California. Prophetically enough, the place was located on Lucas Valley Road, named for an early settler unrelated to George Lucas. The new owner had grand designs for transforming the property into what he referred to as a "filmmaker's retreat," with film editing and sound design studios, screening rooms, and a new Lucasfilm corporate headquarters, all housed in a bucolic farm setting. He wanted it to continue as a viable ranch too, with vineyards, orchards, and grazing lands. Over time, Lucas would buy thousands of adjoining acres and invest hundreds of millions of dollars in pursuit of this vision.

Lucas' filmmaker's retreat was more than just another business investment. It was the tangible expression of his grandest aspirations. Once complete, he dreamed that the as-yet-unnamed center (later dubbed Skywalker Ranch) would serve as a catalyst for film innovation, both technological and artistic. He imagined it as the hub of a counter-Hollywood film community, a collaborative enclave where filmmakers could create works of artistic merit without groveling for studio support or countenancing the meddling of bean-counting executives. His vision had all the idealism of Francis Ford Coppola's struggling American Zoetrope venture, but with the sound financial footing Coppola lacked. Or rather, it had a *potentially* sound financial footing—*if* his *Star Wars* films continued to return handsome profits. If *The Empire Strikes Back* flopped, since he was self-funding the picture, Lucas stood to lose the future Skywalker Ranch and everything else he owned, everything he dreamed of creating. His would be the most meteoric rise and fall in movie history.

Adding to Lucas' anxiety was the realization that, this time, he would not be personally overseeing day-to-day production. He was forced to trust that his handpicked emissaries—producer Gary Kurtz and director Irvin Kershner—would deliver a quality product on time and on budget, or at least close to on time and nearly on budget. Unfortunately, *Empire* was immediately beset by problems no one foresaw and proved to be an even more difficult and far more expensive production than *Star Wars*.

Snowbound

Like *Star Wars*, production of *The Empire Strikes Back* began on location. But, as difficult as shooting in Tunisia had been on the first film, it was a day at the beach compared to filming in Finse, Norway. Ordinarily, early March brought warmer temperatures and the beginning of spring to Northern Europe. The *Empire* crew arrived in Norway with crates full of fake snow, just in case. These were not required. Europe was in the grip of its harshest winter in decades, with subzero temperatures and heavy snow lingering into April.

An advance team had prepared two primary shooting areas: one (nicknamed Camp Kurtz) was located atop the magnificent six-thousand-foot-elevation Hardangerjokulen Glacier, the other halfway up the ascent. Insulated sheds with heaters and other equipment had been installed, but when Kurtz, Kershner, and the rest of the *Empire* company arrived the first week of March 1979, none of these sites or equipment was available. They were all buried in snow. Kershner quickly learned that he could not plan any activity more than a few hours in advance due to the sudden, violent whiteout snowstorms that blew in and blanketed the area for hours and sometimes days at a time. One of those hit Sunday, March 4—the day before shooting was scheduled to begin.

The only actors on the call sheet for the Finse location were Mark Hamill, Peter Mayhew, Denis Lawson (who played Luke Skywalker's wingman, Wedge Antilles), and Des Webb (who appeared inside the Wampa snow monster costume). Carrie Fisher also made the trip, even though she wasn't scheduled to appear, to support Hamill and because she loved to travel. Unable to reach either planned shooting location, Kershner decided to film immediately outside the ski lodge where he and the rest of the company were headquartered. The first day, he filmed Luke staggering and collapsing in the snow after escaping the cave of the Wampa. Although the huge lodge was just a few yards behind him, with the camera facing the banked snow, it looked like Luke was miles from civilization. Although the snow had briefly subsided, allowing Kershner to work, conditions remained terrible—windy, with temperatures ten to twenty degrees below zero Fahrenheit. Camera lenses repeatedly frosted over, and the film sometimes froze and broke while the camera operator changed magazines.

Then it began snowing again and didn't let up for days. Finse, a tiny village with a population of less than one hundred in the off-season, accessible primarily by train, was cut off from the rest of the world when avalanches buried the tracks in snow. Camp Kurtz remained inaccessible. The first unit had only been scheduled to shoot in Norway for one week; Kurtz, Kershner, and Hamill were due back in London for the start of studio filming on Monday, March 12. The director realized that he would be unable to capture most of the footage he came to shoot. The missing shots would have to be faked in the studio or picked up later by a second unit, which would remain in Norway after Kershner's departure.

To try to salvage something from the trip, Kershner summoned Harrison Ford to Finse to shoot the scene where Han Solo saves Luke's life during a snowstorm. This sequence, originally scheduled for filming indoors at EMI, could be shot right outside the hotel. Filming it now would free up a slot in the schedule that could be used to make up some of the location scenes Kershner was forced to abandon. Ford undertook the arduous journey and arrived on March 7, making the last part of the trip in the engine cabin of a locomotive snowplow sent to clear the avalanche. He disembarked in Finse

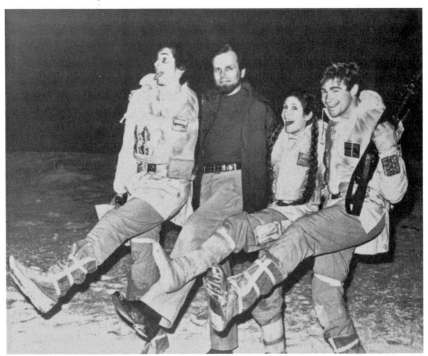

The Empire Strikes Back was a long and tedious shoot, but cast and crew still managed to have fun (at least some of the time). Here producer Gary Kurtz and star Carrie Fisher, center, flanked by a pair of extras, make like the Rockettes.

around midnight, after having downed a bottle of vodka with the engine driver. A bleary-eyed Ford reported for work at 6:00 a.m. the next morning and labored outside in subzero weather in a costume that had been designed for shooting under the hot studio lights. To put it mildly, this lent authenticity to the scene in which Han and Luke fight for survival on the ice planet Hoth.

The first unit stayed through the weekend in Finse, returning to EMI-Elstree Studios in Borehamwood one day late, on Tuesday, March 13. Over the weekend, Kershner shot footage of the Wampa and of Ford and Hamill riding full-size mock-ups of Hoth's beasts of burden and the Tauntaun, among other scenes. The second unit remained in Norway for another thirty days to shoot the huge battle scenes that, with the addition of visual effects, would provide the highlight of *Empire*'s opening act. Eventually, the crew dug out Camp Kurtz and the other site, but work at those locations remained dangerous and uncomfortable. Temperatures sometimes plummeted to thirty below, and the crew and the large number of extras and stuntmen hired for these scenes had to remain alert for sudden snowstorms. If anyone had become lost in a storm, their chances of survival were slim. In the end, only two minor injuries were reported. There were lesser privations, as well. By the time lunch arrived at Camp Kurtz, the hearty meatball stew was frozen solid. And, Kershner reported, it was very difficult to use the bathroom while wearing so many layers of clothing. The second unit finally rejoined the rest of the company in England on April 7.

The Kershner Touch

George Lucas flew to England to observe the first week of production at EMI-Elstree Studios in Borehamwood. He found the studio still in disarray following a fire that had engulfed its Stage 3 while director Stanley Kubrick was filming *The Shining* (see previous chapter). *The Empire Strikes Back* was supposed to take over all eight EMI stages, but Stage 3 was being rebuilt, the immense new soundstage Lucasfilm was funding remained under construction, and Kubrick was still filming his long-overdue *Shining* on other stages. Production designer Norman Reynolds' crews were unable to begin building many of the huge and elaborate sets *Empire* required. It immediately became apparent that the movie would exceed its planned seventy-six-day shooting schedule. Kershner later told publicist Alan Arnold that he had never signed off on the original schedule anyway, because he considered it unrealistic. Now the question became, how late would *Empire* run, and how much would it cost? Kurtz added an extra month to the shooting schedule and hoped it would be enough. It wasn't.

A week later Lucas, who had promised Kershner a free hand in the making of *Empire*, crossed his fingers and returned to California. Before leaving, however, he, Kurtz, and Kershner reviewed the footage from Finse. They all agreed it looked great, but there was disappointingly little of it. This would become a pattern for the remainder of the production as various circumstances conspired to slow filming.

One of the contributing factors was Kershner's methods. Everything he shot looked beautiful, but this was because Kershner worked much more methodically and meticulously than Lucas, using many more complicated camera setups and dolly shots. Kershner had storyboarded the entire film (not just the visual effects scenes) in advance and clung to his plans. Lucas preferred to improvise in the moment, according to each day's demands. Kershner also held shots longer than Lucas, introducing action through dynamic blocking and moving characters around within the frame. Lucas had used shorter, simpler shots, covering a scene from several angles, preferring to create a sense of action through the use of quick cuts during the editing of the film. His camera rarely moved. And, in general, when push came to shove, Lucas was willing to sacrifice aesthetic quality for production efficiency. Kershner was not. As the shoot wore on, this became a point of contention—not between Lucas and Kershner, but between Lucas and Kurtz. Lucas wanted Kurtz to press Kershner to speed up. Kurtz did not think it was his business to tell Kershner how to do his job, especially not since Kershner's product looked so good.

Kershner's approach also differed from Lucas' in other respects. Lucas provided very little guidance to his cast and, for the most part, stuck to the screenplay as written. Kershner was far more collaborative with the actors and often revised dialogue or made other changes based on their input or his own ideas. For instance, it was Kershner's idea to have C-3PO interrupt Han and Leia's romantic interlude aboard the *Millennium Falcon*. As scripted, Leia was supposed to simply pull away from Han. Threepio blundering in not only made the scene more believable, but injected some humor.

However, the director's flexibility could be a two-edged sword. Before filming the scene in which Han is frozen in carbonite, Kershner met with Ford to touch up Han's dialogue. Originally, when Leia tells Han, "I love you!" Han was supposed to answer, "I love you too." Ford suggested that Han simply say, "I know." Kershner loved that line and made the change. But this upset Fisher, who didn't understand why Kershner had met with Ford and not with her. Wasn't this her scene too? Later, when Lucas saw the dailies, he was also unhappy and complained that there wasn't supposed to be a laugh in this sequence. It was one of the few times Lucas questioned Kershner's

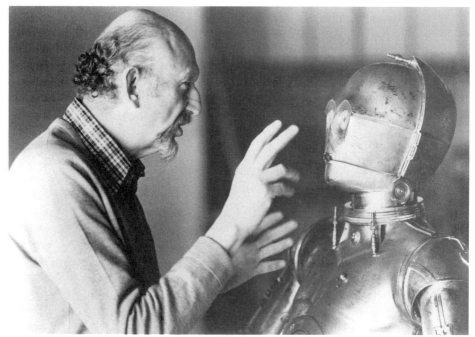

Meticulous director Irvin Kershner (seen here with Anthony Daniels as C-3PO) worked more closely with his cast than George Lucas, eliciting much better performances, but fell dangerously behind schedule.

judgment. Kershner stood his ground, Lucas let it pass, and Han's "I know" became one of the movie's most quotable moments.

To mitigate the schedule impact of Kershner's deliberate shooting style, Kurtz and Kershner split *Empire* into multiple units. This began April 5, when the primary unit led by Kershner began shooting on the Cloud City set, while a second unit, directed by Kurtz, shot additional scenes on the Hoth sets. (Yet another unit was still shooting in Finse at the time.) Whenever a new set became available, Kershner would film on it first, capturing most of the dialogue scenes. Then he would move on to the next soundstage, leaving the second unit to capture any action or visual effects–oriented sequences planned for the set he had just vacated. Later a third and even a fourth unit were added, all working simultaneously on various EMI soundstages. Director of Photography Peter Suschitzky bicycled from building to building with a walkie-talkie, trying to keep up with it all.

Personnel Problems

Despite the problems Kurtz and Lucas had faced with the EMI crew during the filming of *Star Wars*, most of the technicians who had worked on the original film were brought back for the sequel. There was less tension between the filmmakers and the crew this time, perhaps because the older Kershner (then fifty-five) was better able to command the respect of the crew. Following the sensational performance of the first movie, the crew also better understood, and had more faith in, the project they were working on.

Former production designer John Barry, who had left the *Star Wars* team to direct *Saturn 3*, unexpectedly returned to *The Empire Strikes Back* on May 15. Barry had clashed with star Kirk Douglas and producer Stanley Donen on *Saturn 3*, and Donen had replaced him at the helm of that ill-fated sci-fi thriller (see Chapter 13). Barry took over direction of the second unit, but was suddenly taken ill and died on June 1, at age 44. When the medical examiner's report revealed that the cause of death was infectious meningitis, everyone Barry had interacted with had to be screened for the disease. Fortunately, no one else had contracted it. The production took a day off to attend Barry's funeral.

While the rapport among the director, producer, and the crew improved, the relationship between the filmmakers and the cast—and between individual cast members—became strained. *The Empire Strikes Back* was a longer and more strenuous production than the first film, and the easy camaraderie that had carried the cast through the original was not sustainable. All the stars clashed with Kershner at one point or another, and tempers sometimes flared. In an interview with *Starlog* magazine, Hamill said making *Empire* was "nine months of torture for me."

Star Wars had irrevocably altered the lives of Hamill, Ford, and Fisher. They were different people now, and they all felt immense pressure to live up to *Star Wars*. Hamill had married dental hygienist Marilou York, who accompanied him during production. The couple's first child, Nathan, was born in England on June 25. The next day, Hamill, who performed most of his own stunts, severely sprained his thumb while shooting one of the Hoth battle scenes and was forced to miss a week's work. He was happy to spend time with his newborn son, but frustrated that the filming of his climactic lightsaber duel with Darth Vader had to be postponed. Hamill had been taking fencing lessons for eight weeks to prepare for the sequence. Meanwhile, Ford was in stormy temper, having recently separated from his wife, the former Mary Marquardt. They would soon divorce. Fisher's personal life had become tabloid fodder, and she was besieged by paparazzi and gossip reporters throughout her time in England. She also suffered physically with bouts of bronchitis and the flu, as well as the effects of her ongoing drug use, which left her weary and irritable. Then, on June 11, shortly before Carrie Fisher was due to finish her work on the film, Debbie Reynolds received a kidnap

Carrie Fisher and Billy Dee Williams on set at EMI Studios in Borehamwood, England, during the shooting of *The Empire Strikes Back.*

threat against her daughter. Carrie Fisher hired security guards to follow her around during her final week at Borehamwood.

David Prowse was becoming an irritant. The actor remained offended that his voice had been dubbed by James Earl Jones. Now aware that his voice track would not be used, he began to alter Vader's dialogue for comical effect—referring to asteroids as "hemorrhoids," for instance. He had already annoyed Lucasfilm leadership by appearing at science fiction conventions, where he charged money to sign photographs of Darth Vader and sometimes revealed inside information about the new film. Maintaining secrecy about the plot of *The Empire Strikes Back*—in particular about the revelation of Luke's true relationship with Vader—remained a paramount concern. The screenplay was printed on difficult-to-photocopy red paper, and each copy had an individual watermark to indicate, if a script were leaked, whose document had been released. During the filming of the climactic Luke-Vader duel, Prowse was given a script with phony lines ("Obi-Wan killed your father!"). Prowse didn't learn that Vader was Luke's father until he attended press screenings of the finished film and was livid when he realized he had been given bogus dialogue. (Ironically, during convention appearances in London and California in 1977 and '78, Prowse had joked about Vader secretly being Luke's father.)

Then there was Guinness, whose status remained unclear throughout most of the shoot. Kershner made tentative plans to proceed with Ben Kenobi appearing in voice only. Some of the dialogue written for Kenobi was cut, while other lines were given to Yoda. Doctors finally gave Guinness the green light to return to work in late August. His entire performance was filmed in a single three-hour session on September 5.

Reversal of Fortune

By then, *Empire* was in serious financial trouble. On May 20, the production was one day behind schedule. By June 25, it was twenty-six days over. By August 24, it was fifty-two and a half days over. Ultimately production of *The Empire Strikes Back*, originally slated for seventy-six days, would run for six months. Every day was extremely costly. Between London and California, *Empire* had a total of up to three hundred cast and crew members on payroll, with costs running as high as $100,000 per day. On May 26, *Variety* reported that Fox had presold $26 million in guaranteed bookings for the film, but this was well short of the number the film would have to earn for Lucas to break even on his investment.

In May, Lucas went to Bank of America, the lender through which he had financed the film, and obtained an extra $5 million, bringing the budget to $26 million. But that still wasn't enough, and when Lucas tried to secure an additional $6 million in July, he was rebuffed. Bank of America, which had lost a bundle financing Francis Ford Coppola's *Apocalypse Now* when that picture's budget ballooned from $12 to $32 million, refused to loan Lucas another dime. Making matters worse, the *Star Wars* team had learned on June 27 that Alan Ladd Jr., the franchise's champion at Twentieth Century-Fox, was leaving the studio for Warner Brothers. Black Falcon, Lucasfilm's licensing arm, loaned *Empire* another $500,000 but couldn't bridge the budget gap. Lucas feared he might be forced to sell the franchise back to Fox to obtain the funds necessary to complete *Empire*. Fox executives, still stinging from the spanking Lucas gave them during contract negotiations, began licking their chops.

Lucas, who had made periodic, brief visits to EMI since departing for California in early March, returned to England July 16, intending to remain on hand through the final push toward completion. When he left on August 24, filming still wasn't finished. In the meantime, however, Lucas made a decision: Kurtz was out. Although Kurtz was never removed from the payroll and retained the producer's credit on the picture, Howard Kazanjian flew over to serve as line producer for the remainder of the shoot and retained that post throughout postproduction. Lucas was unhappy with Kurtz not only because he was unable to spur Kershner to move with greater speed, but because he had grossly underestimated production costs. Kurtz had projected a 15 percent cost increase in building materials and other basic items needed for the making of *Empire*. But inflation, caused in part by the Oil Crisis of the late 1970s, had driven these costs up 20 to 30 percent. The strengthening British pound also hurt the budget. *Star Wars* had saved a half a million dollars because of a friendly exchange rate, but *Empire* would lose nearly $800,000 because of unfavorable rates. Lucas felt Kurtz should have foreseen and planned for these contingencies. Kurtz resented being brushed aside and left Lucasfilm the following year, joining Jim Henson to coproduce *The Dark Crystal* (1982).

Removing Kurtz did nothing to alleviate the picture's financial crisis, however. "Everything I own, everything I've ever earned, is wrapped up in this picture," Lucas told publicist Alan Arnold on July 19. "If it isn't a success, not only could I lose everything, but I could also end up being millions of dollars in debt. . . . It would probably take me the rest of my life to get back even again." Finally, in late July, Lucas was able to secure up to $25 million of additional financial support from First National Bank of Boston. However, since all Lucas' personal assets were already leveraged, First National would disperse the funds only if Fox agreed to secure the loan. Fox was willing to do this, but in exchange demanded that Lucas give the studio a bigger cut of the profits from *Empire* and accept more studio-friendly terms for his third *Star Wars* film. Even though he felt humiliated, Lucas agreed. At least he would be able to finish *Empire*, and he retained ownership of the franchise.

It remained unclear, however, whether or not he would actually make any money off the picture. In the end, production of *The Empire Strikes Back* would cost just over $30.4 million, nearly triple *Star Wars*' cost. Lucas also had to pay Fox a $20 million distribution fee, plus better than $6 million in interest to Bank of America and First National. In sum, *Empire* needed to make at least $57 million for Lucas to break even. That was more than any previous sequel in film history.

Saving Grace

The Empire Strikes Back wrap party was held August 31 (with picnic tables set up on the Dagobah swamp set), but filming continued into mid-September. Hamill finally finished work on the film September 11, 1979. He was the last member of the principal cast remaining. He spent his final month working on the huge Dagobah set, which featured a three-foot-deep lake, authentic mud and slime, and scores of live snakes (including a twenty-five-foot anaconda). Frank Oz performed as Yoda for twelve days, but Hamill could seldom make out a word the puppeteer was saying because he worked from under the soundstage.

Empire's saving grace was that postproduction ran far more smoothly than it had on *Star Wars*. With the picture running so far behind schedule, Kershner began shipping film to California in May so that Lucas and editor Paul Hirsch could begin assembling the footage. As a result, the first rough cut of the film was ready two weeks after shooting wrapped. New cuts, incorporating more visual effects as they were completed, followed about every two weeks.

With Lucas personally bulldogging the operation, Industrial Light & Magic had completed sixty-six visual effects shots by the time principal photography wrapped. That wasn't many—the screenplay called for more than four hundred effects shots—but it was much better than the one or two that were finished when *Star Wars* had gone into postproduction three years earlier. Lucas had worked in concert with Kershner to prune the screenplay so that ILM didn't waste its resources creating effects shots that would no longer be needed.

Even with Kershner now in California, all major decisions at ILM ran through Lucas, and his sign-off was required on all completed effects shots. ILM developed a new and improved motion-controlled camera, dubbed the Empireflex, as well as the new Quad Optical Printer, which was capable of integrating a greater number of visual elements in the same shot than had ever been composited before. This was necessary for the Hoth battle and asteroid field sequences. Beginning in May, ILM split into two shifts, as it had on the first movie, with teams working nearly around the clock to deliver the shots required. The AT-AT attack sequence and the stop-motion shots of the moving Tauntauns presented the greatest difficulty. The ILM team also had to cope with new headaches. Even though the studio's location was supposed to be a secret (the nondescript building was labeled The Kerner Co.), fans figured out where it was and began digging through the trash looking for souvenirs. As a result, all discarded documents had to be shredded, and film outtakes could not be thrown away.

By October 29, Lucas felt confident enough in *Empire*'s progress to fly to Japan for a meeting with director Akira Kurosawa. Lucas and Coppola had agreed to executive-produce Kurosawa's new samurai epic *Kagemusha* (1980). While all this was going on, Lucas was simultaneously engaged with *Raiders of the Lost Ark*, which director Steven Spielberg began shooting at EMI as soon as *Empire* left.

Other postproduction chores proceeded without serious incident. Pickups and reshoots were filmed in January 1980. These included the shot of R2-D2 being swallowed by the Dagobah swamp monster. The pond on the Dagobah set was too shallow to stage the sequence at EMI, so it was filmed instead in Lucas' swimming pool. Dubbing took place in February. James Earl Jones' voice once again replaced Prowse's. Actor Jason Wingreen—best remembered for his appearance as the train conductor in the classic *Twilight Zone* episode "A Stop at Willoughby"—looped Jeremy Bulloch's Boba Fett dialogue. Lucas, worried that Yoda would sound too much like Miss Piggy or Grover, considered replacing Frank Oz's voice too. Yoda's lines all had to be looped, since Oz's voice (from under the stage) was muffled and largely incomprehensible. Lucas finally decided that no one else would have the same command of the character as Oz, who rerecorded all his dialogue himself.

Work continued right down to the wire. Lucas was still signing off on effects shots on April 11. *The Empire Strikes Back* was sneak-previewed at San Francisco's Northpoint Theater on April 19. The response was favorable but not as wildly enthusiastic as the one that *Star Wars* had generated in the same cinema three years earlier.

The film's world premiere, held in Washington, D.C., on May 19, doubled as a gala fund-raiser for the Special Olympics. The picture opened nationwide May 21, 1980. Although *Empire* fell short of the box office mark set by its predecessor (see next chapter), it became the year's top-grossing film and one of the highest-earning movies ever made. Lucas recovered his investment within the first three months. The Ranch was saved.

18

Only Now, at the End, Do You Understand

Assessing Episode V (1980)

T he *Empire Strikes Back* became the highest-grossing film of 1980, continued the franchise's winning streak in merchandising sales, and earned mostly favorable reviews. It was a tremendous success by any yardstick—except the standard of its predecessor. *Empire* was one of the highest-earning pictures of all time, yet it fell well short of the original film's numbers. Even though it was a far more polished movie than *Star Wars*, *Empire* was initially viewed—by critics and by many fans—as, at best, a qualified success. It was a picture many people enjoyed but few found entirely satisfying.

In later years, however, after the Original Trilogy was complete and viewers were able to consider the series as a whole, *Empire* began to grow in the esteem of critics and the affection of fans. Repeat, close viewing revealed depths and nuances that escaped many viewers the first time around. Qualities that brought audiences up short when *Empire* was new—its darkness and introspection, and its generally more sophisticated, adult-oriented approach to the series' overarching themes—made it stand out in retrospect. In 2010, it was added to the National Film Registry. The movie's rising reputation reached a high-water mark in 2008 when readers of *Total Film* magazine voted *Empire* No. 1 on its list of the best films ever made. Six years later, readers of the British film magazine *Empire* reached the same conclusion, naming *The Empire Strikes Back* the greatest movie ever made (*The Godfather* finished No. 2 and *Star Wars* No. 6). But to reach these giddy heights, *Empire* overcame fierce headwinds in terms of public perception.

By the Numbers

The Empire Strikes Back was greeted with all the hoopla and excitement you would expect for the follow-up to the highest-grossing movie of all time. It opened May 19, 1980, in 127 theaters (nearly four times the number that had initially booked *Star Wars*), including all the largest houses in the biggest cities. Once again, tickets sold out quickly. *Empire* set opening day house records at 125 of those 127 theaters. Television news crews and newspaper reporters turned out to interview fans, many of them wearing costumes or *Star Wars* T-shirts, waiting in epic lines for admission.

Empire raked in $9.6 million its first week. It reigned as the top box office draw in the United States for eleven of its first thirteen weeks, piling up nearly $147 million by July 31. It failed, however, to generate the volume of repeat business that *Star Wars* had commanded. While it became the highest-grossing picture of 1980, it fell more than $100 million short of *Star Wars*' worldwide take. *Empire*'s lifetime gross, including reissues, stands at $538 million, compared to $775 million for *Star Wars*. Moreover, ticket prices had increased by a full dollar in many cities since *Star Wars* was released three years earlier. This meant that, although *Empire* made a fortune, it sold far fewer actual tickets than *Star Wars*. The inflation-adjusted figures reveal the full extent of the disparity in the two films' earnings: $3 billion for *Star Wars*, $1.5 billion for *Empire*. (Despite the smaller returns, Lucas, through an unprecedented profit-sharing program, paid out $5 million in bonuses to his Lucasfilm staff. Every Lucasfilm employee received a cut.)

The Empire Strikes Back didn't incite the same cultural frenzy that accompanied the first film, but that was to be expected. Whatever its virtues, a second *Star Wars* film could not be the revelation the first one had been. There are no second first times. The movie's soundtrack sold well but didn't scale the pop charts the way John Williams' *Star Wars* score had. Author Don Glut's *Empire Strikes Back* novelization made the *New York Times* Best Seller list, but didn't perform as well as Alan Dean Foster's ghostwritten *Star Wars* novelization. Overall, however, merchandising revenue remained robust, in part because this time Lucasfilm was prepared and brought toys, posters, T-shirts, and other wares to market at the same time as the film. Items featuring Yoda, Darth Vader, and Boba Fett were big sellers.

"Good Junk Food"

It's illuminating to compare the initial critical response to *The Empire Strikes Back* with the welcome *Star Wars* received from reviewers. The first film, during the early weeks of its original release, garnered uniformly glowing reviews. But it suffered a savage backlash by some reviewers later, as *Star Wars* mania swept the country (see Chapter 11). Few critics gave *Empire* the kind of gushing praise that had greeted *Star Wars* in its earliest weeks of release, but the negative reviews were—for the most part—more tempered than those that had blasted the original film. The critics neither loved nor hated *Empire*.

The original posters and newspaper advertisements for *The Empire Strikes Back* were based on the promotional art for *Gone with Wind*, with Han and Leia placed like Rhett Butler and Scarlett O'Hara.

Instead, they seemed to find things in the picture to like and to dislike, in varying measures.

Variety critic James Harwood was one of the film's most avid supporters, writing that "*The Empire Strikes Back* is a worthy sequel to *Star Wars*, equal in both technical mastery and characterization, suffering only from the familiarity with the effects generated in the original and imitated too much by others." Gene Siskel of the *Chicago Tribune* and Roger Ebert of the Chicago *Sun-Times* also gave the movie two enthusiastic thumbs up. But others offered backhanded praise. The *Washington Post*'s Judith Martin called *Empire* "good junk food." Vincent Canby of the *New York Times* wrote that "It's a nice movie" but "not, by any means, as nice as *Star Wars*." He went on to characterize *Empire* as "a big, expensive, time-consuming, essentially mechanical operation." Many critics—like many fans—considered the movie's cliff-hanger ending a letdown. Stephen Godfrey of the Toronto *Globe and Mail* wrote that *Empire* was "not as satisfying as the original. A star war can be an exhausting bit of business, especially when, in the end, it turns out to be something of a cheat." Dave Kehr of the *Chicago Reader* wrote that "mainly it's marking time: the characters take a definite backseat to the special effects, and much of the action seems gratuitous, leading nowhere."

Cast members were still defending the movie three years later. Harrison Ford told publicist John Phillip Peecher, for his book *The Making of Return of the Jedi*, "I figure there was at least $11 worth of entertainment in *Empire*.

So if you paid four bucks and didn't get an ending, you're still seven bucks ahead of the game."

Empire received only four Academy Award nominations—winning for Best Visual Effects and Best Sound but losing Best Art Direction-Set Decoration and Best Score. It was shut out of the major categories, such as Best Picture and Best Director, in which *Star Wars* had been nominated. George Lucas was so incensed by these snubs that he resigned his membership in the Academy of Motion Picture Arts and Sciences. *Empire* performed even worse at most of the other awards venues (see Chapter 35).

The S-Word

While making and promoting *The Empire Strikes Back*, George Lucas, Gary Kurtz, Irvin Kershner, and everyone else associated with the film scrupulously avoided using the S-word. The picture was consistently referred to as "the next chapter in the *Star Wars* saga," never as a "sequel." It seemed as if Lucas and friends were trying to use a Jedi mind trick to convince the audience that *Empire* was something other than a continuation of *Star Wars*. But they had good reason for this.

Underlying many of the negative reviews aimed at *The Empire Strikes Back*, and the Academy's lack of respect for the film, was a lingering prejudice—not against *Star Wars* but against sequels. This attitude also contributed to the overall impression that *Empire*, despite its many obvious strengths, failed to equal *Star Wars*. How could it, when sequels were inherently inferior? While it was in production, *Empire*'s nature as a sequel was also the most-cited reason skeptics gave for the film's possible failure. As strange as it may sound today, in the 1970s sequels were box office poison.

Up to that time, most sequels had been cut-rate retreads of the original, made on smaller budgets and with more modest aspirations. There were exceptions, of course, such as *The Godfather, Part II* (1974) and the James Bond films that followed *Dr. No* (1962). But for every *Bride of Frankenstein* (1935) there were a dozen movies like *Son of Kong* (1933)—superfluous knockoffs rushed to market for the express purpose of milking the final drops from the cash cow. Critics sneered at these pictures, and audiences often viewed them with skepticism. Even if a sequel succeeded, it usually placed a film series on a downward slope. The *Planet of the Apes* movies (which, like *Star Wars*, were also released by Twentieth Century-Fox) provide a prime example. The original 1968 classic was made for just under $6 million and grossed more than $33 million. But Fox invested just $3 million in the first sequel, *Beneath the Planet of the Apes* (1970), which returned $17.5 million. The studio continued tightening the budget with each picture, and grosses continued to dwindle. The final film in the original series, *Battle for the Planet of the Apes* (1973), cost $1.8 million and lost money, earning less than $1 million.

The 1970s were strewn with sequels that failed to match their predecessors in terms of quality, box office appeal, or both, including *French Connection II* (1975), *Look What's Happened to Rosemary's Baby* (1976), *Exorcist II: The Heretic* (1977), *Jaws 2* (1978), and *Beyond the Poseidon Adventure* (1979). Lucas' own *More American Graffiti* (1979) premiered while *The Empire Strikes Back* was in production and sank like a stone. It was his first box office failure since *THX 1138* (1971) and not a good portent for his second *Star Wars* picture.

The Empire Strikes Back changed all that. Its success helped destigmatize sequels and demonstrated the possibilities of developing a coherent cinematic universe. It legitimized Lucas' unorthodox strategy of investing even greater resources in a sequel than in an original film. And it road-tested the now-standard practice of building marketing synergy by linking the release of tie-in merchandise with a movie's (feverishly promoted) premiere. Because it profoundly shifted attitudes toward sequels and set the template for Hollywood's current franchise-oriented approach to moviemaking (especially with regard to genre films), some critics now assert that *The Empire Strikes Back* may have been more influential than *Star Wars*. Writing for the pop culture site Nerdist in 2014, Witney Siebold observed that "*The Empire Strikes Back* has become such a ubiquitous and influential presence in fantasy and sci-fi cultures that it can often seem that, in many ways, we haven't grown since. I watch any and all sequels these days, and I see distant reflections of *Empire* all over them."

All the Ingredients . . . and Quality Filmmaking Besides

At a special holiday screening on July 4, 1979, the *Empire Strikes Back* crew saw the film (in working-cut form) for the first time. Even in this condition, missing nearly all its visual effects and without John Williams' score, the picture generated tremendous excitement. Afterward, stills photographer George Whitear told publicist Alan Arnold that "all the ingredients of the original are there, but this time you've got quality filmmaking besides." Unfortunately, it took a while for many other viewers to grasp what Whitear had recognized.

In its finished form, *The Empire Strikes Back* delivered the same kind of jaw-dropping visual effects and pulse-quickening action sequences that had mesmerized fans of *Star Wars*. If anything, *Empire* outdid the original with its exhilarating AT-AT-versus-snowspeeder Hoth battle sequence and the *Millennium Falcon*'s white-knuckle flight into an asteroid field. Plus, the movie concluded with the most thrilling lightsaber duel of the entire series. Although Lucas didn't direct the film, he had personally overseen its visual

This early sequence from *The Empire Strikes Back*, in which Han Solo (Harrison Ford) rescues Luke Skywalker from freezing to death on the ice planet Hoth, was shot just outside the back door of the hotel where the cast and crew were staying in Finse, Norway, during an epic blizzard that wrecked the location shooting schedule.

effects, editing, and sound design. Composer John Williams returned to write another masterful score, incorporating some powerful new themes, most notably the fearsome "Imperial March." This meant all the original film's core strengths were duplicated. *Empire* looked, sounded, and moved like *Star Wars*, not like a second-rate imitation.

Director Irvin Kershner was responsible for most of the new "quality filmmaking" elements Whitear noted. Under Kershner's painstaking direction, *Empire* emerged—special effects aside—as a much more visually appealing film than *Star Wars*. He composed the film with a careful, painterly eye, lending a glossy yet haunted look to the movie's various environs. The snowy vistas of Hoth seem desolate and foreboding. The bogs of Dagobah are eerie and gray, dotted by giant, gnarled Cypress trees and oozing with snakes, swamp monsters, and even stranger threats. Bespin's Cloud City at first appears to be an art deco Shangri-La adrift in purple clouds and bathed in golden-orange sunlight. But beneath this beautiful surface hides a black, infernal underbelly (the steam-belching carbon freeze chamber and the incinerator into which the hog-like Ugnaughts nearly toss Threepio). Each sequence had a unique texture and color palette.

Thanks to Kershner's more collaborative approach with his cast, and his willingness to revise the screenplay, Luke Skywalker, Han Solo, and Princess Leia all grew into better-rounded, more believable characters. Despite limited screen time, new characters Yoda and Lando Calrissian began with fully realized, complex personalities. Even Chewbacca and the droids seemed to display more emotion. Hamill, Ford, and Fisher gave their best *Star Wars* performances in this film, and Frank Oz (as Yoda) and Billy Dee Williams (as Lando) also delivered accomplished portrayals.

Sadly, however, it would take years for Kershner's contributions to the film to be valued. Most critics seemed to believe that George Lucas had directed the film by remote control. He received most of the credit in positive reviews. On the other hand, critics who were disappointed by *Empire* tended to blame Kershner, not Lucas, for the picture's perceived shortcomings. Even Lucas, while acknowledging Kershner's fine work, remained somewhat dismissive of the director's efforts, complaining that Kersh had needlessly overrun his budget. *Star Wars* movies didn't demand refined craftsmanship, he told biographer Dale Pollock bluntly. "It was just a lot better than I wanted to make it," Lucas said. "And I was paying for it." Fortunately, Kershner lived to see critical and popular acclaim belatedly collect around *The Empire Strikes Back*. Kershner also took pride in the fact that when Lucas released his revamped Special Edition versions of the Original Trilogy in 1997, *Empire* was the movie that changed the least.

Screenwriter Lawrence Kasdan also deserves credit for elevating *Empire* to a new, more polished level. The screenplay, attributed to Leigh Brackett and Kasdan but mostly written by Lucas and Kasdan (see Chapter 16), skillfully balanced action and character development, while growing franchise mythology. The script supplied the kind of adrenaline-pumping thrill sequences fans expected, but Kasdan made the most of the scenario's character interludes, particularly with his deft handling of the developing romance between Han and Leia. The screenplay touched on this relationship in a number of different ways and emotional tones, from playful antagonism on Hoth, to surprising tenderness (turned to comic exasperation) aboard the *Falcon*, and finally to heart-wrenching tragedy in the Cloud City carbon freeze chamber. Elsewhere, the script greatly expanded the mythology of the franchise. Most

To preserve the secret of Luke Skywalker's parentage, actor David Prowse (playing Darth Vader) was given phony dialogue to deliver while performing the film's climactic sequence. The correct words were dubbed in later by James Earl Jones.

of what fans know about the Force originates not in *Star Wars* but here, during the scenes in which Yoda trains Luke. And, of course, it was here that the franchise took on new dimensions with the revelation of Luke's true relationship with Vader. During the film's climactic Vader-Luke lightsaber duel, action, character development, and myth building become inseparable.

The climactic revelation of Luke's parentage inspired passionate debate. Was Vader telling the truth, or was he lying? Even though Kershner shot the sequence in a straightforward way, and despite the fact that Luke refers to Vader as "father" and laments (twice), "Ben, why didn't you tell me?," some viewers found this plot twist hard to accept. Young fans found it particularly difficult to grasp the idea that Vader could truly be Luke's father. A throwaway line in which Yoda reminds the spectral Kenobi that "there is another" hope for the rebellion also sparked a great deal of controversy (see Chapter 19). None of these conversations would have happened if Lucas, Kershner, and Kasdan hadn't created characters audiences cared about.

Star Wars for Grown-ups

Despite the many ways that it equaled or surpassed the original, however, many viewers—initially, at least—could only see the ways in which *Empire* was different from *Star Wars*. While still sprinkled with humor, the sequel was more somber in tone. Though by no means slow-moving, its pace was more deliberate. Perhaps most importantly, it built to a conclusion less definite and more fraught than the triumphant finale of the original. As a result, *The Empire Strikes Back* delivered a very different emotional experience than *Star Wars*. It was a movie more likely to inspire philosophical reflection than cheers of exultation.

Many of these differences were part and parcel of being the middle third of a trilogy. Things inevitably go badly for the heroes in the second part of any three-act story. Other differences stemmed from the more adult, character-driven approach Kasdan and Kershner applied to the material. All the major themes of *Star Wars* remained present, but they were internalized. If anything, the overarching conflict (Dark Side versus Good Side/fear versus compassion—see Chapter 29) becomes more overt in *Empire*. But it's fought out not in a massive space battle, but within hearts and minds of Luke Skywalker and other characters. Luke's climactic showdown with Vader is more than just a laser sword fight. Luke's own fear and hatred are his greatest opponents. Those are things that may lure him down the dark path; Vader can only kill him. Yoda urges Luke to avoid conflict with Vader not because he fears that his Jedi skills aren't good enough, but because he fears his commitment to the Jedi way is not yet strong enough to survive the temptation of the Dark Side. Meanwhile, Luke and Leia struggle to overcome another sort of fear, which has driven both of them to lead lives of emotional isolation. And Lando Calrissian, afraid of losing everything he has built on Bespin (and, charitably, of seeing harm come to the thousands of people under his employ or care), tries to protect himself by striking a bargain with the forces of evil.

When viewed through this lens, the cliff-hanger conclusion of *The Empire Strikes Back* remains wholly satisfying. That's because—although Han is carried away in carbon freeze by Boba Fett, Vader survives, and the fate of the rebellion remains in the balance—all of the dramas-within-the-drama are resolved. Luke faces Vader, receives a potentially spirit-crushing revelation, yet refuses to surrender to either hate or ambition. He remains firm in his understanding of right and wrong, and chooses the path of justice rather than vengeance. Han and Leia, even in the face of death—or worse—commit to each other with a kiss and a vow. And Lando, quickly realizing that a bargain with the devil provides no protection at all, turns the tables on the imperials and begins to make amends with his friends.

Thanks to Lawrence Kasdan's witty dialogue and Irvin Kershner's delicate direction, the romantic interludes between Princess Leia (Carrie Fisher) and Han Solo (Harrison Ford) sparkle with life and humor.

As the movie's box office numbers and critical reception indicate, many of these subtleties failed to register with audiences in 1980. They flew over the heads of young patrons, who were a major part of the franchise's fan base. But they remained present, waiting to reward those who returned to *The Empire Strikes Back* in later years. The movie's more introspective scenario, with characters struggling to make moral choices in a time of suffering and temptation, resonated more strongly with viewers as they aged. *Star Wars* became a sensation because it was the perfect film for its moment. *Empire* endures because its themes are timeless.

In sum, *The Empire Strikes Back* was *Star Wars* for grown-ups. With the final film of the Original Trilogy, Lucas would take the franchise in the opposite direction.

19

The Circle Is Now Complete

Writing *Return of the Jedi*

T he cliff-hanger finale of *The Empire Strikes Back* disappointed many viewers, but it also helped make the third *Star Wars* film arguably the most talked-about and eagerly anticipated movie of all time. Tantalizing story threads were left dangling, puzzling mysteries unsolved. Would Han Solo survive? Was Darth Vader *really* Luke Skywalker's father? Would Luke turn to the Dark Side? Would Vader finally be destroyed? And who was the mysterious "another" mentioned by Yoda? Patrons left movie theaters abuzz with these and other questions. Speculation abounded. Uncounted millions of viewers had become emotionally invested in these characters. For many, the three-year wait between Episodes V and VI seemed interminable. But virtually everyone who had seen *Star Wars* and *Empire* would return for the finale, which George Lucas promised would reveal all the answers and tie up the story's loose ends. First, however, Lucas had to figure out what those answers were.

Franchise downsize

Among the many viewers who were not entirely satisfied with *The Empire Strike Back* was the one whose opinion mattered the most: Lucas. As it took shape, the third *Star Wars* movie would emerge, largely, as a response to the second. Lucas believed that the more introspective, adult approach of *Empire* had proven difficult for the young viewers who had made the original picture so successful, paying to see it again and again and again. He was determined to make the movie eventually known as *Return of the Jedi* more kid-friendly. Lucas also felt that, while a darker tone was necessary for the middle chapter of his trilogy, *Empire* had gone too far in that direction. He was adamant that *Jedi* return to the uplifting spirit of the original film and provide a jubilant, happily-ever-after conclusion to his sci-fi fairy tale. These were not purely calculated marketing decisions. George and Marica Lucas adopted an infant daughter in 1981. Parenthood, as it so often does, may have altered George Lucas' perspective.

Lucas also made another momentous decision: *Jedi* would be the last *Star Wars* film. Or at least the last one for a long, long time.

This, too, was a reaction to *The Empire Strikes Back*—not to the finished movie but to its nerve-wracking production. Before making *Empire*, Lucas believed he could hand the keys to the franchise to a trusted collaborator, step away from day-to-day production chores, and be handed, on time and on budget, a film that met his expectations. Then, as the shooting of *Empire* ran months over schedule and costs shot into the stratosphere, Lucas' career flashed before his eyes. Now he realized that the only way to ensure a project would both meet its budget and perfectly align with his vision was to become more actively involved in the making of the film. He dreaded this prospect.

Originally, Lucas had envisioned a long-running *Star Wars* series as the revenue engine for his growing Lucasfilm empire and the funding source for his dreamed-of "filmmaker's retreat," Skywalker Ranch. With *Empire* finished, he was two chapters into a planned nine-movie series. With three years between each film, Lucasfilm would be releasing *Star Wars* pictures for the next twenty-one years. When he believed he could allow other people to make these movies for him, this seemed like a good thing. Now that he believed his personal participation was required, it became an untenable proposition. Then, in 1982, he and director Steven Spielberg scored a sensational success with *Raiders of the Lost Ark*, which outearned *The Empire Strikes Back*. Lucas suddenly had a second blockbuster franchise in his hip pocket. How many more might he be able to dream up? Perhaps Lucasfilm could thrive without *Star Wars*.

"I don't want to spend the rest of my life making *Star Wars* pictures," Lucas told publicist Alan Arnold, as quoted in his book *Once Upon a Galaxy: A Journal of the Making of The Empire Strikes Back*. This would have major ramifications as he began writing the final chapter of the Original Trilogy.

Solving Riddles

The biggest question left hanging at the conclusion of *Empire* was the fate of Han Solo. Arnold, in his book, ventured that Harrison Ford—who felt unchallenged by his role and wasn't under contract to appear in another *Star Wars* film—would not play Solo again. And Arnold wasn't the only one who thought Ford was finished with the series. Lucas and screenwriter Lawrence Kasdan had created Lando Calrissian as a substitute swashbuckler in the event that Ford opted out of the third film. Shortly after the release of *The Empire*

Strikes Back, however, after some wooing by producer Howard Kazanjian, Ford indicated that he would return. Years later, Ford said that finishing the series simply seemed like the morally correct thing to do.

Then there was the sticky issue of identifying who Yoda meant when he referred to "another" hope for the cause of the rebellion. It is unclear what Lucas and Kasdan had in mind when Yoda's enigmatic line was inserted into the screenplay. Lucasfilm was inundated with letters from fans begging to know who Yoda was talking about. Some suggested that this mysterious person could be Han Solo, or Boba Fett, or a lost sibling of Luke's, or a lost sibling of Luke's disguised as Boba Fett, or Luke's mother, or even his father if Vader were lying (perhaps Vader was a *clone* of Luke's father). There was no shortage of theories.

When Mark Hamill was asked about this issue, he guessed that Yoda was referring to a character that could potentially replace Luke in the final film, if for some reason Hamill was unwilling or unable to return for the picture. Like freezing Han in carbonite, he assumed the line was a cagey play by Lucas to prevent any one performer from holding his franchise hostage. This may even have been true. During his DVD audio commentary for *The Empire Strikes Back*, Lucas says that the "another" reference was "designed to make you feel that Luke is expendable. . . . It's a cheap trick but it works." Author Michael Kaminski, in his book *The Secret History of Star Wars*, makes a convincing argument that the "another" Yoda spoke about was originally intended to be a new character who would be introduced in the third film and become the central figure in Episodes VII through IX. If so, that plan had to be scrapped when Lucas decided to scuttle his Sequel Trilogy. He didn't want to introduce any story elements that might compel him to make further *Star Wars* movies.

In the end, the simplest and most elegant solution to the problem was to reveal that the mysterious "another" was indeed Luke's sibling—namely, Leia. This gambit killed two womp rats with one stone, not only solving the mystery of Yoda's final hope but also definitively resolving the romantic triangle between Han, Leia, and Luke. However, it made some of Luke's earlier scenes with Leia retroactively icky, and also raised some puzzling questions about the birth of Darth Vader's offspring, such as: How did Vader know about his son but not about his daughter? How did Uncle Owen and Aunt Beru fit in? Many of these issues would remain unclear until the release of *Revenge of the Sith* in 2005.

Other major questions were resolved by Lucas' decision to conclude the series with Episode VI. The audience needed to be assured that Luke really was Vader's son and provided with a plausible explanation for why Kenobi had misled Luke about his father's identity. Finally, to underscore that the story was truly over, Vader had to die.

The *Jedi* That Might Have Been

Lucas had all these questions on his mind as he sketched out three story outlines in 1980, and again as he wrote his rough draft screenplay, which he delivered on February 24, 1981. This early version, titled *Star Wars Episode Six Revenge of the Jedi*, was radically different from the final screenplay. In many respects, it was more ambitious and original.

Much of the action in this version centers on the capital planet of the Galactic Empire, here called Had Abbadon (later to be known as Coruscant). The entire planet is a giant, smoggy city, which draws most of its natural resources from a relatively unspoiled forest satellite referred to simply as the Green Moon (this is, essentially, Endor). The Green Moon is home to a race of small, furry primitives who are beneath the notice of the Empire: the "Ewaks." It is also the home to two giant laser cannons that defend the imperial Homeworld. Also orbiting Had Abbadon are two new and even more powerful Death Stars, both still under construction.

On Had Abbadon, Darth Vader is summoned to the chamber of the emperor, an underground lair near the planet's core where the imperial throne is encircled by a pool of bubbling lava. Vader's failure to capture or kill Luke Skywalker on Cloud City has drawn the ire of the emperor, who orders Grand Moff Jerjerrod to have his men capture Luke and bring him to the emperor for training. When Vader protests, the emperor uses the Force to momentarily cut off the Sith Lord's air supply and tells him he is fortunate he is being allowed to live. Vader wants to recruit Luke to help him overthrow the emperor; the emperor wants Luke to replace Vader as his hatchet man.

Meanwhile, Princess Leia and a rebel strike team led by Captain Jode makes a secret landing on the Green Moon. They plan to take over the laser cannons, using them to fire on Had Abbadon itself, taking out the force field generator protecting the two Death Stars, and cutting off communications between the space stations and the homeworld. Then, at a prearranged time, the rebel fleet will drop out of hyperspace and destroy the Death Stars. The previous flaw in the Death Star design has been eliminated, so the space stations must be destroyed before they are completed.

Across the galaxy on Tatooine, Luke, Lando, Chewbacca, and the droids rescue Han from the clutches of Jabba the Hutt in much the same manner as in the finished film (although without Leia's help). Luke's battle with the Rancor Monster and the death of Jabba at the Sarlacc Pit are already present in this early version. Next, Luke, Han, and the rest of the gang fly the *Millennium Falcon* to the Grass Planet of Sicemon, where the rebel fleet is massing for the impending attack. On the way, Ben Kenobi and Yoda appear to Luke in a dream. Kenobi explains that Vader was "murdered by the Dark

Luke Skywalker (Mark Hamill) and Chewbacca (Peter Mayhew), improbably, are taken prisoner by the Ewoks in *Return of the Jedi*.

Side" and reveals that Leia is Luke's twin sister. Luke must face Vader again, they say. Kenobi also explains that his time in the Netherworld is running out; he must either return to material form or else become one with the Force. For now, he will remain in the Netherworld and attempt to cloud Vader's ability to use the Force. Yoda has joined Kenobi in the Netherworld and will do the same to the emperor.

On Sicemon, Han learns the details of the rebel plan and wants to rush there to help Leia. Admiral Ackbar cautions against this, as does Luke (at first). Then, while constructing a new lightsaber, Luke has a vision that the attack will fail; Leia is in danger. Luke, Han, Chewie, and the droids rush to the Green Moon in the *Falcon*. On the Green Moon, Leia meets and befriends the Ewaks. As in the finished film, Vader senses Luke as he nears the moon. Luke, Han, Chewie, and the droids are pursued by imperial troops, including a two-legged AT-ST "Chicken Walker." Luke, realizing that his presence poses a threat to the mission, surrenders, enabling the others to escape. He is taken to Grand Moff Jerjerrod, but before Jerjerrod can take him to the emperor, Vader appears. Vader kills Jerjerrod, strangling him with the Force, and takes Luke to the emperor himself.

The final showdown takes place in the subterranean imperial throne room, while on the Green Moon, the Ewaks help the rebels capture the laser cannons and the assault on the Death Stars commences. Luke, aided by Yoda and Kenobi, faces the emperor and Vader. Kenobi and Yoda appear to both Vader and the emperor, and urge them to surrender. Kenobi tells the emperor, "There is no entrance to the Netherworld through the Dark Side." Nevertheless the emperor forces Vader and Luke to fight one another. The emperor tries to goad Luke into turning to the Dark Side to defeat Vader. Luke is too strong for Vader and eventually defeats him, but he refuses to kill. Vader, realizing that his plan has failed, and incensed that the emperor has schemed to try to replace him with his son, launches himself bodily at the emperor. The two of them tumble into the lava and are destroyed. Above, the rebels destroy the Death Stars. The Empire has fallen.

Afterward, the rebels and the Ewaks hold a victory celebration on the moon. Kenobi and Yoda return in the flesh to take part in the festivities.

A second rough draft, which Lucas completed June 12, 1981, fine-tuned the scenario, eliminating Luke's dream sequence (instead, Kenobi and Yoda appear to Luke in spirit form on the Green Moon) and renaming the furry primitives Ewoks. More significantly, this draft also changed Vader's motivation for destroying the emperor. Moved by the exhortations of his son, Kenobi, and Yoda, Vader turns away from the Dark Side. He is redeemed rather than simply defeated.

Script Wars

Unfortunately, many of the most exciting and ambitious elements of the draft scenario would fall away as the screenplay continued to evolve. This process began with a series of story conferences held from July 13 through 17, 1981. Participants in this roundtable discussion included Lucas, screenwriter Lawrence Kasdan, director Richard Marquand, and producer Howard Kazanjian. Kasdan, whose directorial career was taking off (his movie *Body Heat* had earned enthusiastic reviews, and he was developing his second film, *The Big Chill*), agreed to return to *Star Wars* out of gratitude to Lucas. Yet he and Lucas clashed repeatedly throughout these sessions, with Kasdan generally trying to push the story in a darker, more adult direction and Lucas continually pulling it back. Marquand generally took Lucas' side, while Kazanjian remained a wild card. A transcript of the highlights of these sessions, published in J. W. Rinzler's book *The Making of Return of the Jedi*, makes for a fascinating read.

When Lucas jokingly suggested that at the end of the film Luke should put on Vader's mask, destroy the Rebel fleet, and proclaim himself the new

Emperor, Kasdan said, apparently in all seriousness, "That's what I think should happen."

"Come on," Lucas scoffed. "This is for kids."

Kasdan also argued at length that *Jedi* should feature the death of a major character. First he suggested that Luke be killed in battle and that Leia become the one who finishes off the emperor. Lucas quickly vetoed that idea. Later, Kasdan suggested killing Han Solo. But Lucas insisted that viewers would feel let down if Han and Leia didn't wind up together. Still later, Kasdan suggested having Lando—and the *Millennium Falcon*—vaporized during the final battle. "I'm trying to give the story some kind of an edge to it," Kasdan explained, as Lucas became exasperated. Lucas remained adamant that "everybody lives happily ever after and nothing bad happens to anybody. . . . The whole emotion I am trying to get at the end of this film is for you to be real uplifted, emotionally and spiritually, and feel absolutely good about life. That is the greatest thing that we could possibly ever do." Eventually, Lucas agreed that Yoda could die, but only of old age and in a life-affirming way, demonstrating that death was a natural part of the Force and not to be feared.

Virtually every story element was up for grabs at one point or another during the five-day conference. Some were deleted, some were added, and others were changed. Kasdan wanted to eliminate the Ewoks, but Lucas insisted they were essential. He cherished the idea of a low-tech, indigenous people overcoming a technologically superior military force. This had been the driving theme of his *Apocalypse Now* screenplay (although little of this concept survived Francis Ford Coppola's rewrites), and it had also figured prominently in early drafts of *Star Wars* (in which the primitives had been Wookiees rather than Ewoks).

Kasdan also suggested eliminating the Death Stars and having the rebels simply mount an assault on the imperial capital. But Lucas, ever the visual thinker, wanted the climax of the film, like the first one, to feature a gigantic explosion. While numerous methods whereby the rebels could destroy Had Abbadon were bandied about, including igniting the planet's smoggy atmosphere, none of them resulted in the climactic fireball Lucas wanted. Besides, Lucas was having second thoughts about Had Abbadon. Bringing the imperial homeworld to the screen meant building a multitude of huge, expensive sets. Instead, he suggested eliminating Had Abbadon and moving the action to one of the Death Stars. Eventually, the second Death Star was also eliminated, both for budgetary reasons and because it seemed redundant. Moving the final battle from the volcanic depths of Had Abbadon to a Death Star meant that the emperor's death had to be slightly changed, since

Neither Carrie Fisher (left) nor Harrison Ford was pleased with the treatment of their characters in the final screenplay for *Jedi*. Ford requested that Han Solo "commit self-sacrifice," but Lucas insisted on a purely happy ending.

he could no longer be tossed into a lava pit. Instead, he would be thrown into "some type of machinery."

Marquand insisted that Luke must return to Yoda on Dagobah, as he had emphatically promised to do in the previous film, so that sequence was added and the Luke-Yoda-Kenobi conversation moved there. The idea of Kenobi and Yoda returning in flesh and blood was abandoned. Kasdan and Lucas also clashed over whether Darth Vader should be redeemed or simply destroyed; Kasdan complained that Lucas' feel-good ending was "wimpy." Finally, Kasdan wanted Vader's unmasked face to be hideously scarred and mangled. Lucas argued that this would visually undercut the character's redemption; Vader should look damaged but not repulsive.

Diminishing *Return*

Kasdan, armed with Lucas' rough draft and a massive transcript of the story conference, duly set about writing a screenplay. He also had input from the film's cast, gathered by Marquand. Mark Hamill suggested that Luke should give in to the Dark Side and use its power to destroy Vader and the emperor, but be lured back to the Good Side by Leia. Harrison Ford wanted Han Solo to "commit self-sacrifice." Carrie Fisher asked that Leia be softened, complaining that the princess came off like "some kind of space bitch" in *The Empire Strikes Back.* Anthony Daniels hoped C-3PO would play a more meaningful role in *Jedi,* after being reduced to comedy relief in *Empire.* Fisher and Daniels, at least, would get what they wanted.

Kasdan turned in his initial *Jedi* screenplay—labeled a second draft, even though no formal first draft had been recorded—on September 21, 1981. This version was extremely close to the finished film in key respects. Had Abbadon is eliminated; the "Green Moon" orbits a planet named Jus-Endor (later shortened to simply Endor). Many lines from the film first appear here, including Kenobi's explanation that he told Luke the truth about his father's fate "from a certain point of view." Kasdan's script also transformed Kenobi from a White Knight into a tragic figure. He blames himself for Vader's fall and the emperor's rise to power, because he foolishly attempted to train young Anakin Skywalker himself. As a result, when Vader is redeemed, so is Kenobi.

This draft, however, was incomplete. It included blank passages for the major battle scenes, which Lucas was designing along with his Industrial

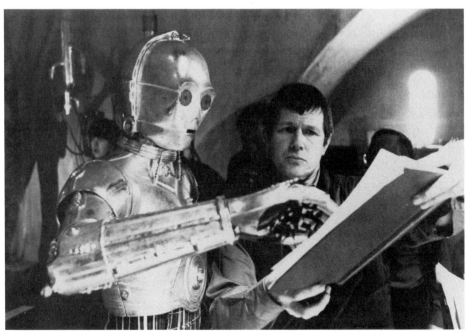

During the early stages of writing *Return of the Jedi,* actor Anthony Daniels (left, as C-3PO) asked director Richard Marquand (right) if Threepio could play a more significant role in the final film of the trilogy. Daniels' wish was granted.

Light & Magic team. Lucas revised Kasdan's draft, filling in those gaps. Then Kasdan polished Lucas' revised version to arrive at the shooting script, which he delivered December 1, 1981. Lucas continued honing the screenplay throughout production. The final dialogue for the Luke-Vader-Emperor duel was written by Lucas during filming.

Before the shooting script could be distributed, however, Kasdan and Lucas had to write some additional scenes—ones they knew would never actually appear on-screen. As part of the *Star Wars* team's extraordinary efforts to ensure the secrecy of the movie's story (see next chapter), fake scenes were written to substitute for those in which Kenobi reveals Leia's true relationship to Luke, and in which the emperor and Vader die. In one of these phony scenes, Luke—rather than Vader—kills the emperor. The real script for these scenes, printed on blue paper, was withheld from the majority of the cast and crew.

In its finished form (blue pages and all), the screenplay eliminated some of the most exciting concepts included in the early drafts, including an assault on the imperial capital. In many ways it repeated the formula from the first movie, beginning on Tatooine and concluding with a space battle and the destruction of a Death Star. *Jedi* also borrowed several other elements from the first two films (see Chapter 21), most notably the climactic Luke-Vader lightsaber duel. As it turned out, there was very little in the third *Star Wars* film viewers hadn't already seen in the first two. The script answered all the lingering questions from *Empire*, but often in the least imaginative ways possible. Even Lucas understood this and seemed resigned to it. In an interview with *Starlog* magazine published prior to the film's release, Lucas explained that *Star Wars* "started out as a simple fairy tale, and that's all it really is. . . . When [*Jedi*] comes out, people will say, 'Oh, my God. How obvious! Why couldn't they think of something more interesting than that?'"

The truth was, they *did* think of something more interesting, but those ideas had been rejected.

20

There Will Be No One to Stop Us This Time

Making *Return of the Jedi*

W ith some trepidation, George Lucas began planning his climactic third *Star Wars* film in the summer of 1980. Caution was warranted. Production of the trilogy's first two installments had been riddled by crises and catastrophes of all sorts. Cost overruns on *Empire* had pushed Lucas to the brink of financial disaster (see Chapter 17). From the outset, Lucas was determined that things would be different with the third picture—which, like *Empire*, he was self-funding. This time, he insisted, the movie would be completed on time and on budget, with no behind-the-scenes drama. In the end, he would have to settle for two out of three.

Lynch Pin

Aside from coming up with a story (see previous chapter), the most important task facing Lucas in these early stages was assembling a crew, beginning with a producer and director. Lucas asked Howard Kazanjian, who had replaced Gary Kurtz as producer of *The Empire Strikes Back* late in filming, to return in that capacity for the concluding film. Kurtz had resigned from Lucasfilm, effective December 11, 1979. Lucas could count on the iron-fisted Kazanjian, unlike the free-thinking Kurtz, to ensure the picture's director would toe the budgetary line. But who would that director be?

By mutual agreement, *Empire* director Irvin Kershner would not return to complete the trilogy. After devoting two years of his life to *Star Wars*, Kershner wanted to return to his own projects. Besides, as much as he admired and respected Kershner, Lucas no longer wanted to collaborate with experienced, strong-willed veterans like his mentor. "We were looking for a director that was rather young, that was flexible, that had not established himself as a great independent filmmaker, that would follow the tradition of *Star Wars*, that would let George be as closely attached as he likes to be on these projects," Kazanjian said in a 1983 interview with *American Cinematographer* magazine. In other words, this time Lucas wanted a director he could control. It was the polar opposite of what he wanted—or thought he wanted—when he asked Kershner to helm *Empire*. Lucas had taken a hands-off approach on that film and watched the project spiral nearly out of control. To prevent that from happening again, Lucas planned to be on set nearly every day of production to provide guidance to his director, and even planned to shoot some second-unit material himself.

Finding a director willing to work with Lucas in that manner wasn't easy. The task was made even more difficult due to a festering conflict between Lucas and the Directors Guild of America. The Guild had fined Lucas $250,000 for placing Kershner's director's credit at the end of *Empire* rather than at the opening. Lucas wanted to maintain a consistent credit format for all the *Star Wars* films and had withheld his own director's credit until the end of the original movie. But the Guild ruled that the opening Lucasfilm logo represented a de facto producer's credit for Lucas, so (according to Guild rules) Kershner had to receive a credit at the beginning too. The Guild issued the fine (which was later reduced by an arbitrator to $25,000) even though Kershner approved placing his credit at the end of the film. Lucas, livid, paid the fine but resigned from the Guild. The upshot of all this was that, unless he went crawling back to the union, it was impossible for Lucas to hire a DGA member to helm *Jedi*. So Lucas' options were limited to non-Guild directors or British filmmakers. This left out his friend Steven Spielberg (who, in any case, was too busy preparing *E.T.: The Extra-Terrestrial*) and scared off other potential candidates who feared running afoul of one of the most powerful trade organizations in Hollywood.

Kazanjian compiled a list of dozens of directors to be contacted about the third *Star Wars* film. Names on the list included relative unknowns such as Canadian John Hough and Englishman Jon Glen, along with well-known filmmakers including Alan Parker and Peter Weir. Lucas and Kazanjian reached out to dozens of candidates, but in the end chose a young American filmmaker—David Lynch, who would later make cult favorites such as *Blue Velvet* (1986) and the TV series *Twin Peaks* (1990–91). Lynch wanted to make a science fiction film, and Lucas had been impressed by the director's first two movies, *Eraserhead* (1977) and *The Elephant Man* (1980). Lucas called Lynch and congratulated him on landing the job, but Lynch called back a few days later to back out. Different sources provide various reasons for why Lynch ultimately declined. Lynch would have had to resign his membership in the DGA and possibly face other repercussions if he directed the film.

He may have had second thoughts about the kind of working relationship Lucas wanted. Or he may have received what he considered a better offer. Shortly afterward, producer Dino de Laurentiis signed Lynch to direct *Dune* (1983), adapted from the Frank Herbert novel that may have been one of the inspirations for *Star Wars* (see Chapter 3). In any case, Lynch's departure was probably for the best. It's difficult to imagine the iconoclastic Lynch and the straitlaced Lucas working together effectively, and Lynch's creepy, subversive style didn't suit *Jedi*—although it's fun to consider what Lynch might have done with the Ewoks.

In Lynch's stead, Lucas opted for his second choice, up-and-coming Welsh filmmaker Richard Marquand (see Chapter 14), who had lobbied hard for the assignment and was elated to win it. Against Kazanjian's advice, Lucas allowed Marquand to select his own cinematographer, Alan Hume, and editor, Sean Barton. Neither had any previous association with *Star Wars* or Lucasfilm. Hume also insisted on shooting with a new Panavision BL3 camera, rather than the old VistaVision equipment that had been used on the first two films. All this would give *Jedi* a slightly different look than its predecessors.

Hard Bargain

Meanwhile, Lucas was trying to nail down financing for the film and to finalize a distribution agreement with Twentieth Century-Fox. The Bank of Boston, which had stepped in to provide completion funds for *The Empire Strikes Back*, agreed to loan The Chapter III Company (the Lucasfilm subsidiary Lucas had formed for the making of *Revenge of the Jedi*) up to $32 million to cover production costs, secured against Lucas' earnings from the first two *Star Wars* films.

Hammering out a deal with Fox was much harder. Alan Ladd Jr. had departed Fox during the making of *The Empire Strikes Back*, and Lucas didn't trust the new studio leadership. Fox executives, on the other hand, felt that Lucas was reneging on his promise to work with them on more studio-friendly terms, a pledge Lucas had made after Fox agreed to secure the funds necessary to complete *Empire*.

When negotiations began in the summer of 1980, Lucas asked Fox to pay a $25 million advance to distribute the film; Fox was willing to pay only $10 million. Another major sticking point was that Lucas, who planned to reissue *Star Wars* and *Empire* theatrically during the run-up to the premiere of *Jedi*, wanted all three films withheld from cable and network television for three years following the release of *Jedi*. Fox wanted to sell the cable and network TV rights to *Star Wars* and *Empire*, which were worth millions, immediately. Over the next year, both sides made offers that were countered and withdrawn. As the negotiation dragged on, additional issues surfaced. Attorneys for the studio argued that, while Lucasfilm by contract owned all sequel rights to *Star Wars*, the studio retained the right to remake the film or to create a *Star Wars* TV series. Lucas' lawyers vehemently denied this, claiming that the term "sequel" covered all possible spin-offs. Later, the two parties haggled over who owned the *Star Wars* characters and their likenesses.

Finally, in September 1981, the frustrated Lucasfilm team informed Fox that it would invoke the "right of first refusal" clause in its contract. Lucas was contractually bound to offer any *Star Wars* sequel to Fox first but was free to take the film elsewhere if Fox declined to distribute it. Fox's inability to come to terms with Lucasfilm, Lucas' attorneys argued, meant that in effect the studio had refused the project; As a result, Lucasfilm was now free to begin shopping the third *Star Wars* film to other studios.

At this point, new Fox majority owner Marvin Davis became involved personally in the negotiations. Davis, an oil magnate with no previous experience in the movie industry, had purchased the studio only months earlier. In late September, Lucasfilm and Fox finally reached an agreement settling all the outstanding issues, including a broadcast holdback for the *Star Wars* films that would last until 1984 (two years sooner than Lucas wanted, but following the premiere of the new movie) and a $2.4 million betterment for the studio on the profits from *Empire*. After the advance was repaid (out of gross receipts), profits would be split on a sliding scale, with Fox receiving between 30 and 40 percent, the studio's share increasing as earnings rose. In the end, the terms were more studio-friendly than those for *Empire*. Fox agreed to advance Lucasfilm $10 million (rather than $25 million) toward production of the movie, payable in two installments. By this time, Lucas had already sunk $2 million of his own money into the picture. He watched every dime spent to make certain that this time he would not have to request additional funds. Final production costs for *Return of the Jedi* tallied $43 million. Taking inflation into account, this was an acceptable increase over *Empire*'s $30.4 million final print cost.

The agreement, officially signed December 4, 1981, also contained an unusual "key man" provision, inserted by Lucasfilm: Fox would retain its rights with regard to *Star Wars* as long as Davis owned the studio. Lucas had the last laugh when, in 1984, Davis sold Twentieth Century-Fox. Lucasfilm attorneys immediately informed Fox that the studio had lost its right of first refusal for any further *Star Wars* films. Lucas was under no obligation to continue partnering with the studio, although ultimately Fox would distribute the later Prequel Trilogy.

Back to Borehamwood

With the distribution deal twisting in the wind, shooting of the third *Star Wars* film, announced as *Revenge of the Jedi*, was postponed from August 1981 to January 1982. Once again interiors would be shot at EMI-Elstree Studios in Borehamwood, London. Norman Reynolds, who returned as production designer, began building sets in December. And again, the production utilized every soundstage at EMI. Simultaneously, in California, the newly formed ILM Creature Shop, under the direction of Phil Tippett, was busy creating a menagerie of monsters and aliens. *Jedi* involved more than twice as many creatures as the two previous *Star Wars* films combined, including the gruesome denizens of Jabba's Palace and an entire village full of Ewoks. The creatures that posed the greatest difficulty were Jabba and the Rancor Monster, which Luke battles in Jabba's dungeon. Jabba was an eighteen-foot-long, one-ton, $500,000 Muppet built by makeup artist Stuart Freeborn (the cocreator of Yoda). Jabba was controlled by three puppeteers and had his own makeup artist. Originally, the Rancor (like the Wampa from *Empire*) was to be portrayed by a man in a suit, but the suit looked unconvincing. So instead the creature was realized as a marionette and later blue-screened into its battle with Luke Skywalker. Most of the other creatures in the film were portrayed by actors in masks or makeup.

Richard Marquand directs Mark Hamill's performance as Luke Skywalker, Jedi badass, in the Jabba's Palace sequence from *Return of the Jedi*.

The only major new human role to be cast was the emperor. Originally, Lucas and Marquand selected seventy-five-year-old Alan Webb to play the malevolent ruler of the Galactic Empire, but Webb was forced to bow out after contracting the flu. The younger Ian McDiarmid, fifty-five, was chosen to replace Webb. Other candidates for the role included Ben Kingsley, who instead appeared in *Gandhi* (1982) and won an Oscar.

Shooting began January 11, 1981, with a sequence eventually deleted from the film: Luke, Leia, Han, Lando, Chewie, and the droids boarding the *Millennium Falcon* amid a sandstorm, following Han's rescue at the Sarlacc nest. These were the last shots taken using a full-sized model of the *Falcon*, originally built for *The Empire Strikes Back*. A few weeks later, the giant prop was burned. The story's concluding Ewok village celebration was also among the earliest scenes shot, from January 20 through 22.

As planned, Lucas appeared on set nearly every day during the making of *Jedi*. He chose camera lenses, selected or approved Marquand's setups, directed second-unit material, and even led a few first-unit scenes. Lucas sometimes suggested ways a scene should be shot more quickly and inexpensively. And he continually pressed Marquand to shoot more "coverage"—additional camera angles of the same scene—to provide greater flexibility during editing. From all accounts, Marquand seemed happy to defer to Lucas in most situations. In publicist John Phillip Peecher's 1983 paperback *The Making of Return of the Jedi*, Marquand compared directing *Jedi* to "having to direct *King Lear* with Shakespeare in the next room." Lucas told Peecher that, "I'm just sort of the overseer. I mean, I try my best to see that the films conform to each other. I try to see that the production moves along and finishes on schedule. . . . But generally, my participation is maybe one-tenth of what it would be if I were directing."

With the exception of Carrie Fisher, who did not hit it off with Marquand, most of the cast and crew got on well with the director, and, unlike with *Empire*, morale remained high throughout production. Fisher, however, was disgruntled for much of the shoot. She felt that Leia had been softened too much in the final screenplay, and she was uncomfortable performing in the soon-to-be-iconic metal bikini costume created for her scenes in Jabba's palace and at the Sarlacc nest. Since the costume was metal, it did not give as she moved, and a prop man was tasked with checking her bosom between takes to make sure nothing had fallen out. In her autobiography, Fisher recalls that during the filming of these scenes she resolved to become a writer. She believed she could write something better than the screenplay she was stuck with, and yearned for a career where no one had to check her breasts every five minutes.

Carrie Fisher hated her "slave girl" metal bikini costume, worn here as Luke and Leia escape Jabba the Hutt's exploding sail barge. But it became one of the most iconic costumes of the series.

Health issues also presented a concern. The flu was sweeping through London at the time, and Lucas, Fisher, Anthony Daniels, and Alec Guinness (not to mention Webb), among other members of the cast and crew, were all stricken at one point or another. Daniels, inside his Threepio mask, suffered miserably. Nevertheless, shooting at EMI wrapped on schedule, April 1, 1982.

California Dreaming

In a break in tradition from previous *Star Wars* pictures, *Revenge of the Jedi* went on location after filming concluded in England. To avoid the expense and other risks of exotic location work, exteriors for *Jedi* were shot at two sites in California. Tatooine exteriors were filmed in the dunes near Buttercup Valley (just across the border from Yuma, Arizona), and Endor sequences—including the speeder bike chase and Ewok battle scenes—were shot in the redwood forest near Crescent City.

The Buttercup Valley location proved treacherous, and several stunt men suffered broken ankles or other injuries during the scene in which Luke, Han, and Chewbacca are nearly fed to the Sarlacc sand monster. Despite extraordinary security measures, word got out that *Star Wars* was shooting at Buttercup Valley, and fans descended on the location and became a distraction. High winds and sandstorms also presented problems, forcing shooting to stop and, at one point, shredding the sails on the huge barge set.

Shooting in Crescent City went more smoothly. However, events conspired to deprive the diminutive Kenny Baker of a moment of glory. Baker, as a thank-you for his tireless and largely unsung work as R2-D2, was also assigned *Jedi*'s most prominent Ewok role, as Wicket—the first Ewok audiences meet and the one who befriends Princess Leia after her speeder bike crash. Unfortunately, on the day of shooting Baker fell ill, contracting food poisoning from a bad chili dog. So instead, Wicket was played by eleven-year-old Warwick Davis, who performed so well in the part that Lucas later cast him in the title role of his epic fantasy *Willow* (1988). Baker appeared in the film in the lesser Ewok role of Paploo.

In addition to playing R2-D2, Kenny Baker also portrayed Paploo the Ewok in *Return of the Jedi.* Unfortunately, Baker lost his showcase scene when he fell ill after eating a bad chili dog.

Lucas' relentless pursuit of efficiency paid off. By May 3, 1982, *Revenge of the Jedi* was a full four days *ahead* of schedule. Principal photography wrapped on May 14 after eighty-eight days of shooting—four more than *Star Wars* but fifty-six fewer than *Empire.*

Spoilers Beyond Imagination

Throughout production, the *Star Wars* team took extreme measures to prevent spoilers (especially the kinship of Luke and Leia, and the fate of Darth Vader) from being leaked. As outlined in the previous chapter, bogus scenes were included in the screenplay in place of the most sensitive sequences. The actors appearing in those scenes received the real script pages, printed on blue paper, a day or two before shooting, so they could memorize their lines. Then the blue pages were collected and shredded. These sensitive scenes were shot on a closed set with a skeleton crew. Employees at Industrial Light & Magic worked from storyboards and were not allowed to read the script at all. But that was only the beginning of Lucasfilm's security precautions.

To throw journalists and fans off the trail of the two California locations, Lucasfilm announced that *Revenge of the Jedi* would be shot at EMI-Elstree Studios (true) and in Tunisia and Germany's Black Forest (both false). To further confound would-be interlopers, Kazanjian booked the Buttercup Valley and Crescent City locations under the name of a fake movie, *Blue Harvest*. Crew members were issued *Blue Harvest* hats and T-shirts emblazoned with the tagline "Horror Beyond Imagination." In addition, a massive eighteen-foot security fence, four acres square, was erected around the Buttercup Valley site. Despite these safeguards, however, area residents quickly figured out that the new *Star Wars* movie was being filmed nearby. The local newspaper ran a story, which was picked up by wire services, and soon fans began descending on the location, gathering outside the fence each morning. Mark Hamill and other cast members signed autographs through the chain link and sometimes mingled with fans at nearby restaurants after shooting wrapped for the day.

The most serious security concerns were internal. Media interest in the film was intense, and there was always the possibility that a crew member could be bribed into leaking a script. Then there was David Prowse, who had been a loose cannon during *Empire* and continued his free-and-easy way with franchise secrets between films. During production, Prowse was kept in the dark about Vader's fate. He was doubled during parts of the climactic fight scene, and another actor, Sebastian Shaw, was hired to play the unmasked Vader. Nevertheless, while attending a science fiction convention in Kansas City, Missouri, Prowse revealed details about the story, including the existence of the Ewoks. Irate Lucasfilm executives considered suing Prowse for violating the terms of his contract, but the publicity arising from legal action was considered more potentially damaging than Prowse's latest security breach.

Despite all these extraordinary efforts, there were significant leaks. The first came when Joe Copeland, Hamill's stand-in during shooting at Buttercup Valley, wrote a story for *Starlog* magazine about his experiences on the film and revealed some plot details. It was a violation of Copeland's contract, but he too avoided a potential lawsuit. The April/May 1983 issue of *Cinefantastique* magazine (published in March) featured an entire article comprised of purported "inside information" about *Jedi*. While many of the would-be spoilers included in the *Cinefantastique* story were erroneous (e.g., it identified the mysterious "another" as Luke's father), the piece revealed that Darth Vader would sacrifice himself to save Luke's life, and it included a crude drawing of an Ewok. Most damaging of all, Marvel Comics issued its one-shot adaptation of the film a month too soon. It appeared April 30, 1983, and immediately sold out; the movie premiered May 25. And Don Glut's *Return of the Jedi* novelization was issued two weeks before the movie's premiere. Anyone who read either book knew the entire story in advance. Finally, on opening day, the Associated Press published a story that revealed many of the film's secrets—all accurate, since the AP writer had attended an advance screening.

"*Jedi* Almost Killed Everybody"

The downside to having Lucas on set every day was that he couldn't be at ILM designing visual effects sequences and signing off on completed shots, as he had done during *Empire*. As a result, when shooting wrapped, nearly all the film's nine hundred visual effects—most of which required creating and compositing many separate elements (multiple spaceships, blaster fire, explosions, etc.)—remained unfinished. Many hadn't even been started. Because shooting had been delayed by six months, the ILM team had less time than usual to complete its work. Plus, they were all exhausted. Between *Star Wars* and *Empire*, ILM had gone on hiatus. Between *Empire* and *Jedi*, however, the shop continued running at full speed and had completed effects for *Dragonslayer*, *Raiders of the Lost Ark* (both 1981), *Poltergeist*, and *E.T.* (both 1982). ILM was so busy it was forced to turn down *Conan the Barbarian* (1982), directed by Lucas' film school buddy John Milius. As the push to complete *Jedi* arrived, many ILMers were running on empty. Nevertheless, Lucas pushed them hard. Unable to work out the effects sequences in advance, he essentially designed them on the fly, adding, deleting, and revising shots as he came up with new ideas or reconsidered old ones.

By mid-October, ILM had eight camera crews working around the clock. As on the previous two films, Lucas personally signed off on every completed visual effects shot—in fact, he signed off on every element of every shot, including space battle scenes featuring dozens of ships. In late November, Lucas caused a major uproar when he requested one hundred additional or revised effects. ILM had completed all but 28 shots on its list; now it suddenly

Nein Nunb (in reality a large puppet operated by Mike Quinn and Richard Bonehill) and Lando Calrissian (Billy Dee Williams) take the controls of the *Millennium Falcon* during the climactic space battle of the Original Trilogy. Screenwriter Lawrence Kasdan wanted to have the *Falcon* and all aboard be destroyed during the final battle, but Lucas refused.

had 128 left, all of which had to be completed by January so that the length of the movie (and of its individual scenes) could be locked, enabling John Williams to record his score in synch with the film. As late as March 1983, Lucas was still ordering that shots be altered or replaced. Visual effects became the only *Jedi* expense to run seriously over budget.

Postproduction also involved unusually extensive pickups and reshoots, beginning in May 1982, when cast members including Hamill and Fisher appeared at ILM to film the speeder bike chase and other footage against a blue screen. Meanwhile, a second unit shot footage for the speeder bike chase and Ewok battle scenes in Crescent City. Hamill returned to ILM in November to shoot an insert of Luke slipping a black glove over his damaged mechanical hand, as well as a scene of Luke building his new lightsaber. This sequence was added because Kazanjian worried that fans would wonder how Luke acquired a new laser sword after losing his at the end of *Empire*.

On January 19, Williams began recording his score with the London Symphony Orchestra at the famous Abbey Road Studio. Dubbing began shortly afterward at the Sprocket Systems studio at Skywalker Ranch. James Earl Jones returned as the voice of Darth Vader and finally agreed to accept a screen credit. Meanwhile, sound designer Ben Burtt was nearly as over-whelmed as the ILM team. *Jedi* featured much more alien dialogue and sound effects than any previous *Star Wars* film. For Episode VI, Burtt invented two new alien languages: Ewok and Huttese.

Editing *Jedi* wasn't simple, either. Marquand and editor Shane Burton, after completing four rough cuts, delivered Marquand's director's cut on August 19. Lucas and Kazanjian screened it and were unimpressed. Marquand's version, even missing nearly all the visual effects footage, ran a flabby 127 minutes and had a different rhythm than the first two movies. Simply put, the cutting wasn't *Star Wars*-y enough. Lucas thanked Marquand and Burton, and then hired Duwayne Dunham to recut the whole thing, under his personal guidance. As usual, Lucas edited some scenes himself and called in Marcia Lucas to assist. Lucas' fine cut (an unfinished product, but more polished than the initial rough cut), completed November 15, also ran 127 minutes but was tighter, and included many more effects sequences. On December 4, Lucas completed a 133-minute version that included placehold-ers for dozens of still-missing effects shots. The final film, with credits, would run 134 minutes.

On April 9, 1983, the movie was sneak-previewed at San Francisco's Northpoint Theater. It was a smash, generating far more enthusiasm than *Empire* had created three years before. Nevertheless, Lucas made some changes. He cut the scene of Luke building his lightsaber and had a final pickup shot filmed and added—of the droids being rescued from the Tatooine sand following the Sarlacc nest sequence.

By the time it was previewed, the picture had undergone one other major revision: It had been retitled. Or, rather, re-retitled. *Return of the Jedi* had been Lucas' original name for the film, but when Kazanjian complained that "Return" was a weak word, Lucas had changed it to *Revenge of the Jedi*. That title was used for the picture's earliest posters, in its first teaser trailer, and in all Lucasfilm press releases until December 1982, when Lucas and Kazanjian reverted back to *Return of the Jedi*. A month earlier, Twentieth Century-Fox market researchers had reported that the *Revenge* title tested poorly. This apparently convinced Lucas his original title was best. Besides, as Lucas would later point out, "Jedi don't take revenge." The last-minute name change created headaches for some *Star Wars* licensees. Toymaker Kenner, for instance, was forced to destroy nearly $250,000 worth of packaging. But there was plenty of pain to go around during postproduction of *Return of the Jedi*.

"*Jedi* almost killed everybody," Lucas said, as quoted in Rinzler's book. "Everything was very, very hard on everybody."

The picture finally reached movie theaters on May 25, 1983—six years to the day from the premiere of *Star Wars*.

21

Not Bad for a Little Furball

Assessing Episode VI (1983)

I n the summer of 1983, America suffered a relapse of *Star Wars* fever. After six long years, the last three spent in the lingering tension created by *The Empire Strikes Back*'s cliff-hanger ending, millions of fans were aching to know the fate of Luke Skywalker, Han Solo, Princess Leia, and Darth Vader. *Return of the Jedi* was far and away the movie event of the year, and possibly the most eagerly anticipated film ever made. Rather than hosting a gala national premiere, charity previews of *Jedi*, benefitting a variety of causes, were held in a dozen cities (from Boston to Los Angeles) May 22 through 24. Passes to these advance screenings were the hottest ticket in the country. As opening day approached, theater operators braced for impact.

The picture opened nationwide on Wednesday, May 25, 1983, playing on 1,002 screens in eight hundred theaters (a massive number for the era). Even though most of those venues ran the film around the clock the first day, lines stretched out the door and around the building in many locations. Once again, patrons—some in costume—waited for hours to secure a seat. At some theaters, fans camped out days in advance. David Maples, dressed as Han Solo, and Patricia Smith, dressed as Princess Leia, were married while waiting in line at the Egyptian Theatre in Los Angeles. Adults skipped work, kids cut school, and parents called in sick and held their children out of school to see *Jedi* on Day One. Predictably, the movie's premiere made the front page of newspapers in many cities. In some places, fans' passion for the intensely anticipated picture turned ugly. Audiences nearly rioted at cinemas in San Diego, North Hollywood, Salt Lake City, and Long Island, New York, where various technical problems disrupted the showing of the movie. And a 70mm print of the film, valued at $12,000, was stolen from the Glenwood Theatre in Overland Park, Kansas, by an armed robber.

As these incidents demonstrate, anticipation for the *Star Wars* finale had spiked to stratospheric and, in some cases, irrational levels. So had expectations for the film. Only a work of consummate genius, incredible power, and extraordinary resonance could have lived up to the hype. *Return of the Jedi* was not that film. But neither was it a bad film.

The Summer of *Jedi*

Jedi raked in a whopping $30 million its first week and dominated the box office during the summer of 1983. Its drawing power derived from both feverish anticipation and feeble competition. Rival studios, leery of getting steamrolled again by *Star Wars*, pushed back the release of their would-be

The original posters and advertising materials for *Return of the Jedi* prominently featured Luke Skywalker's lightsaber and Princess Leia's cleavage.

summer blockbusters until June, July, or August. Even then, most of those pictures—which included *Psycho II*, *Superman III*, the James Bond adventure *Octopussy*, *Twilight Zone: The Movie*, and the *Saturday Night Fever* sequel *Stayin' Alive*—failed to meet expectations. Aside from *Jedi*, the summer's biggest hits were a pair of small-budget sleepers—the Cold War thriller *War Games* with Matthew Broderick and the teen comedy *Risky Business* with Tom Cruise.

With so many other expected hits bombing around it, *Jedi* eventually expanded to more than seventeen hundred screens. By the end of July, it had grossed more than $200 million, but then interest began to cool. Like *Empire*, *Jedi* failed to replicate the volume of repeat business that the original *Star Wars* had inspired. Some fans left disappointed, while others—even though they enjoyed the film—didn't feel compelled to see it more than once or twice. When *Jedi* concluded its original U.S. release in early March 1984, it had tallied $255 million in domestic receipts, making it the top-grossing film of 1983. The Oscar-winning tearjerker *Terms of Endearment*, released in November, finished a distant second with $108 million. *Jedi*'s lifetime worldwide box office earnings stand at $573 million, or just under $1.4 billion when adjusted for inflation. Those are very impressive numbers—higher than

Empire in raw dollars—but the smallest of the Original Trilogy in inflation-adjusted terms.

On the merchandising front, it was a similar story. Millions continued to pour into the Lucasfilm coffers from the sale of *Star Wars* toys, books, games, soundtrack albums, and other products, but *Return of the Jedi* tie-ins didn't move as briskly as had items from the first two films. Don Glut's novelization debuted at No. 1 on the *New York Times* Best Seller list but quickly faded. Kenner's action figures continued to sell well, but its plush Ewok dolls never caught on and were soon relegated to the markdown bin.

"The Dimmest Adventure of the Lot"

Return of the Jedi fared far worse with critics than with audiences, receiving a higher percentage of mixed and negative reviews than either of the first two movies. It's tough to judge what was worse—the dispirited reviews penned by critics who had enjoyed the first two entries or the gleeful lambastings administered by those who had never liked *Star Wars* in the first place. Not all the reviews were bad, of course. *Entertainment Tonight*'s Leonard Maltin loved it, as did Sheila Benson of the *Los Angeles Times*. In the *Chicago Sun-Times*, Roger Ebert wrote that *Jedi* was "magnificent fun" and marveled, "It's a little amazing how Lucas and his associates keep topping themselves." Most other reviewers, including Ebert's TV partner Gene Siskel, were less enthusiastic. Siskel, in his *Chicago Tribune* review, recommended the film but complained that it lacked "the humanity and richly drawn characters that brighten *Star Wars*." Gary Arnold of the *Washington Post* wrote that *Jedi* "was worth the wait" but was disappointed that the film "backs off some of the more tantalizing possibilities suggested by the cliffhanging scenario of *Empire*." Other writers, including Rex Reed of the *New York Post*, Pauline Kael of *The New Yorker*, and Vincent Canby of the *New York Times*, eviscerated the film. Canby called it "by far the dimmest adventure of the lot." Kael claimed that *Jedi*, "an impersonal and rather junky piece of moviemaking," signified everything that was wrong with Hollywood.

Like many fans, most critics complained that *Return of the Jedi* ran short on new ideas. *Newsweek*'s David Ansen called *Jedi* "downright repetitive." Some reviewers complained that Lawrence Kasdan's screenplay failed to develop the lead characters, and that the cast (especially Harrison Ford and Carrie Fisher) seemed uninterested. As they had with Irvin Kershner on *Empire*, many critics singled out director Richard Marquand for scorn. "Richard Marquand fluffs the two or three real opportunities he has, rendering the long-delayed character climaxes with a chilly indifference," wrote Dave Kehr in his *Chicago Reader* critique. And nearly all the film's detractors bemoaned the Ewoks, dismissing the heroic little teddy bears as a blatant merchandising ploy. John Coleman, of the *New Statesman*, felt ripped off and called *Jedi* "one of the biggest cinematic cons of all time."

Return of the Jedi didn't wow awards voters, either. The picture earned five Academy Award nominations (one more than *Empire*), but won only one—a Special Achievement Award for Visual Effects. It lost the awards for Best Art Direction-Set Decoration, Best Sound, Best Effects (Sound Effects Editing), and Best Score. And it performed even worse at most other awards venues (see Chapter 35).

Merits and Demerits

In many respects, the critics were right about *Return of the Jedi*. It's the most flawed leg of the Original Trilogy, and its defects are magnified by its position as the grand finale of the saga, especially its galling dearth of originality. Not only does it mimic the overall structure of the first movie—beginning on Tatooine and concluding with the destruction of a Death Star, followed by a giddy celebration—but it also lifts specific moments from the earlier films. For instance, the Chewbacca-in-handcuffs gambit, first used in the Death Star detention block, is replayed at Jabba's Palace; Luke and Leia make another heroic rope swing, this time from Jabba's crashing sail barge to a nearby skiff; and Jabba's Palace itself is a thinly disguised rehash of the Mos Eisley cantina, complete with band. There's a return trip to Dagobah. Lando's final assault on the Death Star is staged almost identically with the *Dam Busters*–inspired climax of the first movie.

More often than not, the screenplay hashed out by Lucas and Lawrence Kasdan (with input from Marquand and producer Howard Kazanjian) takes the path of least resistance. The answers it provides for the mysteries opened by the previous film are dull and predictable. It addresses the recurring themes of the *Star Wars* series in the most obvious manner possible, as Luke and the emperor literally battle for Luke's soul—and with it, Vader's. The other characters are reduced to little better than puppets or plot devices. As Ansen wrote in *Newsweek*, "the characters have not grown; Princess Leia even seems to have shrunk. She's no longer a commander, just a . . . damsel in distress in a harem outfit." With their roles reduced in stature and complexity, especially in comparison with *Empire*, Harrison Ford, Carrie Fisher, and Billy Dee Williams are left with almost nothing meaningful to play. While Mark Hamill contributes fine work during the picture's climactic duel of lightsabers and wills, he seems out of his depth during the Tatooine sequence playing Luke Skywalker, Jedi Badass. After receiving a major buildup in the last movie, Boba Fett is dispatched early and in a surprisingly offhanded manner—consumed by the Sarlacc monster (followed by a comedy relief burp). This reflects the overall attitude of the screenplay: Fett has been reduced to just another loose end to be tied up. So have most of the other characters.

Jedi has its compensations, however. Despite the familiarity of its constituent parts, the picture's first hour remains riveting. The Tatooine passage—including Luke's battle with the Rancor monster, Han's rescue at the Sarlacc nest, and the speeder bike chase on Endor—are as thrilling as any sequence in the series. Luke's visit with the dying Yoda and his testy encounter with the ghostly Ben Kenobi are emotionally gripping and played with delicacy and conviction by Hamill, Frank Oz, and Sir Alec Guinness. If the rest of the film were as strong as its first hour, *Return of the Jedi* would be at least the equal of its predecessors.

Unfortunately, the picture falters with the arrival of the Ewoks. This isn't entirely the fault of the Ewoks themselves. Most of the film's final seventy-three minutes aren't edited with the same crispness and restless energy as the preceding two and a half films in the series. *Jedi* downshifts to a slower tempo in order to maximize the suspense of the unfolding father-son drama, but

Many critics and fans assumed that the Ewoks were a blatant marketing ploy, but plush versions of characters such as Wicket, left, and Princess Kneesa were soon relegated to the markdown bins.   *Photography by Preston Hewis/ East Bank Images*

this throws off the rhythm of the rest of the film. The Ewoks, however, also present a problem: they're simply too cute. Even when they prepare to roast Han Solo and serve him for dinner (as a Han sandwich, perhaps?), it's impossible to be afraid of the Ewoks. They're so cuddly and adorable that, for a while, they suck all dramatic tension from the narrative. This section of the film contains charming moments—such as Leia's first encounter with Wicket and Threepio's recounting (in Ewok, with sound effects) of the story so far—but for the most part, after the speeder bike chase, *Jedi* drags until the rebel fleet drops out of hyperspace.

The cross-cut finale (switching among Luke, Vader, and the emperor on the Death Star; Han, Leia, and friends on Endor; and Lando aboard the *Millennium Falcon*) lacks the straight-line thrust of the first movie's final battle. But its individual elements are all strong, especially the Luke-Vader-Emperor sequence, a marvelous example of what Alfred Hitchcock referred to as "pure cinema." Vader's internal battle to turn away from the Dark Side, and his ultimate decision to destroy the emperor, unfolds entirely without dialogue. More impressively still, it's told without a human face for the pivotal character; audiences only see Vader's blank, robotic mask. His swirling emotions are

Wicket the Ewok (Warwick Davis) meets R2-D2 (Kenny Baker) in *Return of the Jedi*. The eleven-year-old Davis proved to be a significant discovery for George Lucas; the actor later starred in Lucas' movie *Willow*, among other films.

conveyed entirely through body language, deft editing, and John Williams' tense, haunted musical cues (featuring a ghostly-sounding choir). It's visual storytelling of the highest order.

Return of the Jedi is a treat for the eyes in other ways, too. The picture stands as the magnum opus of mechanical and optical visual effects, a final testament to the beauty of now-lost cinematic arts such as model building, motion-control photography, matte painting, stop-motion animation, puppetry, monster suit making—basically, all the special effects disciplines that were rendered obsolete by computer-generated imagery. Viewers who retain a nostalgic attachment to old school, pre-CGI visual effects can look at *Jedi* (in its non-Special Edition form, anyway) as the zenith of the art form's classic era. No pre-CGI film contains as many wildly imaginative creatures, beautifully realized spaceships, or breathtaking alien landscapes as *Jedi*. In this respect, at least, *Jedi* is a masterwork.

A Certain Point of View

In *Return of the Jedi*, Ben Kenobi cautions Luke Skywalker that "many of the truths we cling to depend greatly on our point of view." So does one's enjoyment of the third *Star Wars* film. Despite its shortcomings, the film remains a rewarding, even enchanting, viewing experience when approached, as Kenobi might say, "from a certain point of view."

Jedi's primary weakness is its lack of ambition. *Star Wars* had been a revelation, and *The Empire Strikes Back* had placed the franchise on a more challenging, adult trajectory. *Jedi* could have continued down that path. Had Luke Skywalker given in to the Dark Side (temporarily), had Han Solo (or even Lando Calrissian) laid down his life for his companions, had the rebels staged an assault on the imperial homeworld rather than against a second Death Star (all ideas that were proposed but rejected; see Chapter 19), the story could have taken on the kind of gravitas and scope worthy of George Lucas' aspirations to mythology. But that wasn't the movie George Lucas wanted to make. He had something much simpler, and cozier, in mind.

"Lucas' apparent reluctance to take any big chances with the scenario in *Jedi*, which shies away from the darker, tangled implications of the unanswered questions in *Empire*, is easy to comprehend," wrote Arnold in his perceptive *Washington Post* review. "He's so protective of the public attachment to his dream world that he resists taking many fresh risks or unfamiliar paths. The stakes are so huge that he'd be foolish to deny the audience a 100 percent reassuring wrap-up. If Lucas had been merely 80 percent reassuring, he might have broken millions of young hearts, and he's obviously loathe to break a single one."

If *Empire* is *Star Wars* for grown-ups, *Jedi* is *Star Wars* for kids. It's not geared for all audiences, like the original, but aimed specifically at young viewers. From a marketing perspective, this was probably a miscalculation. Following the darker *Empire*, it was at best an overcorrection. The audience for *Return of the Jedi* in 1983 consisted, primarily, of viewers who had already seen *Star Wars* and *The Empire Strikes Back*. Fans who had been six when the original came out were now twelve; those who were twelve were now eighteen; those who were eighteen were now twenty-four. *Jedi* was pitched at an age level below all but the youngest members of the core *Star Wars* audience.

However, if *Jedi* leaves something to be desired as the concluding chapter of an epic space opera, it's an absolute triumph when judged in comparison with other children's movies from the 1970s and '80s (like the Benji or Herbie the Love Bug pictures). And it plays best when viewed in the company of children. *Village Voice* critic Andrew Sarris took his young godson to a press screening of *Jedi*. In his review, he reported that the boy thought *Jedi* "was even better than *Star Wars* and *The Empire Strikes Back*. Now that I've thought about it, I tend to agree." I won't go that far, but I can report that my

The climactic father-son duel from *Jedi*—Luke Skywalker (Mark Hamill) vs. Darth Vader (David Prowse)—remains a high point of the Original Trilogy.

six-year-old son loves *Return of the Jedi*, and that watching the movie with him is an entirely different experience than watching it alone, or in the company of other grown-ups. Moments that make me roll my eyes make him squeal with laughter, and I laugh along with him. He is gripped by passages that bore me and bounces up and down on the couch with glee during the exciting parts. His enthusiasm is contagious. Any movie capable of so thoroughly delighting a child can't be as bad as its adult detractors think.

Seen from this point of view—accepting that the *Star Wars* finale was intended to be "Goldilocks and the Three Bears," rather than *The Odyssey*—even some of the picture's faults become merits. In fairy tales, action is often repeated (commonly, three times). So the reuse of familiar elements—including return trips to Tatooine, Dagobah, and the Death Star— accords with this structure. The Ewoks are also easier to accept in a storybook context.

Of course, not everyone is willing or able to approach the film from that perspective. A forgiving attitude improves the experience of watching almost any movie, but many viewers (especially critics) are disinclined to cut any movie that sort of slack. Perhaps that's why, while *Empire* has accumulated greater popular and critical respect over the years, *Jedi* still awaits reappraisal. Some fans love the first two movies but loathe *Jedi*. Critics are even more dismissive. Audience sentiment is ethereal and difficult to quantify, but movie rating websites such as Rotten Tomatoes, Metacritic, and the Internet Movie Database offer some insight. These sites employ different formats and methodologies, but *Jedi* ranks behind the other two films in fan ratings on all three. These sites also aggregate critical opinion, based on published reviews. The gap in those rating is even more severe. *Jedi* trails *Star Wars* and *Empire* by double digits on Rotten Tomatoes' critical "Tomatometer" ratings, and lags almost 40 points behind *Star Wars* on Metacritic's 100-point scale.

Jedi remains the only installment of the Original Trilogy left off the National Film Registry. But its absence should not suggest that *Return of the Jedi* does not belong in the company of its predecessors. It emphatically does. Sure, it's inferior to the first two *Star Wars* films, but so are most other movies. On balance, *Jedi*'s strengths outweigh its weaknesses. Movies don't have to be perfect to be fun, and *Jedi*—for all its faults—remains an enjoyable, sometimes thrilling, and mostly satisfactory conclusion to the *Star Wars* epic. It's the best disappointing movie ever made.

22

Aren't You a Little Short for a Stormtrooper?

Underappreciated Contributors

ilmmaking is a collaborative enterprise, and when movies are as successful as the original *Star Wars* trilogy, there's plenty of credit to go around. Inevitably, however, most of the glory collects around a handful of people, usually a picture's director, its stars, and (to a lesser extent) the screenwriter. In the case of *Star Wars*, the list of frequently name-checked collaborators extends to Industrial Light & Magic leaders such as John Dykstra and Dennis Muren and to composer John Williams. Even so, a handful of people who made pivotal contributions to the franchise have, for various reasons, never received the full measure of recognition they deserve. Without their efforts, the *Star Wars* films might have turned out very differently—if they had been made at all.

Alan Ladd Jr.

Star Wars might never have happened if not for Alan Ladd Jr., who took a chance on George Lucas' wacky space opera idea even after every other studio in Hollywood had rejected the project. Ladd, born October 22, 1937, in Los Angeles, was the son of movie star Alan Ladd and the actor's first wife, Marjorie Jane "Midge" Harrold. His mother and father had been high school sweethearts but divorced in 1941, just as Ladd's career was taking off. The elder Ladd went on to star in the classic Western *Shane* (1953) and teamed with vivacious Veronica Lake for five films, including the noir gems *This Gun for Hire* (1941), *The Glass Key* (1942), and *The Blue Dahlia* (1946). He died of an accidental overdose of alcohol and barbiturates in 1964.

Ladd Jr. was raised primarily by his mother, but stayed with his father on weekends and sometimes visited sets at Paramount Pictures, where his father was under contract. Even when he was with his mother, "I spent all my time watching movie after movie after movie," Ladd said in a 2007 interview. Yet he had no interest in following in his father's footsteps and becoming an actor. Instead, he began his career in film as a talent agent at Creative Management Associates, which he joined in 1963. Ladd's client list included Judy Garland, Warren Beatty, and a former high school classmate, Robert Redford. Five years later, he left CMA and began working as an independent producer. Ladd joined the executive ranks at Twentieth Century-Fox in 1973 and was named chief of creative affairs at the studio three years later. He would eventually climb to the office of president.

Ladd did more than simply give *Star Wars* the green light. He defended the picture when other executives remained skeptical, and helped prevent it from being scuttled as its budget ballooned (see Chapter 7). "Every board meeting I attended, the subject was always *Star Wars*," Ladd recalled in the *Empire of Dreams* documentary. "The costs are rising. It's this, it's that. We've read drafts of scripts that make no sense to us in any way. It was rather unpleasant." Like the rest of the studio's executives, Ladd didn't fully grasp Lucas' ideas. But he believed in Lucas' talent and vision, and didn't try to micromanage the picture. In "the only meeting I had with Laddie about the script, he said, 'Look, it doesn't make any sense to me whatsoever, but I trust you. Go ahead and make it,'" Lucas said, as quoted in a 2014 *Forbes* article. "That was just honest. I mean, it was a crazy movie. Now you can see it [and] know what it is, but before you could see it, there wasn't anything like it. You couldn't explain it. You know . . . it was like this furry dog driving a spaceship. I mean, what is that?"

While at Fox, Ladd also oversaw or greenlit other hits, including *Young Frankenstein, The Towering Inferno* (both 1974), and *Alien* (1979); prestige pictures such as *Julia* (1977, nominated for eleven Academy Awards), *Breaking Away* (1979, six Oscar nominations), and *Norma Rae* (1979, four Academy Award nominations); as well as the cult favorite *The Rocky Horror Picture Show* (1975, zero Oscar nominations). During his tenure as president, he also promoted African American and female executives during an era when both were rarities in Hollywood.

Ladd left the studio during the shooting of *The Empire Strikes Back* to return to independent production, forming the Ladd Company. Although it produced a number of critically acclaimed films, including the Best Picture Oscar winner *Chariots of Fire* (1981), *Blade Runner* (1982), *The Right Stuff* (1984), and *Once Upon a Time in America* (1984), as well as the high-grossing *Police Academy* comedies, the company was not profitable. When MGM-United Artists offered him the posts of chairman and CEO in 1985, he accepted and dissolved the Ladd Company. On Ladd's watch, MGM released movies that included *Moonstruck* (1987) and *Thelma and Louise* (1990), each of which earned six Academy Award nominations and were major hits. Ladd left MGM and re-formed the Ladd Company in 1993. Since then, the company has released just seven films, but those include Oscar champion *Braveheart* (1995) and the two hit *Brady Bunch* comedies. The eighth release of the re-formed Ladd Company, a Western titled *North of Cheyenne*, is in the works.

Throughout his career, Ladd has remained loyal to George Lucas, distributing several Lucasfilm productions, including *Willow* (MGM, 1988). Ladd has been married twice—tying the knot with current spouse Cindra in 1985—and has four daughters. In 2007, he was awarded a star on the Hollywood Walk of Fame, located at 7018 Hollywood Boulevard. His father's star is located at 1601 Vine Street. The Ladds are one of the few father and son tandems to be so honored.

Ralph McQuarrie

Production artist Ralph McQuarrie also played a major role in the development of *Star Wars*. Usually, artists are hired to help better articulate or elaborate on a filmmaker's ideas. But McQuarrie's sketches and paintings went beyond that. During the long and torturous process of developing the screenplay for *Star Wars* (see Chapter 4), McQuarrie's artwork helped Lucas crystalize his own vision. McQuarrie's illustrations also helped Ladd and Lucas to win over leery Fox executives and later to secure the funds necessary to complete the film. His paintings made a far more promising case for the project than Lucas' screenplay, which most readers found incomprehensible.

McQuarrie, born June 13, 1929, in Gary, Indiana, grew up on a farm in Billings, Montana. Later, his family moved to Seattle, where (after high school) he landed a job as a technical illustrator for the Boeing Company. Then he was drafted into the Army and served a tour of duty during the Korean War, surviving a gunshot to the head. After returning to the United States, he used his G.I. Bill education benefits to enroll at the Art Center School in Los Angeles. After graduation, his first job was drawing teeth and dental equipment for a dentistry company. But McQuarrie, a lifelong film fan, wanted to get into the movie business. So he joined with two other artists to form Reel Three, a firm that created artwork for movie posters and animated sequences for CBS television's coverage of the Apollo space program.

While he was at Reel Three in the early 1970s, screenwriter Hal Barwood hired McQuarrie to produce illustrations for a science fiction film he was developing with director-screenwriter Matthew Robbins. This film—known variously as *Galaxy*, *Star Dancing*, and *Home Free*—was never made, but Barwood showed McQuarrie's work to his college buddy George Lucas, who was then preparing to shoot *American Graffiti*. Later, while he was struggling to pull together his ideas for *Star Wars*, Lucas called McQuarrie. Ironically, before working on *Galaxy*, McQuarrie had little interest in science fiction. "When I was young, I'd look at the *Buck Rogers* comic strip, but I didn't think too much about it," McQuarrie said in an interview posted at StarWars.com. "I'd worked for Boeing and was in love with airplanes and spacecraft, and I had an interest in fantasy architecture, although I hadn't thought about doing science fiction."

Nevertheless, his flair for the genre was immediately apparent, and he soon found himself producing hundreds of sketches and dozens of paintings, which went a long way toward defining the look of the emerging *Star Wars* universe. McQuarrie's artwork would guide the development of the picture's sets, props, costumes, makeup, and visual effects. Among other innovations, it was McQuarrie who decided that Darth Vader should wear a mask with a breathing apparatus. He also designed the appearance of C-3PO, R2-D2, Chewbacca, the Sandpeople, the Jawas, and most of the spacecraft seen in the film. "I'd sit with a pencil and dream about whatever I could imagine, sort of grotesque imagery," McQuarrie said. "George would come by every week and a half or two weeks, look at what I'd done, and talk to me about what he'd like to see. I was reading the script to start with, but the script sort of got waylaid. The story was changing in his own mind, so George would just come and talk to me about what he wanted to see."

While *Star Wars* consumed much of McQuarrie's time and energy, he nevertheless found the resources to design the Mother Ship for director Steven Spielberg's *Close Encounters of the Third Kind* (1977). After *Star Wars* and *CE3K* premiered, McQuarrie no longer had difficulty finding employment in the movie business. He went on to work on a dozen more films, most notably *Raiders of the Lost Ark* (1981), *E.T.: The Extra-Terrestrial* (1982), *Star Trek IV: The Voyage Home* (1986), and *Cocoon* (1985), for which he won an Academy Award.

When Lucas began assembling his team to make *The Empire Strike Back*, the first person he hired was McQuarrie. Although Lucas' ideas were better formed this time around, he still considered McQuarrie indispensable. McQuarrie also worked on the ill-fated *Star Wars Holiday Special* and *Return of the Jedi*, although he left the third *Star Wars* film early in preproduction. McQuarrie, at that point in his fifties, was significantly older than Lucas and most of the staff at Industrial Light & Magic, and felt uncomfortable in the increasingly large and corporate ILM/Lucasfilm environment. The more cartoonish look of *Jedi* is due in part to McQuarrie's limited participation. As McQuarrie left, Lucas insisted on thanking him in front of the assembled ILM staff. When McQuarrie said simply that he was one of the first employees Lucas had hired, Lucas corrected him: "No, you were *the* first."

This stunning painting, depicting Y-wing fighters assaulting the Death Star, was one of the works that artist Ralph McQuarrie produced during the making of *Star Wars*. McQuarrie's jaw-dropping art helped convince skeptical Fox executives to invest in the film and established the visual look of the emerging *Star Wars* universe.

McQuarrie's career continued into the early 1990s. Lucas tried to lure McQuarrie out of retirement to serve as a production designer for the Prequel Trilogy, but the artist declined. McQuarrie married Joan Benjamin in 1983 and remained with her until his death in 2012 of Parkinson's disease. Since his death, McQuarrie's *Star Wars* paintings have been displayed in museums, including the touring *Star Wars: The Magic of Myth* exhibition created by the Smithsonian Institution, which appeared at several museums across the United States in the late 1990s and early 2000s. As anyone who has seen them in person can attest, McQuarrie's works are not only important and influential, but beautiful.

Ben Burtt

While McQuarrie originated the look of the *Star Wars* universe, Ben Burtt created its sound. Both were vital. If X-wing fighters had buzzed and sputtered like the spaceships from *Flash Gordon* (1936), or if Chewbacca had yapped like a Pekingese puppy, the illusion would have been shattered. Burtt was a pioneer in the art of sound design, a discipline so new that the Academy of Motion Picture Arts and Sciences didn't recognize it when *Star Wars* was released in 1977. As a result, Burtt received a Special Achievement Award for "sound effects," a description that understated his contributions to the film.

Burtt, born July 12, 1948, in Jamesville, New York, began making 8mm movies in high school. After graduation he enrolled at Allegheny College in Meadville, Pennsylvania. "I majored in physics and was going to be a scientist but couldn't get over my fascination with film," Burtt told *Empire Strikes Back* publicist Alan Arnold. He continued making movies while at Alleghany and won a national student film festival in 1970 for his war movie *Yankee Squadron*, shot at the Old Rhinebeck Aerodrome, an aviation museum in Red Hook, New York, which at the time had working World War I aircraft. Later, Burtt won a scholarship to USC's School of Cinematic Arts, where he earned a master's degree in film production. At USC, Burtt became captivated by the possibilities of movie sound and began working as a teaching assistant under sound instructor Ken Miura. When producer Gary Kurtz, tasked with assembling a crew for *Star Wars*, called Miura and asked for the teacher's best sound mixer, Miura suggested Burtt. Kurtz hired him immediately.

Burtt met with Lucas and discovered the two had similar ideas and ambitions in terms of movie sound. With *THX 1138*'s collage of electronic effects and *American Graffiti*'s wall-to-wall rock 'n' roll soundtrack, Lucas had authored films with distinctive soundscapes. Now he intended to meld the two ideas together, blending a traditional symphonic score with innovative sound mixing, editing, and effects to add greater dimension to the experience of viewing the film. The goal was to completely enfold the viewer in the world Lucas was creating. The brilliant work of Burtt and of composer John Williams (see next chapter) enabled Lucas to fulfill his grand aspirations, creating a sonic panorama that fit together like inserting flap A in slot B. Lucas was ecstatic with the results and, to protect their work, insisted that *Star Wars* be released with Dolby stereo sound (even though most movies were still issued in mono), and later created the THX system (see Chapter 27).

Burtt's extraordinary work encompassed creating alien languages—including Wookiee, Ewok, Huttese, and whatever R2-D2 speaks—from whole cloth (see Chapter 8), as well as the distinctive buzz of lightsabers, the roar of starship engines, the rasp of Vader's respirator, and many other fictional sounds. To create these, Burtt recorded sounds from nature, from machinery, and from everywhere else imaginable, and when he couldn't find a sound, he simply made it himself (vocalizing some of Artoo's beeps and boops). Then he mixed those sounds, slowing them down, speeding them up, running them through a synthesizer, and so on, until he achieved the precise impact Lucas desired. But that was only part of Burtt's genius. He also helped oversee the blending of his work with Williams' to create the immersive sonic experience Lucas wanted.

With *Star Wars*, Burtt first employed two of his distinctive calling cards. The first is the "Wilhelm scream," a vintage sound effect originally recorded for the Gary Cooper Western *Distant Drums* in 1951. Burtt discovered the scream in a library of sound effects and used the anguished shriek when Luke Skywalker shoots a stormtrooper, prior to swinging across the Death Star chasm with Leia. The sound has been reused by Burtt or his admirers in more than two hundred subsequent films, including every *Star Wars* picture. The second Burtt signature was the use of a "black hole," a brief but jarring and total lack of sound, employed immediately before the explosion of the Death Star. Burtt also frequently reused this tactic to powerful effect.

Burtt remained with Lucasfilm for twenty-eight years, leaving in 2005 to join Pixar Animation Studios. After *Star Wars*, he worked as a sound editor, supervisor, or designer on nearly fifty more films and television series and won additional Oscars for his contributions to *Raiders of the Lost Ark*, *E.T.*, and *Indiana Jones and the Last Crusade*. Among numerous other accolades, Burtt has been nominated a total of twelve times for Academy Awards, most recently for Pixar's *Wall-E*. Burtt served as a writer-producer for the animated series *Star Wars: Droids* and penned a teleplay for *The Young Indiana Jones Chronicles*. He directed six IMAX documentary shorts, including the Oscar-nominated *Special Effects: Anything Can Happen* (1996). And he even made on-screen cameos in *Return of the Jedi* (as an imperial officer) and *The Phantom Menace* (1999).

Gary Kurtz

Gary Kurtz occupies a curious place in *Star Wars* lore. He served at the right hand of George Lucas throughout the development of *Star Wars* and became one of its primary architects. But then he fell out of Lucas' favor, and over the years, as history was rewritten to conform to the mythology accumulating around the franchise's origins, Kurtz's contributions have been minimized. The truth is that Kurtz was second only to Lucas among the originators of *Star Wars*. The project wasn't Kurtz's idea, but his efforts enabled Lucas to realize his vision.

Kurtz's first love was music. Born July 27, 1940, in Los Angeles, Kurtz began playing brass and woodwind instruments in high school and won a music scholarship to USC, where he planned to study composition and hoped to eventually find work as a symphony conductor or music teacher.

During his freshman year at the university in 1959, he recorded music for a few projects being made by students in the USC film program. Kurtz, an avid photographer who had shot his own amateur films in high school, liked the people he met from the film school and was intrigued by the possibilities of working in the movie industry. So he switched majors. After graduation, Kurtz estimates that he worked on forty or fifty low-budget independent movies in a three-year period in various low-ranking capacities. In 1966, Kurtz was drafted into the Marines and served for three years in Vietnam, where—due to his background in movies, as well as his pacifist Quaker upbringing—he was assigned to shoot and direct documentary films. He returned from the war in 1969, just as the startling success of Dennis Hopper's *Easy Rider* was breaking open new opportunities for young filmmakers in Hollywood (see Chapter 1).

Kurtz signed with Universal Pictures, where—under the direction of executive Ned Tanen—he helped oversee the production of low-budget movies by young filmmakers; Universal was fishing for the next *Easy Rider*. Kurtz worked as an associate producer on director Monte Hellman's road picture *Two-Lane Blacktop* (1971), which became a cult classic; and on director Paul Magwood's hard-boiled detective pastiche *Chandler* (1971), which did not. Universal canceled its young filmmakers initiative following the disastrous (but prophetically titled) Dennis Hopper vehicle *The Last Movie* (1971). Kurtz worked briefly with Orson Welles on his never-finished film *The Other Side of the Wind*. Then Francis Ford Coppola, who Kurtz had met while preparing *Two-Lane Blacktop*, called and asked if he was interested in joining a project American Zoetrope was producing with screenwriter John Milius and director George Lucas: *Apocalypse Now*. Kurtz and Lucas both dropped out of the project as that film continued its convoluted and painful struggle toward the screen, but the pair had formed a bond. Among many other things, both Kurtz and Lucas were admirers of Akira Kurosawa and Disney comic book artist Carl Barks (see Chapter 3). When Lucas decided to make *American Graffiti* (1973), he brought along Kurtz as producer. (Although Coppola was also listed as producer on *Graffiti*, his credit was mostly ceremonial; "coproducer" Kurtz did all the real work.) In the wake of *Graffiti*'s success, Lucas bounced potential ideas off Kurtz, including a *Flash Gordon* remake, which eventually became *Star Wars*.

Kurtz helped Lucas recruit key crew members, construct a budget, and scout locations for *Star Wars*. He also shot second-unit footage and performed numerous other functions that fell under the famously malleable duties of a movie producer, including running interference between Lucas and Fox executives, and often between the director and troublesome crew members (such as cinematographer Gilbert Taylor). Although the relationship between Lucas and Kurtz was strained at times during the production of *Star Wars*,

Producer Gary Kurtz (left) had George Lucas' back throughout the shooting of *American Graffiti* and *Star Wars*. He's seen here with cinematographer Gilbert Taylor (center) and George Lucas, during the shooting of *Star Wars* in Tunisia.

in part because Lucas was notoriously uncommunicative and had difficulty delegating authority, Kurtz returned to produce *The Empire Strikes Back*.

It was then that the relationship between the two men began to seriously deteriorate. The way Kurtz saw it, his first responsibility was to empower the director to do his best work and ensure that the movie was as good as possible. "If you want to categorize the function of the working producer, it is to provide all the tools so the director can do everything he wants, or at least everything within the limits [in which] you are trying to work," Kurtz explained in a 1977 article for *American Film* magazine. That's what he had done, with tremendous success, for Lucas on *American Graffiti* and *Star Wars*; he did the same for Irvin Kershner on *The Empire Strikes Back*. But Lucas, alarmed by *Empire*'s schedule and budget overruns (see Chapter 17), wanted Kurtz to rein in Kershner, even if it meant sacrificing the quality of the end product. When Kurtz refused, Lucas eventually replaced him with Howard Kazanjian. To this day, Kurtz insists that the cost overruns on *Empire* "were worth it" because the resulting film was so rich and polished. Lucas disagrees.

Kurtz and Lucas also differed on the course the franchise should take following *Empire*. Kurtz wanted to build on the darker, more mature direction of the second film, while Lucas wanted something entirely different and more kid-friendly. In an interview with IGN.com, Kurtz argued that Lucas learned the wrong lessons from the success of *Raiders of the Lost Ark* (1981). "This idea that the roller-coaster ride was all the audience was interested in, and the story doesn't have to be very adult or interesting, seemed to come up because of what happened with *Raiders of the Lost Ark* and the Indiana Jones films," Kurtz said. Because the thinly plotted *Raiders* had made more money than *Empire*, Kurtz says that Lucas became convinced "it didn't matter whether there was a really good story or not. . . . We had serious differences about a lot of that."

Kurtz soon left Lucasfilm to produce Muppet maestro Jim Henson's *The Dark Crystal* (1982). Over the next twenty years, he would complete just nine more film and television projects. At least four proposed Kurtz productions have fallen apart, including an animated feature based on comic book gumshoe *The Spirit*, involving Brad Bird, John Lasseter, and *Spirit* creator Will Eisner. But Kurtz is now enjoying a career resurgence, with two projects (*Road to the Sky* and *13 O'Clock*) in production for 2015 and two more announced for future release.

Kurtz was a vocal critic of *Return of the Jedi* and the *Star Wars* prequels, complaining that the stories were too "simplistic" and that the projects seemed to be overly concerned with marketing and merchandising tie-ins. "There's a lot of undercurrent in *Star Wars* that, if you take it on the surface, a four-year-old can really enjoy it—but there's a lot else going on under there," Kurtz told IGN.com. "It's multi-layered, and *Empire* is as well. That's the thing that bothered me a bit about *Jedi* and certainly about *Episode I*, that those layers, those subtexts—they're all gone. They're not there. . . . There's nothing to ponder. There's no depth in it, and that's where I think the mistake is."

The creative differences that separated Kurtz and Lucas were unfortunate for both parties. Neither would regain the level of artistry they reached together in the 1970s, when together they made *Graffiti*, *Star Wars*, and *Empire*, three of the four best films ever released by Lucasfilm (only *Raiders* rivals that trio). If either *Graffiti* or *Star Wars* had won the Academy Award for Best Picture (both were nominated), the Oscar would have gone to the producer—Kurtz, not Lucas.

Aside from Ladd, McQuarrie, Burtt, and Kurtz, several other contributors also deserve more credit than they generally receive. Production designer John Barry and costume designer John Mollo brought McQuarrie's paintings to life and turned *Star Wars* into a seemingly inhabitable reality. Stuart Freeborn created or cocreated some of the most memorable beings in the

Star Wars universe, including Yoda and Jabba the Hutt. Stunt coordinator Peter Diamond brought vitality and inventiveness to the Original Trilogy's action sequences—including its lightsaber duels and Luke and Leia's swing across the Death Star chasm—without sacrificing safety (some of the more elaborate stunts Diamond created for the trilogy nowadays would be realized through CGI). Finally, the contributions of Lucas' wife, Marcia, should not be underestimated. Not only was she a gifted editor (sharing an Oscar for *Star Wars* with Paul Hirsch and Richard Chew), but she was invaluable as a trusted sounding board and confidant for George Lucas. As the company grew, Marcia became one of the few people at Lucasfilm willing to tell George that he was wrong. Many of the company's productions made after his divorce seemed to suffer from the lack of anyone with the will or authority to tell Lucas that any of his ideas were bad.

23

More Powerful Than You Can Possibly Imagine

The Music of *Star Wars*

I t's impossible to overstate how profoundly a movie's score can influence the audience's viewing experience. An effective score subtly
enhances the emotional impact of the drama unfolding on-screen; a
clumsy or overly busy score can distract and disengage viewers from the story.
Few movies have benefitted more from their scores than the original *Star Wars*
trilogy. But then, few movies have soundtracks as powerful and evocative as
composer John Williams' magnificent *Star Wars* music. His stirring, melodic
themes are as instantly recognizable as any of the characters from the movies
and rank among the most beloved music ever written for motion pictures.

The Man Behind the Music

Williams had already established himself as one of Hollywood's most gifted
composers when George Lucas approached him about scoring *Star Wars*.
Williams, born February 8, 1932, in Floral Park, New York, was the son of a
jazz drummer. When John was sixteen, the Williams family moved to Los
Angeles. After graduating from North Hollywood High School, Williams
enrolled at UCLA as a music composition major and studied privately with
Italian maestro Mario Castelnuovo-Tedesco. He was drafted into the Air Force
in 1952, where he conducted and arranged for the U.S. Air Force Band. When
his military service ended, Williams moved back to New York and enrolled at
the Juilliard School. By night, he played jazz piano in Manhattan clubs under
the name Little Johnny Love and worked as a session musician at New York
recording studios. In 1956, Williams married actress Barbara Ruick, remaining with her until her death in 1974. The couple had three children. Their
youngest son, Mark, sang lead with the rock band Toto. Williams had his own

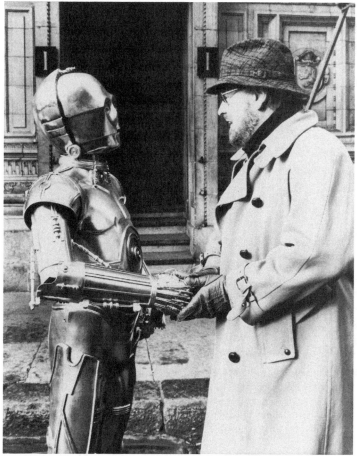

Composer John Williams (right) and friend posed for this publicity shot during the recording of Williams' score for *The Empire Strikes Back.*

brief association with popular music, arranging music and serving as bandleader for Western balladeer Frankie Laine in the early 1960s, the twilight of Laine's career.

However, Williams' greatest love was always symphonic music, and in the late 1950s he returned to Hollywood. Writing and conducting film scores was one way for a classically minded young composer to earn a living, and Williams landed a job as a staff music arranger at Columbia Pictures. He later took a similar position at Twentieth Century-Fox, working as a musician, orchestrator, or conductor on the music for more than a dozen films and TV series. In 1958, he penned the Emmy-nominated theme for an episode of TV's *Alcoa Theatre* and wrote uncredited cues for the juvenile delinquency melodrama *Daddy-O*—his first compositions for the screen.

THE STAR WARS SYMPHONIC SUITE
BY JOHN WILLIAMS

After the *Star Wars* soundtrack climbed to number 2 on the Billboard album chart, composer John Williams went on tour and became an in-demand concert attraction, conducting various orchestras in live performances of the music from Star Wars.

Williams wrote themes for several TV series, including producer Irwin Allen's *Lost in Space*, *Land of the Giants*, and *The Time Tunnel* (his first association with science fiction), and quickly gained a reputation as an imaginative, versatile, and reliable composer. His first major breakthrough arrived in 1967 when Williams' score for *Valley of the Dolls* earned an Academy Award nomination. It was the first of forty-six scores by Williams (so far) to be nominated for an Oscar. He collected the first of his five Academy Awards in 1972 for *Fiddler on the Roof*. By then, Williams had left Fox and was working freelance. In 1975, he wrote the iconic score for Steven Spielberg's *Jaws*, the first of many scores he has written that remain well known even by people not particularly interested in movie music—or even in movies.

While already acclaimed, *Star Wars* launched Williams into a different orbit than his Hollywood contemporaries. His *Star Wars* soundtrack shot up the *Billboard* Hot 100 album chart, peaking at No. 2 (it was denied the top spot by Fleetwood Mac's blockbuster *Rumours*). Twentieth Century-Fox Records had difficulty pressing enough copies to meet demand. Still, the record finished as the sixty-fourth best-selling album of the year, outselling LPs by artists including Donna Summer, Elton John, and Peter Frampton, among others. It remains the best-selling score-only soundtrack recording of all time. Like any rock star with a hit album, Williams went on tour and became an in-demand concert attraction, conducting various orchestras in live performances of the music from *Star Wars* and his other films. Over the next decade and beyond, he cemented his position as America's best-loved film composer with his instantly recognizable themes for *Superman: The Movie* (1978), the Indiana Jones pictures, *E.T.: The Extra-Terrestrial* (1982), *Schindler's List* (1993), and all the subsequent *Star Wars* films, including the forthcoming *Episode VII: The Force Awakens*.

In all, Williams has scored more than eighty films. The only human being nominated for more Academy Awards than Williams is Walt Disney. His Oscar win percentage might be higher if not for the fact that on a dozen occasions, two or more of his scores have been nominated in the same year. In addition to his five Oscars, he has accumulated seventeen Grammys, three Golden Globes, five BAFTA Awards, and two Emmys. He has also written many original concert pieces and had the unique honor of composing the music for the rededication of the Statue of Liberty in 1986. In 2004, Williams' original *Star Wars* score was named to the Library of Congress' National Recording Registry, reserved for recordings that are "culturally, historically, or aesthetically significant" (or, in this case, all three). A year later, the American Film Institute named his *Star Wars* score the most memorable ever composed for an American film.

The Music Behind the Movie

From the beginning, music had been an integral element in George Lucas' vision for *Star Wars*, and his first choice to score the film was Williams, who came enthusiastically recommended by Steven Spielberg. Lucas and Williams met in late 1975 to discuss the movie and exchange ideas about its score. Lucas eschewed electronic music, which had become a sci-fi movie cliché since Louis and Bebe Barron's all-theremin score for *Forbidden Planet* in 1956. Instead, he imagined an original symphonic suite in the Old Hollywood tradition, something along the lines of Erich Wolfgang Korngold's sweeping, tuneful score for *The Adventures of Robin Hood* (1938). Williams agreed that this was the right approach. "The translation of heroic impulses and feelings and reactions, in terms of melodrama and opera, brings you in the direction of the symphony orchestra, rather than synthesizers or computers that might produce a spacey, otherworldly sound," Williams told a National Public Radio interviewer in 2005.

Williams was the perfect choice to compose a score in this style. Like Korngold, he was a master of leitmotif, an operatic technique where individual characters and story elements (such as the Force or the Empire) are given their own musical themes, which recur whenever these characters or concepts appear on-screen or are referred to. Judiciously employed, these cues can generate tremendous emotional power. Once established, the recurring leitmotif can also be used to evoke the presence of these entities even when they remain unseen. By the end of *Jaws*, for instance, the spikey, staccato cue Williams wrote for the monstrous shark could instill terror on its own, without the shark even being shown. Despite Williams' success with *Jaws*, however, traditional symphonic scores were out of fashion in Hollywood at the time. So Williams reveled in the opportunity to create the rousing fanfares and lush romantic themes *Star Wars* would require, and he was excited by the large canvas the picture would provide. Almost no one used as much music as Lucas planned for *Star Wars*. Williams' *Star Wars* score would be 88 minutes long, an extraordinary length for a 121-minute movie.

Williams first viewed the film in early January 1977 and immediately set about composing the music, which was recorded at Anvil Studios in Denham, England, from March 5 through 16, 1977. Williams personally conducted the London Symphony Orchestra during the two-a-day, three-hour sessions, which were supervised by Lionel Newman, head of the Fox music department. It was the first time Williams had worked with a full symphony orchestra. Lucas attended the sessions and was so excited by what he heard that he called Spielberg on the phone and pointed the receiver at the orchestra so his friend could listen to the music as it was recorded. Lucas later said that Williams' score was the only element of *Star Wars* that exceeded his expectations. In the liner notes for a CD boxed set of the *Star Wars* soundtrack recordings, Lucas described Williams' work as "lavish, rich, moving, and thrilling" and wrote that "Every fan of *Star Wars*—and of great music—is in his debt."

Lucas and a team of editors had been struggling to find the tempo and energy the director knew the movie required. Once Williams' music was added to the picture, however, it came together quickly. His score added an entirely new dimension to *Star Wars*, a catalyst that brought all the other elements together. To fully appreciate how important Williams' music is to the film, Google "*Star Wars* without John Williams" and you will find several fan-made and professionally produced clips from the film with its score removed. The movie seems almost unrecognizable without its soaring "Main Title" theme, or the lilting "Princess Leia's Theme," or the jazzy "Cantina Band" music.

But Williams' brilliance was not reserved for those celebrated passages. There's not a clumsy or ineffective note in the entire score, and the lesser-quoted sections serve the picture beautifully. The woodwind-accented "Desert" theme (identified as "Dune Sea of Tatooine/Jawa Sandcrawler" on CD) lends a sense of the exotic and mysterious to our first glimpses of the planet Tatooine. In the "Tractor Beam/Chasm Crossfire" passage, heard as our heroes attempt to reach the *Millennium Falcon* and escape the Death Star, foreboding bass and cellos give way to stabbing violins and pounding tympani, which in turn surrender to a frantic-sounding reprise of the Main

Title; the viewer's pulse quickens almost involuntarily. And Williams' thumping, brassy "TIE Fighter Attack" music may induce nail-biting.

Although it didn't repeat the chart performance of his *Star Wars* soundtrack, Williams' score for *The Empire Strikes Back* was no less evocative or memorable. It introduced several major new leitmotifs, including the ominous "Imperial March," which replaced the more plodding theme Williams had employed for Darth Vader and the Empire in the first film. "Battle in the Snow" (heard during the imperial attack on Hoth) and "Yoda's Theme" (heard as the diminutive Jedi Master raises Luke's X-wing from the swamp) indelibly etch themselves into the viewer's memory. But, once again, less recognizable passages, such as "Lando's Palace" (heard when Han, Leia, Chewie, and Threepio arrive at Cloud City), also work beautifully. This segment begins with a chipper, flutey, almost regal melody that melts into worried-sounding reprises of "Princess Leia's Theme" and the "Main Title," suggesting hidden dangers even before they become fully apparent.

While Williams' score for *Return of the Jedi* included a few memorable new cues—in particular the spooky choral theme (listed as "The Dark Side Beckons" and "The Final Duel" on the soundtrack CD) written for Luke's showdown with Vader and the emperor—it relied heavily on the familiar leitmotifs from the previous films, such as the original *Star Wars* title theme, and the "Imperial March" and "Love Theme" from *Empire*. In an interview posted on the StarWars.com site, Williams called quoting from his previous themes "part of the fun of doing film after film. . . . In each case I've been able to use the earlier material and develop new material that would coexist with it and hopefully feel like a part of the fabric of the film," he said. Williams' evocative redeployment of these familiar themes enables the *Jedi* soundtrack to function like the closing movement of a grand symphony. It isn't a rehash; it's a climactic summing-up.

When George Lucas released his Special Editions of the Original Trilogy in 1997, Williams' scores were—for obvious reasons—among the least-altered aspects of the film. But changes were made, most noticeably to *Return of the Jedi*. Williams replaced the original "Ewok Celebration" music, which featured a chorus chanting in Ewokese ("Yub nub!"), with a vaguely New Agey, woodwind- and percussion-driven "Victory Celebration" theme. More controversially, the music the Max Rebo Band plays in Jabba's Palace was also changed, with the original, New Wavey "Lapti Nek" replaced by the more rhythm-and-blues-inflected "Jedi Rocks." Williams did not write either of these compositions. In retrospect, perhaps Jabba should have booked the band from the Mos Eisley cantina.

Star Wars Goes Disco

While Williams' *Star Wars* soundtrack was ascending the Billboard album charts, a single featuring a very different version of his music—"Star Wars Theme/Cantina Band," by Meco—soared all the way to the top of the *Billboard* Hot 100, reaching that summit on October 1, 1977. This disco version of the *Star Wars* theme sold two million copies and remains the best-selling instrumental single ever released.

"Meco" was the *nom de funque* of record producer Domenico Monardo, an Italian American musician from Pennsylvania who had produced a handful of hit records, including disco diva Gloria Gaynor's Top 10 cover of "Never Can Say Goodbye" (1974). Monardo, who had been a science fiction fan since childhood, reportedly caught *Star Wars* on opening day and saw it four more times during its first week. He was struck with the idea of merging his two passions by creating a disco version of John Williams' *Star Wars* music and quickly pitched the concept to Neil Bogart, founder of Casablanca Records (the label of disco hitmakers such as Donna Summer and the Village People). Although skeptical at first, Bogart eventually agreed, issuing Monardo's *Star Wars* project on a new Casablanca vanity imprint, Millennium Records.

Monardo and his frequent collaborators Tony Bonjiovi, Harold Wheeler, and guitarist Lance Quinn gathered an army of session players and recorded an entire album (*Star Wars and Other Galactic Funk*, credited simply to "Meco") in three weeks during the summer of 1977. The record's liner notes list nearly 150 "musicians from the Milky Way galaxy" among the album's personnel, including guitarists, bass players, keyboardists, drummers and percussionists, string, brass, and woodwind sections, and five autoharp players. The first side of the record was a sixteen-minute suite featuring disco versions of Williams' themes punctuated with droid-like electronic beeps and the sounds of laser blasts created by Suzanne Ciani on a synthesizer. The flip side of the album featured nearly thirteen minutes of generic disco composed by Wheeler and songwriter Solomon Smith. The 3:28 "Star Wars/Cantina Band" single (and a 7:35 dance mix) was culled from Side One.

While the album didn't perform as well as the single, it went platinum (signifying sales of at least one million copies) and demonstrated that there was an audience for sci-fi-oriented dance music. During the height of the craze for Meco's *Star Wars*, a band was assembled to perform live. Although none of the musicians in the Meco show band actually played on the album, the group was booked into discos across the United States in the fall of 1977. Both Meco and John Williams received Grammy nominations for Best Pop Instrumental Recording—Williams for the soundtrack album, Meco for the "Star Wars/Cantina Band" single. Williams deservedly won the award.

Record producer Demenico "Meco" Monardo scored a career-altering smash hit with his disco version of John Williams' *Star Wars* score.

Photography by Preston Hewis/East Bank Images

Star Wars and Other Galactic Funk was so successful that Monardo gave up producing records and became "Meco" full time, working with a rotating group of session musicians to record several more science fiction- and fantasy-themed disco albums (many based on Williams' compositions) over the next eight years, including *Encounters of Every Kind* (1977), *Meco Plays the Wizard of Oz* (1978), *Superman & Other Galactic Heroes* (1978), *Moondancer* (1979), *Music from Star Trek and The Black Hole*, and *Across the Galaxy* (both 1980). He wasn't finished with *Star Wars*, either. An EP titled *Meco Plays Music from The Empire Strikes Back* appeared in 1980, and Meco's "Empire Strikes Back (Medley)" climbed to No. 18 on the Billboard charts, the second-best performance by any Meco recording. Meco issued *Ewok Celebration*, based on Williams' *Return of the Jedi* score, in 1983.

Meco's most unusual project was the oddball holiday album *Christmas in the Stars*, which featured both the song stylings of Anthony Daniels and the first professional recording by future rock star Jon Bon Jovi.

Photography by Preston Hewis/East Bank Images

The fourth Meco *Star Wars* project demands further explanation. Following the success of *Star Wars and Other Galactic Funk* and *Music from the Empire Strikes Back*, Monardo pitched George Lucas the idea of producing a holiday-themed *Star Wars* album. Surprisingly (especially in light of the *Star Wars Holiday Special* debacle two years earlier), Lucas agreed, and Meco's *Christmas in the Stars* was created with the assistance of Lucasfilm. This was not a disco album but a children's record featuring C-3PO, R2-D2, and Chewbacca, with original and traditional Christmas songs. Anthony Daniels provided the voice of Threepio, and Ben Burtt sound effects supplied the "voices" of Artoo and Chewie.

The album cover featured Artoo, Threepio, and other droids gathered around Santa Claus, who was seated in front of a fireplace. Dialogue passages that link the various songs depict the droids and Chewbacca assisting Santa in his workshop. Daniels sings four numbers ("Christmas in the Stars," "Bells,

Bells, Bells," "The Odds Against Christmas," and "Sleigh Ride"). *Christmas in the Stars* also featured the first professional recording by Tony Bonjiovi's eighteen-year-old cousin, Johnny, who would soon change his name to Jon Bon Jovi. The future rock star sings lead on "R2-D2 We Wish You a Merry Christmas," performing with a children's choir. The album's novelty single, "What Can You Get a Wookiee for Christmas (When He Already Owns a Comb)," peaked at No. 69 on the Billboard chart. The warm and fuzzy *Christmas in the Stars* wasn't the hit Meco hoped for, but it retains a corny sort of charm and is much easier to sit through than the *Star Wars Holiday Special.*

After releasing a final Meco album (*Hooked on Instrumentals*) in 1985, Monardo retired from show business and later became a commodities broker. Most of the Meco albums (including *Christmas in the Stars*) are long out of print, but *Star Wars and Other Galactic Funk* was reissued on CD by Hip-O Records in 1999, and a few Meco compilations, such as *The Best of Meco* and *Star Wars Party*, remain available in various formats.

May the funk be with you.

24

Sorry About the Mess

Gaffes and Flubs

Nobody's perfect. And even though every film crew employs a script supervisor and other personnel who are tasked with preventing continuity problems and other gaffes, no movie is mistake free. That certainly includes the three original *Star Wars* pictures, and it's understandable, considering that all three were ambitious productions made under intense pressure, with constrained resources, and in the face of mishaps and minor catastrophes of all sorts (see Chapters 6, 17, and 20).

Still, close inspection of *Star Wars*, *The Empire Strikes Back*, and *Return of the Jedi* reveals that all three films are riddled with sometimes hilarious gaps in continuity, technical snafus, scientific inaccuracies, and lapses in simple logic. The website Movie Mistakes counts 276 errors in the first film alone. George Lucas tried to correct some of the more egregious goofs with his 1997 Special Editions, but he couldn't fix them all and inadvertently introduced a few more. To be fair, many of these flaws are relatively minor and require careful scrutiny or thoughtful reflection to identify. Similar mistakes go unnoticed in most other films, but few movies have been as frequently and closely rewatched, dissected, and analyzed as the Original Trilogy. Devoted fans take a sort of pride in ferreting out these errors and often look on them with a kind of cockeyed affection and amusement. What follows is a representative, although far from comprehensive, sampling of these snafus.

Continuity Errors

The primary responsibility of the script supervisor is to make sure that on-screen details remain consistent from take to take, shot to shot, and scene to scene—so that, for instance, a lightsaber sitting on a table doesn't vanish or change positions when the director cuts to a different camera angle. Nevertheless, these remain the most common types of mistakes that survive a film's final cut, often because they aren't detected until the editing stage (if at all), when nothing can be done about them without undertaking expensive reshoots. There are many of them in the original *Star Wars* films, including the following doozies:

- During the scene in which Ben Kenobi gives Luke his father's lightsaber, Kenobi's brown, hooded cloak disappears and reappears from shot to shot. The cloak is hung (or not) in the alcove where Threepio shuts down to rest. Later in this scene, when Artoo plays Princess Leia's message for Kenobi, the objects on the table where the hologram is projected change in number and position when Lucas cuts to a reverse angle.

- During her rescue from the Death Star detention area, Leia blasts a hole in the garbage chute to provide an escape route. At first the hole is barely large enough for the dainty, 110-pound princess to get through. A second later, it's large enough to accommodate Han, Luke, and the giant Chewbacca. Also during this sequence, the left shoulder armor of Luke's stolen stormtrooper armor vanishes and reappears as different camera angles are employed.

- When we first see Luke Skywalker hanging upside down from the ceiling of the cave of the Wampa ice monster in *The Empire Strikes Back*, his feet are wide apart. But once he recovers his lightsaber, we cut to a closer view in which Luke's feet are close together. Also, the position of the lightsaber in the snow changes from shot to shot as Luke struggles to retrieve it by using the Force.

- When Leia meets Wicket the Ewok in *Return of the Jedi*, she offers him a bite of food. In the wide shot, the food is in her left hand. But when a closer shot is employed, the food has suddenly leapt into the princess' right hand.

- In all three movies the cockpit of the *Millennium Falcon* (seen from outside) has four windows. But seen from inside it only has three. The windows of Darth Vader's TIE Fighter are also configured differently seen from the inside than from the outside.

Equipment Failures and Wardrobe Malfunctions

No, not *that* kind of wardrobe malfunction. To prevent that sort of thing from winding up on film, Carrie Fisher's breasts were restrained with gaffer's tape during filming of *Star Wars*, and a technician was assigned to keep track of her metal-bikini-clad bosom between shots while making *Return of the Jedi*. Still, costumes and props created some of the trilogy's more noticeable (and amusing) continuity issues.

- During their frenzied attempt to escape from the Death Star after rescuing Princess Leia in *Star Wars*, Han and Chewie rush headlong into a squad of stormtroopers. As they turn and run away, the rubber soles of Peter Mayhew's costume are clearly visible. It looks like Chewie has donned a pair of sneakers! The same thing happens during the escape from Cloud City in *Empire*.

- If you look closely, you can see the power cord for Obi-Wan Kenobi's lightsaber (visible running up Alec Guinness' sleeve) during his duel with Darth Vader in the original film.
- At the beginning of Han and Leia's famous romantic exchange at the carbon freeze chamber in *Empire*, Han is wearing a simple white shirt with no jacket. Then, during an insert shot just before he's lowered into the chamber, he's wearing his blue flight jacket. Then the jacket disappears again. Also, throughout this sequence Han's hands are tied. Two Ugnaughts make sure his bonds are secure before he's lowered into the pit. Yet, when his frozen body is retrieved from the chamber, his hands are unbound and raised to shoulder level as if he were trying to escape. Did he manage to free himself in the split-second it took to activate the device?
- Earlier in *Empire*, when Han, Leia, and Chewbacca are captured by Darth Vader, Leia is wearing an elegant brown suit. But when we see her again, she has changed back into her white flight suit. Was she overdressed for interrogation?
- As he awaits being hurled into the Sarlacc nest in *Return of the Jedi*, Lando is wearing a pair of gloves. Later, as he clings to a rope to avoid sliding into the pit, his gloves are gone. But they return when Han pulls him out of the pit.

Screwy Science

George Lucas described *Star Wars* as "space fantasy" rather than science fiction and wasn't overly concerned with scientific accuracy. Even granting that, however, Lucas and screenwriter Lawrence Kasdan made a few glaring scientific blunders.

- In the original film, C-3PO describes his programmed role as "human-cyborg relations." But, aside from Darth Vader, there are no cyborgs (beings that are part human and part robot) in *Star Wars*. In *The Empire Strikes Back* we meet bounty hunter Dengar and Lando's assistant Lobot (whose brain interfaces directly with the Cloud City Central Computer). Plus Luke, technically, becomes a cyborg when he gains a mechanical hand. Still, there don't seem to be enough cyborgs among the population to suggest a major need for liaisons such as C-3PO, and the cyborgs we meet seem perfectly capable of interacting with humans on their own.

Also, Threepio describes his first job as "programming binary load lift-ers," which clearly are mechanical in nature (and "very similar to moisture vaporators in most respects"). Clearly, Threepio should have described his specialty as "human-*android* relations," but apparently Lucas wasn't clear on the difference between cyborgs and androids.

- In maybe the most egregious scientific error from the *Star Wars* films, Han Solo boasts that the *Millennium Falcon* made the Kessel Run "in less than 12 parsecs." The problem with this is that a parsec is an astronomical measure of distance, not time. So this is like boasting that the *Falcon* ran the Indianapolis 500 in less than 500 miles! If he's suggesting that he took some sort of illegal shortcut, this might prove Han is a cunning pilot, but it would not demonstrate that the *Falcon* is a fast ship. Lucas, in the audio commentary for the film, offers a retroactive defense of his use of the word parsec, explaining that what makes the *Millennium Falcon* so fast is its sophisticated navigation system, which enables it to map the shortest route between two points. Accept that if you will. But author Alan Dean Foster, while writing the *Star Wars* novelization, changed "12 parsecs" to "12 standard time units," because he believed Lucas simply didn't know what a parsec was.

- In *The Empire Strikes Back*, Han, Leia, and Chewie exit the *Falcon* in street clothes. They're in the belly of an Exogoth—a sort of giant space-eel—but they *think* they're stepping onto the surface of the asteroid, which has no atmosphere. Yet, while they don breathing apparatus, they don't wear pressure suits to protect them from rapid decompression and the deadly cold (hundreds of degrees below zero Fahrenheit) of outer space. This is the equivalent of Neil Armstrong taking his first step onto the moon in scuba gear and Bermuda shorts.

- Blowing up a Death Star in close proximity to the Endor moon would wipe out the Ewoks too. The explosion of a moon-sized body as nearby as the Death Star could blow the moon's atmosphere completely away, or shower the moon with deadly radiation, or fill its atmosphere with debris, blocking out the life-giving rays of the sun—any one of which would spell certain doom for the inhabitants of the moon. The droids would be okay, and if Han, Leia, and Chewie could make it back to their stolen shuttle before the blast, they might survive too. But all the cute little teddy bears, if their atmosphere survived at all, would likely be shivering in a nuclear winter and dying slow, horrible deaths from radiation poisoning.

- Many of the scientific blunders of *Star Wars* are conventional to movie space opera. For instance, audiences hear the roar of starship engines when in reality they would be silent, at least when viewed from outside the ship. Sound does not travel in the vacuum of space. Similarly, it would be impossible to see a laser fired in outer space, since laser beams are only visible when the air is filled with smoke or other particles, which also do not exist in a vacuum. Besides, lasers move at the speed of light—too fast for our vision to track if fired in short bursts. And, similarly, there can be no fireballs or shattering kabooms in outer space, not even when a Death Star explodes. Nearly all spacefaring SF pictures make these same errors, primarily because the roar of engines and sight of laser blasts make space battles much more exciting. While this sort of thing can be chalked up as dramatic license, it's still bad science.

Plot Holes

These are the most damaging problems of all, since lapses in story logic undermine the credibility of the entire narrative. The frenetic pace of the *Star Wars* films helps disguise these issues, most of which only become apparent later, upon thoughtful reflection.

- Why, if Kenobi was trying to keep Luke's identity secret from Darth Vader, didn't he change the boy's name to Lars (like Uncle Owen or Aunt Beru) or Kenobi or Binks or anything other than Skywalker? Is "Skywalker" supposed to be the galactic equivalent of Smith or Jones?
- At the conclusion of *Star Wars*, the rebels have time to assemble, receive a preflight briefing, and launch their attack on the Death Star only because the fourth moon of Yavin is on the opposite side of the planet from the imperial space station. A countdown tells us how long the rebels have until the Death Star is clear to target the rebel base. So why doesn't the Death Star, which was built to destroy planets, simply obliterate Yavin to clear a shot at the moon? Also, consider that the Death Star reaches the Yavin system shortly after the *Millennium Falcon* arrives. Since the *Falcon* has been moving through hyperspace to get there, this must mean that the Death Star is also capable of faster-than-light travel. So why doesn't the Death Star simply jump through hyperspace to the other side of Yavin and then blow up the moon?
- During the second act of *The Empire Strikes Back*, Luke trains on Dagobah with Yoda, while Han and Leia hide out in the asteroid belt and eventually escape to Bespin. However, Luke's training seems to go on for months, or at least weeks. Han and Leia's adventure seems to last for, at most, a couple of days. Yet they are all reunited at Cloud City. Something doesn't add up, especially since in *Return of the Jedi*, Yoda tells Luke that his training is complete. Either Luke was trained in the ways of the Jedi

(something that usually takes years) in only a few days, or else Han and Leia were holding hands in that asteroid belt for months. Neither option makes much sense.

- At the climax of *Empire*, Luke escapes Darth Vader by allowing himself to fall down Cloud City's massive central ventilation shaft. Why doesn't Vader use the Force to prevent Luke from falling and lift him back onto the platform?

- Making Luke and Leia brother and sister introduces more questions than it answers. Among the many riddles posed by this development is this: Darth Vader can sense Luke Skywalker's presence across the gulf from space, from the Death Star to the forest moon of Endor. He can do this, even when the emperor cannot, because of the special Force bond that exists between father and son. So why is it that in *Star Wars* Vader tortures Leia for hours without realizing she is his daughter?

- Luke's plan to rescue Han from Jabba's Palace hinges on a host of implausibilities. Among other things, the scheme involves goading Jabba into dumping them into the Sarlacc nest and on R2-D2 being assigned to work on Jabba's sail barge (so the droid can fling Skywalker his lightsaber). How could Luke possibly know either of these things would take place? The enraged Hutt is far more likely to simply kill Luke, Han, and Leia on the spot. And what are the chances that Jabba would employ an astromech droid as a waiter? Shouldn't Artoo be patching up one of the gangster's spacecraft?

- The emperor's plan to destroy the rebels is even stupider. Not only does it involve creating a second Death Star that's even more vulnerable than the first one (if the shield generator goes down, the space station is a sitting duck), but the emperor uses himself as bait for this harebrained trap. He doesn't appear to have any sort of backup plan. Also, even though he can sense Luke's feelings, the emperor never notices that Vader is about to switch allegiances and hurl him into the abyss. Oops!

Miscellaneous Mix-Ups

Some of the funniest *Star Wars* snafus defy categorization. These include the following:

- There are several instances in all three movies where, during the editing of the film, footage was flipped to provide a never-filmed reverse angle. For instance, in the middle of Darth Vader's duel with Ben Kenobi from *Star Wars*, because the image was inverted, it appears that the buttons on Vader's chest plate suddenly move from one side to the other. Similarly, when Princess Leia is chained to Jabba the Hutt in *Return of the Jedi*, the birthmark on her back jumps from side to side when a reverse angle is employed.

- In the opening sequence of the first movie, Darth Vader chokes the captain of the *Tantive IV* to death. Yet when he hurls the supposedly lifeless body into a bulkhead, the actor playing the dead man raises his arms to keep from smacking his face against the wall.
- In *Star Wars*, stormtroopers break into the command center where the droids have been hiding while Luke, Leia, and Chewie rescue the princess. The third soldier into the room bonks his head on the door frame like one of Mack Sennett's Keystone Kops.
- In a close-up shot as the disassembled C-3PO rolls down the conveyor belt toward a Cloud City incinerator, the crew filming the scene is clearly visible, reflected in Threepio's shiny metallic noggin.

There are plenty more gaffes, goofs, and flubs to be spotted. Happy hunting.

25

Luke, I Am Your Father

The Quotable (and Misquotable) *Star Wars*

A lthough seldom cited as a source of brilliant dialogue, the original *Star Wars* trilogy remains one of the most-quoted works of the twentieth century, full of instantly recognizable and frequently parodied catchphrases. To say that the language of *Star Wars* has entered the popular vernacular would be a major understatement. Metaphoric references to the Force, Jedi mind tricks, and hyperspace may be casually dropped without fear of misunderstanding. Some words and concepts, including the name *Star Wars* itself—co-opted, to George Lucas' horror, to describe President Ronald Reagan's proposed satellite-based missile defense system—have been widely adopted and accumulated additional definitions. All this speaks to the profound cultural impact of the movies, but it also reflects the steadfast devotion of fans. After all, these words, phrases, and ideas entered the language because fans watched these movies over and over again—in theaters and later on home video—memorizing the dialogue and quoting lines back and forth with one another. (If I say, "When I left you, I was but a learner; now I am the master," you answer with . . . ?)

Given all this, a closer look at some of the films' most famous quotes would seem to be in order.

"A long time ago, in a galaxy far, far away . . . "

Every *Star Wars* film famously opens with these words, printed in blue type against a black background. They precede the title of the film itself. George Lucas' self-conscious mythmaking is at its most obvious here, but the words are beautifully chosen and their impact is both powerful and elegant; they immediately set the fanciful tone for all that follows. The phrase is clearly intended as the equivalent of "Once upon a time. . . . " The link is so self-evident that decades later the writers of the DreamWorks animated *Shrek* film series set the adventures of the loveable ogre and his companions in a fairy-tale world referred to simply as "Far Far Away." This is also one of the most instantly recognizable and durable *Star Wars*-isms. A comprehensive listing of all the various books, movies, TV shows, newspaper and magazine articles, and websites to co-opt the phrase "A long time ago, in a galaxy far, far away" in whole or in part, often for ironic or satirical purposes, would run on for hundreds of pages (and would include this book).

This original "May the Force Be With You" button dates from the summer of 1977. The slogan has been printed on T-shirts, hats, bumper stickers, coffee mugs, and everything else imaginable ever since.   *Photography by Preston Hewis/ East Bank Images*

"May the Force be with you."

This phrase—Jedi-speak for "good luck" or often "goodbye and good luck"—quickly became (and remains) the emblematic catchphrase for *Star Wars*. It appears in every *Star Wars* film and in nearly every *Star Wars* book, comic, and video game. And it has been immortalized (after a fashion) on T-shirts, coffee mugs, key chains, bumper stickers, and every other sort of ephemera imaginable, up to and including being tattooed onto fans' bodies. "May the Force be with you" is spoken four times in the Original Trilogy: twice in *Star Wars* (once by General Dodonna and once by Han Solo), once in *The Empire Strikes Back* (by Luke Skywalker), and once ("May the Force be with us," says Admiral Ackbar) in *Return of the Jedi*.

"I have a bad feeling about this."

This catchphrase/running gag appears twice in *Star Wars* (on first sight of the Death Star, Luke says, "I have a very bad feeling about this;" later, in the trash compactor, Han says, "I got a bad feeling about this"), and it recurs in every subsequent *Star Wars* movie, as well as in countless *Star Wars* novels, comic books, video games, and other media. Leia has the line in *The Empire Strikes Back* (while the *Millennium Falcon* is hidden in the belly of the giant asteroid monster), and both C-3PO and Han say it in *Return of the Jedi* (C-3PO upon entering Jabba's palace and Han when he and Luke are captured by Ewoks). Tellingly, the line does not appear in the ill-conceived *Star Wars Holiday Special*, but it was used in episodes of the *Droids* and *Ewoks* cartoon series of the 1980s, in the *Clone Wars* animated series, and, of course, in the Prequel Trilogy (presumably it will also be repeated in the Sequel Trilogy).

The phrase "I have a bad feeling about this," or some version of it, also appears in countless *Star Wars* novels, comics, video games, role-playing games, and the Star Tours attraction at Disneyland and Disney World. Like the call letters THX-1138 (the name of Lucas' first feature film), the phrase "I have a bad feeling about this" also recurs in other Lucasfilm projects, including the movies *Radioland Murders* (1994) and *Indiana Jones and the Kingdom of the Crystal Skull* (2008), and the *Young Indiana Jones* TV series. And it has been co-opted as an homage to *Star Wars* in numerous other works, including *Star Wars* jokes on TV series including *The Big Bang Theory*, *Robot Chicken*, *Family Guy*, and *Phineas and Ferb*.

"Luke, I am your father."

This is a phantom phrase. Although often "quoted" or parodied, Darth Vader does never actually says this—not in quite this construction, anyway—in *The Empire Strikes Back* or anywhere else. It's a misquote much like "Beam me up, Scotty," which no *Star Trek* character has ever spoken, or "Play it again, Sam," which is never said in *Casablanca*, or "Elementary, my dear Watson," which Sir Arthur Conan Doyle never wrote. The actual exchange from *Empire*:

> Vader: Obi-Wan never told you what happened to your father.
>
> Luke: He told me enough! He told me you killed him!
>
> Vader: No. *I* am your father.

Other Memorable Quotes

In addition to the preceding catchphrases, the original *Star Wars* trilogy abounds with memorable snippets of dialogue. A topically grouped selection follows.

Star Wars Characters, as Described by Star Wars Characters

Aunt Beru: "Luke's just not a farmer, Owen. He has too much of his
   father in him."
Uncle Owen: "That's what I'm afraid of."
                              —Exchange about Luke Skywalker by his
                                        aunt and uncle in Star Wars

"He's quite clever, you know . . . for a human being."
                              —C-3PO, about Luke in Star Wars

"Aren't you a little short for a stormtrooper?"
                              —Princess Leia Organa, about Luke in Star Wars

"A Jedi Knight? Jeez, I'm out of it for a little while and everyone gets
   delusions of grandeur!"
                              —Han Solo about Luke in Return of the Jedi

"Wonderful girl. Either I'm going to kill her or I'm beginning to like her."
                              —Han, on Leia in Star Wars

"This bounty hunter is my kind of scum: fearless and inventive."
                              —Jabba the Hutt, describing the (disguised) Leia
                                        in Return of the Jedi.

"You're far too trusting."
                              —Grand Moff Tarkin, about Leia in Star Wars

"You stuck up, half-witted, scruffy-looking Nerf herder!"
                              —Leia, about Han in The Empire Strikes Back

"He certainly has courage."
                              —Leia, about Han in Star Wars

"Sometimes I amaze even myself."
                              —Han Solo, about Han Solo in Star Wars

"Will someone get this big walking carpet out of my way?"
                              —Leia, on Chewbacca in Star Wars

"I don't know what all this trouble is about, but I'm sure it must be your
   fault."
                              —C-3PO, about R2-D2 in Star Wars

Darth Vader: "When I left you, I was but a learner; now *I* am the master."
Obi-Wan Kenobi: "Only a master of evil, Darth."

—Exchange about Darth Vader from *Star Wars*

"There is good in him. I've felt it."

—Luke, about Vader in *Return of the Jedi*

Luke: "Ben is a great man!"
Han: "Yeah, great at getting us into trouble."

—Exchange about Obi-Wan (Ben) Kenobi in *Star Wars*

"I'm getting too old for this sort of thing."

—Obi-Wan, about himself in *Star Wars*

"You're like . . . family . . . to me."

—Han Solo, about Luke, Leia, and Chewbacca
in the *Star Wars Holiday Special*

On the Force

"The Force is what gives a Jedi his power. It's an energy field created by
all living things. It surrounds us and penetrates us. It binds the galaxy
together."

—Obi-Wan Kenobi, *Star Wars*

"The ability to destroy a planet is insignificant next to the power of the
Force."

—Darth Vader, *Star Wars*

"Hokey religions and ancient weapons are no match for a good blaster at
your side, kid."

—Han Solo, *Star Wars*

"Kid, I've flown from one side of this galaxy to the other, and I've seen a
lot of strange stuff, but I've never seen *anything* to make me believe
that there's one all-powerful Force controlling everything. . . . It's all a
lot of simple tricks and nonsense."

—Han, *Star Wars*

"I find your lack of faith disturbing."

—Vader, *Star Wars*

"You're going to find that many of the truths we cling to depend greatly on our own point of view."

—Obi-Wan, *Return of the Jedi*.

"The Force can have a strong influence on the weak-minded."

—Obi-Wan, *Star Wars*

Luke: "I don't believe it."
Yoda: "That is why you fail."

—Exchange from *The Empire Strikes Back*

Luke: "Master Yoda, you can't die."
Yoda: "Strong am I with the Force, but not that strong."

—Exchange from *Return of the Jedi*

"The Force will be with you, always."

—Obi-Wan, *Star Wars*

On Leadership

"But that's impossible! How will the Emperor maintain control without the bureaucracy?"

—General Tagge (Don Henderson) in *Star Wars*

Moff Jerjerrod (Michael Pennington): "I assure you, Lord Vader, my men are working as fast as they can."
Vader: "Perhaps I can find new ways to motivate them."

—Exchange from *Return of the Jedi*

"I don't know who you are or where you came from, but from now on you'll do as I tell you, okay?"

—Leia, *Star Wars*

"Look, Your Worshipfulness, let's get one thing straight. I take orders from just one person: me."

—Han, *Star Wars*

"Control, control, you must learn control!"

—Yoda, *The Empire Strikes Back*

"Stay on target, stay on target!"

—Gold Five (Graham Ashley), *Star Wars*

"I'd just as soon kiss a Wookiee!" Princess Leia exclaims in *The Empire Strikes Back*. She got her chance in this publicity photo, featuring Carrie Fisher and Peter Mayhew, taken during the shooting of the film.

On Romance

"You could use a good kiss."

—Han, to Leia in *The Empire Strikes Back*

"You like me because I'm a scoundrel. There aren't enough scoundrels in your life."

—Han, to Leia in *The Empire Strikes Back*

"I am your fantasy. I am your experience. So experience me. I am your pleasure. Enjoy me."

—"Holographic Wow" (Diahann Carroll),
The Star Wars Holiday Special

Leia: "I love you."
Han: "I know."

—Exchange from *The Empire Strikes Back*

Han: "I love you."
Leia: "I know."

—Exchange from *Return of the Jedi*

On Adventure

Han: "Together again, huh?"
Luke: "Wouldn't miss it."
Han: "How we doin'?"
Luke: "Same as always."
Han: "That bad, huh?"

—Exchange from *Return of the Jedi*

"Adventure. Heh. Excitement. Heh. A Jedi craves not these things."
—Yoda, *The Empire Strikes Back*

On Ethics

"Luminous beings are we, not this crude matter."
—Yoda, *The Empire Strikes Back*

"No matter how different we appear, we're all the same in our struggle
against the powers of evil and darkness."
—Leia, *The Star Wars Holiday Special*

"Don't give in to hate. That leads to the Dark Side."
—Obi-Wan, *The Empire Strikes Back*

"Anger, fear, aggression. The Dark Side are they. Once you start down
the dark path, forever will it dominate your destiny."
—Yoda, *Return of the Jedi*

Luke: "But how am I to know the good side from the bad?"
Yoda: "You will know . . . when you are calm, at peace, passive."
—Exchange from *The Empire Strikes Back*

Sage Advice

"Try not. Do, or do not. There is no try."

—Yoda, *The Empire Strikes Back*

"Wars not make one great."

—Yoda, *The Empire Strikes Back*

"Always in motion is the future."

—Yoda, *The Empire Strikes Back*

"Don't get cocky."

—Han, *Star Wars*

"If money is all that you love, then that's what you'll receive."

—Princess Leia, *Star Wars*

"Your eyes can deceive you; don't trust them."

—Obi-Wan, *Star Wars*

"Size matters not."

—Yoda, *The Empire Strikes Back*

"Who is the more foolish, the fool or the fool who follows him?"

—Obi-Wan, *Star Wars*

26

Short Help Is Better Than No Help at All

The Ewok Adventures (1984–85) and Saturday Morning Cartoons (1985–86)

A fter the *Star Wars Holiday Special* debacle, the last thing anyone saw coming was another holiday-themed *Star Wars* television event. And yet, not one but two such programs aired, during consecutive Thanksgiving seasons, in 1984 and '85. Even more improbably, the idea for these TV projects originated with George Lucas, who bitterly regretted his first foray into television (see Chapter 15).

What in the world could have inspired Lucas to return to the medium of the franchise's lone belly-flop? Only one thing: Amanda. Lucas' then-three-year-old daughter loved the Ewoks and wanted to see more of them. Eager to please his little girl, he hit on the idea of a one-hour television special featuring the characters, to be broadcast during the holiday season. The show would serve as a Christmas present for Amanda. If anyone else liked it, that was fine too.

The Ewok Adventure (aka *Caravan of Courage*, 1984)

Lucas had no intention of turning his second television venture into a repeat of the *Holiday Special*. Rather than delegating the project to a third-party producer, as he had the *Special*, the Ewok movie would be an in-house Lucasfilm production with visual effects from Industrial Light & Magic. Lucas retained creative control, minding many of the details of the production personally. He supplied the original story; inspected the sets, locations, and costumes; signed off on the visual effects; and even approved (and sometimes rejected) promotional spots for the show.

ABC signed on to broadcast Lucas' Ewok special but insisted it be expanded to a two-hour (with commercials) telefilm. Lucas engaged screenwriter Bob Carrau to expand his simple story into a full teleplay. Originally titled *The Ewok Adventure*, the project took on the retronym *Ewoks: Caravan of Courage* when it was issued on home video to help distinguish the picture from its eventual sequel, *Ewoks: The Battle for Endor*. To direct *The Ewok Adventure*, Lucas tapped his friend John Korty, whose Lucasfilm-branded animated picture *Twice Upon a Time* had premiered shortly after *Return of the Jedi*. To produce, he selected former ILM general manager Thomas G. Smith. Another ILMer, Joe Johnston, served as production designer. The movie was shot primarily in Marin County near Skywalker Ranch, with some work in the California Redwood Forest, where the Endor exteriors from *Return of the Jedi* had been filmed.

Production ran for eight weeks during the summer of 1984, with hours tightly regulated due to child labor restrictions. The Ewoks were played by many of the same actors who had performed in *Jedi*, including young Warwick Davis as Wicket. However, Kenny Baker did not return as Paploo. The picture's human characters were played by journeyman television actors Guy Boyd and Fionnula Flanagan, and thirteen-year-old Eric Walker and five-year-old Aubree Miller, both novices. Flanagan was an Emmy winner, named Outstanding Supporting Actress for her work in the miniseries *Rich Man, Poor Man* (1976). The two Ewok movies remain Miller's only screen credits. Lucas directed reshoots and assisted with the editing of the film.

Even by the standards of made-for-television children's movies, *The Ewok Adventure* is a trifle. The tone is fanciful and the plot is slight, centered on a trio of cute kids (both human and Ewok) who get in and out of various scrapes without ever seeming to be in any real danger. The Towani family—father (Boyd), mother (Flanagan), son Mace (Walker), and daughter Cindel (Miller)—are stranded on the forest moon of Endor following a starship crash. While the kids are away playing, the parents are captured by the Giant Gorax, a thirty-foot-tall, ax-wielding, bat-faced ogre. Mace and Cindel are taken in by a nearby village of Ewoks, who undertake a dangerous cross-country quest to rescue the elder Towanis from the clutches of the Gorax. Along the way, Mace, Cindel, and the Ewoks face various threats (including a giant, rat-faced wolf monster) and gather helpful traveling companions, including a tiny glowing sprite (the *Star Wars* equivalent of Tinkerbell). Cindel develops a friendship with the young Ewok named Wicket (Davis), but the scenario focuses primarily on Mace, who looks and behaves like a sawed-off Luke Skywalker. The final assault on the cave of the Gorax plays out in cartoon fashion, and the story concludes with a joyous family reunion back in the Ewok village. Since much of the dialogue is in Ewokese, Burl Ives narrates the story in the same cheery, sing-song manner in which he recounted the tale of Rudolph, the Red-Nosed Reindeer.

Although made on a modest budget, *The Ewok Adventure* boasts extraordinary production values for a television movie, including mostly impressive visual effects (which won the special an Emmy Award). The sets and costumes—many left over from *Return of the Jedi*—are also first-rate. The Ewoks, whose presence seemed intrusive in *Jedi*, shoehorned into the climax of the Original Trilogy, come off better in this context. Unfortunately, the performers cast in the human roles are uniformly terrible. So, while there is much to recommend about *The Ewok Adventure*, it's likely to satisfy only the youngest viewers. But, of course, that was its intended audience.

The Ewok Adventure aired November 25, 1984, and earned excellent ratings, finishing as the second-highest-rated made-for-TV movie of the year. In addition to its Best Visual Effects award, it earned an Emmy nomination for Outstanding Children's Program (Prime Time), but lost to the PBS *American Playhouse* drama *Displaced Person*, based on a story by Kurt Vonnegut. Random House released a series of children's books based on *The Ewok Adventure*, which sold well. The returns were so good that ABC suggested the picture serve as the pilot for an ongoing Ewoks television series. Lucas nixed that idea but agreed to produce a second Ewok telefilm the following year.

Ewoks: The Battle for Endor (1985)

Lucas assembled a new team to make the second Ewok picture, led by brothers Jim and Ken Wheat, who codirected the film and cowrote the screenplay. Lucas and the Wheat brothers, along with producer Thomas G. Smith and ILM's Joe Johnston and Phil Tippett, hashed out the scenario during a four-day story conference. The Wheat brothers, who had been unimpressed with *The Ewok Adventure*, were eager to take the second film in an edgier direction. Lucas, who had recently watched the Shirley Temple version of *Heidi* (1937) with Amanda, suggested that the story involve an orphan girl and an old man. The cast of the first movie returned for the sequel, although Walker's role was reduced to a cameo. They were joined by Wilford Brimley, a veteran actor whose profile was on the rise after appearing in *Cocoon* (1985); Welsh actress Sian Phillips, best known for her work on BBC series, including *I Claudius* (1976); and towering Dutchman Carel Struycken, who would later play Lurch in the *Addams Family* movies.

Ewoks: The Battle for Endor is an almost shocking departure from the first Ewok telefilm. It's far more frightening and sad than the amiable fluff of *The Ewok Adventure*. The first thing that happens is that a band of Sanysassan Marauders attacks the Ewok village and massacres three-fourths of the recently reunited Towani Family. Cindel (Miller) and Wicket (Davis) escape, but Cindel's father, mother, and brother are killed, and the rest of the Ewoks are taken prisoner. Cindel and Wicket are taken in by Noa (Brimley), another castaway human who has been trapped on the Endor moon for decades, and his pet/companion Teek, a creature that looks like a grinning woodchuck and moves at superspeed. Then Cindel is captured by the Marauders, and Noa, Wicket, and Teek brave the dreaded Sanysassan castle to rescue the girl and free the Ewoks. The picture concludes with a full-scale battle sequence, which plays out in much the same manner as the Ewoks-versus-stormtroopers engagement from *Return of the Jedi.*

Although the story is basically an inversion of the plot of the first movie—instead of the kids rescuing the grown-ups, a grown-up rescues a kid—the tone of the sequel is much darker. The Marauders are

Aubree Miller, as Cindel, poses with Warwick Davis, as Wicket, in this publicity still for *The Ewok Adventure.*

grotesque, skeletal creatures not unlike the bloodthirsty, desiccated knights of the *Blind Dead* horror film series of the 1970s. The other threats presented here—including a small dragon that carries Cindel away—are also much more menacing than anything seen in the previous film. While this makes *The Battle of Endor* a more engrossing experience for adult viewers, it may be too much for the target audience of the previous film. Its initial broadcast was preceded by a parental advisory. Production values are once again high, and the visual effects—including some stop-motion animated creatures—are superior to those in the first film. Even the acting is better, as Brimley supplies a game performance, Davis once again shines, and Miller redeems herself with a surprisingly effective outing.

Ewoks: The Battle for Endor premiered November 24, 1985, on ABC. It performed respectably but not as well as *The Ewok Adventure.* Random House

The Ewok telefilms featured what were, by the standards of 1980s television, superb visual effects. Here, ILM technicians work to make you believe an Ewok can fly.

released another series of children's books based on the special. Fans chose *The Battle of Endor* as the better of the two Ewok movies in a 2001 poll conducted by the official *Star Wars* website. In 2004, Twentieth Century-Fox released the two Ewoks movies on a double-feature DVD, which has since gone out of print.

Even though the two Ewok movies are accepted as *Star Wars* canon, certain elements seem at odds with the theatrical films. Both Ewok yarns involve magic of various sorts—not telepathic or telekinetic Force powers, but the kind of sorcery that (for example) turns a stone into a lizard and then the lizard into a mouse. There is nothing remotely like this in the Original Trilogy or even the Prequel Trilogy. Also, the canonical timeline for the Ewok adventures presents a continuity problem. Although not explicitly stated in the films, *The Ewok Adventure* and *The Battle for Endor* supposedly take place prior to the events of *Return of the Jedi*. Assuming this is the same Wicket seen in *Jedi* (it's the same actor wearing the same Ewok suit), his tribe's behavior toward the humans in *Jedi* becomes inexplicable. Here, the Ewoks become friends of humans. Why would they later try to eat them? Finally, although *The Ewok Adventure* reuses John Williams' famous *Star Wars* title theme, most of the music for these pictures, composed by Peter Bernstein, has a different, and much lighter, impact.

Animated *Ewoks* (1985–86)

A third Ewok movie was tentatively planned but later scrapped in favor of an ongoing animated children's series, *Star Wars: Ewoks*, which premiered September 7, 1985, on ABC. To produce the series, Lucasfilm engaged Canadian animation studio Nelvana, which had created a short animated segment for the *Star Wars Holiday Special* (the only watchable interlude in the entire show). Since then, Nelvana had gained success with its *Strawberry Shortcake* and *Inspector Gadget* cartoons. The show featured Ewok characters from *Return of the Jedi* and the telefilms, including Wicket, Paploo, Chief Chirpa, and Master Logray, as well as new characters, including Wicket's gal pal Kneesa. For the first time, the Ewoks spoke in fluent English (or maybe Ewokese was translated into English).

The *Ewoks* teleplays, written primarily by producers Bob Carrau and Paul Dini, had to conform to network standards for children's programming (e.g., fires could only be started by magic). In general, ABC pressed for lighthearted stories that would appeal to very young viewers. As a result, the show veered away from the darkness of *The Battle for Endor* and even the tone of the relatively lightweight *Ewok Adventure*. Lucas, who was even less involved in the *Star Wars* animated series than he had been in the live-action Ewoks films, did not intervene. As a result, the *Ewoks* cartoon quickly devolved from its *Star Wars* origins into typical Saturday morning pablum. Stories tended to focus on humor and magic. Although in various episodes the Ewoks faced threats including an evil witch, a dragon, a runaway baby giant, a mad scientist, and a tribe of underhanded swamp creatures known as the Duloks, our furry heroes spent much of their time gathering berries, playing games, or attending jolly festivals and tree-related ceremonies. The show became even lighter weight during its second season, when the network requested that most installments contain two eleven-minute stories instead of a single twenty-two-minute adventure.

Star Wars: Ewoks performed well enough to earn a renewal and continued through December of 1986. In all, thirty-five episodes of the series were produced. In the end, the show fell victim to another breed of cuddly critters: Nelvana's own *Care Bears*, which premiered on ABC a week after *Star Wars: Ewoks* but earned far better ratings. Kenner produced a line of *Star Wars: Ewoks* action figures, and Marvel published a tie-in comic book series based on the show. Random House published a series of children's storybooks adapted from episodes of the series. *Star Wars: Ewoks* has never been released in its entirety on home video. A handful of episodes were released on videocassette in the United States and Europe, and in 2004, Fox issued a DVD (now out of print) that featured eight episodes of the series cobbled together to form a pair of eighty-eight-minute animated "movies."

Droids (1985–86)

A second animated series, *Star Wars: Droids*, premiered on ABC the same morning as *Star Wars: Ewoks*. The two shows were conjoined in 1986 for ABC's *Ewoks and Droids Adventure Hour*. Although it lasted only one season (thirteen episodes and a one-hour special were produced), *Droids* holds up better than its longer-running cartoon sibling. The series, also produced by Nelvana, was set prior to the events of the original *Star Wars* and followed C-3PO and R2-D2 as they passed from owner to owner, becoming entangled in various scrapes and adventures. As with *Star Wars: Ewoks*, writers had to work under censor-mandated guidelines: characters could push and shove one another, but not punch; no character could be hit over the head; blasters should not look like real guns; characters must always wear seat belts while riding in a landspeeder, and so on. But ABC exerted less editorial influence over *Droids* than it did over *Ewoks*.

Each *Droids* story arc played out across multiple episodes. In episodes 1 through 4, Threepio and Artoo fall in with a gang of speeder bike racers on the Tatooine-like desert world Ingo. Then they stumble on a secret weapon and find themselves caught between a rebel spy and a ruthless crime lord. In episodes 5 through 8, the droids help a deposed prince recapture the throne of his home world and then fight off an invasion attempt by a band of space pirates. In episodes 10 through 13, the droids and a "merchant scholar" search for the mystic Roon Stones. In a *Raiders of the Lost Ark*-like twist, they must find the powerful stones before they fall into the hands of imperial troops. In the hour-long special "The Great Heep," Threepio and Artoo square off against an evil giant droid, which has assembled itself from the bodies of scrapped droids and feeds on the power supplies of captured R2 units. Most episodes were penned by writer-producers Peter Sauder and Paul Dini. Sound designer Burtt contributed the stories for the "Hidden Planet" story arc and the "Great Heep" special. As with *Ewoks*, George Lucas did not write for this series. The *Droids* opening theme music was composed by Stewart Copeland, best known as the drummer for the rock band the Police.

The animation quality of *Droids* was no better than that of *Ewoks* and no worse than typical Saturday morning cartoon fare of this vintage, although the character designs and backgrounds were unusually imaginative. Anthony Daniels supplied the voice of Threepio, and his endearing, witty performance remains the show's greatest asset. Artoo's "voice" was provided by library sound effects from the *Star Wars* films. Although juvenile and sometimes

The animated *Droids* series (like the *Ewoks* cartoons) never received a full and proper home video release. This out-of-print DVD from 2004 is the best available record of the program, as far as officially released products go.

silly, the *Droids* episodes were fast-paced and more recognizable as *Star Wars* than any of the *Ewoks* projects (live action or animated), with yarns pitting space royalty and humble farm boys against bounty hunters, bandits, and other interstellar lowlifes, and featuring settings like mining camps, cantinas, and pirate hideouts. Minor characters from the Original Trilogy, such as the android bounty hunter IG-88 and the Max Rebo Band (which performs at Jabba the Hutt's palace), sometimes turned up in these tales. Some of the characters, events, and places introduced in the *Droids* series were later referred to in the Prequel Trilogy, while others resurfaced in various *Star Wars* novels, comic books, and video games.

Kenner produced a series of action figures based on the series, and Marvel published a comic book series adapted from it. A *Droids* computer game appeared in 1988, but by then the series had already been canceled. Unfortunately, like *Ewoks*, *Droids* has never been issued in its entirety on home video in any format. Selected episodes, including "The Great Heep" special, were released on videotape in the United States, England, and Germany. A subsequent DVD release included two four-episode story arcs ("The Pirate and the Prince" and "Treasure of the Hidden Planet") spliced together to form a pair of cartoon "movies." Five episodes and the "Great Heep" special were omitted. Even this imperfect DVD, as of early 2015, remains out of print. Of all the currently unavailable *Star Wars* material, the *Droids* cartoons are the most deserving of a proper DVD or Blu-ray release.

27

Stay on Target

A *Star Wars* Miscellany

f this book were a DVD, this chapter would be the deleted scenes. Assembling a concise historical overview of any subject as wide-ranging and much-written-about as *Star Wars* necessitates a great deal of judicious pruning and compressing. Entire tomes have been published about topics covered in a chapter or less in *Star Wars FAQ*. There are many more fascinating, illuminating, or amusing stories than will fit in this or any single book. This chapter collects several items that didn't fit neatly into any of this book's other thirty-seven chapters, but were too captivating or instructive to consign to the proverbial cutting-room floor.

Meet Wedge Antilles (and Friends)

Aside from the principal cast members, one other actor had a speaking role in all three installments of the Original Trilogy: Denis Lawson, who played Luke's sometime wingman Wedge Antilles. Born in Perthshire, Scotland, September 27, 1947, Lawson attended the Royal Scottish Academy of Music and Drama and landed his first professional role in a West End production of *The Metamorphosis* in 1969. He has remained active on the British stage, in BBC-TV productions and in feature films ever since, and his profile has risen over the years. Lawson earned an Emmy nomination for his starring role in a BBC miniseries adaptation of Charles Dickens' *Bleak House* (2005). His *Star Wars* role was supposed to be nothing more than a quick paycheck, but he's been inextricably linked with the franchise ever since. Wedge Antilles was a background character, but he participated in (and survived) the battles of Yavin, Hoth, and Endor, and his presence helped create the illusion of the rebel alliance as a large fighting force with some continuity of personnel. The unassuming rebel pilot became a fan favorite, and the character was fleshed out in many Expanded Universe novels and comic book stories.

Lawson returned as Wedge in *The Empire Strikes Back* and *Return of the Jedi*, and supplied the character's voice in both the *Star Wars: Rogue Leader*

This close-up, from the Hoth battle sequence, demonstrates the level of intensity Mark Hamill brought to his performance in *The Empire Strikes Back*.

video game and *The Lego Movie* (2014), even though Lawson's voice was dubbed by American actor David Ankrum in the original *Star Wars*. Lawson also read the audiobook versions of Timothy Zahn's novels *Heir to the Empire* and *Dark Force Rising*. However, he declined to appear as Reymus Antilles in the Prequel Trilogy and rejected an offer to return as Wedge in the upcoming *Episode VII: The Force Awakens*. Reportedly, Lawson was unwilling to join the cast of the new film unless his role was enlarged and Wedge was treated as something more than walking scenery. Lawson has one other notable connection to the *Star Wars* franchise: He is the real-life uncle of actor Ewan McGregor, who played Obi-Wan Kenobi in the prequels.

In addition to Lawson, a handful of other performers who appeared in minor but memorable roles in the Original Trilogy also remain notable, for one reason or another.

- Garrick Hagon was supposed to have had a much larger role in *Star Wars*, playing Luke's doomed boyhood friend Biggs Darklighter. But his part was trimmed to nearly nothing during postproduction, in part to improve the pacing of the film and in part because George Lucas was unhappy with Hagon's performance. Born September 27, 1939, in London, Hagon grew up in Toronto and performed for seven seasons with the Stratford Shakespeare Festival in Ontario, where he once appeared alongside Alec Guinness in *Richard III*. By the 1970s, he had moved back to England and was earning a living in film, television, and radio. Had Biggs' scenes remained intact, *Star Wars* might have significantly raised the actor's profile. As of 2014, he had racked up better than 150 movie and TV appearances, although mostly in minor roles, including six episodes of *Doctor Who* (1972) and director Tim Burton's *Batman* (1989).

- Rotund actor William Hootkins played the ill-fated, comically named Porkins (aka Red Six) in *Star Wars*. Hootkins was born July 5, 1948, in Dallas, where, as a teenager, he became entangled in the investigation into the assassination of President John F. Kennedy. Hootkins was interviewed by the FBI about Ruth Paine, a woman accused of harboring the wife of assassin Lee Harvey Oswald. Hootkins, who was interested in languages, was taking Russian lessons from Paine. After graduating from high school, Hootkins attended Princeton University, where he majored in Oriental Studies and learned to speak fluent Mandarin Chinese. He also became involved in the school's student-run Intime Theatre. He moved to England in the early 1970s, where he trained at the Royal Academy of Dramatic Arts and began landing roles on the West End stage and in movies and television. Among more than a hundred films and TV series, he appeared in *Flash Gordon* (1980), *Batman* (1989), and *Raiders of the Lost Ark* (1981), in which he famously assures Dr. Jones than the government has "top men" studying the Ark of the Covenant. Hootkins starred as Alfred Hitchcock in the hit West End play *Hitchcock Blonde* in 2003. Plans to move the show to Broadway were canceled when the actor was diagnosed with pancreatic cancer. He died in 2005.

- Kenneth Colley, who portrayed Admiral Piett in both *Empire* and *Jedi*, remains the only actor to appear as the same imperial officer in more than one *Star Wars* film. Born December 7, 1937, in Manchester, England, Colley is a trained Shakespearean actor with a lengthy resume of stage and screen credits, mostly in minor roles. He appeared (very briefly) as Jesus Christ in *Monty Python's Life of Brian* (1979).

- John Ratzenberger, born April 6, 1947, in Bridgeport, Connecticut, remains best known as beer-swilling postman Cliff Clavin from TV's *Cheers* (1982–93). He attended Sacred Heart University in Fairfield, Connecticut, and at age twenty-two worked as a tractor driver at the legendary Woodstock music festival. Ratzenberger moved to London in 1971, where he landed the role of the rebel Major Durlin in *The Empire Strikes Back*, one of dozens of minor parts the actor played before scoring his career-making gig on the classic sitcom. In all, Ratzenberger has appeared in more than 130 films (so far). He is also known for his frequent voice work for animation studio Pixar. He has worked on all fourteen Pixar films so far released, most memorably as Hamm, the piggy bank from the *Toy Story* films.

- Julian Glover, born March 27, 1935, in Hempstead, England, was a Royal Shakespeare Company veteran who at first worked primarily on the stage. He appears in *The Empire Strikes Back* as General Veers, who leads the imperial attack on Hoth. Glover's screen career began in 1959 and remains active today. He's accumulated more than 160 screen credits and is now recognizable from his recurring role as Grand Master Pycelle on the HBO drama *Game of Thrones* (2011–14). He also appeared in the James Bond picture *For Your Eyes Only* (1981) and was the chief Nazi nemesis in *Indiana Jones and the Lost Crusade* (1989).

- No *Star Wars* performer, not even Harrison Ford, has appeared in more blockbuster hits than Warwick Davis. Born Februrary 3, 1970, in Surrey, England, the diminutive actor made his screen rebut as Wicket the Ewok in *Return of the Jedi*, a role he reprised in the telefilms *The Ewok Adventure* (aka *Caravan of Courage*) and *Ewoks: The Battle for Endor*. He has racked up an impressive resume of film credits since then, running to nearly seventy pictures, including the starring role in George Lucas' epic fantasy *Willow* (see Chapter 37) and a recurring role as Professor Flitwick in the Harry Potter movies, in which he delivered convincing and touching performances. In the series finale, *Harry Potter and the Deathly Hallows, Parts 1 and 2*, Davis pulled double-duty, also appearing as Griphook the Goblin. Davis also made a cameo in *Star Wars Episode I: The Phantom Menace* (1999) and will appear in *The Force Awakens*. The three-foot-six actor also starred in the *Leprechaun* horror film series and appeared in the *Chronicles of Narnia* BBC-TV series. In large part based on the *Star Wars* and *Harry Potter* movies, Davis' post-*Jedi* pictures have raked in more than $11.5 billion at the box office—that's $3 billion more than Ford's pictures have earned. Davis married his wife, Samantha, in 1991. They have a son, Harrison, and a daughter, Annabelle. Another son, Lloyd, died shortly after birth. Davis also operates Willow Personal Management, a talent agency for actors of small stature.

Off the Hook

Today when an anticipated blockbuster movie is released, it's promoted not only through posters, trailers, and television ads but with its own website and a distinctive social media footprint. In 1980, home computers and mobile phones were still in their infancy, but the forward-thinking Lucasfilm publicity department launched a promotional campaign using old-fashioned social media: the telephone. Fans were invited to dial 1-800-521-1980 (the seven-digit phone number reflected the picture's nationwide rollout date) to receive a special message from the stars of *Star Wars*.

A series of prerecorded messages from five characters— Luke Skywalker (Mark Hamill), Han Solo (Harrison Ford), Princess Leia (Carrie Fisher),

In addition to stories that didn't fit anywhere else in *Star Wars FAQ,* this chapter also features random photos that were too good to leave out, like this shot from *Return of the Jedi*—possibly the best publicity still ever taken of Peter Mayhew as Chewbacca.

C-3PO (Anthony Daniels), and Darth Vader (James Earl Jones)—were taped during the dubbing of the film. At the time, telephone systems were not fully computerized, and phone prefixes were reserved for specific geographical areas. Since the 521 prefix was for rural Illinois, the *Empire Strikes Back* hotline was set up there. Beginning in February 1980, fans were invited to dial the hotline to listen to the messages, which ran in rotation. Since there was no way to tell which message you would receive when you called, some fans (including the author of this book) dialed the number over and over again to try and hear them all. Craig Miller, who in 1980 was the director of fan relations for Lucasfilm, told a StarWars.com interviewer what happened next:

"The first week the system went live, so many people called the number [that] AT&T couldn't handle it," Miller said.

> They were so overloaded the system couldn't even handle generating busy signals to all of the calls. The 800 system for Illinois crashed and shut down for several hours. AT&T insisted that we add additional phone lines and issue a press release taking the blame for it. Poor us. We contritely agreed to issue a press release to all media saying that we were sorry that *Star Wars* fans were so eager to get information on the sequel . . . that their calls overwhelmed the phone company. And you could call yourself, now that we'd increased the number of phone lines, and listen to the messages. The story, of course, got covered everywhere. Best publicity we could have had.

In case you missed the opportunity to dial in back in 1980, here's a transcription of the messages from the hotline. (Please do not call the phone number, which is now assigned to another party.)

- Voice of C-3PO: "Hello, I am C-3PO and this is the first in a series of messages on the special *Star Wars* telephone line. Each time one of you on Earth calls this number you will receive a message containing information on the continuation of the *Star Wars* saga, *The Empire Strikes Back*. After *Star Wars*, I hoped that all my adventures were over and R2-D2 wouldn't get us into any more trouble with his secret missions, but in *The Empire Strikes Back* it just gets worse. First, there was that dreadful snow planet. I didn't think I'd ever be warm again. And then we were attacked by imperial stormtroopers, and when we got to the Cloud City I just went all to pieces. Oh, dear. I can't go on. Talking about it is too upsetting. You'll just have to see it for yourself when *The Empire Strikes Back* comes to a theater near you on May the 21st, nineteen hundred and eighty."

- Voice of Han Solo: "Before I ran into Ben Kenobi and Luke Skywalker, I had myself a pretty good little operation. They wanted a ride to Alderaan and they were willing to pay enough that I didn't have to ask any questions. Now I'm in the middle of a rebellion. I'm spending half my time dodging Imperial ships and the other half avoiding Her Holiness. Not only that, but Jabba the Hutt's got a price on my head and he's put Boba Fett on my trail. Something tells me it's not going to get any better when *The Empire Strikes Back*."

- Voice of Princess Leia: "The destruction of the Death Star was a major victory for the rebellion, but our battle isn't over yet. Darth Vader and the evil forces of the Emperor keep a stranglehold over the galaxy. But the rebel alliance must and will succeed in forever ridding the galaxy of their scourge. Even now in our secret underground base on the ice planet Hoth, new strategies are being planned. See for yourself in *The Empire Strikes Back*."

- Voice of Luke Skywalker: "Tatooine was just a big ball of dust until Artoo and Threepio showed up. But since then, my life hasn't been the same— from a moisture farmer on a remote desert planet to a leader of the rebellion fighting for freedom throughout the galaxy. But now the rebellion faces even greater odds and I must be ready. I must follow Ben Kenobi's teachings, learn more about the powers of the Force and becoming a Jedi Knight if I'm going to be prepared for a confrontation with Darth Vader. See it when *The Empire Strikes Back*."

- Voice of Darth Vader: "They managed to rescue the Princess and to destroy the Death Star, but this time the rebels won't be so lucky. The power of the Death Star was insignificant compared to the power of the Force, and with Obi-Wan Kenobi gone, I am the master. See it, as *The Empire Strikes Back*."

A Sound Idea

George Lucas invested extraordinary care in the sound design and music for the *Star Wars* films. Despite these efforts, however, most viewers in the late 1970s and early 1980s never experienced the film the way the director intended, due to the sorry state of many cinemas at the time. Some theaters were still using speakers left over from the World War II era, and many operators—especially in smaller markets without another nearby cinema— remained apathetic about niceties such as sound quality. As long as the picture was in focus and patrons could more or less make out the dialogue, that was considered good enough. Twentieth Century-Fox wasn't particularly supportive of Lucas' efforts, either. The studio tried to talk Lucas into releasing *Star Wars* in mono only, since mastering the movie and striking prints in both mono and Dolby stereo sound would increase costs. At the time, most pictures were still released only in mono because most cinemas lacked the capability to present a film in stereo.

The number of stereo cinemas had increased by the time *The Empire Strikes Back* premiered, and the revolutionary sound design and magnificent music of *Star Wars* inspired devoted fans to seek out stereo versions of the film wherever possible. Yet Lucas remained dissatisfied. Shortly after the release of *Empire*, he hired engineer Tomlinson Holman to design and develop a quality assurance system to guarantee that the final chapter of the Original Trilogy, and other Lucasfilm productions, would be presented in a manner befitting the magnificent work of talents like sound designer Ben Burtt and composer John Williams.

The result was the now-ubiquitous THX system, an industry certification signifying that a cinema has the capability to present the film in pristine audio quality. To become THX certified, theaters must meet stringent acoustic, technical, and architectural requirements (governing, for example, the placement of speakers within the auditorium and acceptable levels of background noise). Once those criteria are met, THX provides cinemas with a special surround sound crossover circuit, originally designed by Holman, that must be used to ensure certification. Although the name THX is commonly assumed to derive from Lucas' debut feature, *THX 1138*, it's actually an acronym for Tomlinson Holman Crossover.

"While filmmakers were spending millions of dollars using new computer technology to perfect the sound and picture in the post-production studio, the quality was being lost on movie audiences," said THX resident historian John Dahl, as quoted on the company's website. "By creating a set of standards for theater design and enforcing performance levels of presentation equipment, THX was ensuring that the film experience would translate from studios to every theater." Although primarily concerned with sound, THX also sets standards for viewing angles and lighting levels to ensure image quality.

To promote these new exhibition specifications, Lucasfilm subsidiary Sprocket Systems (THX was not yet a separate corporate entity) launched its Theater Alignment Program in March 1983. Thousands of theater owners were mailed a series of packets that explained the benefits of THX certification, especially when exhibiting films such as the eagerly awaited *Return of the Jedi*. Sprocket Systems employees made personal visits to more than one hundred theaters across the United States. Some theater operators were eager to move forward with the improvements, but many remained skeptical.

A by-product of Lucas' campaign for a moviegoing experience that more faithfully represented the works he was creating was a more educated and demanding viewing public—at least with regard to sound and picture quality. When theater patrons began viewing (and hearing) films in THX-certified theaters, they began voting with their feet—patronizing THX-certified cinemas and abandoning others, especially when queueing up for the visual and audio effects extravaganzas that were fast becoming the industry's most popular fare. Inevitably, more theaters were forced to pursue certification, and new theaters began to be built from the ground up with THX certification in mind (especially with the proliferation of multiplex cinemas in the late 1980s). In later years, the THX certification was expanded to include guidelines for home theater systems, home media (like DVDs and Blu-rays), automobile sound systems, computer speakers, and gaming consoles. Lucas sold the majority interest in THX to computer sound card manufacturer Creative Labs in 2001, but by then he had won his war on poor theater sound.

Outposts of the Lucasfilm Empire

George Lucas' father wanted his son to take over the family business, a stationary store. But as a teenager Lucas didn't want to be in charge of anything other than George Lucas. Instead, he followed a radically different career path: making movies. Ironically, Lucas' success as a filmmaker led him, out of necessity in some cases, to become a respected businessman after all—founding and overseeing some of the most successful enterprises in motion pictures. Here's a rundown of some of the companies Lucas established:

- Before beginning his own Hollywood empire, Lucas helped his friend Francis Ford Coppola found American Zoetrope, which Coppola dreamed of turning into a sort of alternative major studio. For a variety of reasons (many related to the free-spending Coppola's financial issues), that never happened. Even so, American Zoetrope remains an ongoing concern and has produced more than sixty movies since 1969, including films directed by Jean-Luc Godard, Akira Kurosawa, Paul Schrader, Tim Burton, and Kenneth Branagh, as well as every film since then directed by Coppola or his daughter Sofia.

- George Lucas founded his most famous corporate offspring, Lucasfilm Ltd., in 1971. At the time, the company had four employees: Lucas, Kurtz, and secretaries Lucy Wilson and Bunny Alsup. Since then, the company (which now employs nearly one thousand people) has produced twenty-four movies (see Chapter 37), with two more due in 2015, including *Star Wars Episode VII: The Force Awakens*. Over the years, a number of additional companies were spun off from Lucasfilm, including two separate film production firms, Lucasfilm Singapore, which (as the name implies) operates in Asia, and Lucasfilm Animation. In addition, Lucas formed separate limited liability companies for every film produced by Lucasfilm in order to protect himself and the parent company from any extraordinary losses that might be suffered by an individual project. The production companies for the Original Trilogy were called The Star Wars Company, The Chapter II Company (for *The Empire Strikes Back*), and The Chapter III Company (for *Return of the Jedi*). All these companies were dissolved after the films' release. Lucasfilm Ltd. and all the companies still operating under its umbrella were acquired by the Walt Disney Company in 2012. Lucasfilm—like Marvel Comics, another high-profile acquisition made by Disney in recent years—retained its corporate identity but now functions as a Disney subsidiary. Before the sale, Lucas handpicked his successor—Kathleen Kennedy, formerly the leader of Steven Spielberg's production company Amblin Entertainment.

• Lucasfilm also served as the incubator for Pixar Animation Studios. The company came into existence in 1979 as a Lucasfilm department known as the Graphics Group, part of Lucasfilm's Computer Division. It was initially led by Ed Catmull, who Lucas recruited out of the New York Institute of Technology, and focused primarily on designing and building high-end hardware that could be used to create computer-animated visual effects sequences (including ILM's groundbreaking visual effects for *Star Trek II: The Wrath of Khan*, 1982), as well as innovative digital film and sound editing systems. Animator John Lasseter joined the Graphics Group in 1983 and began creating short animated films to demonstrate the capabilities of the Group's products. Three years later, Lucas sold the Graphics Group to Steve Jobs, recently departed from Apple Computer. Strapped for cash in the wake of his divorce, Lucas sold the division to Jobs for $5 million. Jobs sank an additional $5 million into the company, which he renamed Pixar Animation. The company shifted its focus from making equipment to making movies. Almost immediately, Pixar earned its first Academy Award nomination, for Lasseter's short film *Luxo Jr.* (1986). Luxo, an animated desk lamp, became part of the company logo. In 1991, after a handful of other acclaimed shorts, Disney agreed to distribute a Pixar-made feature film. Four years later, *Toy Story* appeared. It earned three Oscar nominations and became the highest-grossing picture of the year, raking in $362 million worldwide. In 2006, Disney announced that it would purchase Pixar, which by then had followed *Toy Story* with other blockbusters, including *A Bug's Life*, *Finding Nemo*, *Monsters Inc.*, and *The Incredibles*. Jobs sold Pixar for $7.4 billion worth of Disney stock. With Disney's acquisition of Lucasfilm in 2012, Pixar and Lucasfilm once again became part of the same corporate family.

• To produce the visual effects needed for *Star Wars*, Lucas was forced to found one of his most successful spin-off ventures, Industrial Light & Magic (see Chapter 5). Kerner Optical, a model shop and practical effects division, was spun off from ILM in 2006 but went bankrupt in 2011, largely due to sagging demand for practical effects in the CGI age.

• Founded almost simultaneously with ILM, and for similar reasons, was the company then known as Sprocket Systems. (For a while, both ILM and Sprocket Systems were united under the single corporate name Lucas Digital.) Sprocket Systems was a state-of-the-art sound mixing and editing facility that produced all the sound effects for the *Star Wars* films, among others. The subsidiary changed its name to Skywalker Sound in

George Lucas has said that, at first, his primary motivation for making *Star Wars* was to create outer space dogfights like the *Millennium Falcon*'s battle with TIE fighters. Here, Han Solo (Harrison Ford) prepares for the incoming attack.

1987 when it moved from its original San Anselmo location to Skywalker Ranch. Like ILM, Sprocket Systems/Skywalker Sound has been an engine for technological innovation within the industry, and a very profitable investment. As mentioned above, THX Ltd. sprang from Sprocket Systems in 1983.

- In early 1978, Lucas founded Black Falcon Ltd. to manage the licensing of various *Star Wars*–related merchandise. Black Falcon was enormously successful and loaned money to the Chapter II Company to help *The Empire Strikes Back* stay afloat during its troubled production (see Chapter 17). In December 1979, Black Falcon was merged back into Lucasfilm Ltd. However, in the 1990s, as a new wave of *Star Wars* books and other merchandise began to appear, the licensing operation was spun off again, as Lucas Licensing. The publishing arm LucasBooks is a subsidiary of Lucas Licensing.

More action figures! A stormtrooper aboard (or, actually, slipped into a hidden slot on top of) Kenner's toy Dewback.

Photography by Preston Hewis/East Bank Images

- Video game company LucasArts, founded in 1982, also enjoyed great success, developing and publishing scores of popular games from the early 1980s into the early 2010s (see Chapter 31). In 2013, LucasArts halted in-house game development but continues to license and publish games created on an outsourced basis.
- Lucas Online, founded in 1997, manages Lucasfilm's online presence—including websites such as starwars.com, indianajones.com, and lucasfilm.com—everything from content to e-commerce.
- Lucas also founded the George Lucas Educational Foundation, which supports innovation in education; and the Lucas Cultural Arts Museum, still in the planning stages, which will house and display Lucas' vast collection of cartoon and pop art. In addition, Lucas has donated hundreds of millions of dollars to his alma mater, USC's School of Cinematic Arts, where the George Lucas Instructional Building is located. After selling Lucasfilm to Disney for a reported $4 billion (half in cash, half in Disney stock), Lucas announced that he would donate the majority of the proceeds to charitable foundations.

28

Mind Tricks

The Science of *Star Wars*

George Lucas had good reasons for referring to *Star Wars* as "space fantasy" rather than by the more exalted term "science fiction." At the time, SF was associated with heavy, downbeat movies (see Chapter 10), which was diametrically opposed to his intent and approach. Perhaps more importantly, branding the picture as sci-fi suggested a degree of fidelity to actual, real-world science. The Merriam-Webster dictionary defines science fiction as "fiction dealing principally with the impact of actual or imagined science on society or individuals or having a scientific factor as an essential orienting component." That traditionalist, "hard SF" approach didn't interest Lucas in the least. He was aiming for the mythic and refused to be hamstrung by minor details like scientific plausibility. This led to some embarrassing gaffes (see Chapter 24), but it also freed the writer-director's imagination to develop his panoramic, vividly rendered, and widely beloved galactic dreamscape—the *Star Wars* universe.

In the nearly forty years since *Star Wars* premiered, however, something unexpected began to happen. New scientific theories suggested that certain aspects of Lucas' universe might not be as far-fetched as they originally seemed. While it's still most fitting to refer to the franchise as "space fantasy," the gap between *Star Wars* and science appears to be closing—in some respects, at least.

Creatures and Alien Worlds

Where Star Wars Was Right: In *Star Wars*, the galaxy teems with life. This much, at least, may be true. A widely publicized study published in May 2014 by Louis Irwin from the University of Texas-El Paso calculated that the Milky Way may contain at least one hundred million planets with complex life-forms. This was just the latest in a series of studies to suggest that life in our galaxy may be widespread. Other scientists have suggested that the number of worlds amenable to complex life may be up to ten times higher than Irwin's estimate.

Where *Star Wars* Went Wrong: Even so, for a variety of reasons, life in our galaxy (or even in one far, far away) is unlikely to function quite like the *Star Wars* universe. For starters, by "complex life," researchers do not necessarily mean intelligent life, only organisms larger and more complex than bacteria or simple microbes. And even if sentient species exist on other planets, *Star Wars* probably doesn't go far enough in imagining what those beings might look like. The franchise's aliens simply aren't alien enough. "Considering that octopi, sea cucumbers, tube worms, and pine trees are all very closely related to us, an alien would look less like us than does a squid," said futurist Dr. Clifford Pickover, as quoted in Jeanne Cavelos' book *The Science of Star Wars.* Not only are there an improbable number of humanoid species in the *Star Wars* movies, but it's extremely unlikely that a multitude of beings from various worlds could share the same atmosphere, much less gather for drinks in the Mos Eisley cantina.

The places from which the *Star Wars* aliens originate also strain credibility due to Lucas' penchant for imagining worlds with a single, planet-wide ecosystem. It's highly improbable that any habitable planet would be covered from pole to pole with desert or snow or swamp or forest, and much more likely that habitable worlds, like the Earth, would contain a multitude of ecological environments that vary from region to region.

If *Star Wars* falls short of the standards of science, however, it succeeds fairly well by the standards of science fiction. Envisioning alien life is one of the greatest challenges science fiction writers undertake. Even the great Isaac Asimov, a chemist by training and a respected scientist in addition to being a legendary SF author, generally shied away from the task in his early works, populating his long-running series of Foundation and Robot novels with human and mechanical characters only. (Later, in his 1972 stand-alone novel *The Gods Themselves,* Asimov created one of the most imaginative of all science fictional aliens—a three-gendered species that exists primarily in a gaseous state, feeding by photosynthesis, and becoming solid only to mate.) *Star Wars* deserves credit for presenting a more diverse and inventive collection of alien creatures (including a dizzying variety of intelligent species, beasts of burden, and monsters) than most science fiction movies and TV shows. Compare *Star Wars* with *Star Trek*, where humans and aliens seem to be differentiated mainly by the shape of their foreheads.

Droids

Where *Star Wars* Was Right: Robots—or, rather, droids— are another ubiquitous feature of the *Star Wars* universe; they come in all shapes and sizes and serve countless functions. Since 1977, robots have become increasingly common in the real world too. In 2013 alone, according to statistics provided by the International Federation of Robotics, more than 178,000 industrial robots were sold worldwide. And that total doesn't include robots produced for medical, military, and personal services, or other specialized uses. The number of robots in the workplace only figures to increase as more industries deploy automated systems. In 2014, for instance, while fast food workers picketed restaurants to demand higher wages, San Francisco-based Momentum Machines introduced a robot it claims is capable of preparing, assembling, dressing, wrapping, and bagging as many as 360 burgers per hour.

Where *Star Wars* Went Wrong: Even so, engineers remain a long way from creating anything resembling C-3PO or R2-D2. Honda spent twenty years developing a bipedal talking robot named ASIMO, introduced in 2004 and advertised as "the world's most advanced humanoid robot." ASIMO (an acronym for Advanced Step in Innovative Mobility and a nod to author Asimov) boasts many remarkable capabilities. According to Honda's ASIMO website, the 4-foot-3, 110-pound robot (which looks a little like a child in a space suit) "can run, walk on uneven slopes and surfaces, turn smoothly, climb stairs, and reach for and grasp objects, . . . has the ability to recognize the face of a select group of individuals, [and] using its camera eyes, . . . can map its environment and register stationary objects."

Yet even ASIMO can't hold a servomotor to the droids in *Star Wars*. ASIMO, according to Honda, "can comprehend and respond to simple voice commands." But as a translator, C-3PO not only has a vast vocabulary but, as Cavelos points out in her book, also possesses extraordinary emotional acuity. "For Threepio to be an effective translator, he needs to be able to recognize the emotion with which someone speaks, translate the speaker's statement into another language, translate the emotion into the equivalent inflection, rhythm, and pitch in another language, and speak the translation with this particular intonation." Programming a robot to speak in six million languages is theoretically possible; programming one to read, comprehend, and respond appropriately to human emotions remains far beyond current science.

Even more impressively, the *Star Wars* droids can reason freely and have complex personalities. Threepio and Artoo are capable of solving problems independently and, although basically honest, remain capable of lying when the situation calls for it (like when stormtroopers break into the Death Star control room where they've been hiding). They also seem to experience a wide variety of genuine emotions, including anxiety, irritation, elation, and affection. Although Threepio and Artoo bicker incessantly, they also demonstrate willingness to sacrifice for one another. "If any of my circuits or gears will help, I'll gladly donate them,"

The science of robotics has made major advances since *Star Wars* debuted in 1977, but droids like C-3PO and R2-D2 remain far beyond current capabilities.

Threepio volunteers near the conclusion of *Star Wars* upon sight of the damaged Artoo. All of this is light years beyond even the most advanced artificial intelligence currently possible in robots or computers. In effect, *Star Wars* droids are sentient beings who happen to be mechanical, rather than biological, in anatomy.

Weapons

Where *Star Wars* Was Right: The blaster, or something very much like it, may soon be real. Since the 1990s, the U.S. military has launched multiple projects aimed at the development of variable-power directed-energy weapons. The Phased Hyper-Accelerated for Shock, EMP, and Radiation (PHASER) initiative attempts to produce a rifle capable of firing a ball of lightning, which could be set to stun or to kill, and could be used to disrupt electronic equipment. Meanwhile, the Multimode Directed Energy Armament System (MDEAS) project tries to construct a weapon that uses a laser pulse to create an ionized channel through which an electric shock could be fired at a target. Again, depending on the voltage, the charge could either stun or kill, and could be used to disrupt enemy electronics. Both of these projects were operational in 2009, according to an article in *Wired*. It's unclear whether they remain ongoing. Another effort, the Pulsed Energy Projectile (PUP) initiative, was abandoned in the early 2000s after six years and more than $14 million. Details on military research and development efforts are usually classified, but it seems that the U.S. military is serious about someday arming soldiers with *Star Wars*-like blasters.

Where *Star Wars* Went Wrong: No one, however, is trying to construct a lightsaber, because it seems to be impossible. To begin with, although frequently referred to as a "laser sword" (even, in his screenplay notes, by George Lucas), it's impossible to construct a blade made of laser light. Lasers emit ultrafocused beams of light, which travel in a straight line until they come into contact with something else. Laser beams, like other light rays, cannot simply stop and stand still. Also, laser beams are invisible, unless the air is full of gas or floating particulates. And besides, it remains unclear whether or not it would be possible to duel with laser swords. Usually, laser beams pass through each other just like flashlight or searchlight beams. However, in 2013, researchers at the Harvard-M.I.T. Center for Ultracold Atoms announced that during an unrelated experiment, they had accidentally transformed photons (the particles that make up light) into hardened molecules capable of smacking into one another. "It's not an inapt analogy to compare this to lightsabers," Professor Mikhail Lukin told the *Harvard Gazette*. "The physics of what's happening in these molecules is similar to what we see in the movies."

On the whole, however, it might be easier to build a lightsaber using plasma instead of laser technology. Under the influence of magnetic fields, plasma can be shaped into filaments and beams. Unfortunately, a familiar problem presents itself: There is no known way to cap the length of a plasma beam. Perhaps residents of the *Star Wars* galaxy have more sophisticated methods for controlling magnetic fields, which makes this possible. Or maybe Jedi knights control the beam using the Force. But until Earth scientists learn the secret, working lightsabers will remain beyond our grasp.

Don't look for the development of a Death Star anytime soon, either. As blogger Sean Goodwin calculated, building a Death Star would require one

Don't look for the construction of a real-life Death Star anytime soon. According to a White House spokesperson, the Obama administration "does not support blowing up planets." (Perhaps this will change following the 2016 elections.)

quadrillion metric tons of steel—which would take more than 833,000 years to mine and manufacture, at the current rate of production. Responding to a (hopefully) facetious proposal posted on the White House website in 2013 requesting that the United States build a Death Star, Paul Shawcross, chief of the Science and Space Branch at the White House Office of Management and Budget, explained that the estimated cost of building a Death Star—"$850 quadrillion dollars"—was too high, given current tight federal budgets. Also, Shawcross added, "the administration does not support blowing up planets." Besides, "Why would we spend countless taxpayer dollars on a Death Star with a fundamental flaw that can be exploited by a one-man starship?"

Hyperspace

Where *Star Wars* Was Right: Um . . .

Where *Star Wars* Went Wrong: Albert Einstein's theory of special relativity, originally published in 1905, determined that travel at speeds faster than light was impossible. But that hasn't stopped generations of science fiction writers from proposing various means of sidestepping Einstein to allow spacecraft to zoom through space at many times the speed of light. That's because faster-than-light travel is invaluable as a storytelling device. It's nearly impossible to write spacefaring SF without it, unless the story is restricted to our own solar system. Even at speeds approaching that of light, it would take years to reach the closest star systems and generations to reach more distant destinations. This clearly won't do for galaxy-spanning space operas, necessitating all the many proposed methods for overcoming Einstein's speed limit. On *Star Trek*, for example, the *Enterprise* employs "warp drive," in which engines literally warp space around the vessel—contracting space in front of the ship and expanding it behind, so that the vessel is propelled forward by the force of a wave in space-time. In Frank Herbert's *Dune* novels, the "Holtzman Effect" enables pilots to shorten interstellar journeys by folding space. Numerous works suggest traveling across great distances via the use of "wormholes," space-time singularities suggested by Einstein's theories.

In *Star Wars*, once ships like the *Millennium Falcon* achieve light speed, they cross into "hyperspace," where wrinkles in the space-time continuum become visible. Pilots like Han Solo follow carefully mapped routes along these wrinkled areas and make precisely calculated jumps across the folds to leap from one point to another without having to travel the enormous distances between the wrinkles. The existence of singularities like wormholes and wrinkles in space is now widely accepted. A paper published in 2014 by a pair of mathematicians at the University of California-Davis demonstrated that wrinkles in space-time are created whenever two shock waves collide. However, these anomalies are believed to be short-lived, unstable, and microscopic in size, not the sort of thing it would be wise or even possible to navigate a starship through.

None of the *Star Wars* films provide a detailed explanation of the (fictional) science behind hyperspace. The current, canonically correct explanation dates from the Prequel Trilogy. Earlier in the 1990s, however, various Expanded Universe works explained the phenomenon differently, stating that when vehicles like the *Falcon* jump to hyperspace, they cross over into an alternate, parallel dimension where our laws of physics don't apply and objects can travel faster than light, and then drop back to normal space when their journey is complete. Like the revised, canonical explanation, this earlier concept relies in part on respected scientific theory. The concept of parallel universes, first proposed by Princeton doctoral candidate Hugh Everett in 1957 and now known as the many worlds theory, has gained traction and become part of the mainstream approach to the study of quantum mechanics. Everett proposed that we exist not as part of a single universe but as part of an infinite multiverse, where every action with more than one possible outcome provides a delta point and "reality" splits off into a different parallel universe for each possible result. If you ever took part in an activity that may have resulted in your death, then in one (or possibly many) of these alternate realities you are dead; if you ever purchased a Powerball ticket, then in at least one of these alternate realities you are rich. And so on. Although some scientists reject Everett's theory, it cannot be mathematically disproven and so far has endured repeated attempts to discredit it. However, no one has yet suggested a way to cross from one of Everett's universes to another. And it doesn't follow that any of those universes would operate under different laws of physics. So, in the end, both explanations of hyperspace contain only the thinnest patina of scientific possibility.

The Force

Where Star Wars Was Right: *Star Wars* got everything right about the Force . . . from a certain point of view.

Where Star Wars Went Wrong: There is absolutely no evidence to support the existence of an energy field that "binds the galaxy together." This is a very old idea, dating as far back as Aristotle (384–322 BCE). The ancient Greeks believed that the world was composed of four basic elements: earth, water, fire, and air. Aristotle proposed the existence of a fifth element, aether, which connected human beings to each other and to everything else in the universe. Among other things, Aristotle believed that aether accounted for the asymmetrical movements of heavenly bodies (since the concept of gravity was as yet unknown) and provided the basis for the "science" of astrology (he ventured that ripples in the aether, created by the motion of the stars and planets, influenced humans here on Earth). Amazingly, aether remained an important scientific theory for the next two thousand years. Then, in 1887, researchers at Case Western Reverse University in Cleveland, Ohio, attempting to measure the effect of aether on objects in motion, instead discovered no evidence of its existence. This experiment, conducted by Albert A. Michelson and Edward W. Morley, led indirectly to the development of Einstein's theories of general and special relativity.

There is also no scientific evidence to support the existence of the phenomena we see in the *Star Wars* films as outward signs of the Force—telepathy, telekinesis, precognition, and ghosts. But that doesn't stop people from believing in such things. A 2006 study conducted at Baylor University found that 28 percent of American men and 31 percent of American women believe in telekinesis, that 39 percent of men and 47 percent of women believe in prophetic dreams, and that 17 percent of men and 25 percent of women believe in ghosts. Judging from the staggering number of "nonfiction" books and television programs produced annually dealing with these and other paranormal topics, those figures may be low.

In the Original Trilogy, before the prequels introduced the idea of "midichlorians" and other pseudoscientific folderol, the Force was treated, and even referred to, as a religion (see Chapter 29). Religious faith, like the belief in paranormal phenomena, exists beyond the scope or measure of empirical science. And, although the number of Americans who identify themselves as religious has been declining, the number of those who believe in God remains high—74 percent, according to a 2013 Harris Interactive Poll. The existence of a deity is impossible to prove or disprove through mathematical formulae or laboratory experimentation, but those who believe see the world though a different lens, which for them represents a deeper truth. So perhaps the Force is better explored theologically than scientifically.

29

Hate Leads to Suffering

The Ethics of *Star Wars*

From the outset, *Star Wars* was intended to be a story with message. "I wanted it [*Star Wars*] to be a traditional moral study . . . there is always a lesson to be learned," George Lucas told *The New Yorker*. But what was the lesson?

At first, detractors and naysayers argued that *Star Wars* had nothing to say (see Chapter 10). More recently, scholars have published papers claiming that it says all kinds of things that Lucas surely never (consciously) intended, labeling the series sexist, racist, anti-Semitic, and crypto-fascist, among other charges. Take, for instance, critic Dan Rubey, who eviscerated the original film for the website Jump Cut. "In the end, *Star Wars* embraces by implication all the things it pretends to oppose," Rubey writes. "The Nuremberg rally scene is a fitting conclusion coherent with the film's fascination with speed, size, and violence, and with the mysticism that cloaks the film's patriarchal power structures. The romance plot incorporates sexism and racism and supports a hierarchical social system that glamorizes those at the top and literally turns those at the bottom into machines."

At the opposite end of the spectrum, people of all political inclinations and religious affiliations have claimed that *Star Wars* supports their ideology: liberals and conservatives alike; Christians, Jews, Muslims, and Buddhists. In his book *Saint Paul at the Movies*, author Robert Jewett asserts that "there is a compelling gospel in this film [*Star Wars*], one that deserves to be compared with Paul's words in [the Biblical Book of] Romans."

None of these possible interpretations necessarily invalidates any of the others. Aside from overt "message pictures" and propaganda films, movies remain open to various thematic readings by different viewers—especially science fiction and fantasy pictures. Perhaps because they're designed to engage our imaginations, sci-fi films often work like inkblot tests; viewers tend to see in them whatever ideas they bring to them in the first place.

Writer Peter Kramer pointed out in a 1999 *History Today* article that certainly was the case with *Star Wars*. He cited a 1986 poll showing that while most viewers considered the Galactic Empire the embodiment of evil, some respondents saw the Empire as representing right-wing dictators, while others saw it representing communism. "When asked whether the movie is in favor of the conservative idea of 'peace through military strength,' conservative respondents overwhelmingly said 'yes,' whereas the majority of moderate and liberal respondents said 'no,'" Kramer reported. "This poll suggests that *Star Wars* allowed everyone to extract from it precisely the political meaning they were most comfortable with."

All of which makes defining the "true" message of the Original Trilogy about as straightforward a task as nailing Jell-O to a wall. I can only offer my take, supported by testimony from Lucas or others involved in the films' creation.

As I see it, then, some of the values reflected in the Original Trilogy would today be categorized as liberal and others as conservative. This is because the series' underlying ideology dates from an era when these political distinctions were understood differently. *Star Wars* expresses the same old-fashioned American ideas espoused by the classic Western and World War II movies of the 1940s and '50s that inspired Lucas in the first place. A half-dozen interrelated themes recur throughout the Original Trilogy.

Freedom Is Inseparable from Responsibility

On the surface, the central conflict in the Original Trilogy appears to be a struggle between freedom and totalitarianism, as the Rebel Alliance fights to overthrow the oppressive Galactic Empire. But this is what Alfred Hitchcock called a "MacGuffin," a device that drives the plot but has little bearing on the actual, deeper concerns of the film. Over the course of Episodes IV through VI, we learn almost nothing about the politics of the Empire. (This is probably good; see the Prequel Trilogy for an alternate approach.) The rebels don't sign declarations or draw up articles of confederation, nor do they give fiery speeches about taxation without representation or violations of civil rights. That's because despite its planet-hopping narrative, the real drama of *Star Wars* doesn't operate on a galactic scale but on an intimate, personal one. Its most important confrontations are fought out in the hearts and minds of a handful of characters, including three members of a single family.

One of the central issues these characters face is whether or not to accept responsibility for their own lives and fates, and toward their fellow beings. The temptation of tyranny is freedom from such responsibility. The knowledge that your life is ultimately under someone else's control brings, in the words of Czech novelist Milan Kundera, a "lightness of being." Under dictatorial rule, the tough decisions are somebody else's worry. Caring for your neighbor is something the state is supposed to do. Democracy forces us to take these matters into our own hands, to shape the course of our lives and our governments.

In the first film, Luke Skywalker has a pair of role models who offer conflicting points of view on these issues. Luke's Uncle Owen wants him to stay home and keep his head down. Obi-Wan Kenobi urges Luke to join the fight, to "learn the ways of the Force and become a Jedi like your father." Luke protests that "It's not that I like the Empire, I hate it, but there's nothing I can do about it right now. It's such a long way from here." Kenobi tells him, "That's your uncle talking." Owen Lars—like, presumably, most subjects of the Empire—is willing to go along to get along, to sacrifice what is right for what is comfortable. As he sees it, the war isn't his concern; he's just trying to make a living. Ultimately, the Empire forces Luke's hand, leaving him little choice but to join Kenobi and the rebels. But once he commits to this path, Luke never again shirks his responsibilities—neither to himself nor to others.

Similarly, Han Solo and Lando Calrissian both learn responsibility through the course of their adventures. At first, while they have no love for the Empire, Han and Lando, like Uncle Owen, see the struggle for freedom as someone else's battle. Since they live on the outskirts of the law, their personal fortunes will not be much different if control of the government changes hands. Although motivated at first by greed, ultimately both Han and Lando find that their concern for the people they care about overrides their financial self-interests. Their story arcs connect three of the films' major themes.

Lucas has often said that one of the lessons he hoped *Star Wars* would impart was that one should, as mythologist Joseph Campbell wrote, "follow your bliss." The first step on that journey is the willingness to accept responsibility, as Lucas explained in a 1999 PBS interview with Bill Moyers. "Myths help you have your own hero's journey, find your individuality, find your place in the world, but hopefully also remind you that you are part of a whole and that you must also be part of the community and think of the welfare of the community above the welfare of yourself," Lucas said.

Love Is Greater than Fear

"Fear is the path to Dark Side," Yoda warns in *The Empire Strikes Back*. "Fear leads to anger. Anger leads to hate. Hate leads to suffering." The Empire rules through fear. After the breakup of the Imperial Senate, Grand Moff Tarkin baldly states that "fear will keep the local systems in line—fear of this battle station." But, again and again in the *Star Wars* films, those who choose love (usually expressed in the form of compassion, but sometimes the romantic variety) ultimately triumph over the powers of fear and darkness. It's not a stretch to say that the Dark Side of the Force is fear, and that the good side is love.

Han Solo's nagging affection for Luke Skywalker drives him to enter the Battle of Yavin at the last minute, clearing the way for Luke to destroy the Death Star. Luke is able to fire the battle station–destroying torpedo because he trusts the advice of his beloved mentor, Ben Kenobi. Yoda fears that Luke is not ready to face Darth Vader at Cloud City. Earlier, in his dreamlike encounter with a spectral Vader, Luke struck out in fear and hatred and received a vision: his face behind Vader's mask (suggesting that if he follows the course of fear, he will replace Vader). However, because he acts out of love for his friends, Luke is able to resist the pull of the Dark Side during his first duel with Vader, even though Vader manipulates Luke's emotions by revealing his true relationship with the younger Skywalker. Meanwhile, Han and Leia overcome the fear of commitment that has driven them to lives of

"Fear is the path to Dark Side," Yoda warns in *The Empire Strikes Back.* "Fear leads to anger. Anger leads to hate. Hate leads to suffering."

emotional isolation. And Lando Calrissian redeems himself by acting against his own self-interests, abandoning a profitable operation he's spent years building in order to save his friends and protect the lives of his employees. Later, on Endor, the rebels are able to take out the Imperial Shield Generator only with the assistance of the Ewoks. They have this help because they treat the furry primitives with kindness and indulgence, even though at first the Ewoks intend to eat them. (Han reaches for his blaster, but Luke dissuades him from drawing his weapon; the Battle of Endor might have gone differently if a panicked Solo had begun massacring teddy bears.) Finally, Luke's unwavering compassion for his father, and his belief that a spark of goodness remains buried deep inside the Sith Lord's heart, ultimately inspires Vader to strike out at the emperor, saving his tortured soul and delivering victory to the rebels. "As they [Luke and Leia] go along, their compassion causes other people to become compassionate," said Lucas, in his DVD audio commentary for *The Empire Strikes Back*.

Empire Strikes Back director Irvin Kershner, in an interview with publicist Alan Arnold, summed up the theme of the *Star Wars* films this way: "It's possible to fight because you love."

Diversity Is Strength

The charge that *Star Wars* is racist dates back to the summer of 1977 when detractors complained that the only person of color in the original film was the villainous Darth Vader, who was not only voiced by an African American actor but was literally black. To counter this criticism, Lucas hired Billy Dee Williams to play Lando Calrissian. And in *Return of the Jedi*, audiences finally saw X-wing cockpits occupied by black, Asian, and female pilots. Although certainly welcome, these steps were not entirely necessary. Those who accused the film of racism were missing the point; they were thinking in real-world terms, not in science fiction terms. In fact, the *Star Wars* films make an emphatic statement against discrimination, but they do so in the vocabulary of space fantasy.

The evil Empire, in the Original Trilogy, is a racial monolith. All its officers are lily-white, most speak with British accents, but, most importantly, all of them are human. Although it sometimes employs alien bounty hunters (who imperial officers revile as "scum"), the Empire remains a distinctly xenophobic, species-ist organization. Although no human rebels of color are seen in the original *Star Wars*, the Alliance welcomes the nonhuman Chewbacca as one of its own (even if, curiously, it fails to award him a medal after the Battle of Yavin). And in the later films, the rebels become even more diverse, with several more species mentioned or shown, most prominently the Calimari

The xenophobic Galactic Empire was willing to employ nonhuman bounty hunters like IG-88 (far left) and Bossk (far right), but considered them "scum."

Admiral Ackbar and Sullustani Nien Nunb, who copilots the *Millennium Falcon* with Lando during the Battle of Endor. "One of the main themes in the film is having organisms realize that they must live together and they must live together for mutual advantage," Lucas told Moyers in 1999. "Not just human beings but all living things in the galaxy are part of a greater whole."

Greed Is Weakness

Characters who are motivated primarily by avarice—especially those who value financial gain more than the lives of others—do not fare well in the *Star Wars* films. Jabba the Hutt, Boba Fett, and the tellingly named Greedo all meet ignominious demises. Meanwhile, characters like Han Solo and Lando Calrissian become truly heroic when they finally place the welfare of others above their personal financial prospects. "I knew there was more to you than money!" Princess Leia exclaims when Han Solo returns after the Battle of Yavin. Solo has risked his life—and a cargo hold full of treasure—to rescue Luke Skywalker and deliver victory to the rebels. In the next film, Calrissian strikes a bargain with the Empire. He's willing to sacrifice

Skywalker—a person he's never met—to gain a secure future for his profitable mining operation. But he feels the sting of guilt when Darth Vader hands over Lando's old friend, Han, to Boba Fett. "This deal's getting worse all the time," he complains. Finally, when Vader announces he will take custody of Leia and Chewbacca, Lando has had enough. He breaks the deal himself, throwing financial considerations aside, to try to save Han, Chewie, and Leia. (The series' anti-greed theme would become even more overt in the Prequel Trilogy, with its venal Trade Federation enabling the transformation of the benevolent Republic into the evil Empire.)

High school English teacher Dan Zehr, in an essay posted on the starwars. com website, draws several meaningful parallels between the *Star Wars* saga and the greatest story of a miser's redemption, Charles Dickens' *A Christmas Carol.* In the Dickens tale, Ebenezer Scrooge "is visited by three spirits and, through these famous encounters, learns to embrace his humanity, and to look beyond himself and his pain. His sense of goodness and compassion, long dormant, is joyfully resurrected, revealing his true self," Zehr writes. "The same could be said of Darth Vader's journey of self-discovery; the Dark Lord must also learn to accept his humanity, and to think beyond his pain and previous life choices, in order to let his inner self turn toward the light."

In the case of George Lucas, however, this theme is more likely to have originated with Disney than with Dickens. Lucas grew up, and remains, a devoted fan of cartoonist Carl Barks' Uncle Scrooge comics (see Chapter 3). While named for Ebeneezer Scrooge (a role he would assume in the 1983 film *Mickey's Christmas Carol*), Donald Duck's parsimonious uncle, although known as "the richest duck in the world," consistently valued his loved ones and the thrill of adventure more than money. Many of the duck's far-flung adventures did nothing to advance his personal fortune. Later stories revealed that Scrooge's love wasn't for wealth as such, but for the sentimental value he placed on every coin in his vast treasury—he could recall how he earned every single one of them (usually some improbable exploit was involved). And the coin that mattered most to him was a simple ten-cent piece—the first dime he ever made. Scrooge's attitude was contrasted with that of the villainous Beagle Boys and rival miser Flintheart Glomhold, who loved only money and would do anything to acquire it.

Not only did Lucas fold this attitude toward money into his *Star Wars* films, he followed it in his life. As George Lucas began amassing a fortune to rival that of Uncle Scrooge, he also began undertaking significant works of philanthropy (see Chapter 27). When he sold Lucasfilm to Disney in 2012, he announced he would donate the majority of the $4 billion proceeds to charity. Lucas' attitude seemed to mirror that of Uncle Scrooge: There's nothing wrong with having a lot of money, unless all you care about is having a lot of money.

God Is Real

One of the more controversial elements of *Star Wars* is the film's apparent argument for a theological view of the universe. Although all manner of science fiction gadgetry is on display, the most powerful thing in the *Star Wars* galaxy is the Force, a metaphysical power accessed through spiritual discipline ("that ancient religion," as one imperial general refers to it). "The ability to destroy a planet is insignificant next to the power of the Force," Darth Vader famously warns. This concept runs counter to most science fiction. More typical of literary and cinematic SF was the attitude of *Star Trek* creator Gene Roddenberry, who believed that mankind could accomplish wonders—but only after it set aside prejudice and superstition, including religion.

Star Wars, on the other hand, was intended to kindle religious curiosity in viewers, as Lucas told Moyers in 1999. "I put the Force into the movies in order to try to awaken a certain kind of spirituality in young people—more a belief in God than a belief in any particular religious system," Lucas said. "I see *Star Wars* as taking all of the issues that religion represents and trying to distill them down into something . . . more easily accessible that people can grab onto to accept the fact that there is a greater mystery out there. . . . I think there is a God. What that God is, or what we know about that God, I am not sure. . . . It is a thin base for theology, that's why I would hesitate to call the Force God."

Good and Evil Remain Valid Concepts

In his address at the ground breaking of the George Lucas Instructional Building at the USC School of Cinema Arts in 1980, Lucas argued that movies have a responsibility to provide moral instruction. "The influence of the church, which used to be all-powerful, has been usurped by film," he said. "Films and television tell us the way we conduct our lives, what is right and wrong. There used to be a Ten Commandments that film had to follow, but now there are only a few remnants, like the hero doesn't shoot anybody in the back."

Taken together, the five themes already outlined in this chapter combined to deliver one more, overriding lesson: that long-cherished concepts of right and wrong—basic ideas about good and evil—had not become irrelevant. If

After the morally murky years of Vietnam and Watergate, *Star Wars* rekindled the idea that the world could still be divided into Good Guys and Bad Guys, or in this case Jedi Knights and Sith Lords.

this seems facile and overly simplistic today, it was a powerful message for American audiences in the summer of 1977. The country had been rocked by the revelation that American soldiers had participated in atrocities like the My Lai massacre in Vietnam, and by the Watergate scandal, in which operatives in the employ of the U.S. government had carried out, and then covered up, criminal activity. The successes of the civil rights and women's liberation movements, and the dawning struggle for gay rights, shook entrenched power structures in many communities, and a sudden economic downturn (including a global fuel shortage) further rattled the country. Reflecting the mood of the nation, many Hollywood films of the early and middle 1970s tended toward cynicism and paranoia. Straightforward stories of heroes and villains were not only out of favor but seemed laughable, relics from a bygone, woefully naïve era.

Star Wars exhilarated audiences, in part because it suggested that moral clarity remained possible. Conservative politicians like Ronald Reagan and

Margaret Thatcher saw this and latched onto it (see Chapter 10). Moreover, with its timeless, mythic structure, the movie inferred a kind of cosmic certitude to its moral center. *Star Wars* held these truths to be self-evident: that love was stronger than hate, and good would always triumph over evil. These were the lessons of the old movie serials, Westerns, and war films, dusted off and repackaged for a new generation that badly needed its sense of right and wrong buttressed.

Jewett, in *Saint Paul at the Movies*, notes that "like most popular films in modern America, particularly ones that attract audiences to see them repeatedly, it [*Star Wars*] reveals the formative values of the culture and to some degree forms those values as well." In his 1983 review of *Return of the Jedi*, *Washington Post* critic Gary Arnold wrote that the original *Star Wars* connected with audiences because it tapped "into inspirational depths that transcend political allegiance" and reflected "politically uncomplicated yearnings—to be in the right, to fight on the side of justice against tyranny." In other words, the movie proposed that the world could still be divided into Good Guys and Bad Guys. It also suggested that as long as we walk the righteous path, adhering to values endorsed by the world's major religions—taking accountability for our own actions and treating other people (of all races and backgrounds) with compassion, valuing the good of our neighbor more than the acquisition of wealth—we would remain the Good Guys.

30

Splinters of the Mind's Eye

Seminal *Star Wars* Fiction

O ver the past thirty-plus years, more than two hundred *Star Wars* novels have seen print. Together with *Star Wars* comic books, video games, and other spin-offs, these books formed what is popularly known as the Expanded Universe, a panoramic fictional landscape spanning nearly twenty-five thousand years of franchise mythology and involving thousands of characters, many of whom originate in the novels rather than the movies. These books have an avid and faithful audience, and often earned spots on the *New York Times* Best Seller list. As Alexandra Alter, who published a report about LucasBooks in the *Wall Street Journal*, told a reporter from National Public Radio, "It's actually gotten to the point where there are really hardcore *Star Wars* fans that prefer the books to the movies." LucasBooks, the publishing division of Lucasfilm, publishes a staggering sixty to seventy *Star Wars* books each year, the content of which is tightly controlled by Lucasfilm's editorial staff and a continuity overseer known as the Keeper of the Holocron. The Holocron is a massive database that tracks all *Star Wars* stories across all media so they can be categorized according to their canonicity. (Yes, really. The current Keeper of the Holocron is a guy named Leland Chee.) But things didn't always work this way. The mighty *Star Wars* literary franchise had relatively humble origins.

Marvel Comics

The first original *Star Wars* fiction arrived in the form of a long-running, best-selling comic series, which helped embattled Marvel Comics avert bankruptcy (see Chapter 12). Marvel's *Star Wars* comics owed their success in large part to fans' insatiable appetite for new stories featuring their favorite characters. The first original story (following a six-issue adaptation of the film) was a thinly veiled reworking of Akira Kurosawa's *Seven Samurai* (or, perhaps more accurately, of John Sturges' Westernized remake, *The Magnificent Seven*) written by Roy Thomas and illustrated by Howard Chaykin. In the four-issue story arc, Han and Chewbacca round up a band of mercenaries and misfits (including a seven-foot-tall, carnivorous green rabbit named Jax) to defend a farming village on a remote planet from marauding bandits.

Over the next few years the stories—mostly written by Archie Goodwin and drawn by Carmine Infantino— pitted Luke, Leia, Han, Chewie, and the droids against space pirates or bounty hunters, or else depicted "untold stories" from the characters' past. Our rebel heroes didn't engage imperial forces again until issue 18, and (excluding flashbacks) Darth Vader didn't reappear until a cameo in issue 21. Almost inconceivably, Vader played a major role in only four issues of the series (numbers 22, 23, 29 and 37) prior to Marvel's six-issue adaptation of *The Empire Strikes Back.*

Marvel's comics also suffered lapses in continuity and errors in terminology (spaceships sometimes engaged "warp drive" instead of entering hyperspace; droids often were referred to as "robots"). They also operated according to the continuity as it was then understood. Lucas was loath to let anyone in on the plots of his *Star Wars* sequels until they were released, so the early Marvel stories introduced a very different Jabba the Hutt, a Luke-Leia romance, and presented Luke's father and Vader as two different people. For all these reasons, the Marvel comics were considered "secondary canon," meaning that writers of later *Star Wars* fiction could refer to certain story elements but must ignore others. In any case, the quality of Marvel's narratives gradually improved, and the artwork (by respected talents such as Al Williamson and Walt Simonson, along with Infantino and others) remained slick and professional throughout.

Meanwhile, from 1979 to 1984, a *Star Wars* comic strip syndicated by the *Los Angeles Times* appeared daily in newspapers nationwide. The strip, which premiered March 12, 1979, was originally written and illustrated by longtime Tarzan comic book artist Russ Manning. In August 1980, after writing and drawing eight story arcs, Manning left the strip due to declining health. He was replaced by the team of writer Archie Goodwin and artist Alfredo Alcala for two arcs (including an adaptation of author Brian Daley's novel *Han Solo at Star's End*). Penciller Al Williamson replaced Alcala in February 1981. Together, he and Goodwin crafted the strip's sixteen remaining arcs. The final strip appeared March 11, 1984. Dark Horse Comics later collected the strip in a series of trade paperbacks.

Marvel lost its license to publish *Star Wars* comics in 1986, and the rights reverted back to Lucasfilm. In the early '90s, Dark Horse Comics purchased the rights and relaunched the *Star Wars* comic book franchise with a succession of miniseries including the acclaimed *Dark Empire* (1991–92) by writer

Tom Veitch and artist Cam Kennedy. Set six years after the events of *Return of the Jedi*, *Dark Empire* became a building block of the emerging Expanded Universe continuity, introducing a villain eventually revealed to be a clone of Emperor Palpatine. The sequel, *Dark Empire II* (1994–95), introduced Han and Leia's son, Anakin Solo, who also became a major figure in the Expanded Universe. In general, Dark Horse's books were more sophisticated than Marvel's, integrating story elements from *Star Wars* novels and video game as well as the movies. The Dark Horse stories were considered "primary canon." But they are not categorically more pure fun to read than Marvel's earlier, scruffier tales.

Splinter of the Mind's Eye by Alan Dean Foster

From this acorn grew the mighty oak that was the Expanded Universe. *Splinter of the Mind's Eye* was the first original *Star Wars* novel issued, published by Del Rey Books on February 12, 1978, while *Star Wars* was still running in many theaters. In 1976, science fiction author Alan Dean Foster, then best known for novels such as *Icerigger* (1974) and the ten-volume *Star Trek Logs* series (1974–78, which novelized screenplays from the *Star Trek* animated TV show), was hired by George Lucas to ghostwrite *Star Wars: From the Adventures of Luke Skywalker*. Like everything else *Star Wars*, this novelization was a blockbuster hit. But Foster's agreement also called for a sequel that might have become the second *Star Wars* film (see Chapter 14).

Lucas, who remained skeptical about the financial prospects for *Star Wars*, asked Foster to develop a story that could be adapted for the screen inexpensively if the film proved to be a mild success—profitable enough, at least, to merit a low-budget sequel. He instructed Foster to keep the number of locations low (the entire story unfolds on a single planet) and leave out Han Solo and Chewbacca (since Harrison Ford was not under contract to appear in the sequel). When *Star Wars* became a box office sensation, Lucas's plans grew far more ambitious, and he discarded the idea of filming *Splinter of the Mind's Eye*.

Foster had access to all of Lucas' various screenplay drafts and story synopses, but was left to his own devices in crafting the story. Foster explained in an email that Lucas simply requested "something that could be filmed on a low budget. He basically said to go write a sequel novel, which is what I did." Lucas made just one change to the story, striking an opening space battle that would have been expensive to film. The resulting story is action-packed, reflecting the style and verve of the first movie. Luke, Leia, C-3PO, and R2-D2 are on an important diplomatic mission when they crash on the forlorn swamp planet Mimban. There they discover a secret imperial mining operation overseen by the sadistic Captain-Supervisor

Grammel and befriend an old woman, Halla, who claims to be a master of the Force. Halla convinces them to help her recover the legendary, lost Kaiburr Crystal, which greatly amplifies the power of the Force. She gives Luke a sliver of the crystal, which falls into Grammel's hands—and eventually draws the attention of Darth Vader. Han Solo and Chewbacca do not appear in the story, but Luke, Leia, and Halla gain a pair of giant, furry allies in Hin and Kee, a pair of Muzzem, which are very Wookiee-like in both appearance and behavior.

Not only is *Splinter of the Mind's Eye* an entertaining yarn, but it points both forward, previewing elements that would emerge in later movies, and back, reviving ideas originally envisioned as part of *Star Wars* but written out of the final screenplay. The swamp planet setting foreshadows the Dagobah passages of *The Empire Strikes Back*, and the presence of an aged master of the Force

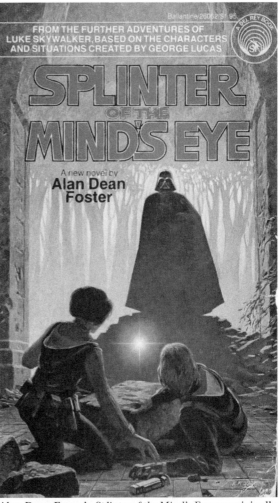

Alan Dean Foster's *Splinter of the Mind's Eye* was originally commissioned by George Lucas as a possible sequel to *Star Wars*.

anticipates Yoda. At one point our heroes encounter a creature known as a wandrella, which is a sort of cross between the giant worms from Dune and the Sarlacc sand monster from *Return of the Jedi*. Luke, Leia, and Halla obtain assistance from a primitive, furry aboriginal species known as the Coway, echoing the assistance Luke Starkiller receives from Wookiees in an early draft screenplay and looking ahead to the role of the Ewoks in *Return of the Jedi*. The Kaiburr Crystal also originates from an early draft screenplay, although it was spelled differently there. (For more on George Lucas' early screenplays, see Chapter 4.) Like *The Empire Strikes Back*, the story concludes with a Luke-versus-Darth lightsaber duel—a confrontation that concludes when one of the combatants loses a limb and tumbles into an abyss (yet survives). When *Splinter* was written, the idea that Luke and Leia were twins had not yet been developed, and sexual tension crackles between the two throughout the story.

Splinter of the Mind's Eye, like Foster's *Star Wars* novelization, was an instant best seller and remains one of the most absorbing and beloved Expanded Universe books. Although never filmed, it was adapted in graphic novel form by writer Terry Austin and artist Chris Sprouse for Dark Horse Comics in 1996. It's the one Expanded Universe novel all *Star Wars* fans should read, if only for a glimpse of the sequel that might have been.

Despite strong sales for the Han Solo and Lando Calrissian novels, written by Brian Daley and L. Neil Smith, respectively, the *Star Wars* literary franchise lapsed into a coma from 1987 until 1991.

Photography by Preston Hewis/East Bank Images

The Han Solo Novels by Brian Daley, and Lando Calrissian Novels by L. Neil Smith

The success of *Splinter of the Mind's Eye* confirmed, if any doubt existed, that there was a readership hungry for *Star Wars* fiction. Author Brian Daley was quickly commissioned to write a trilogy of novels featuring Han Solo and Chewbacca's adventures prior to the events of *Star Wars*. Daley was a young science fiction writer who had published two previous novels. His paperbacks *Han Solo at Star's End, Han Solo's Revenge* (both 1979), and *Han Solo and the Lost Legacy* (1980) are brightly written yarns brimming with action, although they lack the finesse of Foster's work and sometimes resort to preposterous plot devices that threaten the believability of the narrative (even within the fantastic context of the *Star Wars* universe). In Daley's stories, Han and Chewie uncover malfeasance—including widespread kidnapping and slavery—within the Corporate Sector Authority, a corrupt empire-within-the-Empire. The books sold well and the entire trilogy was reissued in omnibus format in 1992. Daley went on to pen radio adaptations of *Star Wars*, *The Empire Strikes Back*, and *Return of the Jedi*, and to cowrite (under the pseudonym Jack McKinney) with James Luceno a long-running series of Robotech novels and the four-volume Black Hole Travel Agency series, among other works. He died of pancreatic cancer in 1996 at age forty-eight.

Between the release of *The Empire Strikes Back* and *Return of the Jedi*, author L. Neil Smith was hired to write a trilogy similar to Daley's Han Solo books but devoted to the backstory of *Star Wars*' other endearing rogue, Lando Calrissian. Like Daley, Smith was an up-and-coming SF writer. *Lando Calrissian and the Mindharp of Sharu*, *Lando Calrissian and the Flamewind of Oseon*, and *Lando Calrissian and the Starcave of ThonBoka* (all 1983) were among his earliest published works. The only character from the films present in these novels is Lando—the most thinly written of the series' major characters, a virtual blank slate. The three books form a trilogy as Lando and his droid, Vuffi Raa, match wits with a sorcerer bent on galactic domination, the revenge-crazed Rentasians (who mistakenly blame Vuffi for the massacre of two-thirds of their population), and the military forces of the Centrality, a semi-autonomous regional government within the Empire. Although diverting and imaginative, Smith's novels lack the action set pieces that are the calling card of the franchise, and—combined with their dearth of familiar characters and settings—seem like *Star Wars* in name only. For instance, even though the primary antagonist is an evil sorcerer, Smith never mentions the Force. Smith has gone on to publish more than thirty novels, including his North American Confederacy series, which includes nine books (so far). Smith has also earned attention as a libertarian political activist. He ran twice for the Libertarian Party's presidential nomination but lost both times. Like *Splinter of the Mind's Eye*, Daley's Han Solo trilogy and Smith's Lando Calrissian novels were both published by Del Rey Books and subtitled "From the Adventures of Luke Skywalker," even though Luke does not appear in any of these six novels.

The Thrawn Trilogy by Timothy Zahn

Although the Foster, Daley, and Smith books sold extremely well, no new *Star Wars* fiction was published for seven years following the final Lando Calrissian novel. The book that ended the drought, Timothy Zahn's *Heir to the Empire*, revolutionized the *Star Wars* literary franchise. Released May 1, 1991, to a public starved for new content after going more than half a decade with no new *Star Wars* movies or novels, *Heir* rocketed to the top of the *New York Times* Best Seller list. It appealed not only to *Star Wars* diehards but to science fiction fans in general, and even to readers who didn't typically read SF but were curious to learn what happened next to Luke, Leia, Han, and their friends. It was the first *Star Wars* novel to depict the events that followed *Return of the Jedi*.

Heir was the opening chapter of the Thrawn Trilogy, which also included *Dark Force Rising* (1992) and *The Last Command* (1993). Set five years after *Return of the Jedi*, the story pits Luke, Leia, Han, Chewie, Lando, and the droids against a new menace—strategic mastermind Grand Admiral Thrawn, who joins forces with the evil clone of a Jedi Master named C'Boath to revive the fortunes of a diminished but not yet destroyed Galactic Empire. *Heir to the Empire* introduced Mara Jade, a former imperial special agent with a personal vendetta against Luke; Leia's childhood friend, Winter; interstellar criminal kingpin Talon Karrde; and a race of assassins known as the Noghri. It also expanded the roles of minor characters from the *Star Wars* films, including Admiral Ackbar and Wedge Antilles. All of these characters would become important to the emerging framework of the Expanded Universe. Zahn also coined the name of the capital planet of the Galactic Empire, Coruscant, which later appeared in the prequel films.

Lucasfilm entered an agreement with Bantam Books to revive the *Star Wars* literary frachise and selected Zahn, who was already a decorated science fiction author, from a list of potential writers suggested by Bantam. The company exercised a degree of editorial control during the process. For instance, Zahn originally planned to make the evil Jedi a clone of Obi-Wan Kenobi, but this was overruled. For the most part, however, Zahn, as he said in a 1991 interview, "was given essentially a blank check to do what I wanted."

The engrossing and vividly written Thrawn Trilogy collectively sold in excess of fifteen million copies worldwide and marked a major advance in the literary franchise. The initial printing of sixty thousand copies sold out in the first week. Previously, the Expanded Universe had consisted of *Star Wars* tie-ins that happened to be books; Zahn's trilogy was high-caliber science fiction that happened to be *Star Wars*. In 2011, National Public Radio polled listeners about their favorite fantasy and science fiction novels. The Thrawn Trilogy finished No. 88 in NPR's Top 100 (J. R. R. Tolkien's *The Lord of the Rings* earned the No. 1 slot, followed by Douglas Adams' *Hitchhiker's Guide to the Galaxy*). The Thrawn Trilogy was later adapted as a Dark Horse Comics miniseries and as a role-playing game. The trilogy also changed the way *Star Wars* authors were compensated. Heretofore, following standard industry practice, writers (including Zahn) had earned a per-copy royalty based on the sales of their novels. Moving forward, however, Lucasfilm began paying authors a relatively generous flat fee but no royalties.

Zahn wrote a two-part sequel known as the Hand of Thrawn Duology (*Specter of the Past*, 1997, and *Vision of the Future*, 1998), which finally ended the war with the Empire and featured the marriage of former enemies Luke Skywalker and Mara Jade. Mara later bore Luke a son, Ben Skywalker. Zahn has written five other non-Thrawn *Star Wars* novels so far, along with several *Star Wars* graphic novels (some connected with the Thrawn series, others not). His non-*Star Wars* works include the long-running Cobra (eight-book), Dragonback (six-book), and Quadrail (five-book) series, along with numerous other SF novels, short stories, and comics.

Author Timothy Zahn's thrilling *Heir to the Empire*, the opening salvo in his Thrawn Trilogy, helped prove that there was still an audience eager for more *Star Wars* stories and served as a major building block for the Expanded Universe.

The robust sales of Zahn's books led to a rapid proliferation of other *Star Wars* novels. *The Glove of Darth Vader*, by Paul and Hollace Davids, appeared in 1992, just a month after Zahn's second Thrawn novel. *Glove* launched a series of six paperbacks known collectively as the Jedi Prince Series, which concluded a month prior to Zahn's final Thrawn installment in 1993. Nearly seventy more *Star Wars* novels and short story collections appeared from 1993 to 1999, when *Star Wars* returned to movie screens with *The Phantom Menace*.

Following the debut of Episode I, the literary franchise truly exploded, with scores of additional books appearing annually. These new books were set before and during the prequel era, during the interim between the two trilogies, as well as the years following the Original Trilogy.

Along with this surge in the *Star Wars* literary franchise came a resurgence of sales of other *Star Wars* merchandise, including action figures and video games (some of which featured characters from the books). The Official Star Wars Fan Club, which had been shuttered since late 1987, reopened. This unexpected renaissance may also have encouraged Lucas to move forward with his plans for the long-delayed Prequel Trilogy.

In the 1990s, however, the Expanded Universe novels focused primarily on continuing the *Star Wars* saga beyond *Return of the Jedi*, with stories set at times ranging from the immediate aftermath of the Battle of Endor (Kathy Tyers' *The Truce at Bakura*, 1993) to fourteen years later (Roger MacBride Allen's Corellian Trilogy, 1995). These books depicted the final battles against the Empire and the establishment of the New Republic, eventually shifting away from the protagonists of the movies to focus on stories about Han and Leia's twin children, Jaina and Jacen; Anakin Solo (who follows his namesake grandfather down the dark path); Ben Skywalker; and other characters originating within the Expanded Universe. Michael J. Stackpole's 1996 book *X-Wing: Rogue Squadron*, the first installment in the ten-volume, multi-author X-Wing series, was the first *Star Wars* novel to include no characters from the films.

Shadows of the Empire

The most ambitious work to appear during the late-1990s flood of *Star Wars* fiction was *Shadows of the Empire* (1996), a multimedia event that included a novel, a comic book miniseries, a video game, a role-playing game, trading cards, and even a soundtrack album—basically, everything except a movie. *Shadows* purported to reveal a previously untold adventure that took place between the events of *The Empire Strikes Back* and *Return of the Jedi*. As such, it was able to include Darth Vader as a major character, becoming the first Expanded Universe story to include Vader since *Splinter of the Mind's Eye*. Han Solo does not appear in the story, since he was still frozen in Carbonite.

Although lively and diverting, *Shadows of the Empire* does not rank among the most compelling *Star Wars* yarns. This is due, in large part, to the frustrating nature of the concept. Since *Shadows* takes place between Episodes V and VI, nothing of consequence can happen without upsetting the established continuity of the series. Leia, Lando, and Luke attempt to rescue Han from Boba Fett before the bounty hunter can deliver him to Jabba the

Hutt, but readers know they will not succeed. Fett fends off attacks by rival bounty hunters, who want to steal the frozen Han and claim the reward, but there's never any doubt that Fett will prevail. Vader desperately searches for Luke, but the audience knows the two will not meet again until the Battle of Endor. *Shadows* also introduces Prince Xizor, a lieutenant of the emperor who's jealous of Vader's status and devises a plot to try to discredit the Dark Lord of the Sith and replace him as the emperor's right hand. But we all know how that will end, too.

The novel (written by prolific SF author Steve Perry), the comic book (written by John Wagner and illustrated by Kilian Plunkett, John Nadeau, and P. Craig Russell), and other media all follow the same interlocking narrative, but each platform offers exclusive story elements. The novel unfolds

Steve Perry's novel *Shadows of the Empire* was part of a multi-platform event that also included a comic book miniseries, a video game, a role-playing game, trading cards, and even a soundtrack album—basically, everything except a movie.

from the shifting points of view of Luke, Leia, Vader, and Xizor. The comic book takes a different perspective, devoting significant attention to Boba Fett and Jix, a spy in Vader's employ, both of whom barely figure in Perry's novel.

Despite its conceptual shortcomings, the various components of *Shadows of the Empire* sold well, and the endeavor proved that the *Star Wars* franchise could create a major "event" even without a new film. A comic book–only sequel, *Shadows of the Empire: Evolution*, appeared in 2000. More importantly,

Shadows provided the template for the far more successful multiplatform *Star Wars: Clone Wars* project, set between the events of Episodes II and III. The original *Clone Wars* (2003–5) included an Emmy-winning animated television and online series, as well as comic books and video games. A second *Clone Wars* series (2008–14) opened with an animated telefilm and included an ongoing cartoon TV series, a novel, two comic books series (one aimed at young readers, another at grown-ups), and five different video games, among other media.

New franchise owner Disney has announced plans for a *Shadows of the Empire*–like multimedia assault that will tie in with the new series of *Star Wars* movies slated to begin in 2015. Along with the Episode VII film will appear an animated TV series, novels, comics, video games, and more. To build momentum, a new cartoon series, *Star Wars: Rebels*, appeared in October 2014, a full year *prior* to Episode VII. Fans should brace for something along the lines of the company's saturation bombing–like deployment of its Marvel Comics properties (Iron Man, Captain America, Thor, the Avengers, Guardians of the Galaxy, etc.) across various platforms.

However, the coming of these new films and related tie-ins spelled death for the vast Expanded Universe beloved by so many readers from 1978 to 2014. One of George Lucas' stated reasons for not filming the third *Star Wars* trilogy was that he didn't want to obliterate the elaborate and widely popular Expanded Universe. But neither could he proceed if he felt beholden to the established EU continuity—otherwise, anyone who had read the books would know the whole story in advance. Producer-director J. J. Abrams, who's in charge of Episode VII, demonstrated an indifference to the continuity of a major SF franchise while making his two *Star Trek* movies. In April 2014, Lucasfilm announced that it was officially decanonizing the entire Expanded Universe. The new, official *Star Wars* canon will be built on Episodes VII through IX and other associated films, TV series, and other projects. This means that, at least for now, fans will have to say goodbye to characters such as Admiral Thrawn, Mara Jade, and Jaina and Jacen Solo, along with the rest of the EU. It was fun while it lasted.

31

Let the Wookiee Win

Star Wars Games

When *Star Wars* premiered in the summer of 1977, there was no home video game industry. Electronic games had not advanced far beyond *Pong*, introduced by Atari in 1972. But that changed dramatically in 1978 after Japanese game maker Taito issued the *Star Wars*-y *Space Invaders*, a $2 billion worldwide sensation that encouraged dozens of other companies to enter the market. The *Star Wars* franchise matured with the emerging video game business. The two seemed tailor-made for one another. While it might be a stretch to suggest that *Star Wars* helped establish a wide audience for electronic games, it certainly didn't hurt. *Star Wars* by nature was well suited to capitalize on the growing game culture, since every film contained multiple action sequences that could be adapted to playable scenarios. Besides, many avid gamers were also *Star Wars* fans.

If *Star Wars* helped shape the video game industry, video games also influenced *Star Wars*. As of January 2014, *Star Wars* video games had earned $2.9 billion. That trails only box office receipts, home video profits, and toy sales among the franchise's various revenue streams. It's a billion dollars more than the wildly successful *Star Wars* books have earned (see previous chapter). And that $2.9 billion counts only video games— not board games, trading card games, role-playing games, or related items. That money helped refill the Lucasfilm coffers following Lucas' costly divorce (see Chapter 37), and enabled him to restart the *Star Wars* series in the late 1990s. In the years since the Original Trilogy, the video game and film industries have grown closer together, with games becoming more cinematic and movies (especially since the advent of CGI) becoming more like video games. Today's blockbusters are designed with video games in mind. The Prequel Trilogy was loaded with game-ready passages, such as the pod race from *The Phantom Menace* (1999).

In the beginning, however, *Star Wars* games were something altogether different.

Board Games

The first *Star Wars* home video game wouldn't appear until 1982, but board games remained popular, and Kenner, alongside its platoons of action figures and other toys, released at least two different games to tie in with each installment of the Original Trilogy. For *Star Wars*, Kenner issued *Escape from the Death Star*, *Adventures of R2-D2*, and *Destroy the Death Star*; for *The Empire Strikes Back*, it released *Hoth Ice Planet Adventure* and *Yoda: Jedi Master*; and for *Return of the Jedi*, it published *Battle at Sarlacc's Pit*, *Wicket the Ewok*, and *Ewoks Save the Trees*.

Most of these products were simple "race" games, where players spun a spinner, rolled dice, or drew from a deck of cards to advance from the game's starting to ending point, encountering various hazards along the way. For instance, in the popular *Escape from Death Star* game (not to be confused with a later role-playing game of the same name), players selected a game piece (each of which featured a pair of characters: Luke and Leia, Han and Chewbacca, C-3PO and R2-D2, or Darth Vader and a stormtrooper) and drew cards that indicated how many spaces to move forward or backward. Players advanced from station to station, first visiting the Death Star Control Room

The Adventures of R2-D2 was one of eight *Star Wars* board games released by Kenner in the late 1970s and early 1980s. *Photography by Preston Hewis/East Bank Images*

to obtain the Death Star plans (it doesn't happen that way in the movie, but whatever), then on to Tractor Beam to deactivate the beam, then the *Millennium Falcon*, and finally, after "battling" TIE fighters (i.e., not landing on unlucky spaces featuring a photograph of a TIE fighter), to the Rebel Base to deliver the plans. The first player to successfully deliver the plans won. In other games, the goal was to accumulate points. In *Battle at Sarlacc's Pit*, for example, players earned "Jedi points" for successfully knocking Gamorrean Guards, Boba Fett, and even Jabba the Hutt into the gaping maw of the Sarlacc sand monster. Once all the enemies were dispatched, the player with the most points won.

In later years, licensed *Star Wars* editions of various other popular board games appeared, including *Monopoly*, *Risk*, *Life*, *Trivial Pursuit*, and a version of *Operation* in which players removed malfunctioning parts from R2-D2. Although not officially branded as such, Tiger Electronics' *Star Wars: Electronic Galactic Battle* game was, essentially, a *Star Wars*-ized version of *Electronic Battleship*, with players trying to find and destroy the opponent's spacecraft. You could play as either the rebels, with X-wings, Y-wings, and such, or as the Empire, with TIE fighters, Star Destroyers, and so on—but, sorry, no Death Star. In addition, a handful of companies have sold *Star Wars* chess sets over the years. Unfortunately, no officially licensed home version of Dejarik holochess (the holographic game played by Chewie and Threepio onboard the *Falcon*) has yet been issued. However, fans have written rules for the game, and a few have created homemade versions of it—some using wooden or metal game pieces, and others as homemade computer games.

Video Games

Custom, homemade *Star Wars* computer games have been around as long as *Star Wars* fans have owned home computers. But the first licensed, Lucasfilm-authorized electric game was Parker Brothers' *Star Wars: The Empire Strikes Back* (1982), created for the Atari 2600 system. A year later, a version was issued for Mattel's Intellivision platform. *Star Wars: The Empire Strikes Back* was a simplistic, scrolling shooter game with primitive graphics. The player flew a snowspeeder and attacked AT-AT walkers, as seen in the Hoth snow battle from the film. The player won the game by destroying five walkers; if the Walkers reached Echo Base and destroyed it, the player lost.

Although sales of *Star Wars: The Empire Strikes Back* were not spectacular, the game performed well enough to encourage the development of more product. Parker Brothers issued *Return of the Jedi: Death Star Battle* and *Return of the Jedi: Jedi Arena* in 1983. In *Death Star Battle*, produced for the Atari 5200 and Atari XE platforms, players piloted the *Millennium Falcon* through a squadron

The very first *Star Wars* home video game ever released was this *Empire Strikes Back* cartridge, made by Parker Brothers for the Atari 2600 system.

Photography by Preston Hewis/East Bank Images

of TIE fighters to destroy the second Death Star. In *Jedi Arena*, made for the Atari 2600 only, players battle one another with lightsabers. A third game, *Return of the Jedi: Ewok Adventure*, was prototyped but never released.

The first *Star Wars* arcade game, produced by Atari and simply named *Star Wars*, also appeared in 1983. This was a sophisticated (by early 1980s standards) first-person shooter/flight simulator featuring color 3-D vector graphics. The player relived the climax of *Star Wars*, taking part in the assault on the Death Star from within the cockpit of an X-Wing fighter. Successful players cleared three levels—overcoming an initial engagement with TIE fighters; then destroying turret guns on the surface of the space station; and finally zooming through a trench and firing a torpedo into the exhaust port to destroy the Death Star. Players continued to be harassed by TIE fighters throughout the second and third levels. The game featured sound effects and snippets of dialogue from the film—including the voices of Mark Hamill, Harrison Ford, James Earl Jones, and Sir Alec Guinness. *Star Wars* was sold as a stand-up console and in a deluxe, sit-down cockpit version. In either configuration, it was a massive hit and remained in production for five years. It became a fixture at many arcades in the United States and the United Kingdom, and fans set video game endurance records (authenticated by the Guinness Book of World Records) playing it.

Parker Brothers released a scaled-down home version in 1984 for Atari and Coleco game systems, and the Commodore 64 computer. In 1987 and '88, it was reconfigured for nine more game systems and reissued. Readers of the website Killer List of Video Games, an online community of video game enthusiasts and preservationists, voted *Star Wars* the fourth-best coin-operated video game of all time (trailing only *Pac-Man*, *Donkey Kong*, and *Galaga*). Atari introduced a second *Star Wars* arcade game, *Return of the Jedi*, in 1984. It featured more lifelike raster graphics and included four levels, some replicating the speeder bike chase scene and others the climactic Death Star battle. A home version was also produced. The true follow-up to the *Star Wars* arcade game was Atari's *The Empire Strikes Back*, released in 1985. It was another 3-D vector graphics first-person shooter/flyer based, like *Star Wars: The Empire Strikes Back*, on the Hoth AT-AT/snowspeeder battle. Neither of Atari's sequels proved as popular as the original *Star Wars* arcade game.

Japanese game maker Namco released an adventure game titled simply *Star Wars* in 1987, created for Nintendo's early Famicom console. The designers of this game seemed completely unconcerned with fidelity to the source material. In it, Luke Skywalker pilots the *Falcon* to various planets to rescue Ben Kenobi, Princess Leia, Han Solo, Chewbacca, and the droids. Each planet is protected by a different Darth Vader, some of which transform into various creatures (a shark, a scorpion, a Wampa, and a dinosaur). Luke has black hair and Chewbacca speaks English. A year later, Mastertronic released a computer game, *Droids: Escape from Aaron*, based on the *Star Wars: Droids* cartoon. This was an adventure game in which Threepio and Artoo escape from the clutches of the Hutt-like Fromm criminal gang. The events depicted in the game did not derive from the TV show but were in keeping with the continuity of the program.

During the 1980s, Lucasfilm simply sold *Star Wars* licenses to various game manufacturers and wasn't always able to exert quality control over the end product. Fed up with the scattershot quality of these games, George Lucas revamped his Lucasfilm Games division to form LucasArts, which designed and manufactured games in-house. Initially, LucasArts partnered with Atari to produce games based on *Labyrinth* (1986) and *Indiana Jones and the Last Crusade* (1989). Later, on its own, LucasArts created original adventure games such as the long-running *Monkey Island* series (1990–2011) for various game systems and computer platforms. Perhaps waiting until Lucas was certain LucasArts had hit its stride, the company didn't release a *Star Wars* game until 1993, but it was worth the wait. *Star Wars: X-Wing*—a combination flight simulator and adventure game, with players battling imperial forces in a trusty rebel fighter—was a smash, spawning multiple expansion packs, collector's editions, and sequels.

More than twenty more *Star Wars* video games were issued prior to the release of *The Phantom Menace* in 1999, including *Star Wars: TIE Fighter* (the first game set from the perspective of the Empire) in 1994, *Star Wars: Dark*

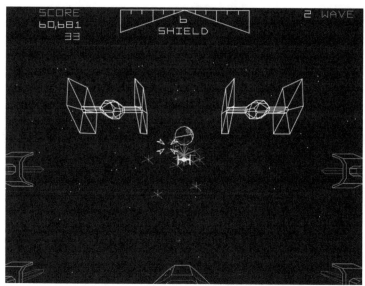

The vector 3-D graphics for the wildly successful original *Star Wars* arcade game were state of the art, circa 1983.

Screen capture courtesy of Killer List of Video Games website, KLOV.com

Forces in 1995, *Shadows of the Empire* in 1996 (part of a multimedia event, see previous chapter), and *Star Wars: Rogue Squadron* (1998), all of which proved very successful. *Star Wars* games have remained the primary focus of LucasArts since the mid-1990s.

In more recent years, the company has expanded into the realms of real-time strategy, role-playing (RPG), and, finally, massively multiplayer online role-playing games (MMORPG) with *Star Wars Galaxies* (2003), *Star Wars: Clone War Adventures* (2010), and *Star Wars: The Old Republic* (2012). LucasArts spent a then-record $200 million developing *The Old Republic*, a pay-to-play download that allows players to interact together online. The game collected one million subscribers within three days of its launch. All three *Star Wars* MMORPG releases were multimedia events, with novel, comic book, and toy tie-ins.

Role-Playing Games

As with video games, role-playing enthusiasts began writing their own *Star Wars* game scenarios long before the first officially licensed *Star Wars* RPG appeared in 1987. With ten years of pent-up demand behind it, West End Games' tabletop *Star Wars: The Role-Playing Game* scored a tremendous success. It spawned more than eighty supplements and sourcebooks for expanded play, as well as four board game spin-offs: *Star Wars: Star Warriors* (1987), *Star*

Wars: Assault on Hoth (1988), *Star Wars: Battle for Endor* (1990), and *Star Wars: Escape from the Death Star* (1990, not to be confused with the Kenner board game).

Perhaps more importantly, *Star Wars: The Role-Playing Game* established much of the backdrop for what would become known as the Expanded Universe. While he was writing his influential Thrawn Trilogy (see previous chapter), author Timothy Zahn was instructed by Lucasfilm to incorporate background material from West End Games' sourcebooks into his story. When Zahn's books shot to the top of the best-seller list, West End Games, in turn, created new materials integrating story elements created by Zahn. Moving forward, Lucasfilm's continuity czar, known as the Keeper of the Holocron, worked to ensure that the rapidly expanding franchise mythology—across novels, role-playing games, video games, and other media—remained consistent. Despite the success of its *Star Wars* products, West End Games went bankrupt in 1998, and Wizards of the West Coast, a division of Hasbro, took over as the producer of *Star Wars* RPGs. In 2011, Fantasy Flight Games acquired the license to produce *Star Wars* role-playing, card, and miniature games.

The line between traditional tabletop RPGs and video games became blurred with the advent of computer role-playing games and MMORPGs, which combine the role-playing concept with immersive computer-animated environments. Two pioneering *Star Wars* computer RPGs, *Star Wars: Knight of the Old Republic* (2003) and the sequel *Star Wars: Knights of the Old Republic—Sith Lords* (2004), were based on the Wizards of the West Coast's *Star Wars* Roleplaying Game.

Star Tours

Online role-playing draws gamers deeper into the *Star Wars* experience, but the *Star Tours* attraction brings fans still closer by combining original short films with a full-fledged flight simulator to create the illusion of traveling to destinations within the *Star Wars* universe. A partnership between Lucasfilm and Disney, promoted as "the Ultimate *Star Wars* Adventure," *Star Tours* opened in December 1986 at Disneyland in Anaheim, California, as part of "Tomorrowland." The attraction expanded to Disney's Hollywood Studios in Orlando and Tokyo Disneyland in 1989, and to Disneyland Park in Paris in 1992.

Star Tours patrons board a full-size mock-up of a "StarSpeeder" spacecraft and experience a voyage to various "tourist sites" across the galaxy, with C-3PO and R2-D2 as guides. At first, visitors traveled only to Endor, but in later years more than fifty additional destinations were added, including (from the Original Trilogy) Alderaan, Bespin, Dagobah, Hoth, Tatooine, Yavin, and even the Death Star. None of these journeys were free of peril, and the StarSpeeder captain was forced to battle TIE fighters, evade imperial Destroyers, or deal with other threats.

Developing *Star Tours* took nearly a year and cost $32 million, almost twice what Walt Disney spent to build the whole of Disneyland in 1955. Lucasfilm produced a first-person point-of-view short film, while Disney "imagineers" purchased four $500,000 military-grade flight simulators and customized them for the attraction. Combined, the movie and the motion simulators create the illusion of interstellar travel. Anthony Daniels appears in the film as Threepio. The original *Star Tours* short also featured Paul (Pee-wee Herman) Reubens as the StarSpeeder captain and a cameo by Warwick Davis as Wicket the Ewok. John Williams offered to write an original score for *Star Tours* but later decided that library cues from his existing scores would be sufficient.

In the early 2010s, the *Star Tours* attraction was replaced by *Star Tours: The Adventures Continue* in the United States and Japan. The revamped ride featured high-definition 3-D graphics, upgraded sound, and improved motion simulators. The original *Star Tours* remains in operation in France. Whereas the original *Star Tours* journeys supposedly took place following the events of *Return of the Jedi*, flights on *The Adventure Continues* take place between Episodes III and IV. This enables the ride to include (in one of multiple possible scenarios) Darth Vader, who menaces passengers as they prepared to leave the spaceport. George Lucas consulted on the scenarios for the attraction's movies, which feature visual effects from Industrial Light & Magic. Each *Star Tours* ride seats up to forty visitors and lasts four and a half minutes. When the ride ends, guests disembark and enter (where else?) the Star Trader gift shop.

In August 2014, Disney CEO Bob Iger announced that the company was planning additional *Star Wars*–based attractions at its theme parks, confirming what many observers had assumed since Disney acquired Lucasfilm in 2012. As of this writing in early 2015, specific details of Disney's plans remained to be announced. It's also unclear whether the new rides will replace or complement *Star Tours: The Adventures Continue*. However, Iger told *Variety* that Disney was "developing designs for a far greater *Star Wars* presence in the parks."

32

Laugh It Up, Fuzzball

Memorable *Star Wars* Parodies

F ew (if any) films have been more frequently lampooned than *Star Wars*. The franchise has been spoofed on film and television, and taken jibes from stand-up comedians, talk show hosts, comic book satirists, and wisenheimers of every other stripe. Through it all, George Lucas has demonstrated the admirable ability to take a joke. Perhaps that's because he understands that this proliferation of parodies amounts to a backhanded testimonial to the franchise's cultural significance. After all, comedians don't get laughs by poking fun at movies nobody has seen (which accounts for the shortage of *More American Graffiti* spoofs). *Star Wars* has always been an easy target, not only because of its many distinctive, colorful, and— let's face it— borderline-silly elements (Laurel and Hardy robots, a giant dog-ape-bear starship copilot, Princess Leia's peculiar hairstyle, etc.), but also because there was never any doubt that audiences would understand the joke. *Everybody* knows *Star Wars*.

Mad Magazine (1977–97)

Star Wars was comedy gold for *Mad* magazine, which published parodies of all three installments of the Original Trilogy and several other satirical features—an average of one piece per year during the franchise's first twenty years, not including references to *Star Wars* that were woven into other *Mad* spoofs. Nearly all of the magazine's best-known talent, including artists Don Martin, Sergio Aragones, and Mort Drucker, took a whack or two at *Star Wars*. All of this delighted Lucas, who grew up reading *Mad* and had hired Drucker to draw the cartoon poster art for *American Graffiti*. When *Mad*'s first *Star Wars* parody, "Star Bores," appeared in late 1977 (in an issued cover-dated January 1978), Lucas fired off a letter to the editor expressing his delight and soon purchased the original artwork from the story. Over the years, Lucas continued to write to congratulate the *Mad* staff on its subsequent *Star Wars* and other Lucasfilm spoofs. "Perhaps most importantly," Lucas wrote in his

Mad magazine published an average of one *Star Wars*-related piece per year from 1977 to 1997, including the hilarious "*Mad Star Wars* Musical" in 1978. George Lucas, a longtime *Mad* fan, sometimes wrote to express his delight with the magazine's jabs at his films.

MAD #203 © E.C. Publications, Inc.
Used by permission of DC Entertainment/ MAD Magazine.

introduction to *Mad About Star Wars*, a book that compiled all *Mad*'s *Star Wars* material, "I have always defended *Mad* from my lawyers."

Like much of *Mad*'s content, its *Star Wars* spoofs were hit-and-miss, usually sophomoric and sometimes crude, but with moments of hilarity and keen insight. Almost every one included an unforgettable zinger or two. In "The *Mad Star Wars* Musical," published in December 1978, Obi-Wan Kenobi croons (to the tune of "The Windmills of Your Mind"): "I know I'll meet Darth Vader and soon after that I'll die/And I'm thinking on the whole that I prefer the *River Kwai*." That line perfectly encapsulated the misgivings of Sir Alec Guinness, both about his character's early dispatch from the story and about the movie's phenomenal popularity. "*Star Wars* Playsets You May Have

Missed," from February 1997, poked fun at the ceaseless merchandising of the franchise by suggesting playsets such as The Dizzy Droid Drag Cantina, featuring cross-dressing action figures, and Jabba the Hutt's bathroom.

The most effective of *Mad*'s *Star Wars* parodies was its October 1983 "Re-Hash of the Jeti." The third *Star Wars* film gave *Mad*'s staff more material than usual to work with, and Drucker and writer Dick De Bartolo cleverly underscored many of the weaknesses that fans and critics complained about in *Return of the Jedi*. For instance, when "Admiral Snackbar" briefs the troops prior to the Death Star attack, he says, "What we'll use is the same top secret attack plan we used in the other *Star Bores* movies!" Then he invites the audience (seen in the panel) to recite the plan along with him. When "Princess Laidup" meets the teddy bear–like "Earwaks," the tribe's leader informs her that "We're the new generation of *Star Bores* merchandising!" "Re-Hash of the Jeti" also poked fun at the idea of "Lube Skystalker" and Laidup being brother and sister, suggesting that all the other characters were also somehow related. At the end of the story, when "Ham Yoyo" asks if he and Laidup can finally get married, she replies, "I'm not sure! I think you're my uncle!!"

Television Spoofs (1977–78)

In the 1970s, as now, the stars of a movie were expected to make personal appearances at news conferences, at premiere screenings, on talk shows, and at other venues to promote a new film. In the case of *Star Wars*, this extended beyond Mark Hamill, Harrison Ford, and Carrie Fisher to include costumed characters like C-3PO, R2-D2, Darth Vader, and Chewbacca, who appeared at shopping malls, comic book stores, and movie theaters (including, famously, the Chinese Theatre in Hollywood), and even in a *Vogue* magazine photo shoot (see Chapter 10). At these appearances the costumed characters were almost never played by the actors from the film. So no one batted an eye when various cast members—costumed and otherwise—were invited to appear on a clutch of television comedy-variety series and specials in late 1977 and '78. Maybe, on occasion, they should have. Although few of these shows have received an official release on home video, most are available online and are Must-Google TV.

The first and most bizarre of these appearances aired on September 23, 1977, as part of the Season Three premiere of the *Donny and Marie* show. Threepio, Artoo, Vader, and Chewie all took part, and (in a rarity) both Anthony Daniels and Peter Mayhew reprised their roles from the film. They appeared alongside singer-songwriter Kris Kristofferson, comedian Red Foxx (star of the recently canceled *Sanford and Son*), game show favorite Paul Lynde, and the show's hosts in an untitled, and nearly unwatchable, ten-minute singing, dancing spoof that remains the most confounding spectacle this side of the *Star Wars Holiday Special*. The skit is nearly plotless: Luke and Leia (Donny and Marie Osmond) and the droids enlist the help of Han Solo (Kristofferson) and Chewbacca to escape from an imperial planet, only to be recaptured by Darth Vader. Foxx plays the disembodied, wisecracking spirit of Jedi Master "Obi-Ben Okefenokee," and Lynde appears as an infuriated imperial officer. Vader is voiced by someone who sounds like Lee ("Tony the Tiger") Marshall, in lieu of James Earl Jones. The skit includes six (inane) musical numbers performed variously by Donny and Marie, Kristofferson, and Lynde, along with a squad of disco-dancing stormtroopers. Daniels and Mayhew comport themselves with dignity, but everything else is abominable.

Soon after, several of the original masks and costumes created by Rick Baker for the Mos Eisley cantina sequence were loaned for use on the short-lived *Richard Pryor Show*, which ran for four episodes in the fall of 1977. Pryor appears alongside the creatures in a five-minute skit titled "*Star Wars* Bar," as the proprietor of a space nightclub. Much of the humor derives from the aliens' grotesque appearances (Pryor tells one creature, "You look just like a nigger from Detroit I know").

Mark Hamill appeared as Luke Skywalker on the 1977 *Bob Hope All-Star Comedy Christmas Special*. In the eight-minute musical skit "Scar Wars," Bart Vader (Hope) kidnaps Santa Claus and holds jolly old St. Nick for ransom. Following some tomfoolery with Hope and guest stars Perry Como and Olivia Newton-John (who is dressed like Princess Leia), Hamill, in full costume, rushes in and uses the Force (that is, the Los Angeles Police Force) to arrest Hope for "malicious mutilation of a marvelous movie." Hardy har har.

When Carrie Fisher hosted *Saturday Night Live* in November 1978, she performed her opening monologue in her Princess Leia costume and later appeared as Leia in the singing beach party spoof "Beach Blanket Bimbo from Outer Space." The sketch, which features the entire Not Ready for Prime Time cast, is a ripping satire of both beach movies and changing sexual mores. For instance, when Leia's name ("Lay-uh") inspires snickers from the guys at the beach, Annette Funicello (Gilda Radner) explains that "This is the fifties, and nice girls don't go all the way." Her boyfriend Frankie Avalon (Bill Murray) helpfully adds, "And we're so horny we'll laugh at anything that even *sounds* dirty!"

Hamill made one of the franchise's most endearing television appearances in 1980, guest-hosting *The Muppet Show* along with C-3PO (Daniels), R2-D2, and Chewbacca (Mayhew). Hamill appears both as Luke Skywalker and as Skywalker's "cousin," Mark Hamill. Luke and the droids are supposedly searching for Chewie, who has been kidnapped. Playing a gung ho Luke, Hamill charges around backstage shouting things like "Remember

Alderaan!" As himself, he does impressions, sings, dances, tells jokes (all badly), and gargles to the tune of a Gershwin number before being run out of the theater by Kermit the Frog. Luke initially declines to appear onstage ("Look, pal, we're on a mission. There's no way we're going to get involved in any third-rate variety show."), but eventually the *Star Wars* characters participate in an extended (eight-minute) "Pigs in Space" sketch. Miss Piggy trades her usual blonde tresses for a twin bun. The crew of the spaceship *Swine Trek* help Luke and the droids free Chewbacca from the clutches of Darth Nader (Gonzo the Great in a Vader-like mask, helmet, and cape), and then everyone sings and dances during a closing musical medley. Threepio tap-dances to "You Are My Lucky Star." That same year, Threepio (Daniels) and Artoo appeared on two episodes of *Sesame Street*. In one installment, Artoo falls in love with a fire hydrant. In the other, the droids sing a counting song with Big Bird.

In the late 1970s, *Star Wars*' costumed characters appeared on several television shows and at many other locations—even the local Wal-Mart. However, the actors in the suits at these events were, with rare exception, *not* the ones who appeared in the film.

The most ambitious *Star Wars* parody to reach television was an ongoing series created by humorist/screenwriter Buck Henry, the man behind the classic spy spoof *Get Smart* (1965–70). Henry's *Quark* (1977–78) starred Richard Benjamin as Adam Quark, the captain of an interstellar garbage scow. The *Quark* pilot was a send-up of *Star Trek*, but by the time the series sold (to NBC), *Star Wars* fever was sweeping the world, and the show was retooled with more of a *Star Wars* vibe. In the second episode, "May the Source Be with You," Captain Quark is assigned to seek out and destroy the planet-sized superweapon of the evil Gorgons (who dress like Darth Vader). Later, the series took swipes at *2001: A Space Odyssey* and *Flash Gordon*. *Quark* premiered as a mid-season replacement series, but despite high production values (including solid visual effects and Emmy-nominated costumes) and the surging popularity of science fiction, the show failed to find an audience and was canceled after just eight episodes.

Film Parodies from *Hardware Wars* (1978) to *Spaceballs* (1987)

Meanwhile, various filmmakers rushed big-screen *Star Wars* satires into production. One of the earliest, funniest, and most enduringly popular of these was writer-director Ernie Fosselius' ultra-cheap *Hardware Wars* (1978), which was structured as a protracted (twelve-minute) trailer. Fosselius cleverly turned his lack of funds into a source of comedy by replacing spaceships with household appliances. Audiences still roar with laughter when his "spacecraft"—including a steam iron, a toaster, an egg beater, and a cassette recorder—zoom through outer space. The costumes and props are also hilariously cut-rate: The Threepio-like robot 4-Q-2 was played by a guy in a Tin Man (from *The Wizard of Oz*) costume, while the Artoo-like Arty Deco was "portrayed" by a canister vacuum cleaner. "Chewchilla, the Wookiee Monster" was a Cookie Monster Muppet dyed brown, and "Fluke Starbucker"'s lightsaber was a flashlight. The arch dialogue and over-the-top performances of *Hardware Wars* are also extremely amusing. As their steam iron "spaceship" is drawn toward a waffle iron "space station," "Ham Salad" tells a panicky Fluke, "Take it easy, kid. It's only a movie." Despite his slim budget, Fosselius hired legendary voice artist Paul Frees, who had narrated the original *Star Wars* trailer, to do the same for *Hardware Wars*. Frees' deadpan delivery makes everything seem even more ridiculous.

Hardware Wars won first place at numerous film festivals and turned a spectacular profit. Shot for just $8,000, the short earned over $1 million. In 1997, a *Hardware Wars* Special Edition (satirizing, of course, Lucas' Special Editions of the Original Trilogy) was issued on DVD. Made without Fosselius' input, this version featured new sequences and digitally enhanced visual effects. In a 1999 interview, George Lucas named *Hardware Wars* as his personal favorite *Star Wars* spoof. *Hardware Wars* was officially recognized by Lucasfilm when it received a Pioneer Award at the Official Star Wars Fan Film Awards in 2003.

While Fosselius was making his delightful short, Brazilian filmmaker Adriano Stuart was shooting the feature-length *Os Trapalhões na Guerra dos Planetas* (*The Bunglers in the War of the Planets*), a picture now commonly referred to as simply the Brazilian *Star Wars*. Unlike the Turkish *Star Wars* (see Chapter 13), this was not a knockoff but a send-up. The locations (including a desert planet and a space cantina), costumes (including a Vader-like evil

Writer-director Mel Brooks lampooned *Star Wars* with *Spaceballs*, featuring (from left) the Chewbacca-like Barf (John Candy), the Threepio-ish Dot Matrix (voiced by Joan Rivers), the Leia-esque Princess Vespa (Daphne Zuniga), and Han Solo substitute Lone Starr (Bill Pullman).

alien), and props are intended to mimic *Star Wars*, but Stuart's approach is pure slapstick. Unfortunately, most of the gags fall flat, in no small measure because of the director's distracting, incessant, and mindless use of slow-motion during the "funny" scenes. On the whole, the ostensibly serious Turkish picture is funnier than the supposedly comedic Brazilian one. *Os Trapalhões na Guerra dos Planetas* was the thirteenth film to star the Bunglers (sometimes translated as "the Tramps"), a four-man comedy troupe who also starred in a long-running Brazilian TV show (1977–1993). Maybe they loved it in São Paulo.

Plenty of other sci-fi spoofs appeared in the 1980s, most of which incorporated elements popularized by *Star Wars* (nervous robots, alien-filled space cantinas, and twin-bun hairdos were recurring features). But most of these weren't *Star Wars* parodies, strictly speaking. *Galaxina* (1980), written and directed by William Sachs, was more a rehash of *Barbarella* (1968), starring former *Playboy* Playmate of the Year Dorothy Stratton as a sexy android. Stratton, tragically, was murdered soon after the film's release. Writer-director Bruce Kimmel's *Naked Space* (1983), starring Leslie Nielsen and Cindy Williams, attempted to do for space flight what *Airplane!* (1980) did for air travel, collecting an almost random assortment of puns and sight gags along with musical numbers and clips from Japanese monster movies. The disappointing *Airplane II: The Sequel* (1982), set on a space shuttle, had covered much of the same territory with marginally better results.

The most thorough, if not most rewarding, *Star Wars* parody arrived in 1987 with Mel Brooks' *Spaceballs*. The scenario—featuring a princess (Daphne Zuniga) rescued by a space cowboy (Bill Pullman) from the clutches of the villainous Dark Helmet (Rick Moranis)—was designed to hew as closely as possible to the original *Star Wars*, while allowing writer-director-producer-star Brooks to take jabs at the second two films and other sci-fi hits along the way. John Candy appears as Barf, the half-man/half-dog copilot of Lone Starr's (Pullman's) spacefaring Winnebago. Brooks plays both the bumbling Skroob, president of the evil Planet Spaceball, and Yogurt, diminutive alien master of a magical power known as the Schwartz. Joan Rivers provides the voice of Dot Matrix, the princess' robot sidekick (a distaff C-3PO). And Dom DeLuise makes a cameo as the cheese-and-pepperoni-covered space pirate Pizza the Hutt.

Despite a fine cast and strong production values, *Spaceballs* does not approach the heights of inspired lunacy achieved by Brooks' best works (*The Producers, Young Frankenstein, Blazing Saddles*), too often relying on outbursts of profanity and sophomoric sexual innuendo to generate laughs. Still, the picture has its moments. At its best, *Spaceballs* operates on the level of a *Mad* Magazine parody. In one hilarious throwaway sequence, Starr and Barf are seated at an outer space diner when actor John Hurt recreates his famous "chest-buster" scene from *Alien* (1979). Only this time, after the creature pops out of his chest, it begins singing and dancing like Michigan J. Frog from the classic Warner Brothers cartoon "One Froggy Evening" (1955).

Spaceballs turned a modest profit but was not the smash Brooks was hoping for. The critical reception was equally tepid. Roger Ebert of the Chicago *Sun-Times* complained that *Spaceballs* "should have been made several years ago, before our appetite for *Star Wars* satires had been completely exhausted." George Lucas penned a congratulatory letter to Brooks following the picture's release. Lucas wrote that he feared he would "bust something from laughing" at *Spaceballs*. The film has acquired a cult following over the years. A sequel, tentatively titled *Spaceballs III: The Search for Spaceballs II*, was proposed but never developed—at least so far. In early 2015, with a new *Star Wars* trilogy on the horizon, Brooks revived talk of a possible *Spaceballs* follow-up. *Spaceballs: The Animated Series* appeared on Canadian television in 2008, with Brooks, Zuniga, and Rivers reprising their roles from the film. The show lasted just thirteen episodes, but the second installment ("Revenge of the Sithee") lampooned the Prequel Trilogy.

Return of the Ewok (1982)

By the time *Return of the Jedi* went into production in 1982, *Star Wars* parodies had become so ubiquitous that the Lucasfilm staff decided to produce one of its own. It took the form of the first *Star Wars* "mockumentary," a satirical biopic about Warwick Davis, the then-eleven-year-old performer who would make his screen debut in *Jedi* as Wicket, the Ewok. Conceived, written, and directed by Davis and assistant director David Tomblin, the twenty-four-minute *Return of the Ewok* was made during the production of *Jedi* with the blessing (and funding) of George Lucas.

Return of the Ewok opens with a fictionalized account of Davis' early life. After failed attempts at careers as a power lifter and soccer goalie, the young man sees the first two *Star Wars* films and decides, "I want to be in the movies." Soon Davis meets with talent agent Maxwell Mercury (Roy Kinnear), who informs him that the only work available is in the new *Star Wars* film.

"You can be an Ewok," Mercury offers.

"An Ewok?" Davis asks. "What's an Ewok?"

"I don't know," the agent replies, "But the money's good and I get 10 percent."

(Kinnear, a veteran character actor, was not part of the *Jedi* cast but was brought in specifically to play this bit.)

Mercury hands Davis his Wicket costume, which he dons before heading to EMI-Elstree Studios, where no one has any idea what an Ewok is. Davis crosses paths with coproducer Robert Watts, Harrison Ford, Mark Hamill, Carrie Fisher (lounging around her dressing room in her metal bikini), C-3PO, R2-D2, Chewbacca, Jabba the Hutt, Boba Fett, and Darth Vader. The line between reality and fantasy becomes blurred at EMI. Although the film's makers and stars play themselves, Anthony Daniels, Kenny Baker, Peter Mayhew, Jeremy Bulloch (Boba Fett), and David Prowse appear (and behave) in character. *Return of the Ewok* includes a rare opportunity to hear David Prowse's undubbed voice as Vader (he shouts, "Come back, Ewok!"). Finally, the all-wise Yoda educates Davis about Ewoks and tells him how to get to Endor (the trip involves a transatlantic flight on Pan Am and a NASA rocket into space).

Unfortunately, *Return of the Ewok* was never finished (if it had been, Prowse's voice probably would have been replaced) and was never officially released. Davis has shown the film during appearances at various science fiction conventions. Portions of it have been broadcast on television specials and posted on the official Starwars.com website, and a snippet from the film (in which Wicket is menaced by Boba Fett onboard the second Death Star) turned up as an "Easter egg" bonus feature on the 2004 DVD release of the

Original Trilogy. However, the short has been widely bootlegged and posted to various Internet sites. An official, polished release of *Return of the Ewok* is long overdue.

Even though it was never completed, *Return of the Ewok* established the precedent for later official spoofs. *R2-D2: Beneath the Dome*, a twenty-minute mockumentary about everybody's favorite astromech droid, was shot during *Star Wars Episode II: Attack of the Clones* and released in 2001. The *Lego Star Wars* movies, based on the Lego toy line and released directly to DVD, could also be categorized as self-parody. Another official satire—an animated series titled *Star Wars: Detours* (billed as "a comedic look at the *Star Wars* universe")— was planned but canceled when Disney purchased Lucasfilm.

Later Spoofs

Star Wars parodies continued to appear on both the large and small screens throughout the 1990s, kicking into hyperdrive following the advent of the Prequel Trilogy in 1999. Amateur filmmaker Kevin Rubio's ten-minute short *Troops* parodied both *Star Wars* and the reality TV drama *Cops*, supposedly depicting the everyday lives of stormtroopers. *Troops* proved wildly popular and spurred an outpouring of additional fan films, many of them satirical. One of those was Joe Nussbaum's eight-minute short *George Lucas in Love* (1999), which spoofed both *Star Wars* and the Oscar-winning *Shakespeare in Love* (1998), depicting how various events from Lucas' adolescence prefigured and inspired the Original Trilogy. One of the wittiest and most charming *Star Wars* parodies, *George Lucas in Love* won several awards and earned a congratulatory note from Lucas. The twenty-nine-minute *Thumb Wars* (1999) featured characters such as Black Helmet Man and Princess Bunhead played by finger puppets. The list goes on and on.

Various animated and live-action television series, including (but not limited to) *Family Guy*, *Robot Chicken*, *Phineas and Ferb*, *South Park*, *Pinky and the Brain*, and even *Friends* also mounted *Star Wars* spoofs. Lucas participated in the *Robot Chicken* parody, appearing as himself in a promo for the first of three *Star Wars*–themed *Robot Chicken* episodes. (Seated on a psychiatrist's couch, Lucas says that he was emotionally traumatized by—what else?—the *Star Wars Holiday Special*.) *Family Guy* offered irreverent and wickedly funny send-ups of all three installments of the Original Trilogy in various episodes ("Blue Harvest," 2007, targeted the original film; "Something, Something, Something, Dark Side," 2010, took aim at *The Empire Strikes Back*; and "It's a Trap!," 2011, took on *Return of the Jedi*).

But the spoofs weren't limited to film and television. Musician Weird Al Yankovic scored a hit with "The Saga Begins" (1999), which set a satire of

The Phantom Menace to the tune of Don McLean's "American Pie" ("My, my, this here Anakin guy/May be Vader someday later/Now he's just a small fry . . ."). Canadian actor Charles Ross' "One Man Star Wars Trilogy" found off-Broadway success, opening in Toronto in 2001 and touring various cities for the next six years. The inevitable hardcore porn parodies eventually appeared as well. And the number of online spoofs—ranging from polished works from websites such as How It Should Have Ended and Honest Trailers to sundry and pervasive Internet memes—are too numerous to count. By 2012, *Star Wars* spoofs were so common they began appearing in advertising, including a Volkswagen television commercial featuring a boy in a Vader costume using his "Force powers" to start his father's Passat. With a new round of *Star Wars* movies and TV series now emerging, the next cycle of *Star Wars* parodies can't be far behind. Fans can only hope that the next round of spoofs features at least one send-up as funny as *Hardware Wars*, and that none of them involve the Osmonds.

33

I Am Altering the Deal

Remastering and Revising the Original Trilogy

To celebrate the twentieth anniversary of *Star Wars*, and to build momentum for the upcoming *Star Wars Episode I: The Phantom Menace* (1999), George Lucas decided to rerelease the Original Trilogy to movie theaters. This much was a familiar gambit; he had reissued *Star Wars* in 1979, anticipating the premiere of *The Empire Strikes Back*, and rereleased both earlier films in 1982, in advance of *Return of the Jedi*. Lucas had made minor alterations to the films for these previous reissues. But this time he had something much bigger in mind—a wholesale reconstruction of the trilogy, including a visual effects face-lift, retouched sound and music, and the integration of both previously deleted and newly created footage.

In interviews, Lucas argued that the existing versions of his *Star Wars* films didn't fully represent his artistic vision because when they were made the technology did not yet exist to put that vision on the screen, and because he was limited by tight budgets. As far back as a 1981 interview with *Starlog* magazine, Lucas estimated that *Star Wars* had realized only about 25 percent of what he had imagined, because he was forced to make so many compromises during production. Twenty years later he had the technological capability and financial wherewithal to do whatever he wanted. Lucas convinced Fox to sink $10 million (nearly as much as it cost to make the movie in the first place) into revising *Star Wars*, and Lucasfilm invested $2.5 million apiece into refurbishing *Empire* and *Jedi*.

He also insisted, to the dismay of many fans, that the new *Star Wars* Special Editions were intended to replace, not merely enhance, the original versions. "There will only be one [version of the films]," Lucas said in an interview with the American Society of Cinematographers trade magazine. "Films never get finished, they get abandoned. At some point, you're dragged off the picture kicking and screaming while somebody says, 'Okay, it's done.' That isn't really the way it should work. Occasionally, [you can] go back and get your cut of the video out there, which I did on both *American Graffiti* and *THX 1138*. . . . I think it's the director's prerogative, not the studio's, to go back and reinvent a movie."

Of course, Lucas never asked fans if they wanted their favorite movies reinvented, and the resulting Special Editions proved controversial. Traditionalist fans wondered why the films had to change at all, while preservation-minded viewers argued that the original versions should be saved for posterity along with the Special Editions. At first, many fans didn't believe Lucas would really try to obliterate the original versions of the *Star Wars* films, movies to which many had a profound emotional connection. The backlash didn't fully erupt until the films were released on DVD. (The following chapter outlines the troubled history of the original versions on home video.)

Controversy aside, the Special Editions packed cinemaplexes across the United States and around the world in early 1997. The films were reissued about a month apart—*Star Wars* on January 31, *Empire* on February 27 and *Jedi* on March 14. *Jedi*'s rerelease was pushed back a week to keep from stepping on the previous reissues, which were still raking in ticket sales in many cities. Some of the revisions played well, others did not. And, despite Lucas' assertion that the 1997 Special Editions would be the final version of these films, he continued to tinker with the movies, making further changes when they were issued to DVD and Blu-ray. For good measure, he also made changes to the Prequel Trilogy when those films were issued to DVD and Blu-ray. Here's an overview of some of the more important revisions made to the Original Trilogy over the years.

Early Theatrical Reissues

Even though the movie played for more than a year in some cities, *Star Wars* was rereleased in 1978, 1979, 1981, and 1982. The 1981 reissue was the first to feature noticeable changes from the original, although most of the alterations were subtle. The most dramatic change was to the title of the movie itself. For the first time, *Star Wars* gained the subtitle *Episode IV: A New Hope*, which was added to the opening title crawl. This brought the original film into greater continuity with *The Empire Strikes Back*, whose subtitle had included the designation *Episode V*. The additional line of text meant that the crawl had to begin on a different, earlier musical cue.

Most of the other changes made to the film with this reissue were to its sound effects and, in some instances, dialogue. For instance, when Luke, Ben, and the droids approach the Mos Eisley cantina, music from the bar spills out into the street. This music wasn't heard in the original version. Additional beeps and growls are dubbed in throughout the film to give R2-D2 and Chewie more "dialogue" (inside the cantina, for instance, Chewbacca growls at two passing stormtroopers). Different sound effects are used in several instances, including: the klaxon aboard the rebel ship overtaken by Vader; the whine of the *Millennium Falcon*'s engines as it drops out of hyperspace; and the audible jolt as the Death Star captures the *Falcon* in its tractor beam. Many of the sound effects used in the *Falcon*'s dogfight with the TIE fighters and in the climactic assault on the Death Star were also enhanced or replaced.

In some cases, dialogue has been overdubbed with alternate takes. This happens when C-3PO says, "Use the comlink? Oh my, I forgot, I turned it off"; when Luke says, "What good will it do us if he gets himself killed?"; and with lines from Han and Luke during their exchange as Han loads his reward aboard the *Falcon*. Perhaps most notably, during the final battle Luke says, "Blast it, Wedge! Where are you?" instead of "Blast it, Biggs! Where are you?," writing his childhood friend—most of whose scenes had been cut in postproduction—further out of the picture. Although recorded in stereo, a mono mix was released in 1977 in many theaters that had not yet installed stereo audio equipment. The 1981 rerelease was stereo-only.

The Empire Strikes Back was also slightly altered for its 1982 rerelease—mostly minor revisions to sound effects and dialogue. For example, near the end of the film an establishing shot of the rebel fleet and Lando's line "When we find Jabba the Hutt and that bounty hunter we'll contact you" are both removed. *Return of the Jedi* was not theatrically reissued prior to its 1997 Special Edition.

The Special Editions

Lucas began discussing possible revisions to *Star Wars* with Dennis Muren at Industrial Light & Magic in 1993. Lucas wanted to commemorate the upcoming twentieth anniversary of the franchise (then still four years away) by rereleasing all three installments of the series. Updating some of the visual effects and possibly adding new or deleted material to the original film, he reasoned, would excite devoted fans and draw them back to theaters, even though by then the movies were readily available on home video. At first, the plan was to update the first picture only and to revise only fifteen to twenty shots. But the idea of "fixing" *Star Wars*, of altering the films so they more perfectly aligned with his original intentions, proved irresistible to Lucas. The project quickly grew in scope and ambition.

This publicity still, created for the 1997 release of the *Star Wars* Special Edition, demonstrates some of the CGI additions made to the Mos Eisley spaceport sequence in the original films.

An exhaustive accounting of all the alterations Lucas ultimately made to *Star Wars*, *The Empire Strikes Back*, and *Return of the Jedi* for their 1997 Special Editions could fill an entire book. I have included only the most dramatic and controversial changes here. While certainly Lucas was within his rights as an artist and a producer to make whatever changes he wanted to his work, audiences were also within their rights to embrace or reject his revisions, many of which failed to enhance the viewing experience, especially those made to the original film.

Star Wars

For openers, Lucas updated many of the visual and sound effects to bring them up to then-current industry standards. The destruction of Alderaan and the Death Star, for instance, is far more spectacular in the Special Edition. Most fans wouldn't have batted an eye if Lucas stopped there, but he went much further. New computer-animated characters are added to several scenes set on Tatooine. Stormtroopers are seen riding Dewbacks (those big lizard-like creatures) while searching for the droids. Mos Eisley spaceport is a much larger and busier place in the Special Edition, with new shots showing bustling streets full of Banthas, droids, aliens, and imperial troops. These additions slow the pace of the film and also work against the idea that Tatooine is a forlorn, backwater planet. Indeed, the place now seems so bustling and lively that it's hard to understand why Luke complains about living there.

The most notorious change, of course, is that during Han Solo's cantina showdown with the bounty hunter, Greedo shoots first but improbably misses Solo at point-blank range. This not only stretches the bounds of credulity but changes our impression of Han Solo. In his book *Han Solo at Star's End* (one of the first *Star Wars* novels), author Brian Daley has Han say, "I happen to *like* to shoot first." Having Greedo shoot first softens what had been a defining moment for the formerly ruthless mercenary and changes the arc of the character. This scene is quickly followed by another major revision, the restoration of a deleted exchange between Han and Jabba the Hutt (with a CGI Jabba replacing the original human version, played by Declan Mulholland) at Docking Bay 94. This is the most problematic of all the Special Edition changes to *Star Wars* because it slows the narrative's momentum and seems pointless since Han and Jabba simply repeat the conversation Han just had moments earlier with Greedo. The picture needed one of these scenes, not both.

The Empire Strikes Back

Empire—which was, in many respects, the best-crafted entry in the trilogy to begin with—suffered the least from Lucas' Special Edition futzing. In fact, the alterations—most of which are subtle, smoothly integrated, and effective—actually enhance certain elements of the film. Once again, many visual and sound effects were refreshed. Also, a few minor lines of dialogue were altered. For instance, Vader's urgent command "Bring my shuttle" is changed to the more sanguine "Alert the Star Destroyer to prepare for my arrival." And on Dagobah, when the swamp monster spits out Artoo, Luke's line "You're lucky you don't taste very good" is changed to the less jokey "You were lucky to get out of there." Newly created footage shows the Wampa ice creature gnawing on a carcass in its cave (where Luke waits as a possible second course). This was a rare instance of Special Edition changes actually making the film seem more violent and dark; for the most part, the revisions softened and lightened the tone of the films. And finally, windows were added to several shots on Bespin, creating lovely backgrounds in a few scenes. This not only increased the pictorial beauty of the film but addressed one of director Irvin Kershner's complaints about the picture: Wouldn't a city floating in the clouds have more windows?

Return of the Jedi

The Special Edition alterations to *Return of the Jedi* were neither as beneficial as those to *The Empire Strikes Back* or as problematic as those to *Star Wars*. Curiously, once again, most of the changes involved the sequences set on Tatooine. These include: newly shot footage of the slave woman Oola (Femi Taylor) in the pit with the Rancor monster; a herd of Banthas seen roaming the dunes in a new establishing shot; and a beefed-up Sarlacc monster, now equipped with CGI tentacles and a beak. In addition to enhanced visual and sound effects, the most noticeable changes this time around involved—of all things—John Williams' musical score. The original musical performance at Jabba's Palace—a New Wave–inflected, synthesizer-driven dance number known as "Lapti Nek"—was replaced with a longer, bluesier song titled "Jedi Rocks." Since the new composition involved an additional voice, a new alien singer (Joh Jowza), was digitally added to the Max Rebo Band, along with *eight* other new members. Several new shots (including a close-up of a vocalist's lips) were inserted.

At the close of the film, following the destruction of the second Death Star, the original closing theme was also replaced. The original "Ewok Celebration" music was a primitive, woodblock-and-vocal piece known to fans as "The Yub Nub Song." Its replacement, retitled "Victory Celebration," is a more richly arranged, New Agey melody with what sounds like pan flute and an entirely different ("Ya ya ya") vocal. Many fans prefer "Lapti Nek" to "Jedi Rocks," but the revised, more sweeping "Victory Celebration" makes a more fitting conclusion for an epic space opera than the original music, which sounded like an outtake from the soundtrack to *Fraggle Rock*. The new "Victory Celebration" plays over an extended sequence that shows celebrations erupting spontaneously across the galaxy—on Bespin, Tatooine, and Coruscant, the previously unseen capital planet of the Galactic Empire.

DVD and Blu-ray

As mentioned, Lucas continued to make adjustments to *Star Wars*, *The Empire Strikes Back*, and *Return of the Jedi* when the Special Editions appeared on DVD in 2004 and on Blu-ray in 2011. For the most part, the changes were intended to provide greater continuity between the Original Trilogy and the Prequel Trilogy, although in some cases the alterations seemed completely arbitrary. Again, most of the changes were minor in nature and mostly focused on visual and sound effects, or specific lines of dialogue (e.g., Ben Kenobi's throaty roar that frightens away the Sand People in *Star Wars* is changed to a whooping howl).

However, a handful of the DVD alterations remain noteworthy. In *Star Wars*, the Han-Greedo shootout was changed again, with Greedo and Han firing at almost the same time (but Greedo still first). In *The Empire Strikes Back*, the emperor (seen in a flickering, holographic cameo) is played by Ian McDiarmid, who assumed the role in *Return of the Jedi* and continued in the part through the prequels. The original footage, featuring actor Clive Revill, was replaced by footage of McDiarmid shot during the making of *Revenge of the Sith* (2005). Similarly, Boba Fett's dialogue, originally provided by Jason Wingreen, is now voiced by Temuera Morrison, who played Jango Fett and the Clone Troopers in *Attack of the Clones* (2002).

Three notable—or notorious, depending on your point of view—"improvements" were made to the final scenes of *Return of the Jedi*. Cosmetic changes (including a change of eye color) were made to the face of actor Sebastian Shaw during Darth Vader's unmasking scene, to make Shaw's features appear more similar to those of actor Hayden Christensen, who played Anakin Skywalker in *Attack of the Clones* and *Revenge of the Sith*. Shaw is removed entirely, and replaced by Christensen, from the scene in which a ghostly Anakin appears to Luke alongside the spectral Obi-Wan and Yoda. Although Obi-Wan and Yoda appear as they did at the time of their deaths, Anakin inexplicably looks young and strong. And finally, the scenes of interplanetary jubilation now include a shot from Naboo, homeworld of Princess Amidala and Jar Jar Binks. As viewers watch the jubilation, a Gungan voice (which sounds like Jar Jar) exults, "We'sa free!"

The movies underwent another round of minor revisions when the films debuted on Blu-ray. The Han-Greedo scene in *Star Wars* was altered yet again, so that the two fire at virtually the same time. And in *Return of the Jedi*, the Ewoks now have CGI eyelids, enabling them to blink. Before selling Lucasfilm to Disney in 2012, Lucas had announced plans to reissue all six *Star Wars* films yet again, this time in 3-D. That effort was delayed, however, following Disney's decision to move forward with production of *Star Wars* Episodes VII through IX. If the Original Trilogy is eventually released in 3-D, it may face yet another round of tweaks and tucks, for better or worse.

34

We Would Be Honored if You Would Join Us

Star Wars Home Viewing

It may difficult now to remember—or, for readers younger than thirty, to imagine—but once upon a time there was no such thing as home video, Netflix, or cable television. To see a movie, you had to go to the theater, or else hope to catch a TV broadcast. (A film might run on network television, with commercials, for one night only, a year or more after it left theaters.) *Star Wars* appeared during the waning days of this bygone era, which meant that fans unable to undertake a monthly or weekly pilgrimage to the cinema to revisit their favorite film had to make due with substitutes such as the novelization ghostwritten by Alan Dean Foster, the Marvel Comics adaptation, View-Master reels, and the like, all of which sold briskly. Your author's favorite was *The Story of Star Wars*, a 1977 record album that offered an abridged version of the story narrated by Roscoe Lee Browne, with dialogue, sound effects, and music from the film. The gatefold dust jacket included a sixteen-page booklet full of color stills from the movie. Also released on 8-track, cassette, and reel-to-reel tape by Twentieth Century-Fox Records, *The Story of Star Wars* went gold, serving as yet another testament to the public's unquenchable thirst for all things *Star Wars*.

Despite the popularity of these products, however, what fans really wanted was the movie itself. Naturally, once available, it became a huge seller. As of this writing, the franchise had racked up a staggering $3.8 billion in revenue from home video sales and rentals, across all formats. Nevertheless many hardcore fans believe that Lucasfilm has let them down in this regard, especially since the advent of DVD.

8mm and 16mm Film

Since the 1930s, movie fans had been able to purchase 8mm and 16mm reductions of theatrical films for home viewing. Beyond a coterie of diehard

Before the advent of videotape, fans who wanted a home experience of *Star Wars* had to make due with substitutes like *The Story of Star Wars* record album, which told the story of the film with the help of dialogue clips, sound effects, and selections from John Williams' score.   *Photography by Preston Hewis/East Bank Images*

collectors, however, few people actually did so, in part because the hobby was cost-prohibitive—feature-length films were very expensive (running hundreds of dollars apiece) and also required investment in a movie projector and a screen, if not converting a room or basement into a home theater. Beginning in the late 1940s, however, companies such as Castle Films and Ken Films enjoyed success marketing more affordable 8mm and 16mm abridgments of popular films, "digests" that edited movies to as few as eight or twelve minutes and could be shown on less expensive 8mm or, later, Super 8 projectors. The most popular abridgements were of horror and science fiction movies, although comedies and cartoons also sold well.

Star Wars first became available for home viewing from Ken Films in 8mm and Super 8 "digests," which featured up to sixteen minutes of clips from the movie. This earliest edition, released in late 1977, contained just eight minutes of footage. It was the least expensive option available, printed in black-and-white and without sound. Even so, it cost $5.97 (about $23 in inflation-adjusted terms).

Ken Films released the first *Star Wars* abridgement in 1977. It ran just two hundred feet (about eight minutes) and was made available in black-and-white silent, color silent, and color sound versions priced from $5.97 to $22.88 (that's $23 to $88 in inflation-adjusted terms). This digest contained footage of the escape from the Death Star and the *Millennium Falcon*'s dogfight with TIE fighters. Toymaker Kenner sold this same 8mm short in a blue plastic "movie viewer." The user looked through a tiny hole and cranked the film forward by hand. These products marked the first release of *Star Wars* for home viewing in any format.

With its initial abridgement flying off the shelves, Ken Films quickly cobbled together two longer digests, each priced at $54.95 (about $211 today) in their color-sound versions. The first of these abridgements included the opening of the film and several early scenes on Tatooine, then cut abruptly to the rescue of Princess Leia from the Death Star detention block and the ensuing TIE fighter dogfight (reusing the footage from the eight-minute short). The other ran seventeen minutes and included the cantina scene and the destruction of the Death Star. Later, Ken Films issued a pair of Super 8 abridgments from *The Empire Strikes Back*, both running seventeen minutes. This time the footage ran in sequential order so that, when shown back-to-back, the viewer could enjoy a thirty-four-minute version of the film.

No Super 8 abridgments were produced for *Return of the Jedi*. By then, new formats had rendered pricey 8mm digests obsolete—or nearly obsolete, anyway. Some companies continued to produce products for Super 8 collectors—an increasingly high-end, niche market. In 1989, Britain's Derann Film Service released *Star Wars*—the entire film—in a pristine Super 8 anamorphic widescreen color stereo-sound version that remains the Holy Grail for *Star Wars* 8mm film collectors. Britain's Classic Home Cinema did the same for *The Empire Strikes Back* in the late 1990s. These releases are highly prized not only for their exceptional picture and sound quality, but because they present the films in their original, unaltered versions, the availability of which would soon become a matter of ongoing controversy.

A sticker on the box for the 1992 VHS release of the Original Trilogy warned viewers that this was their last chance to purchase the films in their original, unaltered state.

Betamax and VHS

Sony's first Betamax home video systems went on sale in the spring of 1975. A year later, JVC's first Video Home System (VHS) recorders entered the market. Most Hollywood studios sat out the ensuing format war, hesitant to manufacture home versions of its product on either Betamax or VHS until the market sorted itself out. The earliest *Star Wars* product offered on home video was the made-for-TV, behind-the-scenes documentary *The Story of Star Wars*, released by Magnetic Video on VHS and Betamax in 1979. Twentieth Century-Fox, aware that it was sitting on a gold mine, finally released *Star Wars* on VHS and Beta in May 1982. Initially, like most early home video releases, the tapes were very expensive (around $100), and sold primarily to the proprietors of video rental stores. But in 1984, *Star Wars* was reissued in both formats, re-priced for "sell through" at under $40. This industry jargon meant that the movie was marketed to individual viewers for the first time. (Some diehards paid movie store prices to acquire the film two years earlier.) Fox issued *The Empire Strikes Back* at the same time and same price point, and *Return of the Jedi* followed in 1986. As more people bought videocassette players, the price of tapes continued to drop.

In 1992, the trilogy was issued for the first time as a boxed set on VHS (by then, Betamax was dead). Priced at $49.99, the trilogy was available in both "pan-and-scan" or, for the first time on video, letterboxed widescreen format. Three years later, the original, unaltered trilogy was released for the final time on videotape. The video box set was affixed with a sticker declaring, "Last Chance to Own the Original *Star Wars*." It was at this point that, for many fans, it began to sink in that George Lucas was serious about replacing the original versions of the *Star Wars* films with his altered Special Edition versions. (See the preceding chapter for more details on the Special Editions.)

Five years later, the trilogy was issued yet again (for the third time in six years) in its Special Edition form and has been available in this format only ever since, to the consternation of many fans. The 1997 Special Edition was also the last videotape release of these films. Individual movies were sold separately during each of the 1990s trilogy releases. Numerous other *Star Wars* products, including three volumes each of the *Droids* and *Ewoks* cartoon series, the made-for-TV Ewoks movies, and four different documentaries, were also issued on VHS and/or Betamax. Notable in its absence was the *Star Wars Holiday Special*, still unreleased to home video in any format.

Laser Disc and Other Formats

Cinemaphiles looking for a higher-end audio-video presentation during the videotape era turned to laser disc. Although the disc had to be flipped in the middle of the movie because each side could hold only about an hour of audio-video information, the sound and picture quality of laser surpassed both VHS and Beta. However, in order to make the movies fit onto a single, two-sided laser disc, both *Star Wars* (released on laser in 1982) and *Empire* (issued in 1982) were time-compressed (slightly sped up), reducing the original 121-minute original film to 118 minutes, and the first sequel from 124 to 120 minutes. The 136-minute *Jedi* was issued on laser in 1986 in a full-length, double-disc version. Widescreen editions followed in 1989. The films were reissued as a trilogy in 1993, 1995, and 1997. *The Making of Star Wars* and the two made-for-TV Ewoks movies were also issued on laser.

Many variant laser disc editions were produced for Japan, France, and other countries where the format was more popular. In the United States, laser remained a niche product. In 2013, thirty minutes of previously unseen *Empire Strikes Back* outtakes (mostly from scenes set on Dagobah) were discovered on a laser disc created to demonstrate Lucasfilm's EditDroid editing system, which entered the market in the 1980s. A fan purchased a copy of the ultra-rare disc on eBay for $699 and promptly posted the raw footage to YouTube. It has been all over the Internet since, despite Lucasfilm's attempts to stamp it out.

Wary of missing a trick, Fox also issued the *Star Wars* films in numerous other, now obsolete formats, including:

- Capacitance Electronic Disc (CED)—CED was an early analog video system using discs played with a needle, like a phonograph record. Introduced by RCA in 1981 as a rival to both VHS and Beta, the format failed to gain wide acceptance, in part because it was impossible to buy blank CEDs and record with them. Nevertheless *Star Wars* was released on CED in 1982, *Empire* in 1984, and *Jedi* in 1986. The CED versions of *Star Wars* and *Empire* were the same time-compressed versions that were offered on laser.

- Video High Density (VHD)—Another analog video disc, similar to CED but smaller in size, VHD was introduced in 1981 by JVC, which marketed the format primarily in Japan. *Star Wars* made its VHD debut in 1983, followed by *Empire* in 1984 and *Jedi* in 1986.

- Video Compact Disc (VCD)—The first digital home video platform, VCD was a forerunner of DVD. Although popular in Asian markets such as Malaysia and Singapore, the format never caught on in the United States. The Original Trilogy was released, and widely bootlegged, in this format in 2000.

DVD and Blu-ray

The first *Star Wars* movies issued on DVD were the prequels *The Phantom Menace* (in 2001) and *Attack of the Clones* (in 2002), which was released alongside the mockumentary *R2-D2: Beneath the Dome*. The Original Trilogy made its DVD debut in 2004, appearing in both full screen and non-anamorphic widescreen editions. This release featured the altered Special Edition versions of the films, with additional tweaks new to this edition. Lucas would continue to tinker with the films as they were reissued. (The preceding chapter includes a detailed rundown of all these alterations.)

Lucasfilm relented to pressure from fans and reissued the Original Trilogy on DVD In 2006, this time including the films in both their Special Edition and original, unaltered form. However, the original versions were treated as "bonus material" and not afforded the same degree of care and consideration as the Special Edition versions. While the altered versions were presented in sparkling, state-of-the-art, anamorphic widescreen transfers, the unaltered versions were offered in mealy, non-anamorphic transfers that appeared to have been ported over from the previous VHS release. Fans cried foul, but as of this writing, this marked the final release of the Original Trilogy in its unaltered form. This same set—minus the original versions—was repackaged and reissued in 2008.

The Prequel and Original Trilogies were remastered—with a new batch of alterations—and issued together as part of the *Star Wars: The Complete Saga* set on Blu-ray disc in 2011. After acquiring Lucasfilm in 2013, Disney reissued these same masters as separate sets (devoted to the original and prequel trilogies) on Blu-ray and DVD. In both 2011 and 2013, the Original Trilogy was again offered only in its rejiggered form. Many other *Star Wars* products, including the made-for-TV Ewoks movies and selected episodes of the *Ewoks* and *Droids* cartoon series, have also been issued on DVD.

What all this means is that, by the time the *Star Wars* films were available in affordable editions that recreated their proper aspect ratios, with high-definition picture quality and THX stereo sound, they were no longer offered in their original, pre-Special Edition form. This has forced many fans to choose between audio-video quality and content. Anyone interested in seeing the films as they were first experienced by audiences in 1977, 1980, and 1983 must make due with substandard presentations, or resort to extralegal measures. Enthusiasts have produced cleaned-up "de-specialized editions" of the three films integrating footage from various sources, and posted them on the Internet. However, making and viewing these versions remains, technically at least, a crime.

It's conceivable that Disney's purchase of Lucasfilm could clear the way for authorized, remastered, anamorphic, hi-def releases of the films in their original theatrical form. *Star Wars* fans have been clamoring for such a release for over a decade now, and Disney (except in the case of *Song of the South*) usually gives the people what they want. So far, however, no official announcement has been made on this topic. Until something better comes along, fans are advised to hang on to their 2004 DVDs, or older videotape or Super 8 versions. And keep their fingers crossed.

35

Medal Ceremony

Honors and Awards Won and Lost

he importance and validity of film awards may be debated—and often are, especially by people whose favorite movies seldom win awards. But, if nothing else, these annual events indicate how movies are regarded by specific audiences—industry insiders, technical professionals, critics, and fans. In the case of the original three *Star Wars* films, the record provides further evidence that, for the most part, these pictures were well respected within the industry and by most critics, and adored by viewers in general and science fiction fans in particular.

It's illuminating to compare the Academy Awards history of the original three *Star Wars* films with that of other science fiction, fantasy, and action-adventure film series. Between them, *Star Wars*, *The Empire Strikes Back*, and *Return of the Jedi* accumulated nineteen Oscar nominations and won eight awards. The James Bond series has tallied only ten nominations and four wins, even though there have been twenty-three (or twenty-five, depending on whether or not you count *Never Say Never Again* and the 1967 *Casino Royale*) Bond films, compared to those three original *Star Wars* pictures. The *Star Trek* series (twelve films) has gathered fourteen Oscar nominations and won one award. The *Alien* series (six movies, including the two Alien vs. Predator films) collected ten nominations and won three awards. The *Terminator* series (four films) garnered six nominations and four wins, all for *Terminator 2: Judgment Day* (1991). George Lucas' other film series, starring Indiana Jones and running four films, accumulated fourteen nominations and seven wins. The only comparable film series more decorated than *Star Wars* is Peter Jackson's *Lord of the Rings* trilogy, which piled up twenty-nine Academy Award nominations and won sixteen Oscars, including Best Picture (for *The Lord of the Rings: The Return of the King* in 2003). All this indicates that, at least in the minds of Oscar voters, the original *Star Wars* trilogy stands as one of the finest examples of epic fantasy-adventure filmmaking.

It's also revealing to revisit the major awards the original three *Star Wars* films lost (including those for which *The Empire Strikes Back* and *Return of the*

Jedi didn't even earn nominations), and consider how these films stack up against the winners and nominees.

Here's a rundown of the Academy Awards and many other honors won (and lost) by the Original Trilogy and related works.

Star Wars (1977)

Although many critics and fans consider *The Empire Strikes Back* a more polished film, the original *Star Wars* remains the most decorated picture in the history of the franchise (so far).

Star Wars won seven Academy Awards, for Best Art Direction (this award was shared by production designer John Barry, art directors Norman Reynolds and Leslie Dilley, and set decorator Roger Christian), Best Costume Design (John Mollo), Best Sound (Don MacDougall, Ray West, Bob Minkler, and Derek Ball), Best Film Editing (Paul Hirsch, Marcia Lucas, and Richard Chew), Best Visual Effects (Robert Blalock, John Dykstra, Richard Edlund, Grant McCune, and John Stears), and Best Music (John Williams), as well as a Special Achievement Award for sound effects, given to Ben Burtt. But the film was denied all the major awards for which it was nominated—Best Picture, Best Director, Best Original Screenplay, and Best Supporting Actor (Sir Alec Guinness). In one of the biggest upsets in Oscar history, the Academy Award for Best Picture went to Woody Allen's *Annie Hall*, one of the lowest-earning films ever to win the award (the picture has a lifetime gross of $38 million, nearly all of that accumulated *after* winning Best Picture). Allen also won for Best Director and, along with cowriter Marshall Brickman, Best Original Screenplay. The Best Supporting Actor award went to Jason Robards for his performance as author Dashiell Hammett in director Fred Zinnemann's Nazi-era drama *Julia*. Had Lucas accepted a credit for his contributions to the editing of *Star Wars*, he would have won an Oscar. Instead, he left empty-handed.

Even though it lost in the highest-profile categories, *Star Wars*' Oscar performance remained a major achievement. It was the first full-blooded science fiction film ever honored with a Best Picture nomination. Earlier nominees had included Stanley Kubrick's political satire *Dr. Strangelove, or How I Learned to Stop Worrying and Love the Bomb* (1964), categorized by some as science fiction, and Kubrick's *A Clockwork Orange* (1971), which featured a dystopian near-future setting but functioned primarily as social commentary. Kubrick's monumental *2001: A Space Odyssey* (1968), like every other previous SF classic, was snubbed by the Academy.

Star Wars returned similar results from the Golden Globe Awards, where it won for Best Score but lost in the Best Picture-Drama, Best Director, and

Mark Hamill and Anthony Daniels (as C-3PO) made a red carpet appearance at the 50th Annual Academy Awards in April 1978.

Best Supporting Actor categories. Director Herbert Ross' backstage-at-the-ballet soap opera *The Turning Point* was named Best Picture-Drama, and Ross also won Best Director. The Best Supporting Actor nod went to Peter Firth for *Equus*, director Sidney Lumet's picture about a policeman investigating the blinding of six horses. In hindsight, *Star Wars'* Golden Globe losses are more galling than its Oscar defeats. *Annie Hall*, despite its relatively feeble box office performance, remains a classic of 1970s cinema and a career high-water mark for one of the decade's most celebrated directors. But *The Turning Point* and *Equus* haven't aged well and are now nearly forgotten.

At the BAFTA (British Academy of Film and Television) Awards, Britain's answer to the Oscars, the pattern continued. *Star Wars* claimed awards for Best Score and Best Sound, but lost in the Best Film, Best Costume Design, Best Film Editing, and Best Production Design/Art Direction categories. *Julia* was named Best Film, while *Death on the Nile* won for Costume Design, *Midnight Express* for Film Editing, and *Close Encounters of the Third Kind* for Production Design/Art Direction. *Star Wars* performed better at other international awards ceremonies, being named Best Foreign Language Film at Japan's Hochi Film Awards and winning Germany's Goldene Leinwand ("Golden Screen") Award, which is based on ticket sales.

Despite the backlash the film suffered from a minority of critics, *Star Wars* was also honored by important critics' societies. The Los Angeles Film Critics awarded *Star Wars* and John Williams its prizes for Best Picture and Best Score, respectively. The National Board of Review named *Star Wars* to its annual Top Ten Films list. *Star Wars* won Best Picture, Best Director, and Best Supporting Actor (Guinness) at the Utah Film Critics Association Awards. Demonstrating the breadth of its appeal, *Star Wars* was also named Favorite Motion Picture at the People's Choice Awards, which are selected by fans.

Various technical societies also bestowed nominations on the picture, including the Directors Guild of America, American Cinema Editors, the Writer's Guild of America, and the British Society of Cinematographers. At the Grammy Awards, Williams' score won three awards but lost the prestigious Album of the Year to Fleetwood Mac's pop juggernaut *Rumours*. It was unusual for a symphonic recording even to be nominated in this category.

As you might expect, *Star Wars* cleaned up at awards geared specifically to the science fiction audience. It was named Best Dramatic Presentation at the prestigious Hugo Awards, voted on by attendees at the annual World Science Fiction Convention (WorldCon) and named for *Amazing Stories* editor Hugo Gernsback, who coined the term "science fiction." At the Saturn Awards, handed out annually since 1972 by the Academy of Science Fiction, *Star Wars* hauled in a dozen awards, including Best Science Fiction Film, Best Writing, Best Supporting Actor (Guinness), and Best Music, along with a sweep of the various technical awards. Cinematographer Gilbert Taylor was given a Special Award for his contributions to the film, which was ironic given his dismissive attitude toward the project and personality conflicts with George Lucas. Actors Mark Hamill, Harrison Ford, Carrie Fisher, and Peter Cushing also earned Saturn nominations. The Science Fiction Writers of America, who don't typically honor works outside the realm of literary SF, also graced *Star Wars* with a special Nebula Award.

The preceding list is limited to awards presented during the 1977–78 awards season. *Star Wars* has continued to garner accolades over the decades, frequently finishing at or near the top when fans and sometimes critics are asked to name their favorite movies or science fiction films. A comprehensive survey of these honors would run on for several more pages, but two stand out. In 1989, *Star Wars* was named to the U.S. Library of Congress' National Film Registry, as "a culturally, historically, and aesthetically important" movie. And in 1997 *Star Wars* finished No. 15 on the American Film Institute's "100 Years . . . 100 Movies" ranking of the 100 Greatest American Movies of All Time. When AFI voters were repolled ten years later, *Star Wars* moved up to No. 13, finishing just below John Ford's Western classic *The Searchers* (1956), one of Lucas' inspirations, and just above Alfred Hitchcock's *Psycho* (1960). In both polls it was the highest-ranked science fiction film on the list.

The *Star Wars Holiday Special* (1978)

The *Star Wars Holiday Special* (1978) didn't win, wasn't nominated for, and didn't deserve any awards. During production, however, producers believed that the special's elaborate and expensive Wookiee treehouse set and plethora of alien makeups might earn the show Emmy nominations in the art direction and makeup categories. As it turned out, everyone involved was so mortified by the final program that they made no effort to lobby Emmy voters for nominations, probably hoping that the world would forget the *Holiday Special* entirely. The Emmy for Art Direction in a Limited Series or Special went to *Studs Lonigan*, a miniseries about a family of Irish immigrants during the prohibition era. The makeup award went to *Backstairs at the White House*, a miniseries about maids and other servants employed at the presidential residence. Ironically, the Emmy for Outstanding Comedy-Variety or Music Program went to Gary Smith and Dwight Hemion—the same production team behind the *Star Wars Holiday Special*— for *Steve* [Lawrence] *and Eydie* [Gormé] *Celebrate Irving Berlin*, another of Smith-Hemion's many variety shows.

The *Empire Strikes Back* (1980)

Although it's become the most critically renowned *Star Wars* film, much of the respect now afforded *The Empire Strikes Back* collected around the movie in later years. Various factors prevented many reviewers, and some fans, from fully appreciating the picture's virtues during its original release. One of those factors was a then-endemic prejudice against sequels among Hollywood insiders (see Chapter 18), which hurt the film's chances with Oscar voters. Only one sequel had ever before earned a Best Picture nomination—1974 Oscar champion *The Godfather, Part II*. (The Best Picture–nominated *Broadway Melody of 1936* was the second in a series of four similarly plotted backstage musicals, but not a true sequel.) Even though Hollywood became much more sequel-friendly over the years, as of this writing (in early 2015) only four more sequels have earned Best Picture nominations: *The Godfather, Part III* (1990), *The Lord of the Rings: The Two Towers* (2002), *The Lord of the Rings: The Return of the King* (2003, the only other winner of the award), and *Toy Story 3* (2010).

All this helps account for why the most polished picture in the history of the franchise earned a relatively meager four nominations and was shut out of the major categories at the 53rd annual Academy Awards. At the ceremony, which was postponed by a day following the attempted assassination of President Ronald Regan, *Empire* won for Best Sound (an award shared by Gregg Landaker, Steve Maslow, Peter Sutton, and Bill Varney) and received a Special Achievement Award for visual effects (shared by Richard Edlund, Brian Johnson, Dennis Muren, and Bruce Nicholson). It was also nominated for Best Art Direction-Set Decoration but lost that award to director Roman Polanski's period drama *Tess*, and for John Williams' score, which lost to Michael Gore's music from *Fame*. Director Robert Redford's sensitive family drama *Ordinary People* won Best Picture and Best Director. Other Best Picture nominees that year included *Tess*, Martin Scorsese's *Raging Bull*, David Lynch's *The Elephant Man*, and Michael Apted's *Coal Miner's Daughter*. Lucas, irate about the lack of respect shown his film, resigned his membership in the Academy of Motion Picture Arts and Sciences.

Lucasfilm had lobbied for Best Picture and Best Director nominations, and Best Supporting Actor nominations for Frank Oz, Anthony Daniels, and David Prowse and James Earl Jones. The Screen Actors Guild ruled that Oz and the Prowse-Jones team were ineligible. The Guild did not consider puppeteers to be actors, and it forbade two actors from being nominated for playing the same role in the same film. Daniels was eligible but he didn't receive a nomination. Had SAG ruled differently, Oz was the most likely of the three to have received a nomination. Instead, the Oscar went to Timothy Hutton for *Ordinary People*. The other nominees were Judd Hirsch for *Ordinary People*, Michael O'Keefe for *The Great Santini*, Joe Pesci for *Raging Bull*, and Jason Robards for *Melvin and Howard*. All of those were fine performances, but none of them have left the kind of impact on popular culture as Yoda, Darth Vader, or C-3P0.

Empire's fortunes were even worse at the other major awards venues. It earned just one Golden Globe nomination, for Williams' score, which it lost (to Dominic Frontiere's compositions for *The Stunt Man*). At the BAFTA Awards, Williams' score won, but *Empire* lost in the categories of Best Production Design/Art Direction and Best Sound. Williams' score was nominated for two Grammys, winning for Best Album of Instrumental Score Written for a Motion Picture or Television, but losing for Best Pop Instrumental Performance. Internationally, *The Empire Strikes Back* won only Germany's box office–based Golden Screen Award.

The film was not honored by any of the major critics' circles, and—almost inconceivably—only one professional organization, the Writers Guild, nominated it for an award. But *The Empire Strikes Back* was named Favorite Motion Picture at the People's Choice Awards. And science fiction fans loved it. *Empire* won the franchise a second Hugo Award. At the Saturn Awards, it won Best Science Fiction Film, Best Actor (Hamill), Best Director (Irvin Kershner), and Best Special Effects. It was also nominated for Best Supporting Actor (Billy Dee Williams), Best Writing, Best Music, and Best Costumes. Kershner's victory was impressive, since it came over Kubrick (director of

Best Horror Film winner *The Shining*), Brian De Palma (for *Dressed to Kill*), and Ken Russell (for *Altered States*).

The clearest evidence of the growing appreciation that *The Empire Strikes Back* has enjoyed over the years is that in 2010 it was named by the Library of Congress to the National Film Registry, placing two-thirds of the Original Trilogy among those films deemed worthy of preservation for their outstanding cultural, historical, and aesthetic merits.

Return of the Jedi (1983)

Although *Return of the Jedi* is almost universally regarded as the weakest installment in the Original Trilogy, it returned a similar collection of awards as *The Empire Strikes Back* and outperformed its immediate predecessor at certain venues.

Jedi earned five Academy Award nominations (one more than *Empire*), winning another Special Achievement Award for Visual Effects (to Edlund, Muren, Ralston, and Tippett), but losing the awards for Best Art Direction-Set Decoration, Best Sound, Best Effects (Sound Effects Editing), and Best Score. The Academy's choice for Best Picture of 1983 was director James L. Brooks' weepy dramedy *Terms of Endearment*. The other nominees included *The Big Chill*, directed and cowritten by *Return of the Jedi* screenwriter Lawrence Kasdan, as well as Peter Yates' *The Dresser*, Philip Kaufman's *The Right Stuff*, and Bruce Beresford's *Tender Mercies*.

John Williams' *Return of the Jedi* score won a Golden Globe, while *Empire* had failed to garner any Golden Globe nominations. And *Jedi* snagged four BAFTA nominations (one more than *Empire*), winning the award for Best Special Visual Effects and losing for Best Makeup Artist, Best Production Design/Art Direction, and Best Sound. At the Grammy Awards, Williams' score was nominated for Best Album of Original Score Written for a Motion Picture or Television, as had been his *Empire Strikes Back* soundtrack. *Jedi* also won the franchise's third Golden Screen Award in Germany. And it was named Best Family Feature Motion Picture at the seventh annual Youth in Film Awards in 1984.

Return of the Jedi continued *Star Wars*' mastery of the People's Choice Awards, where it was named Favorite Motion Picture. And *Jedi* completed the franchise's clean sweep of the major science fiction awards. It claimed another Hugo Award for Best Dramatic Presentation, making it the most-honored film series in the history of the award—a very impressive achievement. The other Hugo winners from the intervening years of the original *Star Wars* trilogy—*Superman: The Movie* (1978), *Alien* (1979), *Raiders of the Lost Ark* (1981), and *Blade Runner* (1982)—suggest how competitive the category was during this era. Incidentally, for the sake of comparison, the *Star Wars* Prequel Trilogy didn't receive any Hugo nominations. At the Saturn Awards, *Jedi* won Best Science Fiction Film, Best Actor (Hamill), Best Costumes, Best Makeup, and Best Special Effects, and earned additional nominations for Best Actress (Fisher), Best Supporting Actor (Williams), Best Director, Best Writing, and Best Music.

Perhaps *Return of the Jedi* will someday receive the kind of critical reassessment that *The Empire Strikes Back* has enjoyed, but that hasn't happened yet. As noted in Chapter 21, *Jedi* is the only one of the three original *Star Wars* films not included on the National Film Registry. This is an oversight that should eventually be corrected, if only because it makes little sense to enshrine only two-thirds of a trilogy, leaving out the final chapter of the story. *Return of the Jedi* was a major pop culture event, and it remains a picture of cultural, historical, and aesthetic importance, even if it's not quite the equal of its predecessors.

The Ewok Movies (1985–86)

Star Wars acquitted itself far better with its second made-for-television production than it had with its first. *The Ewok Adventure* (1984), also known as *Caravan of Courage*, earned an Emmy nomination for Outstanding Children's Program (Prime Time). It lost that award to a PBS *American Playhouse* drama titled *Displaced Person*, based on a story by Kurt Vonnegut about a black German World War II orphan. *The Ewok Adventure* won the Emmy for Outstanding Visual Effects. That award was shared by Jon Berg, John Ellis, Christopher Evans, Harley Jessup, Dennis Muren, Michael Pangrazio, and Phil Tippett. The follow-up telefilm *Ewoks: The Battle of Endor* (1985) was, if anything, even more ambitious than the original, yet it received no Emmy nominations. The Emmy winner that year for Outstanding Children's Program (Prime Time) was a Canadian-made adaptation of author Lucy Maud Montgomery's *Anne of Green Gables*. The animated *Droids* and *Ewoks* television series also failed to garner any awards.

Still, in all, for a franchise whose cinematic value remains debatable (at least in the minds of certain critics), *Star Wars* has a packed trophy case.

36

Always in Motion Is the Future

W hen *Star Wars* was unleashed on this galaxy in May 1977, Sir Alec Guinness and Peter Cushing were the only cast members moviegoers knew by name. By the end of the summer, Mark Hamill, Harrison Ford, and Carrie Fisher had become three of the most recognizable people on Earth, permanently altering the trajectories of their careers—and their lives. Darth Vader, C-3PO, R2-D2, and Chewbacca became world-famous too, of course, but the performers inside those iconic costumes remained unknown to most viewers. Their anonymity was by Lucasfilm design, but David Prowse, Anthony Daniels, Kenny Baker, and Peter Mayhew found ways to translate their *Star Wars* affiliation into lucrative opportunities of various sorts. Inevitably, *Star Wars* left its mark on the lives of Guinness and Cushing too.

Mark Hamill

At first, the stars of *Star Wars* struggled to escape the shadows of Luke Skywalker, Han Solo, and Princess Leia (see Chapter 11). A gruesome automobile accident, resulting in reconstructive facial surgery (see Chapter 8), made the challenge even tougher for Mark Hamill. Most of the parts he was offered following *Star Wars* were fresh-faced Luke Skywalker types, but Hamill no longer had the youthful glow he exuded in his star-making role. Nevertheless, Hamill's best non-*Star Wars* leading role dates from this difficult period: Private Griff, from director Sam Fuller's uncompromising World War II epic *The Big Red One* (1980), which costarred Lee Marvin, Robert Carradine, and Hamill. The movie flopped when it first appeared, slashed to 113 minutes by United Artists, but benefitted from critical reassessment when Fuller's original 162-minute cut was issued by Warner Brothers in 2004. One of the film's primary strengths is Hamill's subtle, rangy performance as a soldier who's reluctant to kill until he discovers the horrors of a Nazi concentration camp.

In the years immediately following *Return of the Jedi*, Hamill alternated between starring roles in low-budget sci-fi, horror, and action films such as *Slipstream* (1989, produced by Gary Kurtz), *Midnight Ride* (1990), and *Time Runner* (1993), and guest appearances on television shows like *Amazing Stories* (1986), the revived *Alfred Hitchcock Presents* (1987), and *The Flash* (1991), where he appeared as supervillain The Trickster in two episodes. New horizons opened for Hamill, an avid comic book collector, after being cast as the voice of the Joker in *Batman: The Animated Series* (1992–94), a part he reprised in numerous subsequent animated Batman series and movies. Hamill's devilish yet childlike Joker caused a minor sensation, and soon offers for more voice work came pouring in. Comic book fans still debate who made the best Joker: Cesar Romero, Jack Nicholson, Heath Ledger, or Hamill.

Although he had extensive voice credits already, that aspect of Hamill's career suddenly kicked into hyperdrive. Hamill has displayed terrific flair and versatility in

Mark Hamill created his second action figure–worthy character with his astonishing performance as the Joker on *Batman: The Animated Series*. The role helped the actor's second career as an in-demand voice artist ascend to new heights.

Photography by Preston Hewis/East Bank Images

his scores of subsequent animated projects, and his voice work has not been confined to cartoons. One of his most lucrative endeavors was providing the voice of protagonist Maverick Blair for the award-winning *Wing Commander* video game series (1990–2004). Hamill's deal included a profit share in the franchise, which spawned a series of novels, an animated television series (1996), and even a live-action feature film (1999). *Star Wars* and *Wing*

Commander residuals, along with his other paychecks, have enabled Hamill to be selective about his roles and demand top pay. During a conversation with me at the Emerald City Comicon in Seattle in 2004, actor Wil Wheaton (who also has extensive voice credits) explained that in the world of Saturday morning cartoons, all the voice talent works for Guild scale "unless you're Mark Hamill."

But Hamill never strayed too far from *Star Wars* and has often appeared at conventions and other official franchise functions. He voiced the villainous Darth Bane in the series finale of *Star Wars: Clone Wars* (2014). And, along with Harrison Ford and Carrie Fisher, Hamill returned to his most famous role for the upcoming *Star Wars Episode VII: The Force Awakens*. Hamill remains devoted to his wife, Marilou, whom he married between production of *Star Wars* and *The Empire Strikes Back*. They now have three children: Nathan (born during production of *Empire*), Griffin (born in 1983), and Chelsea (born in 1988).

Harrison Ford

By the time the Original Trilogy ended, Harrison Ford had already established himself as a major star, not only based on his work as Han Solo but by headlining *Raiders of the Lost Ark* (1981) and *Blade Runner* (1982). Three more Indiana Jones movies (so far) and many more action blockbusters followed, including two appearances as Tom Clancy's Jack Ryan (in *Patriot Games*, 1992, and *Clear and Present Danger*, 1994). With his classic good looks and easygoing yet charismatic screen presence, Ford is one of the few performers of his generation who likely would have been a movie star during Hollywood's Golden Age. He's a latter-day Tyrone Power. Like Power, however, Ford has struggled to gain recognition as an actor rather than merely as a dashing leading man.

Yet Ford's filmography contains several roles that demonstrate the actor's abilities are not limited to swashbuckling action fare. When the screenplay has supplied the opportunity, he has repeatedly risen to complex, challenging parts with subtlety, skill, and conviction. He won his lone Academy Award nomination for director Peter Weir's *Witness* (1985), in which he played Detective John Book, assigned to protect a young Amish boy who has witnessed a murder. Book begins to question his outlook on life when he moves in with an Amish family, and he begins a tentative romance with the boy's widowed mother (Kelly McGillis). Ford's brilliant, delicate performance earned him a BAFTA Award for Best Actor, but he lost the Oscar to William Hurt (for *Kiss of the Spider Woman*). Ford was also very impressive in Weir's *The Mosquito Coast* (1986), playing a paranoid inventor who moves his family to the South American jungle, with catastrophic consequences; in Roman Polanski's Hitchcockian thriller *Frantic* (1988), as a surgeon plunged into

Harrison Ford cemented his position as an A-list leading man with his role as Indiana Jones in *Raiders of the Lo st Ark* and its sequels.

international espionage when he accidentally picks up the wrong suitcase at the airport; in Mike Nichols' *Working Girl* (1988), in a supporting part that showcased Ford's underutilized comedic gifts; in Alan J. Pakula's twisty courtroom thriller *Presumed Innocent* (1990), about a prosecutor accused of murder; and in Nichols' *Regarding Henry* (1991), playing an amnesia patient who doesn't like what he learns about himself as his memories return. Ford deserved, but was denied, a second Oscar nomination for director Andrew Davis' *The Fugitive* (1993). Tommy Lee Jones won an Academy Award as U.S. Marshall Sam Gerard, who tracks escapee Richard Kimball (Ford), a man out to prove he was wrongly convicted of his wife's murder. Jones was named Best Supporting Actor, but he and Ford were, essentially, the film's two leads.

Ford divorced his first wife, Mary Marquardt, shortly after completion of *The Empire Strikes Back*. From 1983 to 2004 he was married to screenwriter Melissa Mathison. After the breakup of that union, Ford entered a long-term relationship with actress Calista Flockhart, whom he married in 2010. Ford fathered two children with Marquardt (Benjamin and Willard) and two with Mathison (Malcolm and Georgia), and is now father to Flockhart's previously adopted son, Liam. Ford has three grandchildren. An outspoken supporter of various conservationist and environmentalist groups, Ford also serves as vice-chair of Conservation International, a green lobby group.

Carrie Fisher

By the time *Return of the Jedi* wrapped, Carrie Fisher was growing disenchanted with film work, although she continued to take supporting roles in pictures such as Woody Allen's *Hannah and Her Sisters* (1986) and Rob Reiner's *When Harry Met Sally* (1989), and to make guest appearances on various TV series. Many of her post-*Star Wars* performances reveal a flair for comedy untapped by her role as Princess Leia. But Fisher's most significant work was offscreen.

After vowing to become a writer during the making of *Jedi* (see Chapter 20), Fisher published her first novel in 1987. The semi-autobiographical *Postcards from the Edge* scaled the *New York Times* Best Seller list, and a follow-up, *Surrender the Pink*, appeared in 1990. Between those two works, Fisher penned the screenplay for Mike Nichols' 1990 film adaptation of *Postcards*, which starred Meryl Streep and Shirley MacLaine. Her later novels include *Delusions of Grandma* (1993), *Hollywood Moms* (2001), and *The Best Awful There Is* (2004). She has also accumulated another ten screenwriting credits, including writing material for the Academy Award broadcasts in 1997, 2002, and 2007.

Fisher achieved sobriety after being diagnosed with bipolar disorder, an ordeal that became fodder for her bracingly funny one-woman play *Wishful Drinking*, which debuted at the Geffen Playhouse in Los Angeles in 2006. The show was a smash, and Fisher revived it at numerous venues (including a short run on Broadway) through 2010. A book adaption of the play appeared in 2008 (the cover featured a twin-bunned Princess Leia, apparently passed out, still holding a martini glass). The show was filmed and broadcast on HBO in 2010. She earned a Grammy nomination for the audiobook version of *Wishful Drinking*. In 2012, she published a second best-selling memoir, *Shockaholic* (the cover of which featured a scandalized Princess Leia doll hiding its eyes).

While promoting *Wishful Drinking* and *Shockaholic* in various television and print interviews, Fisher was candid about her history of addiction (to alcohol and prescription drugs), mental illness, and her tempestuous romantic relationships. She and singer-songwriter Paul Simon were in an on-gain, off-again romance beginning in 1977. She was briefly married to Simon from August 1983 to July 1984. After that marriage ended, Fisher entered a long-term relationship with casting agent Bryan Lourd. The couple had a daughter, Billie, together in 1992, but Lourd later left Fisher for a relationship with a man. Fisher told *Vanity Fair* that she briefly started taking drugs again in 2005 after political lobbyist Greg Stevens died of an OxyContin overdose while in her home. Fisher's written works radiate with the incisive wit and emotional honesty that have carried her through these and other personal crises.

Billy Dee Williams

Perhaps because he didn't join the cast until *The Empire Strikes Back*, or perhaps because Lando Calrissian remained a supporting character, *Star Wars* didn't materially alter the career of Billy Dee Williams. Unlike Hamill, Ford, Fisher, and even Guinness, he didn't become inexorably imprinted on the viewing public as his *Star Wars* alter ego. Playing Lando raised his profile, but it neither opened new doors nor closed old ones. After *Jedi*, Williams returned to the career he had before, as one of the most popular and reliable black leading men in Hollywood. Unfortunately that was not (and still is not) quite the same thing as being one of the most popular and reliable leading men in Hollywood. In the later 1980s, as he entered his fifties, Williams began to accept more supporting parts and television roles, including a recurring role on the prime-time soap *Dynasty*. He also appeared memorably as crusading district attorney Harvey Dent in Tim Burton's *Batman* (1989). Williams has not been announced as part of the cast of *The Force Awakens*. He provided the voice of Lando for *Star Wars* video games and cartoons, including *Star Wars: Rebels* (2014). Williams has been married three times and has been with his current wife, Teruko Nagami, since 1972. Their daughter Hanako was born in 1973. Williams is also an accomplished fine artist whose paintings have been displayed in the Smithsonian Institution, the National Portrait Gallery, the Schomburg Museum, and various other galleries and museums across the country.

David Prowse

David Prowse's relationship with *Star Wars* remains conflicted. While enjoying the attention and opportunities that playing Darth Vader brought him, Prowse still seethes with resentment that his voice was replaced by that of James Earl Jones, and at other perceived grievances. He defiantly signs autographs "David Prowse IS Darth Vader." As early as 1979, during production of *The Empire Strikes Back*, Prowse told publicist Alan Arnold that "I had the raw end of the deal. It seemed to me that there was a concerted effort to preserve Darth Vader's anonymity at my expense. Yet I had played him and . . . I was determined to get the credit for it."

Prowse was correct that Lucasfilm executives intentionally kept the profile of *Star Wars*' costumed performers low—even going so far, in an early press release, as suggesting that C-3PO and R2-D2 were actual robots. The logic was brutally simple: If the actors playing Vader, the droids, and Chewbacca remained unknown, they could be rehired inexpensively or replaced if necessary. At most promotional appearances in the 1970s—including the footprint ceremony in front of the Chinese Theatre in Hollywood and a *Vogue* magazine photo shoot—other actors appeared in the Vader suit. Prowse defiantly hired his own publicity agent and began speaking and signing autographs at science fiction conventions across the United States and in Europe. His paid appearances at these events only increased tensions between the actor and Lucasfilm executives, especially since Prowse was prone to leak details of upcoming films (see Chapters 17 and 20).

Nevertheless, conventions and other *Star Wars*–related projects have sustained him financially since *Return of the Jedi*. "I now make a comfortable living attending science fiction conventions, meeting fans in person and selling autographs, et cetera," Prowse told London's *Daily Telegraph* in 2011. "I also run a small business selling autographs and photographs from my website." Following *Jedi*, Prowse has tallied a meager eleven screen credits, including documentaries in which he appeared as himself. And one of those documentaries—*The People vs. George Lucas* (2010)—resulted in Prowse being banned from all official *Star Wars* events and Lucasfilm-sponsored functions. Prowse later complained that he grants scores of interviews each year and had no idea that this one would wind up in a Lucas-bashing documentary. Prowse had his say when he published a memoir titled *Straight from the Force's Mouth* in 2011. A year later, about the time that Disney announced it would move forward with *Star Wars Episode VII*, in which Prowse will not appear, the actor complained loudly (and not for the first time) that he receives no royalties from his film appearances as Darth Vader. (Prowse, unlike some other cast members, was never granted a partial profit share.) This probably ensures that his love-hate relationship with the franchise will continue indefinitely.

Anthony Daniels

Anthony Daniels quietly turned playing C-3PO into a cottage industry. During the Original Trilogy era he emceed *The Making of Star Wars* TV special; appeared on *The Muppet Show* (alongside Hamill), *Sesame Street*, and *The Donnie and Marie Show*; joined Hamill, Ford, and Fisher in the ill-fated *Star Wars Holiday Special*; made an antismoking PSA; and performed in the BBC radio serial adaptations of all three films. And Daniels has hardly had a break since. He returned as C-3PO in the *Droids* animated series (1985), the *Star Tours* attraction at Disney World (1986–2010), the Prequel Trilogy, the *Clone Wars* animated series, and the Lego *Yoda Chronicles* cartoons, as well as in sundry video games and promotional projects. He will appear again as Threepio in *The Force Awakens*. Daniels also agreed to participate in a live-action series tentatively titled *Star Wars: Underworld*, first announced in 2005, but that project was scrapped when Disney purchased Lucasfilm and decided to move forward with Episode VII. Somehow, Daniels also found time for dozens of roles (not as C-3PO) on various British television shows, including a recurring part on the crime drama *Prime Suspect* (1995), starring Helen Mirren. Daniels is married to actress Christine Savage and has a son.

Actor Anthony Daniels poses with his alter ego in this publicity still. Not only has Daniels portrayed C-3PO in every *Star Wars* film, he's made scores of additional appearances as the character on various TV shows, cartoons, documentaries, and other venues.

Kenny Baker

Like Anthony Daniels, Kenny Baker has appeared in every *Star Wars* movie made so far, a streak that will continue with *Episode VII*. He also acted in *Flash Gordon* (1980), *Time Bandits* (1981), *Amadeus* (1984), *Labyrinth* (1986), and *Willow* (1988), among other film and television appearances. Between movies, like Prowse and Peter Mayhew, Baker earns a comfortable living appearing at science fiction conventions and other special events. When his cabaret act with Jack Purvis, the Mini Tones, disbanded, he worked for a while as a stand-up comedian. In 2009, he self-published *From Tiny Acorns: The Kenny Baker Story*. Baker married his wife, Eileen, who was also a little person, in 1970 and remained with her until her death in 1993. He and Eileen had two full-sized children.

Peter Mayhew

When *Star Wars* premiered in 1977, Peter Mayhew was still living at home with his parents. The film's success not only gave him the wherewithal to find his own place, but the motivation to move out since fans began knocking on the door day and night asking for Chewbacca's autograph. Between *Star Wars* and *Empire*, Mayhew resumed his job as an orderly at Mayday Hospital in suburban London. After *Return of the Jedi*, however, Chewbacca became Mayhew's livelihood, thanks to the sci-fi convention circuit. Seven of his thirty-three post-*Jedi* film credits are as Chewbacca. He appeared as the beloved Wookiee in *Star Wars Episode III: Revenge of the Sith* (2005), as part of the *Star Tours* attraction, as a Top 10 list presenter on the *Late Show with David Letterman* (2005), and in an episode of *Glee* (2011). He will also appear in *The Force Awakens*. Most of the rest of his screen appearances—twenty-four of them since the Original Trilogy ended—have been as himself, talking about Chewbacca on various television programs and documentaries, including the forthcoming *Standing in the Stars: The Peter Mayhew Story*. Mayhew has written an autobiographical graphic novel, *Growing Up Giant*, and a children's book, *My Favorite Giant* (both 2013). His tremendous height (seven feet, three inches) is the result of the genetic disorder Marfan syndrome, which was successfully treated when he was in his teens. He endured double knee replacement surgery in 2013. Mayhew, who became a naturalized U.S. citizen in 2005, now lives in Texas. His nonprofit Peter Mayhew Foundation partners with organizations such as the Make-a-Wish Foundation and the Children's Cancer Fund to comfort children facing serious illnesses.

Sir Alec Guinness

The phenomenal success of *Star Wars* baffled and sometimes disturbed Sir Alec Guinness (see Chapter 11), but it also gave him financial independence and the ability to become more selective about his film roles. Because of this, and due to declining health, the actor made just eight more movies after *Return of the Jedi*, but three of those were memorable. He played the eccentric Professor Godbole in director David Lean's epic *A Passage to India* (1984); received a British Academy of Television Award nomination in the title role in the BBC drama *Monsignor Quixote* (1985), based on a Graham Greene novel; and earned an Academy Award nomination as William Dorritt in the Charles Dickens adaptation *Little Dorritt* (1988). That film remains notable for its extreme length, running six hours. Guinness died of liver cancer on August 5, 2000, at age eighty-six. His wife of sixty-two years, actress Merula Salaman, passed away two months later, also of cancer. The couple was survived by their son, Matthew, born in 1940.

Peter Cushing

When *Star Wars* debuted, Peter Cushing was nearer the end of his career than Guinness. His health was faltering, and he remained emotionally devastated since the death of his wife, Helen, in 1971. In his autobiography, Cushing wrote that he considered suicide the night of his wife's death, and that life seemed empty without her. "Time is interminable, the loneliness is almost unbearable, and the only thing that keeps me going is the knowledge that my dear Helen and I will be reunited again someday," he told an interviewer from Britain's *Radio Times* in 1972. "To join Helen is my only ambition." Because Cushing declined a profit share in *Star Wars*, preferring a fixed salary, he didn't enjoy the financial windfall Guinness received. Instead, he soldiered on, making fourteen more film and television appearances between 1978 and 1986, mostly low-budget schlock like *Son of Hitler* (1978) or cameos like his bit in *Top Secret!* (1984). The lone bright spot was the high-toned horror send-up *House of the Long Shadows* (1983), which costarred Cushing and fellow horror movie stars Vincent Price, Christopher Lee, and John Carradine. Cushing was diagnosed with prostate cancer in 1982 but declined surgery. Illness forced him to retire from the screen in 1987, but he continued his secondary career, painting and selling fine art watercolors. He also wrote and illustrated a whimsical children's book, *The Bois Saga*, which was published shortly before his death. Cushing finally joined his beloved Helen on August 11, 1994. He was eighty-two.

37

Oh, He's Not Dead. Not Yet.

T he fall of 1983 should have been the sweetest of times for George Lucas. After completing his epic *Star Wars* trilogy, a monumental achievement, he planned to settle into quiet family life with his wife and two-year-old adopted daughter Amanda, and oversee the completion of his bucolic Camelot at Skywalker Ranch. But none of those things turned out the way Lucas hoped. Even though it was a huge hit, *Return of the Jedi* was unable to match, let alone top, the sensational returns for his original *Star Wars* film, and it drew the harshest criticism of the Original Trilogy (see Chapter 21). By then, however, Lucas had bigger heartaches. During post-production of *Jedi*, Marcia Lucas informed her husband that she had fallen in love with another man and wanted a divorce. It was all the emotionally devastated Lucas could do to complete the film. The dissolution of his marriage, in turn, had serious ramifications for his company and for the future of the *Star Wars* franchise.

Marcia Lucas, who had endured long separations from her workaholic husband since the making of the first *Star Wars* movie, met artist Tom Rodrigues while George Lucas was in England shooting *Jedi*. Rodrigues, ten years younger than Marcia, was overseeing the installation of an elaborate stained glass dome at the new Lucasfilm headquarters at Skywalker Ranch. In June 1983, just weeks after the premiere of *Jedi*, George and Marcia appeared at a Lucasfilm staff meeting and, holding hands, informed shocked employees that they were ending their fifteen-year marriage. The Lucases were co-owners of the company. News reports and other accounts indicate that Marcia Lucas received at least $35 million, and perhaps as much as $50 million, in the ensuing settlement. Initially, George and Marcia agreed to share custody of their daughter Amanda, but George gained primary custody a year later after Marcia bore Tom Rodrigues a daughter, Amy, in 1985. (Marcia and Tom married in 1988 but divorced in 1995, following a two-year separation.)

Steven Spielberg told *60 Minutes* in 1999 that Lucas' divorce "pulverized" his friend. Lucas scaled back his working hours, delegating more of his authority to trusted associates and devoting more time to raising his daughter. As a single parent, he adopted another daughter, Katie, born in 1988, and a son named Jett, born in 1993. Lucas began a long-term relationship with singer Linda Ronstadt in 1984, but the romance ended in the late 1980s. Lucas later explained that he wanted marriage but Ronstadt did not.

Aside from altering its founder's personal priorities, the divorce had another direct consequence for Lucasfilm: Lucas no longer had the personal fortune to self-finance a *Star Wars* movie. It would take more than a decade to rebuild his wealth to the point where he could resume the series on his terms, which were the only terms he would consider for a *Star Wars* film. By then, fortunately, breakthroughs in CGI enabled Lucas to realize more of his imagined universe at a lower cost. And perhaps most importantly, Lucas finally was prepared, emotionally, to undertake the rigors of making *Star Wars* movies again.

Lucas' Skywalker Ranch never became the independent filmmaking hub he originally envisioned. The high cost of renting space at the state-of-the-art facility priced out small-time moviemakers. The pictures made there were mostly things like *Star Wars*—big-budget, major studio blockbusters with elaborate visual and audio effects. That's what the facilities there were designed to create.

Through it all, however, Lucas continued making movies. Although in the wake of *Star Wars* he often spoke about making personal, unconventional films—for instance, he told *Starlog* magazine in 1981 that "I'm going to make films that are very experimental. They're not really theatrical films."—Lucas has never gotten round to producing those pictures. Instead, he was the primary creative force behind six non-*Star Wars* feature films and one television series released between 1978 and 1997, when he returned to directing with the Prequel Trilogy. He also served as executive producer (sometimes without credit) on a dozen more films, mostly made by friends and close associates. Lucas' non-*Star Wars* projects included blockbusters, bombs, and everything in between. But most of these works proved to be remarkable for one reason or another.

More American Graffiti (1979)

George Lucas never wanted to make *More American Graffiti*. The end credits of the original *Graffiti* had revealed the fates of the picture's lead characters, rendering any sequel superfluous. But *American Graffiti* had been a colossal hit, and Universal demanded a follow-up. When executives informed Lucas that the studio planned to move forward with the project with or without his participation, Lucas caved. The only thing he wanted less than an *American Graffiti* sequel was an *American Graffiti* sequel made without his involvement.

The project suffered a serious blow when Richard Dreyfuss, who had recently won an Oscar for his work in *The Goodbye Girl* (1977), refused to reprise his role as Curt Henderson. This meant that the sequel would proceed without the original film's best-realized and most emotionally complex character. The rest of the principal cast—including Ron Howard, Cindy Williams, Charles Martin Smith, Mackenzie Phillips, and Paul Le Mat—signed on, but Howard, Williams, and Phillips were available for only a few weeks during the summer hiatus from their respective TV series *Happy Days*, *Laverne and Shirley*, and *One Day at a Time*. Lucas' friends Willard Huyck and Gloria Katz, who had cowritten the original *Graffiti* with Lucas, were also unavailable, busy developing the romantic comedy *French Postcards* (1979). So Lucas turned to writer-director Bill Norton, another of his former USC classmates, to helm the project and tapped Howard Kazanjian to produce. Due to the schedule constraints of his cast, Norton had just forty-four days to shoot the film.

The original *Graffiti* had taken place on a single eventful night in 1962. The sequel tells four stories set during four consecutive New Year's Eves from 1964 to 1967. Each segment was shot in a distinct visual style, employing different film stocks (including 16mm) and aspect ratios (even split-screen). This was intended to reflect the splintering impact the Vietnam War has on the lives of the protagonists, who appear together only briefly, at the beginning of the 1964 story. But the fragmented look of the film also underscores the scattershot, underdeveloped nature of Norton's screenplay, which not only fails to cohere but whose component pieces are leaden and depressing, especially compared to the effervescent, feel-good original. Characters who came off as quirky but likable in the original here seem shallow and annoying. Most of the jokes misfire. Even the wall-to-wall rock music soundtrack fails to provide a significant emotional lift. In retrospect, the picture's inventive structure and obvious artistic aspirations were probably better suited to drama than comedy.

More American Graffiti was virtually ignored by viewers. It grossed a paltry $8 million (compared to the original's $140 million) and received scathing reviews. *Variety* critic Dale Pollock considered the movie a noble failure, calling it "one of the most innovative and ambitious films of the last five years, but by no means one of the most successful." Janet Maslin of the *New York Times* was less impressed, writing that "*More American Graffiti* is so grotesquely misconceived that it nearly eradicates fond memories of the original."

The Indiana Jones Franchise

Lucas first conceived of a swashbuckling archeologist-adventurer—originally named Indiana Smith—in 1975, and hashed out the preliminary story concept with writer-director Philip Kaufman. It was Kaufman who suggested that the story involve the lost Ark of the Covenant. Lucas and Kaufman went their separate ways before completing a screenplay—Lucas to make *Star Wars* and Kaufman to direct the Clint Eastwood Western *The Outlaw Josey Wales* (1976). Eastwood soon fired Kaufman and took over as director himself.

Two years later, following the release of *Star Wars*, George and Marcia Lucas took a Hawaiian vacation with Steven Spielberg and Amy Irving. As they sat on the beach, Spielberg told Lucas that he wanted to make a James Bond film. Lucas told Spielberg he had something even better: Indiana Smith. In that moment the Lucas-Spielberg collaboration was born, and with it one of cinema's most successful franchises. The development of what became the Indiana Jones series is nearly as fascinating as that of *Star Wars* and could fill a book all its own (*Indiana Jones FAQ?*).

Raiders of the Lost Ark (1981)—a joyous, thrill-packed serial pastiche—set the tone for the series. *Raiders* earned $389 million, garnered rave reviews and eight Oscar nominations (winning four awards), established Harrison Ford as a major star, and confirmed that there was more to Lucasfilm than *Star Wars*. *Indiana Jones and the Temple of Doom* (1984), conceived while both Lucas and Spielberg were struggling through romantic break-ups, emerged with a mean-spirited edge that put off some viewers and many critics. It grossed $333 million but earned mixed notices. *Indiana Jones and the Last Crusade* (1989), which introduced Sean Connery (James Bond himself) as Jones' father, returned to the gentler spirit of *Raiders*. It raked in $474 million and recaptured the goodwill of fans and reviewers alike.

The Indiana Jones project that may have had the greatest personal impact on Lucas was the least successful, *The Young Indiana Jones Chronicles*. Conceived by Lucas as a quasi-educational program, the lavishly produced television series incorporated figures and incidents from world history. The show followed young Indiana—played by both Corey Carrier (as an eight- to ten-year-old Jones) and Sean Patrick Flanery (Jones, aged sixteen to twenty-one)—as he accompanied his archaeologist father on travels around the globe, finding adventure at every stop. The show ran on ABC for two seasons (1992–93), but the network canceled it due to weak ratings and exorbitant production costs. The Family Channel aired four *Young Indiana Jones* TV movies from 1994 through '96. Lucas invested himself deeply in the project, writing an extensive outline of Jones' life, as well as thumbnail story concepts for seventy episodes (only twenty-eight of which were produced). He even ghost-directed some sequences for the program. *Young Indiana Jones* seemed to rekindle Lucas' interest in hands-on filmmaking. By the time the final Family Channel movie aired, Lucas had decided to return to directing and was moving ahead with his long-delayed *Star Wars* Prequel Trilogy.

Howard the Duck (1986)

For a decade, from his breakout success with *American Graffiti* in 1974 through the *Star Wars* trilogy and the first two Indiana Jones films (1981 and '84), George Lucas had the Midas touch. He seemed to be able to sense what audiences wanted, sometimes before they realized it themselves. The quickly forgotten *More American Graffiti* (which he didn't want to make) had been his only setback. And then came *Howard the Duck*.

Lucas exercised less authorial control over *Howard* than the *Star Wars* or Indiana Jones films, or the later *Willow*. He was not significantly involved in the writing of the screenplay or in the editing of the film. But it was his idea to adapt this offbeat Marvel Comics title for the big screen, and as executive producer he pushed to make *Howard the Duck* a live-action picture, even though director Willard Huyck and screenwriter Gloria Katz wanted to do it as an animated feature. He was also front-and-center in promoting the movie and received an above-the-title screen credit ("George Lucas presents . . .").

George Lucas' (and Industrial Light & Magic's) attempt to bring *Howard the Duck* to the screen was such a disaster that the film's title character was never seen on the original movie posters or promotional stills. Even the Special Edition DVD cover played it coy.

Lucas first proposed a *Howard the Duck* film in the

mid-1970s, and Huyck and Katz penned a rough draft screenplay at that time. But the project was placed on the back burner for several years, and by the time Lucas, Huyck, and Katz returned to it, the timing was all wrong. Created by writer Steve Gerber and artist Val Mayerik in 1973, *Howard the Duck* was the closest Marvel came to the underground "comix" of that era. Subversive and silly in equal measure, Gerber's stories blended social satire, superhero parody, and absurdist surrealism. The character enjoyed a meteoric rise in popularity, even appearing in a short-lived syndicated newspaper strip (1977–78), but this soon waned. A product of the counterculture that briefly escaped into the mainstream, Howard seemed out of place in the Reaganized America of the mid-1980s. But if 1986 was too late for a *Howard the Duck* movie, it was also too early, since the technology did not exist to create a believable live-action version of the character. Industrial Light & Magic's Creature Shop, under the direction of Phil Tippett, did its best with puppets and rubber suits but was unable to come up with a convincing solution. The rest of the picture's visual effects also fell below the usual ILM standard. And the screenplay, cowritten by Huyck and Katz, was even worse: clumsy, tone deaf, and nearly plotless, it completely misses the singular charm of Gerber's stories. Some story elements—especially the overtly sexual relationship of Howard and his human girlfriend, Beverly (Lea Thompson)—were a poor fit for the family-friendly Lucasfilm brand. Although the picture features lively performances by Thompson, Jeffrey Jones, and Tim Robbins, and top-shelf sound design by Ben Burtt, it never stood a chance at the box office.

Made for $30 million, *Howard the Duck* earned just $16 million. Audiences were baffled by it, and critics giddily lambasted both the film and the suddenly tarnished Golden Boy, Lucas. Even Lucas defender Gene Siskel wondered in his *Chicago Tribune* critique, "Who was this stupid film made for?" *Howard the Duck* quickly gained a (deserved) reputation as one of the most notorious bombs in Hollywood history. Ironically, however, that very critical drubbing also created a new audience for the picture—fanciers of so-bad-it's-good cinema. With that crowd, it has emerged as an unlikely cult favorite.

Willow (1988)

The most ambitious picture Lucas made following the Original Trilogy was *Willow*, a self-conscious attempt at mythmaking and franchise-building designed to prove that epic fantasy could translate to a live-action movie. When Wicket Ufgood (Warwick Davis), a "Nelwyn" dwarf, comes into custody of a human infant marked for death by wicked sorceress Queen Bavmorda, he undertakes a dangerous journey to ensure the child's safety. Along the way, he collects a small group of friends, including a mad swordsman (Val Kilmer),

George Lucas, seen here with (from left) director Ron Howard, toddler Dawn Downing, and Warwick Davis, hoped to launch a third blockbuster franchise with *Willow*.

a bewitched sorceress (Patricia Hayes), a pair of inches-tall "Brownies" (Kevin Pollack and Rick Overton), and Bavmorda's daughter (Joanne Whalley). Together they face Bavmorda's ruthless army as well as magical menaces, including giant doglike beasts; trolls, and a two-headed, fire-breathing monster.

Willow came together in much the same way as the second and third *Star Wars* films and the Indiana Jones pictures: Lucas created the original story and fleshed out a screenplay with the movie's director (Ron Howard) and screenwriter (Bob Dolman). Since starring in *American Graffiti*, Howard had established himself as a bankable director with hits such as *Splash* (1984) and *Cocoon* (1985). Dolman was a Canadian television writer best known for his work on *SCTV* (1981–84). Alan Ladd Jr., Lucas' former champion at Twentieth Century-Fox, green-lit the film for his new employer, Metro-Goldwyn-Mayer. *Willow* was shot at EMI-Elstree Studios in Borehamwood, England, and on location in Wales and New Zealand. Diminutive star Warwick Davis had played Wicket in *Return of the Jedi* and both Ewok TV movies.

Willow has its rewards, chief among them Davis' endearing performance in the title role and Adrian Biddle's lush cinematography. But Dolman's lumpy screenplay suffers from lapses in both pacing and logic. The limitations of mechanical and optical effects, and then-rudimentary CGI, also undercut key sequences (the film's climactic duel of sorceresses fizzles). Although it turned a modest profit (earning $22 million over its $35 million budget), *Willow* was not the sequel-spawning smash Lucas, Ladd, and MGM had hoped for. It would take another thirteen years (and advances in CGI) for the movies to produce the first true fantasy blockbusters, with the advent of the *Harry Potter* (2001–2011) and *Lord of the Rings* (2001–2003) series. *Willow* received mixed reviews, with most critics praising its production values and visual effects but lamenting its weak screenplay. It also earned a pair of Academy Award nominations, for Best Visual Effects and Best Sound Effects, but lost both to another ILM production, *Who Framed Roger Rabbit*. With *Willow*, Lucas swung for the fences but had to settle for a single.

Radioland Murders (1994)

Following the breakthrough success of *American Graffiti* in 1973, Lucas frequently mentioned two projects he wanted to tackle next: One was a space opera in the style of *Flash Gordon*, and the other was a slapstick farce in the tradition of classic film comedians like Laurel & Hardy and Abbott & Costello. "It's been a long time since anybody made a really goofy comedy that had people rolling in the aisles," Lucas said in a 1974 interview with *Film Quarterly*. "It's very hard to do, which is why nobody does it, but it's a challenge. It's like climbing that mountain."

Or, if you do it wrong, like falling off a cliff.

Lucas began sketching out rough ideas for a comedy murder mystery set during the Golden Age of radio while writing *American Graffiti*. His story *Radioland Murders* was inspired in part by the classic comedy *Who Done It?* (1942), in which Bud Abbott and Lou Costello play aspiring radio writers who try to solve a series of murders at the station where they are employed (as soda jerks), but accidentally become the prime suspects. In *Radioland Murders*, a radio writer attempts to solve a series of murders at his station, only to be blamed for the crimes. Lucas wrote a treatment in 1973, and his friends Willard Huyck and Gloria Katz penned a first draft the following year. But with the advent of *Star Wars* and Indiana Jones, *Radioland Murders* was put on hold. Steve Martin and Cindy Williams were approached about starring in the film in 1979, but the project was again delayed. The screenplay went through several more rewrites before finally going into production in October 1993 under the direction of British comedian Mel Smith. Lucas decided to use the film to test-drive his new, cutting-edge editing system, known as Sabre.

The mystery plot of *Radioland Murders* is interwoven with musical numbers and "botched" (i.e., parodied) radio shows supposedly being broadcast live on the station. Brian Benben, then the star of the HBO comedy series *Dream*

On (1990–1996), and Mary Stuart Masterson, who had recently costarred in *Benny & Joon* (1993), headline a cast loaded with familiar character people, including Christopher Lloyd, Jeffrey Tambor, Ned Beatty, Michael Lerner, Michael McKean, Robert Klein, Corbin Bernsen, Bobcat Goldthwait, and Harvey Korman. Various other performers, including Rosemary Clooney, George Burns, and Billy Barty, make cameo appearances as radio performers. The multitude of guest stars was made possible in part by the Sabre editing system, which enabled Smith to paste together scenes involving actors who weren't physically present on set at the same time.

Radioland Murders does a remarkable job of aping the broad comedic style (including the often corny jokes) of slapstick comedy films from the 1940s. Unfortunately, it was promoted not as slapstick but as a revival of the more sophisticated screwball comedy form of the 1930s, which was more character-driven and relied on subtle wordplay. There is nothing subtle or sophisticated about *Radioland Murders*, which falls one pie fight short of the Keystone Kops. The picture was also hurt by comparisons to Woody Allen's much funnier *Radio Days* (1987), also set during the Golden Age of radio. *Radioland Murders* has its moments, but overstays its welcome and eventually grows tiresome. The comedies of Abbott & Costello generally ran about 80 minutes; *Radioland Murders* lasts nearly two hours.

The picture became Lucasfilm's biggest box office loser. Made for a thrifty $15 million, it earned just $1.3 million. Opening on 844 screens, it made nearly $900,000 its first week, only to suffer a then-record 78 percent drop in earnings in week two. It vanished from theaters shortly afterward. Critics hated it. *Time* magazine's Richard Schickel called it "an all-around disaster." *Variety*'s Brian Lowry equated *Radioland Murders* with *Howard the Duck*. Caryn James of the *New York Times* wrote, "Even George Lucas makes mistakes, and *Radioland Murders* is one of his whoppers."

Movies with Friends

In addition to the movies he authored or coauthored as an executive producer, George Lucas also used his clout—and sometimes his money—to help friends and associates bring projects to the screen. The degree of his participation in these productions varied widely.

In 1979, Lucas and Francis Ford Coppola convinced executives at Twentieth Century-Fox to provide completion funds for **Kagemusha** (1980), a samurai epic from Lucas' idol Akira Kurosawa, and to distribute the film in the United States. Kurosawa's movie had run over budget, and Japan's Toho Studio was unable to provide the money necessary to finish the picture. *Kagemusha* operated on a colossal scale, employing five thousand costumed extras for one remarkable battle scene. It also featured some of Kurosawa's most beautiful production design and cinematography, earning Oscar nominations for Best Art Direction and Best Foreign Language Film. It also became the highest-grossing Japanese film of 1980.

A year later, Lucas helped screenwriter Lawrence Kasdan land his first directorial assignment, helming his self-written neo-noir thriller **Body Heat** (1981). The film was one of the first produced by the Ladd Company, founded by former Fox production chief (and *Star Wars* booster) Alan Ladd Jr. Lucas agreed to serve as an executive producer and offered to personally cover cost overruns up to $250,000. But he declined a screen credit because he believed the steamy thriller was not appropriate for his family-friendly Lucasfilm brand. Kasdan delivered *Body Heat* on budget (for $9 million), and it became a sleeper hit, grossing more than $24 million and garnering enthusiastic reviews.

The animated fantasy **Twice Upon a Time** (1983) was the brainchild of John Korty, an independent filmmaker from Northern California whose studio (in a converted barn) inspired Lucas to create his Skywalker Ranch. Lucas helped Korty (who would soon direct *The Ewok Adventure*) secure a distribution deal with the Ladd Company. *Twice Upon a Time*, animated through the manipulation of paper cutouts and still photographs, depicts a conflict between rival factions responsible for manufacturing dreams: The Frivoli create pleasant dreams, but the denizens of the Murkworks produce nightmares. It was the first animated movie branded with the Lucasfilm logo but came and went almost unnoticed. The picture received only a limited U.S. release and was quickly withdrawn, eventually reemerging in reedited form (with a completely different dialogue track) on cable television and home video.

Cinematographer and sometime director Haskell Wexler, who helped Lucas get into USC, made **Latino** (1985), a small-budget film about an American Vietnam veteran sent to aid the Contra rebels in Nicaragua in their fight against the Sandinista government. The American (Robert Beltran) switches allegiances after he falls in love with a Nicaraguan journalist. The politically charged film's commercial prospects were snuffed out when the Iran-Contra scandal broke shortly after the debut of *Latino*.

Mishima: A Life in Four Chapters (1985) was a Japanese-American coproduction from writer-director Paul Schrader. Lucas and Coppola helped Schrader secure half the picture's $5 million budget from Warner Brothers, and Toho supplied the other half. It's an ambitious, unorthodox film about Japanese author Yukio Mishima, which combines biographical interludes with adaptations of three of the writer's stories. Unconventional and at times willfully difficult, *Mishima* earned mixed reviews on its initial release but has since gained favor with critics and intellectually minded viewers. In 2008, it was released on DVD by the Criterion Collection.

Lucas assisted Jim Henson with **Labyrinth** (1986), an oddball musical-adventure-fantasy starring David Bowie, Jennifer Connelly, and a cast of Muppets. Henson began the project with illustrator Brian Froud, with whom he had made *The Dark Crystal* (1982, produced by Gary Kurtz). But the team struggled to develop a workable script. Lucas, among other writers, helped Henson revise the screenplay. Later, Lucas played a major role in editing the picture. "I did the first cut, and then George was heavily involved on bringing it to the final cut," Henson told *Starlog* magazine. With its Japanese-inspired costumes and imagery, *Labyrinth* plays like a kabuki *Wizard of Oz*. Connelly plays a teenage girl trying to rescue her younger brother from the clutches of the evil goblin king (Bowie). *Labyrinth*, produced at a cost of $25 million, was a commercial disappointment in the United States, where it earned just $12 million, although it performed better overseas and eventually turned a profit. Reviews were mixed, but the picture has developed an avid cult following. There is nothing else quite like it.

Lucas was a fan of the experimental films of director Godfrey Reggio and backed his *Powaqqatsi: Life in Transformation* (1988), the middle leg of the Qatsi Trilogy, following *Koyaanisqatsi: Life Out of Balance* (1982) and preceding *Naqoyqatsi: Life as War* (2002). Made without dialogue and set to the electronic

From left: Jim Henson, David Bowie, and George Lucas combined their unique talents to make the one-of-a-kind musical fantasy *Labyrinth*.

music of composer Philip Glass, *Powaqqatsi* depicts the encroachment of modern culture and "progress" on the lives of the poor in Brazil and Africa. Like the other Qatsi films, it was an art house hit and was later released on DVD and Blu-ray by the Criterion Collection. Lucasfilm's involvement with *Mishima* and *Powaqqatsi* are the closest Lucas came to making the "experimental" films he so often spoke about.

Lucas repaid Coppola for his assistance with *American Graffiti* by helping fund *Tucker: The Man and His Dream* (1988), a slickly produced, sentimental biopic about automaker Preston Tucker (Jeff Bridges). Coppola had yearned to make *Tucker* since the early 1970s, but by the time he got around to the project, Coppola's American Zoetrope company was financially strapped. Lucas, who also admired Tucker (an auto industry maverick), stepped in as an executive producer and helped his friend secure a deal with Paramount Pictures, which had originally rejected the project. Although the movie bombed, making just $19 million, it earned mostly favorable reviews and remains one of Coppola's most entertaining pictures of the 1980s.

Lucas partnered with Steven Spielberg to back Don Bluth's animated dinosaur yarn **The Land Before Time** (1988). Bluth, a former Disney animator, sold Spielberg and Lucas on his idea for, basically, a prehistoric version of *Bambi*, starring talking dinosaurs. After his mother is killed by a T-Rex, a young Apatosaurus named Littlefoot falls in with four other dinosaur orphans who are searching for the Great Valley. There they hope to find safety. *The Land Before Time*, made for $12 million, was a major hit, earning $82 million and spawning thirteen direct-to-home-video sequels and a TV series, as well as toys, video games, and other merchandise. Lucas, Spielberg, and Bluth were not involved creatively in any of those later ventures. *The Land Before Time* outperformed Disney's *Oliver & Company*, released the same year, and earned mostly positive reviews.

Lucas returned to active filmmaking with *Star Wars Episode I: The Phantom Menace* (1999). After finishing the Prequel Trilogy and overseeing the related *Clone Wars* animated series, Lucas reteamed with Spielberg for a fourth Indiana Jones entry, *Indiana Jones and the Kingdom of the Crystal Skull* (2008), and made the World War II drama *Red Tails*, about the Tuskegee Airmen. He produced, cowrote, and directed reshoots for *Red Tails*.

In 2006, after completing the Prequel Trilogy, Lucas began dating Mellody Hobson, then chair of DreamWorks Animation. The couple was married on June 22, 2013, and their daughter, Everest, was born via a gestational surrogate in August 2013. Lucas' three elder children all made cameo appearances in the Prequel Trilogy. Amanda is now a professional mixed martial artist.

Katie Lucas has written episodes of the *Star Wars: Clone Wars* and *Star Wars: Rebels* animated series.

After selling Lucasfilm to Disney in 2012, Lucas claimed he was retiring, telling the *New York Times* that he was "moving away from the business, from the company, all this kind of stuff." He cited fan backlash over his Special Edition alterations to the Original Trilogy, and the dismissive critical response to the Prequel Trilogy, among the reasons for his retirement. "Why would I want to make any more [*Star Wars* movies] when everybody yells at you all the time and says what a terrible person you are?" he said.

Despite his supposed retirement, however, in January 2015, Lucas released his first animated feature, a fantasy about fairies and goblins titled *Strange Magic*, loosely adapted from Shakespeare's *A Midsummer Night's Dream* and set to an *American Graffiti*-like rock soundtrack. Lucas wrote the original story and served as executive producer for the film, which was directed by Gary Rydstrom. "Just like *Star Wars* was designed for 12-year-old boys," Lucas told *Wired* magazine, "*Strange Magic* was designed for 12-year-old girls." It did not, however, generate *Star Wars*-like business. *Strange Magic* earned scathing reviews and failed to attract an audience.

If and when the seventy-year-old Lucas actually retires, the movies will lose a restless creative spirit and a true visionary.

38

The Force Will Be with You, Always

The *Star Wars* Legacy

he 2002 fantasy film *Reign of Fire* depicts a world where humans have been reduced to a primitive state—huddled together in caves, scratching out a meager existence—by the return from hibernation of fire-breathing dragons. The picture received mixed reviews and disappointed at the box office (made for $60 million, it earned just $82 million worldwide), but *Reign of Fire* includes at least one remarkable scene:

On a candlelit stage in the survivors' underground bunker, leader Quinn (Christian Bale) and his friend Creedy (Gerard Butler) act out a story to amuse the children. The two men, wearing samurai-like costumes, battle with painted wooden swords (one red, one blue).

Quinn: "Join me, the Black Knight says, and we can end this conflict forever."

Creedy: "I'll never join you, the white knight says. You killed my father!"

Quinn: "The Black Knight stares through the holes in his shiny mask and he speaks words that burn into our hero's heart forever: *I* am your father."

The children gasp in astonishment, then cheer with delight.

Afterward, one of them asks, "Did you make that up, Mr. Quinn?"

There's a kernel of truth in this sequence. If some sort of calamity—nuclear holocaust, meteor strike, global pandemic, or even dragon attack—somehow obliterated movies, television, video games, the Internet, and all our other modern media, people would go back to telling stories around the campfire. Inevitably, the stories told would be the ones people knew best and cared about most deeply—the exploits of legendary heroes and villains. Naturally, one of those stories would be the *Star Wars* saga.

Like fairy tales and nursery rhymes, the story of Robin Hood, or the twentieth-century myths of Tarzan and Superman, *Star Wars* has become indelibly ingrained in our popular consciousness. It's a tale people absorb almost by osmosis simply by living on planet Earth, and which has become part of our way of seeing the world. As Roger Ebert wrote in a 1999 retrospective review of *Star Wars*, "George Lucas' space epic has colonized our imaginations, and it is hard to stand back and see it simply as a motion picture, because it has so completely become part of our memories."

This doesn't mean that the *Star Wars* brand will forever remain a widely popular, wildly lucrative concern. The franchise has already endured one fallow period.

In the late 1970s, although it had its detractors, *Star Wars* had been as close to universally beloved as imaginable. It seemed to appeal to almost everybody. This was by design. "Instead of going for a specific niche audience and playing that audience off against other audiences and making that audience feel special as opposed to the other audiences, . . . [like] the old classic movies, the *Star Wars* movies tried to bring everyone together," *Washington Post* film critic Stephen Hunter observed during in an appearance on *PBS NewsHour* in 2005. "And the consequence is a movie that can be enjoyed by bald geezers like me and kids with pins in their noses, who otherwise would have very little to talk about, I'm afraid."

However, the series lost some of its luster following *Return of the Jedi* (1983), which many viewers considered a less than entirely satisfactory conclusion to the *Star Wars* saga. During the long wait that followed—with only a pair of *Ewoks* telefilms and two short-lived Saturday morning cartoon shows (see Chapter 26) to sate fans' desire for new material—interest dwindled. The Official Star Wars Fan Club closed up shop in 1987. Publication of *Star Wars* novels and comic books ceased, and sales of action figures and other collectibles plummeted. When the U.S. Library of Congress added the original film to its National Film registry in 1989, the honor was considered posthumous. Although fondly remembered, *Star Wars* was looked upon as something that used to be, rather than something that is.

The publication of Timothy Zahn's best-selling novel *Heir to the Empire* in 1991 resuscitated the moribund franchise, ushering in the Expanded Universe and jump-starting sales of *Star Wars* merchandise of all sorts. Throughout the 1990s, *Star Wars* regained its currency in popular culture. Many observers expected, and fans hoped, that the long-awaited Prequel Trilogy would enable the franchise to recapture the near-universal popularity it had achieved in the late 1970s. That didn't happen. Instead, the prequels proved divisive.

All three movies—*Episode I: The Phantom Menace* (1999), *Episode II: Attack of the Clones* (2002), and *Episode III: Revenge of the Sith* (2005)—packed theaters and spawned a merchandising frenzy. *The Phantom Menace* (1999), in terms of raw dollars (not adjusting for inflation), remains the highest-grossing film of the series with worldwide earnings of over $1 billion. *Star Wars* ephemera

Although it divided fans and failed to impress critics, *Star Wars Episode I: The Phantom Menace*—starring, in the foreground from left to right, Liam Neeson as Qui-Gon Jinn, Ewan McGregor as Obi-Wan Kenobi, and Jake Lloyd as the young Anakin Skywalker—remains the highest-grossing movie in the series in raw dollars (without adjusting for inflation). The picture raked in more than $1 billion worldwide.

has been ubiquitous ever since (it's nearly impossible to make a simple trip to the grocery store without stumbling across some *Star Wars*–branded treat or trinket). Every *Star Wars* picture contains admirable elements and gripping sequences, and the prequels have devoted adherents. Esteemed cultural critic Camille Paglia, in her 2012 book *Glittering Images*, argues that *Revenge of the Sith* is a work of genius on par with the tomb of Queen Nefertari in Egypt and the Acropolis in Greece. She also asserts that George Lucas is "the greatest artist of our time."

However, most critics and many fans found *The Phantom Menace* and the other prequels profoundly disappointing. Arguably, the second trilogy did more harm than good to the prestige of the franchise. The Original Trilogy was hardly flawless (see Chapters 10, 18, 21, and 24), but the inherent weaknesses in the series are greatly magnified in Episodes I through III. Lucas' shortcomings as a screenwriter and an acting coach are painfully apparent. But the biggest problem with the prequels is that their lack of any paradigm-shifting, "I am your father"-level revelations make them seem superfluous. Like J. R. R. Tolkien's *The Silmarillion*, they simply fill in the backstory. One can still watch the Original Trilogy (or read *The Hobbit* and *The Lord of the Rings*) and miss nothing essential by skipping their protracted preambles. Worse still, the backstory Lucas provides diminishes much of the mystery and power of the earlier films. (Midi-chlorians, really?)

Many longtime fans found the prequels, frankly, embarrassing. They felt, in a strange way, betrayed by them. Writer Brian Shaw, in a web essay *defending* the Prequel Trilogy, writes, with only slight exaggeration, that *The Phantom Menace* "inspired many spirited and geeky debates as to whether or not Lucas' new film had, in fact, ruined our childhoods. . . . An alarmingly high percentage of *Star Wars* fans out there believe that the Prequel Trilogy, the three movies created between 1999 and 2005, are garbage." The release of the prequels happened to coincide with the explosion of social media, and a preposterous amount of server space is now devoted to housing blogs, columns, memes, and fan-made videos excoriating the Prequel Trilogy, including the popular (and highly amusing) "Mr. Plinkett Reviews" and "What if Star Wars Was Good?" YouTube videos.

Now a feverishly promoted new wave of *Star Wars* movies is on the way, beginning with *Episode VII: The Force Awakens*. *Star Wars* fans who felt let down by the prequels have their fingers crossed that the sequels will help the franchise regain lost respect. The new *Star Wars: Rebels* cartoon series—by far the most satisfying animated *Star Wars* product so far produced—provides reason to hope. At the time of this writing (in early 2015), little information has been released about the new film. There's no way to tell how good or bad, acclaimed or reviled *The Force Awakens* will be, or how it will rank in the canon of *Star Wars* films. Better than *Return of the Jedi*? Better at least than *The Phantom Menace*? Or maybe (cringe) worse?

Whatever these films prove to be, they figure to be different from what has come before. In early 2015, George Lucas told the website Cinema Blend that although Disney's purchase of Lucasfilm included all his original concepts

Reportedly, the upcoming *Episode VII: The Force Awakens* will reunite the heroes of the original film: Luke Skywalker (Mark Hamill), Princess Leia (Carrie Fisher), Chewbacca (Peter Mayhew), and Han Solo (Harrison Ford).

for the Sequel Trilogy, "they came to the decision that they didn't want to do those. So they made up their own."

If the Sequel Trilogy and other new *Star Wars* ventures are successful, it will, naturally, bolster the franchise brand. But even if they flop, the ongoing power and cultural relevance of the Original Trilogy will continue undiminished. If critics sneer at the new *Star Wars* films, they may take some retroactive shots at the Original Trilogy for good measure. That doesn't matter. At this point, the original *Star Wars* films are critic-proof. If things really go south (it's at least theoretically possible), the sale of *Star Wars* products could fall off; Disney might even regret buying the franchise.

The series' box office fortunes, critical reputation, and financial power may be at risk, but the cultural legacy of *Star Wars* is indestructible. Even though the Prequel Trilogy was poorly received by critics, and remains divisive even among diehard fans, there are no indications that the *Star Wars* myth is slipping from the public consciousness. Character names, plot points, and even lines of dialogue from the Original Trilogy still can be dropped in casual conversation, or referred to magazine articles or political stump speeches without a note of explanation. Even people who have avoided seeing the movies (and it takes a conscious effort to do so) can usually identify Darth Vader and Yoda, and know that Vader is the father of Luke Skywalker. In 2002, the Oxford English Dictionary added the words "Jedi," "Force," and "Dark Side" to its unabridged edition. *Star Wars* has literally entered the vernacular.

Like other great myths, *Star Wars* has become an object of study at universities across America and around the world. "A hundred years from now someone will be sitting here discussing the impact of *Star Wars* and they will be seeing different things in it than we are seeing today, just as today we have classes in the university on Homer," New York University professor Joan Breton Connelly writes in her book *Star Wars: The Legacy Revealed*. But most importantly, a hundred years from now audiences will still be watching *Star Wars* (perhaps in a Lucas Family–approved Holographic Special Edition), and they will continue to be dazzled, thrilled, and inspired by it. "It's bad guys versus good guys, and everyone wants to see that story," director (and *Star Wars* fan) Kevin Smith told CNN. "That story will never grow tired, never grow old."

In the late 1980s and early 1990s, toymaker Kenner introduced a slogan to help boost flagging sales of its action figures: "*Star Wars* is forever!" It was truth in advertising.

Bibliography

Books

Arnold, Alan. *Once Upon a Galaxy: A Journal of the Making of The Empire Strikes Back*. New York: Del Rey, 1980.

Baxter, John. *George Lucas: A Biography*. London: HarperCollins, 1999.

Bordwell, David and Thompson, Kristin. *Film History: An Introduction, Third Edition*. New York: McGraw-Hill, 2010.

Bouzereau, Laurent. *Star Wars: The Annotated Screenplays*. New York: Del Rey, 1997.

Bresman, Jonathan. *Mad About Star Wars: Thirty Years of Classic Parodies*. New York: Del Rey, 2007.

Cavelos, Jeanne. *The Science of Star Wars*. New York: St. Martin's, 2000.

Clark, Mark. *Star Trek FAQ: Everything Left to Know About the First Voyages of the Starship Enterprise*. Milwaukee, WI: Hal Leonard, 2012.

Daley, Brian. *Han Solo and the Lost Legacy*. New York: Del Rey, 1980.

Daley, Brian. *Han Solo at Star's End*. New York: Del Rey, 1979.

Daley, Brian. *Han Solo's Revenge*. New York: Del Rey, 1979.

Fisher, Carrie. *Wishful Drinking*. New York: Simon & Shuster, 2008.

Foster, Alan Dean. *Splinter of the Mind's Eye*. New York: Del Rey, 1978.

Guinness, Alec. *A Positively Final Appearance*. New York: Penguin, 2001.

Jewett, Robert. *Saint Paul at the Movies: The Apostle's Dialogue with American Culture*. Louisville, KY: Westminster/John Knox, 1993.

Kaminsky, Michael. *The Secret History of Star Wars: The Art of Storytelling and the Making of a Modern Epic*. Kingston, Ontario: Legacy, 2008.

Kline, Sally (Ed.) *George Lucas Interviews*. Jackson: University of Mississippi, 1999.

Miels, Linda and Pye, Michael. *The Movie Brats: How the Film Generation Took Over Hollywood*. New York: Holt, Rinehart and Winston, 1979.

Paglia, Camille. *Glittering Images: A Journey Through Art from Egypt to Star Wars*. New York: Vintage, 2013.

Peecher, John Phillip (Ed.). *The Making of Return of the Jedi*. New York: Del Rey, 1983.

Perry, Steve. *Shadows of the Empire*. New York: Bantam, 1996.

Pollock, Dale. *Skywalking: The Life and Films of George Lucas*. New York: Harmony, 1983.

Rinzler, J. W. *The Making of Return of the Jedi*. New York: Del Rey, 2013.

Rinzler, J. W. *The Making of Star Wars*. New York: Del Rey, 2007.

Rinzler, J. W. *The Making of The Empire Strikes Back*. New York: Del Rey, 2010.

Sansweet, Stephen J. *Star Wars: From Concept to Collectibles*. San Francisco: Chronicle, 1992.

Sansweet, Stephen J. *Star Wars: The Ultimate Action Figure Collection*. San Francisco: Chronicle, 2012.

Smith, L. Neil. *Lando Calrissian and the Flamewind of Oseon*. New York: Del Rey, 1983.

Smith, L. Neil. *Lando Calrissian and the Mindharp of Sharu*. New York: Del Rey, 1983.

Smith, L. Neil. *Lando Calrissian and the Starcave of ThonBoka*. New York: Del Rey, 1983.

Stradley, Randy (Ed.). *Star Wars Omnibus: Shadows of the Empire*. Milwaukie, Oregon: Dark Horse, 2010.

Taylor, Chris. *How Star Wars Conquered the Universe: The Past, Present, and Future of a Multibillion Dollar Franchise*. Philadelphia, Pennsylvania: Perseus, 2014.

Thomas, Roy and Goodwin, Archie (Eds). *Star Wars Omnibus: A Long Time Ago, Vol. 1*. Milwaukie, OR: Dark Horse, 2010.

Thomas, Roy and Goodwin, Archie (Eds.). *Star Wars Omnibus: A Long Time Ago, Vol. 2*. Milwaukie, OR: Dark Horse, 2010.

Thomas, Roy and Goodwin, Archie (Eds.). *Star Wars Omnibus: A Long Time Ago, Vol. 3*. Milwaukie, OR: Dark Horse, 2011.

Thomas, Roy and Goodwin, Archie (Eds.). *Star Wars Omnibus: A Long Time Ago, Vol. 4*. Milwaukie, OR: Dark Horse, 2011.

Thomas, Roy and Goodwin, Archie (Eds.). *Star Wars Omnibus: A Long Time Ago, Vol. 5*. Milwaukie, OR: Dark Horse, 2012.

Zahn, Timothy. *Dark Force Rising*. New York: Bantam, 1992.

Zahn, Timothy. *Heir to the Empire*. New York: Bantam, 1991.

Zahn, Timothy. *The Last Command*. New York: Bantam, 1993.

DVDs, Blu-rays, and CDs

2001: A Space Odyssey. Warner DVD, 2011.

Adventures of Indiana Jones, The. Paramount DVD, 2003.

Adventures of Young Indiana Jones, The, Volume One—The Early Years. Paramount DVD, 2007.

Adventures of Young Indiana Jones, The, Volume Two—The War Years. Paramount DVD, 2007.

Adventures of Young Indiana Jones, The, Volume Three—The Years of Change. Paramount DVD, 2008.

Air Force. Warner DVD, 2007.

American Graffiti. Universal DVD, 2011.

Battle Beyond the Stars. Shout! Factory DVD, 2011.

Battle of the Stars. DVD, Private copy.

Black Hole, The. Disney DVD, 2004.

Body Heat. Warner Blu-ray, 2014.

Christmas in the Stars. RSO Records, 1980.

Dam Busters, The. Anchor Bay DVD, 2005.

Flash Gordon Serials Collection. Image DVD, 1996.

Galaxina. Mill Creek DVD, 2011.

Good, the Bad, and the Ugly, The. MGM DVD, 2007.

H. G. Wells' The Shape of Things to Come. Blue Underground DVD, 2004.

Hidden Fortress, The. Criterion DVD, 2001.

Howard the Duck. Universal DVD, 2009.

Indiana Jones and the Kingdom of the Crystal Skull. Paramount DVD, 2008.

Kagemusha. Criterion DVD, 2008.

Labyrinth. Sony DVD, 1999.

Land Before Time, The. Universal, 2003.

Magnificent Seven, The. MGM DVD, 2001.

Message from Space. Shout! Factory DVD, 2013.

Mishima: A Life in Four Chapters. Criterion DVD, 2008.

More American Graffiti. Universal DVD, 2003.

Naked Space. DVD, Private copy.

Powaqqatsi: Life in Transformation. MGM DVD, 2002.

Radioland Murders. Universal DVD, 2006.

Return of the Ewok. DVD, Private copy.

Sanjuro. Criterion DVD, 2007.

Saturn 3. DVD, Private copy.

Searchers, The. Warner DVD, 2007.

Seventh Voyage of Sinbad, The. Sony DVD, 2008.

Spaceballs. Twentieth Century Fox DVD, 2000.

Star Odyssey. DVD, Private copy.

Star Wars (original 1977 version). 16mm print, Private copy.

Star Wars Animated Adventures: Droids. Twentieth Century Fox DVD, 2004.

Star Wars Animated Adventures: Ewoks. Twentieth Century Fox DVD, 2004.

Star Wars and Other Galactic Funk. Mercury Records (Rhino Reissue), 1999.

Star Wars Episode I: The Phantom Menace. Twentieth Century Fox DVD, 2000.

Star Wars Episode II: Attack of the Clones. Twentieth Century Fox DVD, 2002.

Star Wars Episode III: Revenge of the Sith. Twentieth Century Fox DVD, 2005.

Star Wars Ewok Adventures. Twentieth Century Fox DVD, 2004.
Star Wars Holiday Special. DVD, Private copy.
Star Wars Trilogy. Twentieth Century Fox Blu-ray, 2013.
Star Wars Trilogy. Twentieth Century Fox DVD, 2004.
Star Wars Trilogy. Twentieth Century Fox VHS, 1995.
Starcrash. Shout! Factory DVD, 2010.
Story of Star Wars, The. 20th Century-Fox Records, 1977.
THX 1138. Universal DVD, 2004.
Tucker: The Man and His Dream. Paramount DVD, 2000.
Twice Upon a Time. DVD, Private copy.
War of the Planets. DVD, Private copy.
War of the Robots, DVD, Private copy.
Willow. Twentieth Century Fox Blu-ray/DVD, 2013.
Yojimbo. Criterion DVD, 2007.

Websites

http://www.airspacemag.com/daily-planet/100-million-planets-our-galaxy-may-harbor-complex-life-180951598/?no-ist
http://anthonydaniels.com/index.html
https://archive.org/details/starlogmagazine
http://www.baylor.edu/content/services/document.php/33304.pdf
http://blogs.indiewire.com/theplaylist/wedge-antilles-actor-dennis-lawson-says-star-wars-episode-vii-would-have-bored-him-he-passed-on-returning-20140512
http://www.brainpickings.org/index.php/2014/05/30/star-wars-influences-mashup/
http://www.brianonstarwars.com/2014/05/star-wars-prequels-are-just-as-good.html
https://ca.movies.yahoo.com/person/john-dykstra/biography.html
http://www.canada.com/ottawacitizen/news/story.html?id=c782db39-0f36-4ad1-bdf2-27a115ecb422
http://collider.com/jj-abrams-lawrence-kasdan-star-wars-episode-7-writing/
http://www.comicbookresources.com/?page=article&old=1&id=186
http://www.complex.com/style/2014/05/star-wars-in-fashion
http://www.cnn.com/2007/SHOWBIZ/Movies/05/23/star.wars.30/
http://content.time.com/time/magazine/article/0,9171,921233,00.html
http://www.darthvader-starwars.com/index.htm
http://www.denofgeek.com/movies/star-wars/26133/richard-marquand-interview-return-of-the-jedi-star-wars
http://www.ejumpcut.org/archive/onlinessays/JC18folder/starWars2.html

http://www.emmytvlegends.org/interviews/people/rick-baker
http://entertainment.time.com/2012/05/25/
    happy-35th-anniversary-star-wars/
http://www.forbes.com/sites/judebrennan/2014/05/01/the-man-who-green-
    lit-star-wars-the-most-important-movie-mogul-youve-never-heard-of/
http://www.harrisinteractive.com/NewsRoom/HarrisPolls/tabid/447/ctl/
    ReadCustom%20Default/mid/1508/ArticleId/1353/Default.aspx
http://www.historytoday.com/peter-kramer/ronald-reagan-and-star-wars
http://www.ifr.org/industrial-robots/statistics/
http://www.ign.com/articles/2002/11/11/an-interview-with-gary-kurtz
http://www.in70mm.com/news/2003/star_wars/
http://www.imdb.com/
http://www.kennercollector.com/kenner-history/
http://www.kennybaker.co.uk/
http://motherboard.vice.com/blog/
    in-1980-the-star-wars-casts-emempireem-hotline-broke-att
http://www.movieguide.org/news-articles/hollywood-demographics-2.html
http://www.moviemistakes.com/
http://www.nationalcathedral.org/about/darthVader.shtml
http://news.harvard.edu/gazette/story/2013/09/seeing-light-in-a-new-way/
http://www.npr.org/2013/07/16/202368713/
    use-the-books-fans-star-wars-franchise-thrives-in-print
http://www.npr.org/templates/story/story.php?storyId=4661664
http://www.nydailynews.com/entertainment/tv-movies/george-
    lucas-irvin-kershner-empire-strikes-back-director-mentor-article-
    1.450774#ixzz3AlhVtl00
http://www.nytimes.com/2012/01/22/magazine/george-lucas-red-tails.
    html?ref=global-home&_r=0
http://www.petermayhew.com/
http://www.physics.org/article-questions.asp?id=59
http://ratzenberger.com/
http://www.rogerebert.com/scanners/
    how-star-wars-changed-the-world-as-we-knew-it
http://www.salon.com/2007/04/12/castaneda/
http://www.starpulse.com/Celebrity/Dennis_Muren-spb3526991/
    Biography/
http://www.starwars.com/
http://www.starwarsholidayspecial.com/
http://starwarsinterviews1.blogspot.com/2010/01/howard-kazanjian-
    interview.html
http://starwars.wikia.com/wiki/Main_Page

http://staticmultimedia.com/content/film/features/feature_1115643931

http://statisticbrain.com/star-wars-total-franchise-revenue/

http://www.telegraph.co.uk/finance/personalfinance/
   fameandfortune/8784832/Stars-Wars-actor-Dave-Prowse-aka-Darth-
   Vader-talks-money.html

http://www.theasc.com/magazine/starwars/articles/sped/uni/pg1.htm

http://www.theasc.com/magazine/starwars/articles/starwars/mm/index.
   htm

http://www.theatlantic.com/entertainment/archive/2011/09/
   why-the-first-star-wars-is-still-the-best-star-wars/245128/

http://www.thedigitalbits.com/columns/history-legacy– showmanship/
   remembering-return-of-the-jedi-30th

http://www.the-numbers.com/

http://www.theraider.net/features/interviews/alan_ladd.php

http://www.theworldsbestever.com/2013/04/03/the-force-of-fur/

http://www.tvparty.com/70starwars.html

http://www.vanityfair.com/magazine/2008/12/star_wars_special200812

http://www.vanityfair.com/online/oscars/2010/10/irvin-kershner

http://variety.com/2014/biz/news/significant-star-wars-presence-planned-
   for-disney-theme-parks-1201276296/

http://www.washingtonpost.com/blogs/post-politics/wp/2013/01/12/
   white-house-rejects-death-star-petittion/

http://whatculture.com/film/52-reasons-why-star-wars-might-just-be-the-
   greatest-film-of-all-time.php

http://www.wired.com/2015/01/george-lucas-strange-magic/

https://www.youtube.com/

http://www.youtube.com/watch?v=2F7Wwew8X4Y

https://www.youtube.com/watch?v=8B4meZDKLQg

http://www.youtube.com/watch?v=RuNQ9pA6avw

Index

THE FAQ SERIES

AC/DC FAQ
by Susan Masino
Backbeat Books
978-1-4803-9450-6 .... $24.99

Armageddon Films FAQ
by Dale Sherman
Applause Books
978-1-61713-119-6 .... $24.99

Lucille Ball FAQ
*by James Sheridan
and Barry Monush*
Applause Books
978-1-61774-082-4 .... $19.99

The Beach Boys FAQ
by Jon Stebbins
Backbeat Books
978-0-87930-987-9 .... $22.99

Black Sabbath FAQ
by Martin Popoff
Backbeat Books
978-0-87930-957-2 .... $19.99

Johnny Cash FAQ
by C. Eric Banister
Backbeat Books
978-1-4803-8540-5 .... $24.99

Eric Clapton FAQ
by David Bowling
Backbeat Books
978-1-61713-454-8 .... $22.99

Doctor Who FAQ
by Dave Thompson
Applause Books
978-1-55783-854-4 .... $22.99

The Doors FAQ
by Rich Weidman
Backbeat Books
978-1-61713-017-5 .... $24.99

The Eagles FAQ
by Andrew Vaughan
Backbeat Books
978-1-4803-8541-2 .... $24.99

Fab Four FAQ
*by Stuart Shea and
Robert Rodriguez*
Hal Leonard Books
978-1-4234-2138-2 .... $19.99

Fab Four FAQ 2.0
by Robert Rodriguez
Backbeat Books
978-0-87930-968-8 .... $19.99

Film Noir FAQ
by David J. Hogan
Applause Books
978-1-55783-855-1 .... $22.99

Football FAQ
by Dave Thompson
Backbeat Books
978-1-4950-0748-4 .... $24.99

The Grateful Dead FAQ
by Tony Sclafani
Backbeat Books
978-1-61713-086-1 .... $24.99

Prices, contents, and availability
subject to change without notice.

Jimi Hendrix FAQ
by Gary J. Jucha
Backbeat Books
978-1-61713-095-3 .... $22.99

Horror Films FAQ
by John Kenneth Muir
Applause Books
978-1-55783-950-3 .... $22.99

James Bond FAQ
by Tom DeMichael
Applause Books
978-1-55783-856-8 .... $22.99

Stephen King Films FAQ
by Scott Von Doviak
Applause Books
978-1-4803-5551-4 .... $24.99

KISS FAQ
by Dale Sherman
Backbeat Books
978-1-61713-091-5 .... $22.99

Led Zeppelin FAQ
by George Case
Backbeat Books
978-1-61713-025-0 .... $19.99

Modern Sci-Fi Films FAQ
by Tom DeMichael
Applause Books
978-1-4803-5061-8 .... $24.99

Morrissey FAQ
by D. McKinney
Backbeat Books
978-1-4803-9448-3 .... $24.99

Nirvana FAQ
by John D. Luerssen
Backbeat Books
978-1-61713-450-0 .... $24.99

Pink Floyd FAQ
by Stuart Shea
Backbeat Books
978-0-87930-950-3 .... $19.99

Elvis Films FAQ
by Paul Simpson
Applause Books
978-1-55783-858-2 .... $24.99

Elvis Music FAQ
by Mike Eder
Backbeat Books
978-1-61713-049-6 .... $24.99

Prog Rock FAQ
by Will Romano
Backbeat Books
978-1-61713-587-3 .... $24.99

Pro Wrestling FAQ
by Brian Solomon
Backbeat Books
978-1-61713-599-6 .... $29.99

Rush FAQ
by Max Mobley
Backbeat Books
978-1-61713-451-7 .... $24.99

Saturday Night Live FAQ
by Stephen Tropiano
Applause Books
978-1-55783-951-0 .... $24.99

Seinfeld FAQ
by Nicholas Nigro
Applause Books
978-1-55783-857-5 .... $24.99

Sherlock Holmes FAQ
by Dave Thompson
Applause Books
978-1-4803-3149-5 .... $24.99

Soccer FAQ
by Dave Thompson
Backbeat Books
978-1-61713-598-9 .... $24.99

The Sound of Music FAQ
by Barry Monush
Applause Books
978-1-4803-6043-3 .... $27.99

South Park FAQ
by Dave Thompson
Applause Books
978-1-4803-5064-9 .... $24.99

Bruce Springsteen FAQ
by John D. Luerssen
Backbeat Books
978-1-61713-093-9 .... $22.99

Star Trek FAQ
(Unofficial and Unauthorized)
by Mark Clark
Applause Books
978-1-55783-792-9 .... $19.99

Star Trek FAQ 2.0
(Unofficial and Unauthorized)
by Mark Clark
Applause Books
978-1-55783-793-6 .... $22.99

Quentin Tarantino FAQ
by Dale Sherman
Applause Books
978-1-4803-5588-0 .... $24.99

Three Stooges FAQ
by David J. Hogan
Applause Books
978-1-55783-788-2 .... $22.99

U2 FAQ
by John D. Luerssen
Backbeat Books
978-0-87930-997-8 .... $19.99

The Who FAQ
by Mike Segretto
Backbeat Books
978-1-4803-6103-4 .... $24.99

The Wizard of Oz FAQ
by David J. Hogan
Applause Books
978-1-4803-5062-5 .... $24.99

Neil Young FAQ
by Glen Boyd
Backbeat Books
978-1-61713-037-3 .... $19.99

HAL•LEONARD®
PERFORMING ARTS
PUBLISHING GROUP

FAQ.halleonardbooks.com